ACPL ITEM
DISCARDED

D0459611

648
F26
2132390

The fastest, cheapest, best
way to clean everything

**DO NOT REMOVE
CARDS FROM POCKET**

ALLEN COUNTY PUBLIC LIBRARY

FORT WAYNE, INDIANA 46802

You may return this book to any agency, branch,
or bookmobile of the Allen County Public Library.

DEMCO

By The Editors of
Consumer Guide®

The Fastest, Cheapest, Best Way to Clean Everything

Simon and Schuster
New York

ALLEN COUNTY PUBLIC LIBRARY
FORT WAYNE, INDIANA

Copyright © 1980 Publications International, Ltd. All rights reserved.
This book may not be reproduced or quoted in whole or in part by mimeograph or
any other means or for presentation on radio or television without written permission
from:
Louis Weber, President
Publications International, Ltd.
3841 West Oakton Street
Skokie, Illinois 60076
Permission is never granted for commercial purposes.

Manufactured in the United States of America
1 2 3 4 5 6 7 8 9 10

Library of Congress Catalog Card Number: 80-81316
ISBN 0-671-25500-2
Published by Simon and Schuster
A Division of Gulf + Western Corporation
New York, New York 10020

Contributing Editors: Betty Silverman and Judy Lawrence
Cover Photos: Mel Winer
Cover Design: Frank E. Peiler

Publications International, Ltd., has made every effort to ensure the accuracy and
reliability of the information, instructions, and directions in this book; however, it is in
no way to be construed as a guarantee, and Publications International, Ltd., is not
liable in case of misinterpretations of the directions, human error, or typographical
mistakes.

Contents

2132390

Introduction 9

Inside the House 11

Ceilings	Acoustical Tile 11
	Ceiling Tile 12
	Painted 12
	Papered 12
	Plaster 12
	Spray-On Acoustical Finish 12
Countertops	Acrylic 12
	Ceramic Tile 13
	Marble 14
	Marble, Cultured 14
	Plastic Laminate 15
	Wood 16
Fireplaces	Chimney and Flue 17
	Firebox 18
	Fire Screen 19
	Glass Enclosure 19
	Grate and Cast Iron Tools 20
	Mantel and Hearth 20
	Tools 22
Floors	Asphalt Tile 23
	Brick 25
	Ceramic Tile, Glazed 27
	Ceramic Tile, Unglazed 28
	Concrete 30
	Cork 31
	Flagstone and Slate 32
	Linoleum 34
	Marble 36
	Quarry Tile 38
	Rubber Tile 39
	Terrazzo 42
	Vinyl 43
	Wood 45

Radiators, Heat Vents, and Returns 47

Walls	Brick 48
	Ceramic Tile 49
	Decorator Tile 50
	Metal Tile 50
	Mirror Tile 51
	Painted 51
	Paper 51
	Vinyl 52
	Wood Paneling 52

Windows 54
Woodwork 55

Contents

Home Furnishings **58**

Bedding	Bedspread	58
	Blanket	59
	Comforter and Quilt, Down-Filled	60
	Comforter and Quilt, Wool-, Cotton-, and Synthetic Filled	61
	Mattress and Box Spring	62
	Pillow	63
	Sleeping Bag	65

Carpets and Rugs **66**

Furniture	Metal	69
	Plastic	70
	Upholstery, Fabric	70
	Upholstery, Leather	71
	Upholstery, Vinyl	72
	Wood, Oiled	72
	Wood, Painted	73
	Wood, Polished	73
	Wood, Specialty	74

Lampshades **74**

Mirrors **76**

Objets d'Art	Alabaster	76
	Bone	77
	Candlesticks	77
	Fabric Flowers	77
	Ivory	78
	Jade	78
	Marble	79
	Paintings	80
	Porcelain	80

Pianos **81**

Slipcovers **83**

Television Sets **84**

Window Coverings	Blinds	85
	Curtains	86
	Draperies	87
	Shades, Window	88
	Shutters	90

Bathrooms **91**

	Bathtubs and Washbasins	91
	Countertops	93
	Hardware	95
	Shower Curtains	96
	Showers and Shower Stalls	97
	Toilets	99

Kitchenware **101**

Cookware	Aluminum	101
	Cast Iron	103

Contents

Clay 103
Copper 104
Enamelware 106
Glass and Ceramic-Glass 106
Nonstick Coated 107
Stainless Steel 108

Dinnerware **109**
Flatware and Cutlery **111**
Glassware **112**
Preparation, Storing,   Metal 113
and Serving Utensils   Plastic and Rubberware 113
Woodenware 114

Large Appliances **116**

Automatic Dishwashers **116**
Clothes Washers and Dryers **118**
Freezers **119**
Microwave Ovens **121**
Rangehoods **122**
Refrigerators **124**
Stoves   Ceramic Cooktops 126
Ovens 126
Stovetops and Exteriors 128
Trash Compactors **129**

Small Appliances **131**

Blenders and Food Processors **131**
Coffeemakers **132**
Electric Can Openers **133**
Electric Irons   Soleplate 134
Water Reservoir 135
Garbage Disposers **135**
Hot Trays **136**
Toaster Ovens and Broilers **137**
Toasters **138**
Waffle Irons   Baked Enamel 139
Metal 139

Natural Fabrics **140**

Cotton 140
Linen 141
Silk 141
Wool 142

Synthetic Fabrics **143**

Acetate 143

Contents

Acrylic 143
Fiberglass 144
Modacrylic 145
Nylon 145
Polyester 146
Rayon 146
Spandex 147
Triacetate 147

Wearing Apparel **148**

Diapers **148**
Gloves **150**
Outerwear   Down-Filled 150
                     Polyester Fiber-Filled 151
                     Wool 151
Rainwear   Cloth 152
                     Rubber, Plastic, and Vinyl 153
Shoes   Fabric 154
                     Leather and Vinyl 155
                     Suede 157
Sweaters **158**

Personal Items **160**

Eyeglasses **160**
Hairbrushes and Combs **161**
Jewelry   Costume 162
                     Pearl 163
                     Precious Metal 164
                     Precious Stone 165
Wigs and Hairpieces Human Hair 167
                     Synthetic 168

Metals **169**

                     Aluminum 169
                     Brass 170
                     Bronze 172
                     Chromium 173
                     Copper 174
                     Gold 176
                     Iron 177
                     Pewter 178
                     Platinum 179
                     Silver 180
                     Stainless Steel 182
                     Tin 183
                     Zinc 184

Outside the House **186**

Awnings **186**

Contents

Barbecue Grills 187
Brick 189
Garbage Cans 190
Outdoor Furniture   Aluminum, Painted 191
                                  Aluminum, Unpainted 192
                                  Vinyl and Plastic 193
                                  Wood 194
                                  Wrought Iron 195
Window Screens 195

Automobiles 197
                                  Carpets 197
                                  Chrome 198
                                  Floor Mats 199
                                  Paint 200
                                  Tires 202
                                  Upholstery, Cloth 203
                                  Upholstery, Vinyl and Leather 204
                                  Vinyl Tops 205
                                  Windows and Windshields—Glass and Plastic 206
                                  Wood Grain Trim 207

Miscellaneous 208
                                  Books 208
                                  Drains 210
                                  Paintbrushes and Paint Rollers 212
                                  Records 214
                                  Tools 215

Tools of the Trade 217
                                  Brooms 217
                                  Brushes 217
                                  Carpet Sweepers 218
                                  Cloths 218
                                  Dishpans 219
                                  Dustmops 219
                                  Dustpans 219
                                  Floor Scrubbers/Polishers/Rug Shampooers 219
                                  Gloves 220
                                  Mitts 220
                                  Mops 220
                                  Pails 221
                                  Paper Towels 221
                                  Pumice 221
                                  Scouring Pads, Fiber 221
                                  Scouring Pads, Steel 222
                                  Scouring Pads, Synthetic 222
                                  Scrapers 222
                                  Sponges 223
                                  Stepladders or Step Stools 223

Contents

Vacuum Cleaners and Attachments 223
Window Cleaners 224

Recommended Basic Products 225

All-Purpose Cleaners 225
Liquid Dishwashing Detergents 226
Common Household Products 227

Laundry 228

Sorting 228
Preparing the Wash   Prewash Spot and Stain Removers 229
                         Presoaks 230
Laundry Products   Water Conditioners 230
                         Detergents and Soaps 231
                         Bleach 234
                         Fabric Softeners 235
Using an   Loading the Machine 236
Automatic Washer   Water Temperature............................ 236
                         Water Level 237
                         Machine Cycle 237
Using a Wringer Washer 237
Hand Washing 238
Drying Clothes   Machine Drying 238
                         Line Drying 239
Solving Washing   Brown Stains 240
Problems   Excessive Wear............................... 240
                         Gray and Dingy Fabric 240
                         Greasy Spots 240
                         Harsh-Feeling Fabrics 241
                         Linting 241
                         Scorching During Ironing 241
                         Static Electricity 241
                         Yellowing 241

Spots and Stains 242

Stain Removing Agents to Have on Hand 243
Stain Removing Equipment 245
Stain Removing   Absorbing 245
Techniques   Flushing 246
                         Freezing 246
                         Scraping 246
                         Sponging 246
                         Tamping 246
How to Remove Staining Substances 247

Directory of Manufacturers 275

Index 279

Introduction

Cleaning is always a chore. But that's no reason why *learning* about cleaning—how to clean efficiently; how to work with particular materials without damaging them; how to get rid of dirt, grease, grime, etc.—has to be difficult or time consuming.

The Fastest, Cheapest, Best Way to Clean Everything has been specially prepared to tell you—at a glance—what to do and what not to do when cleaning anything: your home, your car, your clothing, and more. A book that will seldom sit long on a shelf, it presents only the information you really need to know to get your things clean. And it presents that information in concise but complete lists of **"Do's"** and **"Don'ts"** so that you can quickly absorb the essentials and get on with your work.

But you need more than "how to" instructions. You also need a guide to "what with." You need brand-name recommendations of those products that will provide the results you're seeking every time you clean. *The Fastest, Cheapest, Best Way to Clean Everything* is the *only* book that supplies the "what with" information you need.

Cleaning Styles

Not everyone cleans the same way. Product recommendations, therefore, must vary according to the cleaning style of the individual. For example, you may be the sort of person who simply wants to put cleaning chores behind you as rapidly as possible. You find little enjoyment in lavishing great quantities of time and attention on things that need cleaning, and you're probably willing to pay a premium price for a product that can make your kitchen, bath, floors, etc., look presentable in the briefest period possible. If this describes your attitude toward cleaning, then you should look at the products under the **Fastest** headings.

Or you might be the sort of person who is far more conscious of what you spend for cleaning products. You not only look for the least expensive brands to buy, but you also take true delight in mixing your own cleaning solutions whenever possible to beat the brand-name game altogether. Like your time-conscious counterparts, you simply want your home, furnishings, car, and so forth to look dirt-free; but unlike the first group, you are willing to devote some time and energy in order to minimize out-of-pocket expenses. If you take this approach, then you'll find the information you want under the **Cheapest** headings.

Finally, you might be someone to whom time and money matter little when it comes to getting things clean. A quality-conscious person, you want products—sometimes so specialized as to be difficult to find in ordinary supermarkets and hardware stores—that will do more than merely make things look good. You want products that will care for, preserve, and protect your possessions while getting rid of unwanted dirt, grease, grime, etc. A product fulfilling these criteria seldom can be made at home, usually costs more than its clean-only competition, and frequently demands a good deal of time and attention in terms of application. It is a product for cleaning perfectionists, those who take pride in keeping what they own in top shape no matter how expensive or time consuming the task may be. If you're one of these cleaning perfectionists, then you'll find the very finest cleaning products—the only ones you'd consider using—under the **Best** headings.

Introduction

How to Use the Book

Even though you can probably think of a dozen areas that need cleaning immediately, take a few minutes to examine the chapters on basic cleaning products and "tools of the trade." The information you'll discover in these chapters will make every cleaning chore you ever tackle both safer and more successful.

The bulk of the book is divided into sections, such as "Inside the House," representing major areas of cleaning responsibility, with chapters on specific cleaning targets. In most cases these chapters are subdivided (for example, "Ceilings" is broken down into acoustical tile, ceiling tile, painted, papered, plaster, and spray-on acoustical finish), and the subdivisions are presented in alphabetical order. Each topic within a chapter, of course, has its own instructional material and its own fastest, cheapest, best product recommendations.

Those recommended products, as you might expect, represent only a fraction of the total number tested. The other products—many of which are quite serviceable—appear in list form immediately following the fastest/cheapest/best recommendations, with capsule commentaries on their ease of use and quality of performance. Each list is structured so that the first entry is the most preferable, the next somewhat less, and on down in descending order of performance.

The determination of recommended products and the structure of the lists of other products tested were based upon actual testing of all the products in situations as similar as possible to those you are likely to encounter. It should be understood, however, that product formulations can be altered over time and that they frequently vary from one region of the country to another. It is possible, therefore, that you might obtain different results from those presented on the following pages.

There is one constant, though, that applies to every product mentioned in this book as well as to any other cleaning product you may encounter: Always read and follow the manufacturer's directions. Your personal safety, the safety of the objects you are cleaning, and the results you expect the product to provide are all contingent on your doing what the product label tells you to do.

Get Started!

You've probably already categorized yourself as a "fastest," "cheapest," or "best" cleaner. But no matter what your style, your chores only get bigger and more difficult the longer you wait. Therefore, turn the page and get started!

Inside the House

Ceilings

Many ceiling surfaces are washable. Some ceilings, especially the acoustical type, need special treatment, but all benefit from routine care.

Do's

- Lift cobwebs off ceilings monthly with a cloth covering a mop or broom or with a vacuum brush attachment.
- Wash or clean ceilings before walls if you are cleaning a whole room.
- Protect furniture and floors with dropcloths or newspaper while you clean.
- Use a sponge mop to clean ceilings so you won't need a ladder.

Don'ts

- **Do not** crush cobwebs onto the ceiling or they will leave marks.
- **Do not** allow water or cleaning agents to drip onto furniture or floors.
- **Do not** allow drips to run down walls.

Acoustical Tile

Made of porous material, acoustical tile absorbs noise. Vinyl-coated acoustical tiles can be washed with an all-purpose cleaner solution (see Recommended Basic Products) applied with a sponge. Noncoated tiles generally are not washable and can be spot cleaned using the recommended products. When an overall cleaning is needed, an application of special acoustical tile paint is recommended.

Fastest and Cheapest

Absorene (Absorene Manufacturing Co., Inc.), a pink substance that resembles modeling clay, spot cleans nonwashable acoustical tiles well. Knead a small portion until soft and pliant, squeeze it into an oblong shape, and apply with long even strokes in one direction only. After five or six strokes, fold the piece over to cover the soil, and use until it is completely dirty. Continue cleaning with another piece of the dough.

Read manufacturer's cautions and warnings before using any product.

Best

Banish smudges and dirt on light-colored acoustical tile with **Like Magic All Purpose Cleaner** (Sterling Products). Apply a very small amount of this pink paste to the surface with a damp terry cloth and work in a circular motion to loosen the soil. As a final step, wipe the tiles clean with a dry cloth.

Ceiling Tile

Vinyl-coated ceiling tile can be cleaned with an all-purpose cleaner solution (see Recommended Basic Products). Refer to Acoustical Tile above for products and techniques for nonwashable tile, with the exception that special acoustical tile paint is not necessary when repainting vinyl-coated tile.

Painted

Painted ceilings are cleaned the same way as painted walls. (See Walls—Painted.)

Papered

Ceilings covered with some sort of wall covering, whether paper, vinyl-coated paper, or vinyl cloth, are all cleaned the same way as walls covered with the same material. (See Walls—Paper, Vinyl.)

Plaster

Decorative plaster ceilings, as opposed to flat, painted plastered ceilings, are really noncleanable because of the unpainted surface and deep texture. When a plaster ceiling becomes dirty, the best treatment is to vacuum it using the brush attachment and paint it.

Spray-On Acoustical Finish

This rough, sound-absorbing finish is often used in new construction and remodeling. While it is relatively cheap and quick to apply, it is a noncleanable ceiling treatment. When it becomes dirty the best thing to do is vaccum it using the brush attachment and respray it.

Countertops

Countertops in the kitchen, bath, family room, and workshop are made from many different materials. A good care program will keep them sparkling clean and free of stains.

Acrylic

Acrylic countertops can be scrubbed with scouring powders or steel wool if necessary to remove stains or scratches and still retain its good looks. For routine cleaning, any of the products listed for Marble, Cultured can be used.

Ceramic Tile

Glazed or unglazed ceramic tile can be used for countertops in the kitchen or bath. Unglazed tiles should be treated periodically with a sealer to keep stains out of the slightly porous surface. Glazed ceramic tile is virtually stainproof, but that isn't true of the grout.

Do

- Use an old toothbrush or nailbrush to help clean grout.

Don'ts

- **Do not** use harsh abrasive cleaners that might scratch the glaze.
- **Do not** apply wax or polish to glazed tiles.
- **Do not** drop heavy objects on the tile—it can crack or chip.

Fastest

Tile 'n Grout Magic (Magic American Chemical Corp.) cleans both types of ceramic tile and the grout quickly. Scrub the aerosol foam onto the tile with the handy plastic brush built in the top of the can and rinse clean with a damp sponge for beautiful results.

Cheapest

The following recipe makes an inexpensive and good cleaner for ceramic tile: ½ cup vinegar, 1 cup clear ammonia (see Recommended Basic Products), ¼ cup baking soda (see Recommended Basic Products), and 1 gallon warm water. **Caution:** Wear rubber gloves and work in a well-ventilated area when using this powerful solution. Apply to the countertop with a sponge and rinse with clear water. Wipe dry to prevent dull waterspots.

Best

20 Mule Power Industrial Strength Bathroom Cleaner (United States Borax & Chemical Corporation) is the best tile cleaner. Spray the liquid directly on the surface, allow to penetrate, and use a synthetic scouring pad (see Tools of the Trade) to loosen the dirt. A clear water rinse finishes the job. **Caution:** Wear rubber gloves to avoid skin contact with this powerful cleaner and take care not to breathe in the mist as it is being sprayed on the tile.

Other Products Tested

Lysol Basin/Tub/Tile Cleaner (Lehn & Fink Products Division of Sterling Drug Inc.)—very good performance; pump spray; moderate odor.
X-14 Instant Mildew Stain Remover (White Laboratories)—spray cleaner that removes mildew stains and soil from grout; no scrub, no rinse; good performance, but not a general cleaner.

Read manufacturer's cautions and warnings before using any product.

Countertops

Arm & Hammer Baking Soda (Church & Dwight Co., Inc.)—powder mixed with equal part water to make a paste; apply to grout with damp cloth; scrub with toothbrush; good cleaner; rinse with water.
Clorox Bleach (The Clorox Company)—liquid; mild solution will clean grout when scrubbed with toothbrush; ¼ cup bleach to 1 quart water; rinse with clear water; good performance; strong odor.
Dow Disinfectant Bathroom Cleaner (The Dow Chemical Co.)—aerosol; moderately good cleaner; pleasant pine odor.
Afta Tile Cleaner (Afta Solvents Corporation)—moderately good cleaner with built-on spray brush head; moderate odor.

Marble

Marble countertops are easily cared for. See Objets d'Art—Marble for care instructions and recommended cleaning products.

Marble, Cultured

Cultured marble is a synthetic product that resembles real marble in beauty. Used for bathroom countertops as well as molded lavatories and shower stall panels, this acrylic material is easy to care for.

Do

- Avoid abrasive cleaners and steel wool pads—they will scratch the surface.

Don't

- **Do not** allow a lighted cigarette to touch the surface—it will leave a permanent burn mark.

Fastest

Use **Bon Ami Deluxe Polishing Cleanser** (Faultless Starch/ Bon Ami Company) for a fast cleanup of cultured marble surfaces. Apply directly onto wet surface. This mild powder gets rid of dirt and soap film but does not damage the surface. Rinse well with clear water and buff dry with a soft cloth for a beautiful shine.

Cheapest

Mix ½ cup vinegar, 1 cup ammonia, and ¼ cup baking soda in 1 gallon hot water. **Caution:** Wear rubber gloves and work in a well-ventilated area when using this powerful solution. Apply it to the cultured marble with a large sponge, rinse with clear water, and buff dry. Dirt and soap film are quickly and inexpensively removed.

Best

Soft Scrub Cleanser (The Clorox Company), a mildly abrasive liquid cleanser, is the best product for cleaning cultured marble. Squeeze this mild cleaner onto a sponge or directly onto the surface to dissolve scum and dirt, leaving a clean finish after rinsing with clear water and wiping the counter dry.

Other Products Tested

Lysol Basin/Tub/Tile Cleaner (Lehn & Fink Products Division of Sterling Drug Inc.)— pump spray; very good cleaner; moderate odor.
Dow Disinfectant Bathroom Cleaner (The Dow Chemical Co.)—aerosol; moderately good cleaner; pleasant pine odor.

Plastic Laminate

Called by many trade names, such as Formica, plastic laminate is used extensively for countertops throughout the house. It comes in a glossy, matte, or textured surface.

Do

- Apply an appliance wax or light furniture wax to brighten dull surfaces.

Don'ts

- **Do not** use abrasive cleaners and steel wool—they will mar the surface.
- **Do not** cut directly on the surface with knives.
- **Do not** set hot pans down on the surface—this causes burn marks.

Fastest

For general cleaning, wipe regularly with a damp cloth or sponge. **Scotch-Brite Household Scrub 'N Sponge** (3M) works particularly well. Moistened slightly with water, the white fiber side is just abrasive enough to loosen greasy smears and other soil. Turning the scrubber over, use the sponge side to wipe the surface damp-dry.

When a spot or stain persists, apply **Bon Ami Deluxe Polishing Cleanser** (Faultless Starch/Bon Ami Company) with a wet sponge; it cleans the spot without damaging or scratching the surface. Then rinse and damp-dry the countertop.

Cheapest

Nothing can be cheaper than a damp cloth or sponge for general cleaning, but baking soda (see Recommended Basic Products) is the cheapest way to rid countertops of stains. Just sprinkle the soda on the stain, rub in with a damp cloth or sponge, and rinse with clear water. This method even removes the stain left by the dye used to mark prices on food products.

Read manufacturer's cautions and warnings before using any product.

Countertops

Best

Soft Scrub Cleanser (The Clorox Company), a mild liquid abrasive, is an excellent way to clean soil and stains from these countertops. Squeeze a small amount directly onto the surface and rub in with a damp sponge. Rinse with clear water for a beautifully clean counter.

Other Products Tested

Formula 409 All Purpose Cleaner (The Clorox Company)—spray liquid; performs fast and efficiently; no rinsing; wipe off with a dry cloth.
Jubilee Kitchen Wax (S. C. Johnson & Son, Inc.)—aerosol foam; very good cleaner and wax; moderate odor; flammable.
Lemon Behold Furniture Polish (The Drackett Company)—aerosol furniture polish; very good wax finish; especially good for wood grain plastic laminate; moderate odor; flammable.
Glass Plus (Texize Chemicals Company)—spray liquid; very good cleaner; moderate odor.
Parsons' Clear Detergent Ammonia (Armour-Dial Inc.)—liquid; dilute ½ cup in 1 gallon warm water; good for grease film; strong odor.
Amway Zoom Spray Cleaner Concentrate (Amway Corp.)—spray concentrate diluted with equal part water; good for grease film; rinse with clear water; eye irritant.
Grease Relief (Texize Chemicals Company)—spray used full strength; cuts grease and dirt quickly; rinse with clear water.
Mica-Lustre (Multi-Care Corporation)—green liquid with silicone; expensive; good dressing that cleans and polishes; pleasant odor; reduces surface static electricity.
Countertop Magic (Magic American Chemical Corp.)—aerosol foam; moderately good cleaner; moderate odor.

Wood

Do's
- Oil periodically for moisture protection.
- Clean up after each use with a damp sponge.
- Remove stains with a solution of ¼ cup chlorine bleach in 1 quart warm water. Rinse, dry, and coat with oil.
- Get rid of odors by rubbing the surface with a slice of lemon.

Don't
- **Do not** set hot pans down on wooden countertops—they can leave burn marks.

Fastest and Cheapest

Baking soda (see Recommended Basic Products) cleans and deodorizes wooden surfaces. Mix ½ cup baking soda in 1 quart warm water and rub it on the wooden countertop, using a synthetic scouring pad (see Tools of the Trade). Rinse well with clear water and pat dry to remove excess moisture. When completely dry, restore the finish by using boiled linseed oil or salad oil, rubbed in with a steel wool pad.

Treat the countertop with two coats, applied 24 hours apart, and blot up the excess oil after application.

Best

Martens Wood Preservative (Martens Mfg., Inc., A Div. of Foley Mfg. Co.) is an excellent product for restoring the surface of wooden countertops. First, lightly sand any heavily soiled areas of the wood. Then set the plastic bottle in a pan of hot tap water for a few minutes to make sure the contents are completely liquified, pour a small amount of the preservative onto the surface, and rub it in with a lint-free cloth. Let it penetrate for 30 minutes and wipe off any excess.

Fireplaces

Whether you have a small fireplace set into the corner of your den, or one that spans the entire length of a wall, a fireplace needs regular care and cleaning to assure a safe and efficient fire. Creosote, a flammable, tar-like substance that accumulates in the chimney and flue, can be removed by the homeowner, eliminating the worry of at least one potential fire hazard.

Do's

- Give your fireplace and its accessories routine cleaning throughout the wood-burning season to eliminate that end-of-the-year accumulation of soot, ashes, and creosote tars.
- Vacuum or dust the hearth area weekly to prevent dust and soot build-up.
- Burn only seasoned, well-dried wood to minimize dangerous creosote build-up.
- Inspect the firebox, flue, and chimney yearly for creosote accumulation.

Don'ts

- **Do not** use water to drown a fire unless it is an absolute emergency. This makes a paste of the ashes that is difficult to remove.
- **Do not** sweep or vacuum the fireplace until all the embers have been extinguished for at least 12 hours.
- **Do not** use an abrasive cleanser inside the fireplace. Many leave a flammable residue and wear away firebrick.
- **Do not** use your fireplace as an incinerator. Paper products and green wood leave a dangerous creosote residue inside the chimney.

Read manufacturer's cautions and warnings before using any product.

Chimney and Flue

Your fireplace's chimney and flue must be cleaned properly at least biannually to assure a safe fire.

Do's

- Only clean your chimney when the roof is completely dry.
- Use every precaution—this can be a dangerous job.
- Wear rubber-soled shoes for good traction on the roof.
- Seal the fireplace opening in the room with a scrap sheet of plywood or heavy plastic held in place by masking tape. Make sure there are no leaks.
- Use a flashlight to inspect the chimney for obstructions.

Don'ts

- **Do not** sweep your chimney on a windy or rainy day.
- **Do not** remove the fireplace covering until the dust and soot have settled for about 2 hours.
- **Do not** lean into the chimney.

Fastest, Cheapest, and Best

After you seal the fireplace opening in your room, take a burlap bag and fill it with wadded paper. Place a brick or two in the bottom for added weight. Drop the bag into the chimney suspended on a rope that is at least five feet longer than the chimney and move it up and down inside of the chimney. Follow this procedure around the perimeter of the chimney.

After the dust and soot has settled for about 2 hours, remove the plywood or plastic from the fireplace opening, hold a plastic garbage bag under the damper as you open it to catch the soot, and vacuum the firebox.

Firebox

The firebox is the area that contains the fire; it is commonly constructed of either metal sheeting or firebrick. Since the heat of the fire keeps the firebox clean (in much the same way a self-cleaning oven works), very little upkeep is required.

Do's

- Gently scrub the walls of the firebox opening with a stiff-bristled brush (not a wire brush) only to the height of the lintel (the heavy steel brace that supports the masonry above the fireplace opening).
- Clean firebrick the same way as metal sheeting, but use gentle strokes on firebrick as it crumbles easily.
- Scrub the firebox with a dry brush to remove caked ashes.
- Sweep up dry soot and ashes from the floor of the firebox regularly.
- Dispose of ashes in a fireplace that has an ash pit by removing the grate and brushing the ashes and soot into it.
- Shovel the bulk of the ashes into a bag if your fireplace doesn't have an ash pit; vacuum the remaining light ashes.

Don'ts

- **Do not** bend any edges of a metal firebox where it joins the flue. Bent edges leave openings to the wall studs or supports where fire could spread.
- **Do not** use water on firebrick as it may cause the porous material to lose its heat-retaining qualities.

Fire Screen

Most fire screens are black painted metal, though a few are brass-plated and may be cleaned like brass fireplace tools.

Fastest, Cheapest, and Best

To clean the fireplace screen, mix ½ cup vinegar and 1 gallon warm water. Add 1 teaspoon ammonia (see Recommended Basic Products). Dip a cloth into the solution and wipe down both sides of the screen. Rinse with a cloth dipped in clear, warm water.

Glass Enclosure

Glass enclosures for the fireplace present a special cleaning problem. They are constructed of a heat-resistant, tempered glass. To clean the glass and metal edging facing the room, also see Windows.

Do

- Clean the glass facing the fire after every second fire to remove the residue of soot and fumes.

Fastest

Smoke stains on the inside can be removed with the following recipe: mix ½ cup vinegar with 1 gallon clear, warm water. Add 1 tablespoon clear ammonia (see Recommended Basic Products). Either spray this solution on the glass, or wipe it on with a cloth dipped in the solution. Rinse with clear, warm water and dry with a clean, dry cloth. Repeat several times if the enclosure is really dirty.

Best

The best product for removing smoke, soot, and creosote from glass fireplace enclosures is **Butcher's Fireplace & Stove Glass Cleaner** (The Butcher Polish Co.). This pump spray container makes applying the product directly onto the glass surface easy; wipe off the product and dirt with a dry cloth or paper towels, repeating the procedure on heavily soiled areas. For baked-on soot, scrape the glass very carefully with a glass scraper to avoid scratching the surface.

Read manufacturer's cautions and warnings before using any product.

Fireplaces

Other Products Tested

Formula 409 All Purpose Cleaner (The Clorox Company)—pump spray; removes smoke and grease; wipe immediately from glass; rinsing needed; pleasant odor.
Glass Plus (Texize Chemicals Company)—pump spray glass cleaner; no rinsing; moderate odor; use with a grease remover.
Grease Relief (Texize Chemicals Company)—pump spray that removes smoke and grease, but leaves a film that is difficult to remove; rinsing needed.

Grate and Cast Iron Tools

Like the chimney, the grate, usually made from cast iron, can also accumulate a build-up of creosote tars or sap from burning green wood. Tools that are made of cast iron may be cleaned using the same procedures and products as for the grate.

Fastest

To remove all the build-up that isn't permanently burned on, take the grate or tool outside and hose it down. Sprinkle a little **Comet Cleanser** (Procter & Gamble) on the surface and scrub with a stiff-bristled brush. Rinse very well to insure that any residue is washed off.

Cheapest

Scrub the surface with a stiff-bristled brush. This should remove any caked-on ashes and soot, but will not take off tars.

Best

Take the grate outside and hose it down, then scrub with **Brillo Steel Wool Soap Pads** (Purex Corporation). It may take several pads, but it will remove all the soot that can be removed. Ordinarily, no precautions need to be taken, but since this job requires a lot of pads, wear rubber gloves to protect your hands from abrasion.

Other Products Tested

Mr. Muscle Overnight Oven Cleaner (The Drackett Company)—toxic, use outdoors; not designed for fireplace grates, but is a fair cleaner for tar; rubber gloves required; must set overnight; rinse thoroughly to remove *all* residue.

Mantel and Hearth

The trim surrounding a fireplace is commonly made from wood or masonry tile. Also popular are brick, marble, or ceramic tile (also see Walls—Brick, Objets d'Art—Marble, and Walls—Ceramic Tile).

Do

- Clean painted wooden mantels regularly by removing smoke and dust.

Don't

- **Do not** mar the finish as you clean a stained or varnished mantel. Treat it as you would a fine piece of furniture.

Cheapest, Masonry Tile

Masonry tile may be cleaned inexpensively by sprinkling a little dry baking soda (see Recommended Basic Products) onto the tile. Rub it with a bristle brush to absorb most stains and clean the tile. Vacuum away the dry powder.

Best, Masonry Tile

Red Devil Fireplace Cleaner (Meeco Mfg. Inc.) mixed with three parts water to one part cleaner for tough stains, or five parts to one for regular maintenance, cleans masonry tile best. Spray on with a trigger-spray bottle; rinse well with clear water and wipe clean. Allow the surface to dry. If shadows appear after use on white stone or brick tiles, brush well with a dry brush after the surface has dried completely.

Other Products Tested

Soft Scrub Cleanser (The Clorox Company)—mild liquid abrasive; pleasant odor; can cause permanent scratching to tile if used too often or rubbed too hard.

Cheapest, Painted Wood

An inexpensive way to clean painted wood on your mantel is to mix 2 tablespoons of a gentle dishwashing detergent (see Recommended Basic Products) in 1 gallon warm water. Wipe with a cloth or sponge. Don't let any excess run off. Clean from the bottom up to avoid streaking.

Best, Painted Wood

Spray **Fantastik Multi-Surface Spray Cleaner** (Texize Chemicals Company) directly onto a soiled painted surface and wipe with a clean cloth, damp sponge, or paper towel. Spray only a small portion at a time, as any dripping will streak the painted surface.

Other Products Tested

Amway Zoom Spray Cleaner Concentrate (Amway Corp.)—spray; dilute or use full strength for tough spots; very effective, but more expensive than similar products.
Formula 409 All Purpose Cleaner (The Clorox Company)—pump spray; no rinsing, but

Read manufacturer's cautions and warnings before using any product.

Fireplaces

must be wiped immediately as it can leave a film; pleasant odor.
Soft Scrub Cleanser (The Clorox Company)—mild liquid abrasive; rinse or wipe clean; pleasant odor; may scratch surface if rubbed too hard or too long.

Fastest, Varnished or Stained Wood

For varnished or stained wood, spray **Complete All Purpose Polishing Cleaner** (S. C. Johnson & Son, Inc.) directly onto the surface, holding the bottle about six inches away from the surface. Wipe with a soft cloth.

Cheapest, Varnished or Stained Wood

For a varnished or stained mantel, spray **Lemon Behold Furniture Polish** (The Drackett Company) onto a cloth or directly onto the mantel. Wipe dry. A bit of elbow grease is required to remove any film and get a glossy shine.

Best, Varnished or Stained Wood

On varnished or stained mantels, apply **Formby's Furniture Cleaner** (Formby's Inc.) to the surface and rub into the wood. If desired, this can be followed up with an application of **Formby's Lemon Oil Furniture Treatment** (Formby's Inc.) for added protection. About once a year, an application of any brand of carnauba wax can be applied to the surface for a beautiful finish, but the buffing requires a lot of work.

Other Products Tested

Lemon Pledge (S. C. Johnson & Son, Inc.)—aerosol; pleasant odor; easily smudged or smeared.
Old English Lemon Creme Furniture Polish (Boyle-Midway Inc.)—aerosol; pleasant odor; can leave an oily film if not completely rubbed in.

Tools

The andirons and fire tools are usually brass or brass-plated. Cast iron tools are cleaned with the same procedures and products listed in Grate and Cast Iron Tools. If the tools are brass, there are many products that can restore them to their original beauty with little time and effort.

Fastest

Apply generous amounts of **Amway Metal Cleaner** (Amway Corp.) with a sponge or soft cloth. Rub gently to clean. While still wet, rinse off with warm water. Wipe dry and polish with a clean, soft cloth. This product is not recommended for use on simulated brass, as it can remove the finish.

Cheapest

For routine cleaning and dusting, spray a little **Windex Glass Cleaner** (The Drackett Company) on a dry cloth and wipe the metal clean.

Best

Apply **Tarni-Shield Copper & Brass Cleaner** (3M) liberally with a soft cloth. For the best tarnish protection, rub thoroughly. Rinse in clear water and let stand 2 to 5 minutes. Buff dry to a high luster with a clean, soft cloth.

Other Products Tested

Tarn-X (Jelmar Co.)—liquid; wipe on and rinse immediately in hot water; does not give as brilliant a shine as other products listed; strong odor.

Floors

Floors come in a variety of materials. Knowing the specific materials that your floors are made of will be an important factor in their care, since floors can be damaged by using the wrong cleaning method or product.

Asphalt Tile

This tile recovers well from indentations, but grease, oil, and solvents such as kerosene, gasoline, naphtha, and turpentine, or harsh cleaning preparations, strong soaps, and scouring can damage the surface.

Do's

- Wipe up spills and clean sticky spots immediately.
- Protect heavy traffic areas with mats or throw rugs.
- Use plastic casters and cups on furniture legs to minimize scratches and indentations.
- Protect the floor when moving heavy furniture.
- Sweep, dust-mop, or vacuum heavy traffic areas, entrances, and frequently used rooms regularly.
- Vacuum asphalt floors thoroughly each week to pick up loose dirt. Use a crevice tool or small brush attachment to clean around baseboards, radiators, and other hard-to-reach places.
- Damp mop weekly. If you use a cleaner/polish that cannot withstand this treatment, you must reapply the cleaner/polish instead of just damp mopping.
- Remove heel marks by dipping grade 000 steel wool in your liquid floor wax. Rub the spot gently and wipe with a damp cloth.
- Let floor dry completely before walking on it.
- Occasionally, remove wax build-up with a recommended cleaner or wax stripper.

Floors

Don'ts

- **Do not** use solvent-based products. They can soften and damage the tile.
- **Do not** shake a water-based liquid polish before using.
- **Do not** scour or use very hot water or strong soaps.
- **Do not** allow grease, oil, or solvents to contact the tile.
- **Do not** flood the floor with water. Excess water can seep into the seams and loosen adhesives that hold the flooring down.
- **Do not** use chemically treated or oiled mops and dust cloths that leave a sticky, dust-collecting film.
- **Do not** use rubber compound floor protectors on furniture legs.
- **Do not** attempt to push or pull heavy articles across an unprotected asphalt tile floor.

Fastest

Mop & Glo (Lehn & Fink Products Division of Sterling Drug Inc.) works fast on asphalt tile. This cleaner/polish requires only one step, using a sponge mop and pail of water. It's convenient to apply with the handy plastic squeeze bottle with a flip-top opening and gives a sparkling clean shine. However, it does not last as long as most self-polishing liquids and requires frequent re-application.

Cheapest

A home recipe is the cheapest way of cleaning and removing wax from this type of floor and does a great job. Mix ¼ cup **Spic and Span** (Procter & Gamble), 1 cup clear ammonia (see Recommended Basic Products), and ½ gallon cool or cold water. **Caution:** Wear rubber gloves and work in a well-ventilated area when using this powerful solution. Apply to the floor with a sponge mop, using pressure for heavily soiled areas; rinse with cool clear water for spotless results. Apply two thin coats of **Klear Floor Finish** (S. C. Johnson & Son, Inc.), allowing the floor to dry between coats and before walking on it. Apply the wax with a long-handled wax applicator that has a washable chenille pad.

Best

Oakite All Purpose Cleaner (Oakite Products, Inc.) is a phosphate-free, powder cleaner that rates highest for cleaning and removing wax from asphalt tile. Dissolve ½ cup in 1 gallon warm water and apply to the floor with a sponge mop. Although the label does not say it is necessary, rinse the tile with clear water to make sure no film remains to dull the finish. When the floor is dry, apply two thin coats of **Klear Floor Finish** (S. C. Johnson & Son, Inc.). Klear is a water-based, self-polishing liquid that gives an even, high gloss and good scuff resistance over a long period of time. Detergent mopping doesn't affect its shine.

Other Products Tested

CLEANER/POLISHES. Step Saver (S. C. Johnson & Son, Inc.)—liquid with ammonia, very good cleaner; moderate gloss; pleasant odor.

POLISHES—SELF-POLISHING. Hard Gloss Glo-Coat (S. C. Johnson & Son, Inc.)—liquid with moderate gloss; very good scuff resistance; no hazing; stands up well to detergent washing.
Stanhome Super Floor Finish (Stanley Home Products, Inc.)—moderate-gloss liquid; very good scuff resistance; no hazing; stands up well to detergent washing.
Super Bravo Floor Finish (S. C. Johnson & Son, Inc.)—self-polishing liquid; excellent shine; stands up to detergent washing.
Beacon Floor Wax (Lehn & Fink Products Division of Sterling Drug Inc.)—moderate-gloss liquid; good scuff resistance; fair when washed with detergent.
Lundmark's Acrylic Floor Wax (Lundmark Wax Company)—high-gloss liquid; fair scuff resistance; stands up well to detergent washing.
Future Acrylic Floor Finish (S. C. Johnson & Son, Inc.)—high-gloss liquid; fair scuff resistance; stands up well to detergent washing.

WAX STRIPPERS AND CLEANERS. Parsons' Wax & Acrylic Remover (Armour-Dial Inc.)—liquid; use undiluted; excellent stripper and cleaner.
Mex Multi-Purpose Cleaner (United Gilsonite Laboratories)—powder; very good performance; good stripper; excellent cleaner in weaker solution.
Trewax Instant Wax Stripper & Floor Cleaner (Trewax Company)—liquid; very good as stripper; excellent cleaner.
Lundmark High Power Wax Remover (Lundmark Wax Company)—good wax stripper and cleaner.

Brick

Brick flooring appears to be very durable, due to its hard, fired surface. But it is actually quite porous and stains easily. For this reason, it must be sealed and waxed. Also see Fireplaces and Walls—Brick.

Do's

- Wipe up spills and clean sticky spots immediately.
- Protect heavy traffic areas with mats or throw rugs.
- Use plastic casters and cups on furniture legs to minimize scratches.
- Protect the floor when moving heavy furniture or appliances.
- Seal the floor with a commercial sealer.
- Sweep, dust-mop, or vacuum heavy traffic areas, entrances, and frequently used rooms regularly.
- Weekly, vacuum all floors thoroughly to pick up loose dirt. Use a crevice tool or small brush attachment to clean around baseboards, radiators, and other hard-to-reach places.
- Damp mop weekly with a sponge mop or string mop.
- Strip the wax build-up and rewax occasionally if you use a water-based, self-polishing liquid wax.
- Apply a wax-stripping product with a scrub brush or floor-scrubbing machine with a brush attachment.
- Rinse the floor thoroughly with clean water after applying the stripper according to the manufacturer's directions.
- Apply wax to the floor. You can use either a water-based, self-polishing wax or a paste wax.
- Apply a solvent-based polish over a water-based one if desired.
- Allow the floor to dry completely before walking on it.

Floors

Don'ts

- **Do not** let acids come in contact with the floor.
- **Do not** shake a water-based liquid polish before using.
- **Do not** scour or use strong soaps.
- **Do not** apply a water-based polish over a solvent-based polish.
- **Do not** use chemically treated or oiled mops and dust cloths that leave a sticky, dust-collecting film.
- **Do not** use abrasives.
- **Do not** use varnish or lacquer as a sealer.
- **Do not** use rubber compound floor protectors on furniture legs.
- **Do not** attempt to push or pull heavy articles across an unprotected floor.

Fastest and Cheapest

By using this homemade solution in conjunction with a water-based, acrylic self-polishing wax, you can care for a brick floor quickly and inexpensively. Most acrylic liquid waxes are self-sealing, so you can skip the application of a sealer. This method is not as effective as the stripper, sealer, wax treatment. Clean and strip the floor with the following solution: ¼ cup **Spic and Span** (Procter & Gamble), 1 cup clear ammonia (see Recommended Basic Products), and ½ gallon cool or cold water. **Caution:** Wear rubber gloves and work in a well-ventilated area when using this powerful solution. Apply to the floor with a sponge mop, using pressure for heavily soiled areas; rinse with cool, clear water for spotless results. Then apply two thin coats of **Future Acrylic Floor Finish** (S. C. Johnson & Son, Inc.).

Best

Strip off the wax build-up with undiluted **Parsons' Wax & Acrylic Remover** (Armour-Dial Inc.). Apply with a scrub brush or a brush attachment on a floor scrubbing machine. Rinse the floor thoroughly with clean water. Seal with **Trewax Beauty Sealer** (Trewax Company). Then apply two thin coats of **Klear Floor Finish** (S. C. Johnson & Son, Inc.). Klear is a water-based, self-polishing liquid that gives an even, high gloss and good scuff resistance over a long period of time. Detergent mopping doesn't affect its shine. Allow to dry thoroughly between coats. Use a long-handled wax applicator with a lamb's wool pad.

If you wish to use paste wax, apply **Johnson Paste Wax** (S. C. Johnson & Son, Inc.), which provides a high-luster finish that can be renewed simply by rebuffing. Apply the wax to the brushes of an electric floor care machine with a spatula in small amounts. Slowly operate the machine back and forth to apply an even, thin coat. Allow floor to dry and then buff.

Other Products Tested

POLISHES—SELF-POLISHING. Hard Gloss Glo-Coat (S. C. Johnson & Son, Inc.)—liquid with moderate gloss; very good scuff resistance; no hazing; stands up well to detergent washing.

Stanhome Super Floor Finish (Stanley Home Products, Inc.)—moderate-gloss liquid; very good scuff resistance; no hazing; stands up well to detergent washing.

Super Bravo Floor Finish (S. C. Johnson & Son, Inc.)—self-polishing liquid; excellent shine; stands up to detergent washing.

Beacon Floor Wax (Lehn & Fink Products Division of Sterling Drug Inc.)—moderate-gloss liquid; good scuff resistance; fair when washed with detergent.

Lundmark's Acrylic Floor Wax (Lundmark Wax Company)—high-gloss liquid; fair scuff resistance; stands up well to detergent washing.

Future Acrylic Floor Finish (S. C. Johnson & Son, Inc.)—high-gloss liquid; fair scuff resistance; stands up well to detergent washing.

WAX STRIPPERS AND CLEANERS. **Mex Multi-Purpose Cleaner** (United Gilsonite Laboratories)—powder; very good performance; good stripper; excellent cleaner in weaker solution.

Trewax Instant Wax Stripper & Floor Cleaner (Trewax Company)—liquid; very good as stripper; excellent cleaner.

Lundmark High Power Wax Remover (Lundmark Wax Company)—good wax stripper and cleaner.

BUFFABLE WAXES AND POLISHES. **Butcher's Bowling Alley Paste Wax** (The Butcher Polish Co.)—easy to apply and buff up by hand or electric polisher; rebuffs well to remove slight scuff marks.

Trewax Clear (Trewax Company)—paste; to be buffed with electric floor polisher; excellent shine.

Non-Slip Liquid Floor Wax (Trewax Company)—for use with electric floor polisher; excellent shine; can be buffed after damp mopping.

Ceramic Tile, Glazed

Highly glazed ceramic tile requires little more than a regular dusting and mopping. Also see Countertops—Ceramic Tile.

Do's

- Vacuum floor regularly. Use attachments to get all dust, dirt, and debris out of hard-to-reach areas.
- Damp mop with an all-purpose cleaner.
- Use a synthetic scouring pad and non-abrasive cleaner for stubborn spots.
- Dry floor with a soft cloth to avoid streaks.

Don't

- **Do not** use abrasive powders or steel wool pads.

Floors

Fastest, Cheapest, and Best

The following home recipe is the fastest, cheapest, and best way to clean a glazed ceramic tile floor. It does a great job. Mix ¼ cup **Spic and Span** (Procter & Gamble), 1 cup clear ammonia (see Recommended Basic Products), and ½ gallon cool or cold water. **Caution:** Wear rubber gloves and work in a well-ventilated area when using this powerful solution. Apply to the floor with a sponge mop, using pressure for heavily soiled areas; rinse with cool, clear water for spotless results. Dry with a soft cloth.

Ceramic Tile, Unglazed

Do's
- Wipe up spills and clean sticky spots immediately.
- Protect heavy traffic areas with mats or throw rugs.
- Use plastic casters and cups on furniture legs to minimize scratches.
- Protect the floor when moving heavy furniture or appliances.
- Seal the floor with a commercial sealer. Apply a water-based wax to the floor.
- Sweep, dust-mop, or vacuum heavy traffic areas, entrances, and frequently used rooms regularly.
- Weekly, vacuum all floors thoroughly to pick up loose dirt. Use a crevice tool or small brush attachment to clean around baseboards, radiators, and other hard-to-reach places.
- Damp mop weekly with a sponge mop or string mop.
- Strip the wax build-up and rewax occasionally.
- Apply a wax-stripping product with a scrub brush or floor-scrubbing machine with a brush attachment.
- Rinse the floor thoroughly with clean water, after applying the stripper according to the manufacturer's directions.
- Apply wax to the floor.
- Apply a solvent-based polish over a water-based one if desired.
- Allow the floor to dry completely before walking on it.

Don'ts
- **Do not** let acids come in contact with the floor.
- **Do not** shake a water-based liquid polish before using.
- **Do not** scour or use strong soaps.
- **Do not** apply water-based polishes over solvent-based polishes.
- **Do not** use chemically treated or oiled mops and dust cloths that leave a sticky, dust-collecting film.
- **Do not** use abrasives.
- **Do not** use varnish or lacquer as a sealer.
- **Do not** use rubber compound floor protectors on furniture legs.
- **Do not** attempt to push or pull heavy articles across an unprotected floor.

Fastest

Strip off the wax build-up with undiluted **Parsons' Wax & Acrylic Remover** (Armour-Dial Inc.). Rinse the floor thoroughly with clean water. Apply **Trewax Terrazzo and Slate Sealer/Finish** (Trewax Company) and buff if you wish.

Cheapest

By using this homemade solution in conjunction with a water-based, acrylic self-polishing wax, you can care for an unglazed ceramic tile floor quickly and inexpensively. Most acrylic liquid waxes are self-sealing, so you can skip the application of a sealer. Clean and strip the floor with the following solution: ¼ cup **Spic and Span** (Procter & Gamble), 1 cup clear ammonia (see Recommended Basic Products), and ½ gallon cool or cold water. **Caution:** Wear rubber gloves and work in a well-ventilated area when using this powerful solution. Apply to the floor with a sponge mop, using pressure for heavily soiled areas; rinse with cool, clear water for spotless results. Then apply two thin coats of **Future Acrylic Floor Finish** (S. C. Johnson & Son, Inc.).

Best

Strip off the wax build-up with undiluted **Parsons' Wax & Acrylic Remover** (Armour-Dial Inc.). Rinse the floor thoroughly with clean water. Seal with **Trewax Beauty Sealer** (Trewax Company). Then apply two thin coats of **Klear Floor Finish** (S. C. Johnson & Son, Inc.). Klear is a water-based, self-polishing liquid that gives an even, high gloss and has good scuff resistance over a long period of time. Detergent mopping doesn't affect its shine. Allow to dry thoroughly between coats. Use a long-handled wax applicator with a lamb's wool pad.

Other Products Tested

POLISHES—SELF-POLISHING. **Hard Gloss Glo-Coat** (S. C. Johnson & Son, Inc.)—liquid with moderate gloss; very good scuff resistance; no hazing; stands up well to detergent washing.
Stanhome Super Floor Finish (Stanley Home Products, Inc.)—moderate-gloss liquid; very good scuff resistance; no hazing; stands up well to detergent washing.
Super Bravo Floor Finish (S. C. Johnson & Son, Inc.)—self-polishing liquid; excellent shine; stands up to detergent washing.
Beacon Floor Wax (Lehn & Fink Products Division of Sterling Drug Inc.)—moderate-gloss liquid; good scuff resistance; fair when washed with detergent.
Lundmark's Acrylic Floor Wax (Lundmark Wax Company)—high-gloss liquid; fair scuff resistance; stands up well to detergent washing.
Future Acrylic Floor Finish (S. C. Johnson & Son, Inc.)—high-gloss liquid; fair scuff resistance; stands up well to detergent washing.

WAX STRIPPERS AND CLEANERS. **Mex Multi-Purpose Cleaner** (United Gilsonite Laboratories)—powder; very good performance; good stripper; excellent cleaner in weaker solution.
Trewax Instant Wax Stripper & Floor Cleaner (Trewax Company)—liquid; very good as stripper; excellent cleaner.

Read manufacturer's cautions and warnings before using any product.

Floors

Lundmark High Power Wax Remover (Lundmark Wax Company)—good wax stripper and cleaner.

BUFFABLE WAXES AND POLISHES. Non-Slip Liquid Floor Wax (Trewax Company)—for use with electric floor polisher; excellent shine; can be buffed after damp mopping.

Concrete

Floors made of common concrete, like those found in unfinished basements and in garages, are very porous and soak up stains quickly. Both painted and unpainted concrete floors are treated the same way.

Do's

- Seal basement concrete floors.
- Vacuum basement concrete floors thoroughly.
- Wash basement concrete floors with a strong all-purpose cleaner solution.
- For garage concrete floors, soak up oil and grease stains immediately with an oil-absorbing product, such as **Oil-Dri** (Oil-Dri Corp. of America).
- Use a stiff broom to sweep out dirt, dust, and litter.
- Using a stiff broom, scour the surface with a strong all-purpose cleaner solution and flush with clean water.
- Work from the back of the garage and flush out remaining dirt with a garden hose.

Don't

- **Do not** let stains set for even a short time on any concrete floor.

Fastest and Cheapest

After removing loose surface dirt by sweeping and hosing (garages) or vacuuming (basements), use this homemade cleaning solution: ¼ cup **Spic and Span** (Procter & Gamble), 1 cup clear ammonia (see Recommended Basic Products), and ½ gallon cool or cold water. **Caution:** Wear rubber gloves and work in a well-ventilated area when using this powerful solution. Apply to the floor with a sponge mop, using pressure for heavily soiled areas; rinse with cool, clear water for spotless results. Let the floor dry. Basement floors must be sealed; use **Trewax Beauty Sealer** (Trewax Company).

Best

Use the above procedure, but use ½ cup **Oakite All Purpose Cleaner** (Oakite Products, Inc.) in 1 gallon warm water; then seal with **Trewax Beauty Sealer** (Trewax Company).

Other Products Tested

CLEANERS. Mex Multi-Purpose Cleaner (United Gilsonite Laboratories)—excellent cleaner; performs close to Oakite.

Cork

Water and water-based products are taboo on cork tile floors. You must use only solvent-based cleaners and polishes for maintaining this porous tile flooring.

Do's

- Wipe up spills and clean sticky spots immediately.
- Protect heavy traffic areas with mats or throw rugs.
- Use plastic casters and cups on furniture legs to minimize scratches and indentations.
- Use an appliance dolly to move heavy furniture and appliances over a cork floor.
- Seal the floor with a varnish, shellac, or lacquer.
- Dust-mop or vacuum heavy traffic areas, entrances, and frequently used rooms regularly.
- Vacuum all floors thoroughly weekly. Use a crevice tool or small brush attachment to clean around baseboards, radiators, and other hard-to-reach places.
- Remove heel marks by applying a solvent-based wax, polish, or cleaner to a rag and rubbing the mark.
- Apply a liquid or paste solvent-based wax. Use a wood cleaner first, if necessary.
- About twice a year, rewax with a solvent-based liquid or paste wax. No stripping is necessary, because the solvents in the new wax will strip off the old wax.
- Make sure the room is well-ventilated when using solvent-based waxes and polishes.
- Shake solvent-based liquid polishes vigorously before using.
- Buff when the flooring appears dull to renew the shine.

Don'ts

- **Do not** use water or detergents on cork floors.
- **Do not** use water-based products on cork floors.
- **Do not** allow grease, oil, acids, alkalies, or abrasives to contact the floor.
- **Do not** use chemically treated or oiled mops and dust cloths that leave a sticky, dust-collecting film.
- **Do not** use rubber compound floor protectors on furniture legs.
- **Do not** attempt to push or pull heavy articles across an unprotected floor.

Fastest and Cheapest

Bruce One Step (Armour-Dial Inc.) cleans and polishes a cork floor quickly. After vacuuming the floor, pour this solvent-based liquid on a small area and rub lightly with a clean, dry wax applicator. Working on a small section at a time, stroke the floor in one direction. Blot up excess liquid with a clean cloth. This self-polishing liquid gives the floor a beautiful gloss.

Best

Wood Preen (The Kiwi Polish Company Pty. Ltd.), a liquid cleaner and wax, is the best product for cleaning cork floors. After vacuuming floors, apply with a dry wax applicator or cloth on a small area at a time. Let soak 3 minutes and wipe up excess before it dries. When dry, buff with a floor polisher. Although it is not self-polishing, it cleans and buffs up to a beautiful shine and will buff up nicely when scuff marks appear.

Read manufacturer's cautions and warnings before using any product.

Floors

Other Products Tested

CLEANERS. **Bruce Deep Cleaner** (Armour-Dial Inc.)—liquid; excellent cleaner; leaves light wax finish.
Trewax Wood Cleaner (Trewax Company)—liquid; very good cleaner for general or spot cleaning; leaves a surface that needs to be rewaxed or polished.

POLISHES—SELF-POLISHING. **Bruce Acrylic** (Armour-Dial Inc.)—liquid; very good to excellent performance.
Bissell One Step Wood Floor Care (Bissell Inc.)—liquid; very good cleaner; high gloss.

POLISHES—BUFFABLE. **Bruce Clean & Wax** (Armour-Dial Inc.)—liquid to be used with electric floor polisher; excellent performance and shine.
Johnson Paste Wax (S. C. Johnson & Son, Inc.)—paste to use with a soft cloth or an electric polisher for application and buffing; high-luster finish; can be rebuffed.
Butcher's Bowling Alley Paste Wax (The Butcher Polish Co.)—easy to apply and buff by hand or electric polisher; rebuffs well to remove slight scuff marks.
Trewax Clear (Trewax Company)—paste; to be buffed with electric floor polisher; use after wood cleaner application; excellent shine.

Flagstone and Slate

These natural stone flooring materials are similar in that they have rough, porous surfaces and are set into grout. They must be sealed for protection.

Do's

- Wipe up spills and clean sticky spots immediately.
- Protect heavy traffic areas with mats or throw rugs.
- Use plastic casters and cups on furniture legs to minimize scratches.
- Protect the floor when moving heavy furniture or appliances.
- Seal the floor with a commercial sealer.
- Sweep, dust-mop, or vacuum heavy traffic areas, entrances, and frequently used rooms regularly to remove dust and litter.
- Vacuum all floors thoroughly weekly to pick up loose dirt. Use a crevice tool or small brush attachment to clean around baseboards, radiators, and other hard-to-reach places.
- Damp mop weekly with a sponge mop or string mop, using either clear water or an all-purpose cleaner solution in warm water.
- Wring the mop until it doesn't drip, and apply it to the floor in slow, even strokes, with just enough pressure to loosen and pick up dirt.
- If a water-based, self-polishing liquid wax is used, occasionally strip the wax build-up and rewax.
- Apply a wax-stripping product with a scrub brush or floor-scrubbing machine with a brush attachment.
- After applying the stripper according to manufacturer's directions, rinse the floor thoroughly with clean water.
- Apply wax to the floor. You can use either a water-based, self-polishing wax or a paste wax. Test a paste wax in a corner to see if it will discolor the flooring.
- If a solvent-based paste wax is used, rewax to both strip the old wax and renew the shine.

Don'ts

- **Do not** let acids come in contact with the floor.
- **Do not** shake a water-based liquid polish before using.
- **Do not** scour or use strong soaps.
- **Do not** apply water-based polishes over solvent-based polishes.
- **Do not** use chemically treated or oiled mops and dust cloths that leave a sticky, dust-collecting film.
- **Do not** use abrasives.
- **Do not** use varnish or lacquer as a sealer.
- **Do not** use rubber compound floor protectors on furniture legs.
- **Do not** attempt to push or pull heavy articles across an unprotected floor.

Fastest

Strip off the wax build-up with undiluted **Parsons' Wax & Acrylic Remover** (Armour-Dial Inc.). Rinse the floor thoroughly with clean water. Apply **Trewax Terrazzo and Slate Sealer/Finish** (Trewax Company) and buff.

Cheapest

A home recipe is the cheapest way of cleaning this type of floor. Mix ¼ cup **Spic and Span** (Procter & Gamble), 1 cup clear ammonia (see Recommended Basic Products), and ½ gallon cool or cold water. **Caution:** Wear rubber gloves and work in a well-ventilated area when using this powerful solution. Apply to the floor with a sponge mop, using pressure for heavily soiled areas. Rinse with the floor thoroughly with clean water. Apply **Trewax Terrazzo and Slate Sealer/Finish** (Trewax Company) and buff.

Best

Strip off the wax build-up with undiluted **Parsons' Wax & Acrylic Remover** (Armour-Dial Inc). Rinse the floor thoroughly with clean water. Seal with **Trewax Beauty Sealer** (Trewax Company). Then apply two thin coats of **Klear Floor Finish** (S. C. Johnson & Son, Inc.), allowing the floor to dry thoroughly between applications. Use a long-handled wax applicator with a lamb's wool pad.

Or, if you prefer to use a paste wax, apply **Trewax Clear** (Trewax Company) to the brushes of a floor polishing machine with a spatula in small amounts. Slowly operate the polisher back and forth to apply an even, thin coat. When dry, buff floor.

Other Products Tested

POLISHES—SELF-POLISHING. Hard Gloss Glo-Coat (S. C. Johnson & Son, Inc.)— liquid with moderate gloss; very good scuff resistance; no hazing; stands up well to detergent washing.
Stanhome Super Floor Finish (Stanley Home Products, Inc.)—moderate-gloss liquid; very good scuff resistance; no hazing; stands up well to detergent washing.

Read manufacturer's cautions and warnings before using any product.

Floors

Super Bravo Floor Finish (S. C. Johnson & Son, Inc.)—self-polishing liquid; excellent shine; stands up to detergent washing.
Beacon Floor Wax (Lehn & Fink Products Division of Sterling Drug Inc.)—moderate-gloss liquid; good scuff resistance; fair when washed with detergent.
Lundmark's Acrylic Floor Wax (Lundmark Wax Company)—high-gloss liquid; fair scuff resistance; stands up well to detergent washing.
Future Acrylic Floor Finish (S. C. Johnson & Son, Inc.)—high-gloss liquid; fair scuff resistance; stands up well to detergent washing.

WAX STRIPPERS AND CLEANERS. Mex Multi-Purpose Cleaner (United Gilsonite Laboratories)—powder; very good performance; good stripper; excellent cleaner in weaker solution.
Trewax Instant Wax Stripper & Floor Cleaner (Trewax Company)—liquid; very good as stripper; excellent cleaner.
Lundmark High Power Wax Remover (Lundmark Wax Company)—good wax stripper and cleaner.

BUFFABLE WAXES AND POLISHES. Johnson Paste Wax (S. C. Johnson & Son, Inc.)—provides a high luster after buffing; rebuffing brings back original shine.
Butcher's Bowling Alley Paste Wax (The Butcher Polish Co.)—easy to apply and buff up by hand or electric polisher; rebuffs well to remove slight scuff marks.
Non-Slip Liquid Floor Wax (Trewax Company)—for use with electric floor polisher; excellent shine; can be buffed after damp mopping.

Linoleum

Linoleum must be waxed to shine and stand up to foot traffic effectively.

Do's

- Wipe up spills and clean sticky spots immediately.
- Protect heavy traffic areas with mats or throw rugs.
- Use plastic casters and cups on furniture legs to minimize scratches and indentations.
- Protect the floor when moving heavy furniture or appliances.
- Sweep, dust-mop, or vacuum heavy traffic areas, entrances, and frequently used rooms regularly to remove dust and litter.
- Vacuum linoleum floors thoroughly each week to pick up loose dirt. Use a crevice tool or small brush attachment to clean around baseboards, radiators, and other hard-to-reach places.
- Damp mop weekly.
- Remove heel marks by dipping grade 000 steel wool in your liquid floor wax. Rub the spot gently and wipe with a damp cloth.
- Occasionally, remove wax build-up with a recommended all-purpose cleaner or stripper.
- Always test a corner before stripping to make sure the product won't permanently damage the flooring. This is particularly true of older linoleum.
- Use an all-purpose cleaner solution or water-based cleaner/polish for routine care. Read the product label for precautionary measures.
- Apply two thin coats of water-based, self-polishing wax if an all-purpose cleaner solution is used.

Don'ts

- **Do not** use solvent-based products. They can soften and damage the linoleum.
- **Do not** shake a water-based liquid polish before using.
- **Do not** scour or use very hot water or strong soaps.
- **Do not** allow grease, oil, or solvents to contact the linoleum.
- **Do not** flood the floor with water.
- **Do not** use chemically treated or oiled mops and dust cloths that leave a sticky, dust-collecting film.
- **Do not** use rubber compound floor protectors on furniture legs.
- **Do not** attempt to push or pull heavy articles across an unprotected linoleum floor.

Fastest and Cheapest

Mop & Glo (Lehn & Fink Products Division of Sterling Drug Inc.) works fast on linoleum. This cleaner/polish requires only one step, using a sponge mop and pail of water. It's convenient to apply with the handy plastic squeeze bottle with a flip-top opening for a clean shine. However, it doesn't last as long as most self-polishing liquids, and requires frequent reapplications.

Best

Dissolve ½ cup **Mex Multi-Purpose Cleaner** (United Gilsonite Laboratories) in 1 gallon very warm water. Apply to the floor with a damp, squeezed-out mop. Rinse with clear water. This product cleans as well as strips wax efficiently. Then apply two thin coats (let dry between coats) of **Klear Floor Finish** (S. C. Johnson & Son, Inc.). Klear is a water-based, self-polishing liquid that gives an even, high gloss. It has good scuff resistance over a long period of time and can be detergent washed without losing its shine. Apply with a long-handled wax applicator with a washable, reusable chenille pad.

Other Products Tested

POLISHES—SELF-POLISHING. Hard Gloss Glo-Coat (S. C. Johnson & Son, Inc.)—liquid with moderate gloss; very good scuff resistance; no hazing; stands up well to detergent washing.
Stanhome Super Floor Finish (Stanley Home Products, Inc.)—moderate-gloss liquid; very good scuff resistance; no hazing; stands up well to detergent washing.
Super Bravo Floor Finish (S. C. Johnson & Son, Inc.)—self-polishing liquid; excellent shine; stands up to detergent washing.
Beacon Floor Wax (Lehn & Fink Products Division of Sterling Drug Inc.)—moderate-gloss liquid; good scuff resistance; fair when washed with detergent.
Lundmark's Acrylic Floor Wax (Lundmark Wax Company)—high-gloss liquid; fair scuff resistance; stands up well to detergent washing.
Future Acrylic Floor Finish (S. C. Johnson & Son, Inc.)—high-gloss liquid; fair scuff resistance; stands up well to detergent washing.

WAX STRIPPERS AND CLEANERS. Parsons' Wax & Acrylic Remover (Armour-Dial Inc.)—liquid; use undiluted; excellent stripper and cleaner.
Oakite All Purpose Cleaner (Oakite Products, Inc.)—use ½ cup per gallon of very warm

Floors

water; rinse with clear water even though not indicated in directions.
Trewax Instant Wax Stripper & Floor Cleaner (Trewax Company)—liquid; very good as stripper; excellent cleaner.
Lundmark High Power Wax Remover (Lundmark Wax Company)—good wax stripper and cleaner.

Marble

Marble is available with a polished or nonpolished finish. Nonpolished marble is quite porous, stains easily, and must be sealed. Polished marble is less porous but can still be stained; a sealer is recommended for this finish also.

Do's

- Wipe up spills and clean sticky spots immediately.
- Protect heavy traffic areas with mats or throw rugs.
- Use plastic casters and cups on furniture legs to minimize scratches.
- Protect a marble floor when moving heavy furniture or appliances.
- Seal the floor with a commercial sealer.
- Sweep, dust-mop, or vacuum heavy traffic areas, entrances, and frequently used rooms regularly to remove dust and litter.
- Weekly, vacuum marble floors thoroughly to pick up loose dirt. Use a crevice tool or small brush attachment to clean around baseboards, radiators, and other hard-to-reach places.
- Damp mop weekly with a sponge mop or string mop, using either clear water or an all-purpose cleaner solution in warm water.
- If you use a water-based, self-polishing liquid wax, occasionally strip the wax build-up and rewax.
- Apply a quality wax-stripping product with a scrub brush or floor-scrubbing machine with a brush attachment. After applying the stripper according to the manufacturer's directions, rinse the floor thoroughly with clean water.
- Use a non-abrasive powder and a synthetic scouring pad on stubborn spots.
- Test a paste wax in a corner to see if it will discolor the marble.
- If you use a solvent-based paste wax, rewax to both strip the old wax and renew the shine.
- Apply either two thin coats of a water-based, self-polishing wax or a paste wax, such as used on wood floors.
- Allow the floor to dry completely before walking on it.

Don'ts

- **Do not** let acids or alkalies come in contact with the floor.
- **Do not** shake a water-based liquid polish before using.
- **Do not** scour or use strong soaps.
- **Do not** apply water-based polishes over solvent-based polishes.
- **Do not** use chemically treated or oiled mops and dust cloths that leave a sticky, dust-collecting film.
- **Do not** use abrasives.
- **Do not** use varnish or lacquer as a sealer.
- **Do not** use rubber compound floor protectors on furniture legs.
- **Do not** attempt to push or pull heavy articles across an unprotected floor.

Fastest and Cheapest

Vacuum the floor, then damp mop with an all-purpose cleaner solution (see Recommended Basic Products). Wring the mop so it is not dripping wet and apply to the marble in slow, even strokes, with just enough pressure to loosen and pick up dirt. Buff dry with a clean, dry cloth to prevent streaking.

Best

Strip off wax build-up with undiluted **Parsons' Wax & Acrylic Remover** (Armour-Dial Inc.). Rinse the floor thoroughly with clean water. Seal with **Trewax Beauty Sealer** (Trewax Company). Apply **Trewax Clear** (Trewax Company), a paste wax, and buff. The combination of Trewax Beauty Sealer and Trewax Clear provides a well-sealed floor that buffs up to an attractive, long-lasting shine.

Other Products Tested

POLISHES—SELF-POLISHING. Hard Gloss Glo-Coat (S. C. Johnson & Son, Inc.)—liquid with moderate gloss; very good scuff resistance; no hazing; stands up well to detergent washing.
Stanhome Super Floor Finish (Stanley Home Products, Inc.)—moderate-gloss liquid; very good scuff resistance; no hazing; stands up well to detergent washing.
Super Bravo Floor Finish (S. C. Johnson & Son, Inc.)—self-polishing liquid; excellent shine; stands up to detergent washing.
Beacon Floor Wax (Lehn & Fink Products Division of Sterling Drug Inc.)—moderate-gloss liquid; good scuff resistance; fair when washed with detergent.
Lundmark's Acrylic Floor Wax (Lundmark Wax Company)—high-gloss liquid; fair scuff resistance; stands up well to detergent washing.
Future Acrylic Floor Finish (S. C. Johnson & Son, Inc.)—high-gloss liquid; fair scuff resistance; stands up well to detergent washing.

WAX STRIPPERS AND CLEANERS. Oakite All Purpose Cleaner (Oakite Products, Inc.)—powder; contains no phosphates; highly efficient cleaner; mix ½ cup to 1 gallon very warm water; although not listed in directions, rinse with cool water.
Mex Multi-Purpose Cleaner (United Gilsonite Laboratories)—powder; very good performance; good stripper; excellent cleaner in weaker solution.
Trewax Instant Wax Stripper & Floor Cleaner (Trewax Company)—liquid; very good as stripper; excellent cleaner.
Lundmark High Power Wax Remover (Lundmark Wax Company)—good wax stripper and cleaner.

BUFFABLE WAXES AND POLISHES. Johnson Paste Wax (S. C. Johnson & Son, Inc.)—provides a high luster after buffing; rebuffing brings back original shine.
Butcher's Bowling Alley Paste Wax (The Butcher Polish Co.)—easy to apply and buff up by hand or electric polisher; rebuffs well to remove slight scuff marks.
Non-Slip Liquid Floor Wax (Trewax Company)—for use with electric floor polisher; excellent shine; can be buffed after damp mopping.

Quarry Tile

Because this unglazed clay tile is very porous, quarry tile should be well-sealed with as many as three coats of sealer, and further protected by a high-quality wax.

Do's

- Wipe up spills and clean sticky spots immediately.
- Protect heavy traffic areas with mats or throw rugs.
- Use plastic casters and cups on furniture legs to minimize scratches.
- Protect a quarry tile floor when moving heavy furniture or appliances.
- Seal the floor with a commercial sealer.
- Sweep, dust-mop, or vacuum heavy traffic areas regularly.
- Weekly, vacuum quarry tile floors thoroughly to pick up loose dirt. Use a crevice tool or small brush attachment to clean around baseboards, radiators, and other hard-to-reach places.
- Damp mop weekly.
- Strip the wax build-up and rewax occasionally, if you use a water-based, self-polishing liquid. Rewaxing will both strip the old wax and renew the shine if you use a solvent-based product.
- Apply a wax-stripping product with a scrub brush or floor-scrubbing machine with a brush attachment. After applying the stripper according to manufacturer's directions, rinse the floor thoroughly with clean water.
- Use a non-abrasive powder and a synthetic scouring pad for stubborn spots.
- Test a paste wax in a corner to see if it will discolor the tile.
- Apply either a water-based, self-polishing wax or a paste wax, such as those used on wood floors.
- Allow the floor to dry completely before walking on it.

Don'ts

- **Do not** let acids or alkalies come in contact with the floor.
- **Do not** shake a water-based liquid polish before using.
- **Do not** scour or use strong soaps.
- **Do not** apply water-based polishes over solvent-based polishes.
- **Do not** use chemically treated or oiled mops and dust cloths that leave a sticky, dust-collecting film.
- **Do not** use abrasives.
- **Do not** use varnish or lacquer as a sealer.
- **Do not** use rubber compound floor protectors on furniture legs.
- **Do not** attempt to push or pull heavy articles across an unprotected floor.

Fastest and Cheapest

Strip off the wax build-up with undiluted **Parsons' Wax & Acrylic Remover** (Armour-Dial Inc.). Rinse the floor thoroughly with clean water. Apply **Trewax Terrazzo and Slate Sealer/Finish** (Trewax Company) and buff if you wish.

Best

Strip off the wax build-up with undiluted **Parsons' Wax & Acrylic Remover** (Armour-Dial Inc.). Rinse the floor thoroughly with clean water. Seal with **Trewax Beauty Sealer** (Trewax Company). Then apply two coats of **Klear Floor Finish** (S. C. Johnson & Son, Inc.). Let dry between coats. Use a long-handled wax applicator with a lamb's wool pad.

Or apply **Trewax Clear** (Trewax Company), a paste wax, in small amounts to the brushes of a floor polishing machine with a spatula. Slowly operate the polisher back and forth to apply an even thin coat. Allow the floor to dry and buff.

Other Products Tested

POLISHES—SELF-POLISHING. **Hard Gloss Glo-Coat** (S. C. Johnson & Son, Inc.)—liquid with moderate gloss; very good scuff resistance; no hazing; stands up well to detergent washing.
Stanhome Super Floor Finish (Stanley Home Products, Inc.)—moderate-gloss liquid; very good scuff resistance; no hazing; stands up well to detergent washing.
Super Bravo Floor Finish (S. C. Johnson & Son, Inc.)—self-polishing liquid; excellent shine; stands up to detergent washing.
Beacon Floor Wax (Lehn & Fink Products Division of Sterling Drug Inc.)—moderate-gloss liquid; good scuff resistance; fair when washed with detergent.
Lundmark's Acrylic Floor Wax (Lundmark Wax Company)—high-gloss liquid; fair scuff resistance; stands up well to detergent washing.
Future Acrylic Floor Finish (S. C. Johnson & Son, Inc.)—high-gloss liquid; fair scuff resistance; stands up well to detergent washing.

WAX STRIPPERS AND CLEANERS. **Oakite All Purpose Cleaner** (Oakite Products, Inc.)—powder; contains no phosphates; highly efficient cleaner; mix ½ cup to 1 gallon very warm water; although directions do not indicate, rinse with cool water.
Mex Multi-Purpose Cleaner (United Gilsonite Laboratories)—powder; very good performance; good stripper; excellent cleaner in weaker solution.
Trewax Instant Wax Stripper & Floor Cleaner (Trewax Company)—liquid; very good as stripper; excellent cleaner.
Lundmark High Power Wax Remover (Lundmark Wax Company)—good wax stripper and cleaner.

BUFFABLE WAXES AND POLISHES. **Johnson Paste Wax** (S. C. Johnson & Son, Inc.)—provides a high luster after buffing; rebuffing brings back original shine.
Butcher's Bowling Alley Paste Wax (The Butcher Polish Co.)—easy to apply and buff up by hand or electric polisher; rebuffs well to remove slight scuff marks.
Non-Slip Liquid Floor Wax (Trewax Company)—for use with electric floor polisher; excellent shine; can be buffed after damp mopping.

Rubber Tile

The procedure for caring for rubber tile is similar to that for asphalt tile. However, rubber tile can be damaged by strong sunlight and is more susceptible to damage by strong cleaners.

Floors

Do's

- Wipe up spills and clean sticky spots immediately.
- Protect heavy traffic areas with mats or throw rugs.
- Use plastic casters and cups on furniture legs to minimize scratches and indentations.
- Protect a rubber tile floor when moving heavy furniture.
- Sweep, dust-mop, or vacuum heavy traffic areas regularly.
- Vacuum all floors thoroughly each week to pick up loose dirt. Use a crevice tool or small brush attachment to clean around baseboards, radiators, and other hard-to-reach places.
- Damp mop weekly. If you use a cleaner/polish that cannot withstand damp mopping, you must reapply the cleaner/polish.
- Remove heel marks by dipping grade 000 steel wool in your liquid floor wax. Rub the spot gently and wipe with a damp cloth.
- Test any cleaner or stripper in a corner before using on the entire floor.
- Use an all-purpose cleaner solution or water-based cleaner/polish for routine care. Read the product label for precautionary measures.
- Occasionally, remove wax build-up with a recommended cleaner or wax stripper.
- If you use an all-purpose cleaner solution, follow it with two thin coats of self-polishing wax; allow to dry between coats.

Don'ts

- **Do not** use solvent-based products. They can soften and damage the tile.
- **Do not** shake a water-based liquid polish before using.
- **Do not** scour or use very hot water or strong soaps on the tile.
- **Do not** allow grease, oil, or solvents to contact the tile.
- **Do not** flood the floor with water. Excess water can seep into the seams and loosen adhesives that hold the flooring down.
- **Do not** use chemically treated or oiled mops and dust cloths that leave a sticky, dust-collecting film.
- **Do not** use rubber compound floor protectors on furniture legs.
- **Do not** attempt to push or pull heavy articles across an unprotected rubber tile floor.

Fastest

Mop & Glo (Lehn & Fink Products Division of Sterling Drug Inc.) works fast on rubber tile. This cleaner/polish requires only one step, using a sponge mop and pail of water. It's convenient to apply with the handy plastic squeeze bottle with a flip-top opening for a clean shine. However, it does not last as long as most self-polishing liquids and requires frequent reapplications.

Cheapest

A home recipe is the cheapest way of cleaning this type of floor and does a great job. Mix ¼ cup **Spic and Span** (Procter & Gamble), 1 cup clear ammonia (see Recommended Basic Products), and ½ gallon cool or cold water. **Caution:** Wear rubber gloves and work in a well-ventilated area when using this powerful solution. Apply to the floor with a sponge mop, using pressure for heavily soiled areas; rinse with cool, clear water for spotless results. Let the floor dry, and then apply **Klear Floor Finish** (S. C. Johnson & Son, Inc.).

Best

Oakite All Purpose Cleaner (Oakite Products, Inc.) is a phosphate-free powder cleaner that rates highest for cleaning rubber tile. Dissolve ½ cup in 1 gallon warm water and apply to the floor with a sponge mop. Although the label does not say it is necessary, rinse the tile with clear water to make sure no film remains to dull the finish. When the floor is dry, apply two thin coats of **Klear Floor Finish** (S. C. Johnson & Son, Inc.). Klear is a water-based, self-polishing liquid that gives an even, high gloss and good scuff resistance over a long period of time. Detergent mopping doesn't affect its shine.

Other Products Tested

CLEANER/POLISHES. **Step Saver** (S. C. Johnson & Son, Inc.)—liquid with ammonia; very good cleaner; moderate gloss; pleasant odor.

POLISHES—SELF-POLISHING. **Hard Gloss Glo-Coat** (S. C. Johnson & Son, Inc.)—liquid with moderate gloss; very good scuff resistance; no hazing; stands up well to detergent washing.
Stanhome Super Floor Finish (Stanley Home Products, Inc.)—moderate-gloss liquid; very good scuff resistance; no hazing; stands up well to detergent washing.
Super Bravo Floor Finish (S. C. Johnson & Son, Inc.)—self-polishing liquid; excellent shine; stands up to detergent washing.
Beacon Floor Wax (Lehn & Fink Products Division of Sterling Drug Inc.)—moderate-gloss liquid; good scuff resistance; fair when washed with detergent.
Lundmark's Acrylic Floor Wax (Lundmark Wax Company)—high-gloss liquid; fair scuff resistance; stands up well to detergent washing.
Future Acrylic Floor Finish (S. C. Johnson & Son, Inc.)—high-gloss liquid; fair scuff resistance; stands up well to detergent washing.

WAX STRIPPERS AND CLEANERS. **Parsons' Wax & Acrylic Remover** (Armour-Dial Inc.)—liquid; use undiluted; excellent stripper and cleaner.
Mex Multi-Purpose Cleaner (United Gilsonite Laboratories)—powder; very good performance; good stripper; excellent cleaner in weaker solution.
Trewax Instant Wax Stripper & Floor Cleaner (Trewax Company)—liquid; very good as stripper; excellent cleaner.
Lundmark High Power Wax Remover (Lundmark Wax Company)—good wax stripper and cleaner.

Read manufacturer's cautions and warnings before using any product.

Terrazzo

This flooring is made of about 70% marble chips that are set in cement. Terrazzo is ground and polished to provide a durable finish. However, it does stain fairly easily, so it must be well-sealed.

Do's

- Wipe up spills and clean sticky spots immediately.
- Protect heavy traffic areas with mats or throw rugs.
- Use plastic casters and cups on furniture legs to minimize scratches.
- Protect a terrazzo floor when moving heavy furniture.
- Seal the floor with a commercial sealer.
- Sweep, dust-mop, or vacuum heavy traffic areas, entrances, and frequently used rooms regularly to remove dust and litter.
- Vacuum all floors thoroughly each week to pick up loose dirt. Use a crevice tool or small brush attachment to clean around baseboards, radiators, and other hard-to-reach places.
- Damp mop with a sponge mop or string mop, using either clear water or an all-purpose cleaner solution in warm water.
- Occasionally, if you use a water-based, self-polishing liquid wax, strip the wax build-up and rewax. If you use a solvent-based paste wax, rewaxing will both strip the old wax and renew the shine.
- Apply a wax-stripping product with a scrub brush or floor-scrubbing machine with a brush attachment.
- Rinse the floor thoroughly with clean water after applying the stripper according to manufacturer's directions.
- Test a paste wax in a corner to see if it will discolor the tile.
- Apply wax to the floor. You can use either a water-based, self-polishing wax or a paste wax, such as those used on wood floors.

Don'ts

- **Do not** let acids come in contact with the floor.
- **Do not** shake a water-based liquid polish before using.
- **Do not** scour or use strong soaps.
- **Do not** apply water-based polishes over solvent-based polishes.
- **Do not** use chemically treated or oiled mops and dust cloths that leave a sticky, dust-collecting film.
- **Do not** use abrasives to clean terrazzo.
- **Do not** use varnish or lacquer as a sealer.
- **Do not** use rubber compound floor protectors on furniture legs.
- **Do not** attempt to push or pull heavy articles across an unprotected floor.

Fastest and Cheapest

Strip off the wax build-up with undiluted **Parsons' Wax & Acrylic Remover** (Armour-Dial Inc.). Rinse the floor thoroughly with clean water. Apply **Trewax Terrazzo and Slate Sealer/Finish** (Trewax Company) and buff if desired.

Best

Strip off the wax build-up with undiluted **Parsons' Wax & Acrylic Remover** (Armour-Dial Inc.). Rinse the floor thoroughly with clean water. Seal with **Trewax Beauty Sealer** (Trewax Company). Then apply two thin coats of **Klear Floor Finish** (S. C. Johnson & Son, Inc.) and allow the floor to dry between coats. Use a long-handled wax applicator with a lamb's wool pad.

Or apply **Trewax Clear** (Trewax Company), a paste wax, with a spatula in small amounts to the brushes of a floor polishing machine. Slowly operate the machine back and forth to apply an even, thin coat. Allow the floor to dry and then buff.

Other Products Tested

POLISHES—SELF-POLISHING. Hard Gloss Glo-Coat (S. C. Johnson & Son, Inc.)—liquid with moderate gloss; very good scuff resistance; no hazing; stands up well to detergent washing.
Stanhome Super Floor Finish (Stanley Home Products, Inc.)—moderate-gloss liquid; very good scuff resistance; no hazing; stands up well to detergent washing.
Super Bravo Floor Finish (S. C. Johnson & Son, Inc.)—self-polishing liquid; excellent shine; stands up to detergent washing.
Beacon Floor Wax (Lehn & Fink Products Division of Sterling Drug Inc.)—moderate-gloss liquid; good scuff resistance; fair when washed with detergent.
Lundmark's Acrylic Floor Wax (Lundmark Wax Company)—high-gloss liquid; fair scuff resistance; stands up well to detergent washing.
Future Acrylic Floor Finish (S. C. Johnson & Son, Inc.)—high-gloss liquid; fair scuff resistance; stands up well to detergent washing.

WAX STRIPPERS AND CLEANERS. Mex Multi-Purpose Cleaner (United Gilsonite Laboratories)—powder; very good performance; good stripper; excellent cleaner in weaker solution.
Trewax Instant Wax Stripper & Floor Cleaner (Trewax Company)—liquid; very good as stripper; excellent cleaner.
Lundmark High Power Wax Remover (Lundmark Wax Company)—good wax stripper and cleaner.

BUFFABLE WAXES AND POLISHES. Johnson Paste Wax (S. C. Johnson & Son, Inc.)—provides a high luster after buffing; rebuffing brings back original shine.
Butcher's Bowling Alley Paste Wax (The Butcher Polish Co.)—easy to apply and buff up by hand or electric polisher; rebuffs well to remove slight scuff marks.
Non-Slip Liquid Floor Wax (Trewax Company)—for use with electric floor polisher; excellent shine; can be buffed after damp mopping.

Vinyl

If your vinyl floor is "no-wax" vinyl, you should omit the stripping and waxing discussed below for general maintenance. However, "no-wax" floors do lose their shine in high-traffic areas after a time and require a gloss-renewing product available from the manufacturer of your floor or **Brite For No-wax Floors** (S. C. Johnson & Son, Inc.).

Floors

Do's

- Wipe up spills and clean sticky spots immediately.
- Protect heavy traffic areas with mats or throw rugs.
- Use plastic casters and cups on furniture legs to minimize scratches and indentations.
- Protect the floor when moving heavy furniture.
- Sweep, dust-mop, or vacuum heavy traffic areas, entrances, and frequently used rooms regularly.
- Vacuum all floors thoroughly each week to pick up loose dirt. Use a crevice tool or small brush attachment to clean around baseboards, radiators, and other hard-to-reach places.
- Damp mop weekly.
- Remove heel marks by dipping a synthetic scouring pad in your liquid floor wax. Rub the spot gently and wipe with a damp cloth.
- Occasionally, remove wax build-up with a recommended cleaner or wax stripper.
- Use an all-purpose cleaner solution or water-based cleaner/polish for routine care. Read the product label for precautionary measures.
- Apply two thin coats of self-polishing wax if an all-purpose cleaner solution is used, allowing the floor to dry between coats.

Don'ts

- **Do not** use solvent-based products.
- **Do not** shake a water-based liquid polish before using.
- **Do not** scour with anything abrasive or use very hot water or strong soaps on vinyl tile.
- **Do not** allow grease, oil, or solvents to contact the tile.
- **Do not** flood the floor with water. Excess water can seep into the seams and loosen adhesives that hold the flooring down.
- **Do not** use chemically treated or oiled mops and dust cloths that leave a sticky, dust-collecting film.
- **Do not** use cleaners that contain pine oil.
- **Do not** use rubber compound floor protectors on furniture legs.
- **Do not** attempt to push or pull heavy articles across unprotected vinyl floors.

Fastest

Mop & Glo (Lehn & Fink Products Division of Sterling Drug Inc.) works fast on vinyl flooring. This cleaner/polish requires only one step, using a sponge mop and pail of water. Apply with the handy plastic squeeze bottle with a flip-top opening for a sparkling clean shine. However, it does not last as long as most self-polishing liquids, and requires frequent reapplications.

Cheapest

A home recipe is the cheapest way of cleaning this type of floor and does a great job. Mix ¼ cup **Spic and Span** (Procter & Gamble), 1 cup clear ammonia (see Recommended Basic Products), and ½ gallon cool or cold water. **Caution:** Wear rubber gloves and work in a well-ventilated area when using this powerful solution. Apply to the floor with a sponge mop, using pressure for heavily soiled areas; rinse with cool, clear water for spotless results. Let the floor dry, and then apply two thin coats of **Klear Floor Finish** (S. C. Johnson & Son, Inc.).

Best

Oakite All Purpose Cleaner (Oakite Products, Inc.) is a phosphate-free powder cleaner that rates highest for cleaning vinyl floors. Dissolve ½ cup in 1 gallon warm water and apply to the floor with a sponge mop. Although the label does not say it is necessary, rinse the tile with clear water to make sure no film remains to dull the finish. When the floor is dry, apply **Klear Floor Finish** (S. C. Johnson & Son, Inc.). Klear is a water-based, self-polishing liquid that gives an even, high gloss and good scuff resistance over a long period of time. Detergent mopping doesn't affect its shine.

Other Products Tested

CLEANER/POLISHES. **Step Saver** (S. C. Johnson & Son, Inc.)—liquid with ammonia; very good cleaner; moderate gloss; pleasant odor.

POLISHES—SELF-POLISHING. **Hard Gloss Glo-Coat** (S. C. Johnson & Son, Inc.)—liquid with moderate gloss; very good scuff resistance; no hazing; stands up well to detergent washing.
Stanhome Super Floor Finish (Stanley Home Products, Inc.)—moderate-gloss liquid; very good scuff resistance; no hazing; stands up well to detergent washing.
Super Bravo Floor Finish (S. C. Johnson & Son, Inc.)—self-polishing liquid; excellent shine; stands up to detergent washing.
Beacon Floor Wax (Lehn & Fink Products Division of Sterling Drug Inc.)—moderate-gloss liquid; good scuff resistance; fair when washed with detergent.
Lundmark's Acrylic Floor Wax (Lundmark Wax Company)—high-gloss liquid; fair scuff resistance; stands up well to detergent washing.
Future Acrylic Floor Finish (S. C. Johnson & Son, Inc.)—high-gloss liquid; fair scuff resistance; stands up well to detergent washing.

WAX STRIPPERS AND CLEANERS. **Parsons' Wax & Acrylic Remover** (Armour-Dial Inc.)—liquid; use undiluted; excellent stripper and cleaner.
Mex Multi-Purpose Cleaner (United Gilsonite Laboratories)—powder; very good performance; good stripper; excellent cleaner in weaker solution.
Trewax Instant Wax Stripper & Floor Cleaner (Trewax Company)—liquid; very good as stripper; excellent cleaner.
Lundmark High Power Wax Remover (Lundmark Wax Company)—good wax stripper and cleaner.

Wood

Maintaining the integrity and beauty of wood floors involves using only solvent-based cleaners and polishes. Water should never be used on this type of floor. If the floor is sealed with polyurethane, no further treatment, including waxing, is necessary.

Floors

Do's

- Wipe up spills and clean sticky spots immediately.
- Protect heavy traffic areas with mats or throw rugs.
- Use plastic casters and cups on furniture legs to minimize scratches and indentations.
- Use an appliance dolly to move heavy furniture and appliances over a wood floor.
- Seal the floor with a varnish, shellac, polyurethane, or lacquer.
- Dust-mop or vacuum heavy traffic areas, entrances, and frequently used rooms regularly.
- Vacuum wood floors thoroughly weekly. Use a crevice tool or small brush attachment to clean around baseboards, radiators, and other hard-to-reach places.
- Remove heel marks by applying a solvent-based wax, polish, or cleaner to a rag and rubbing the mark.
- Apply a liquid or paste solvent-based wax. Use a wood cleaner first, if necessary.
- Shake solvent-based liquid polishes vigorously before using.
- Make sure the room is well-ventilated when using solvent-based waxes and polishes.
- About twice a year, rewax with a solvent-based liquid or paste wax. No stripping is necessary, because the solvents in the new wax will strip off the old wax.
- Buff to renew the shine.

Don'ts

- **Do not** use water or detergents on wood floors.
- **Do not** use water, detergents, or water-based products on wood floors.
- **Do not** allow grease, oil, acids, alkalies, or abrasives to contact the floor.
- **Do not** use chemically treated or oiled mops and dust cloths that leave a sticky, dust-collecting film.
- **Do not** use rubber compound floor protectors on furniture legs.
- **Do not** attempt to push or pull heavy articles across an unprotected floor.

Fastest and Cheapest

Bruce One Step (Armour-Dial Inc.) cleans and polishes a wood floor quickly. After vacuuming the floor, pour this solvent-based liquid on a small area and rub lightly with a clean, dry wax applicator. Working on a small section at a time, stroke the floor in the direction of the grain. Blot up excess liquid with a clean cloth. This self-polishing liquid gives the floor a beautiful gloss.

Best

Wood Preen (The Kiwi Polish Company Pty. Ltd.), a liquid cleaner and wax, is the best product for cleaning wood floors. After vacuuming floors, apply with a dry wax applicator or cloth on a small area at a time. Let soak 3 minutes and wipe up excess before it dries. When dry, buff with a floor polisher. It cleans and buffs up to a beautiful shine and will buff up nicely when scuff marks appear. **Caution:** This is a combustible mixture; use in a well-ventilated area.

Other Products Tested

CLEANERS. Bruce Deep Cleaner (Armour-Dial Inc.)—liquid; excellent cleaner; leaves light wax finish.

Trewax Wood Cleaner (Trewax Company)—liquid; very good cleaner for general or spot cleaning; leaves surface that needs to be rewaxed or polished.

POLISHES—SELF-POLISHING. Bruce Acrylic (Armour-Dial Inc.)—liquid; very good to excellent performance.
Bissell One Step Wood Floor Care (Bissell Inc.)—liquid; very good cleaner; high gloss.

POLISHES—BUFFABLE. Bruce Clean & Wax (Armour-Dial Inc.)—liquid to be used with electric floor polisher; excellent performance and shine.
Johnson Paste Wax (S. C. Johnson & Son, Inc.)—paste to use with a soft cloth or an electric polisher for application and buffing; high-luster finish; can be rebuffed.
Butcher's Bowling Alley Paste Wax (The Butcher Polish Co.)—easy to apply and buff by hand or electric polisher; rebuffs well to remove slight scuff marks.
Trewax Clear (Trewax Company)—paste; to be buffed with electric floor polisher; use after wood cleaner application; excellent shine.

Radiators, Heat Vents, and Returns

Whether the source of heat in the room is from a standing radiator, a baseboard unit, a portable heater, a register, or a heat-distributing device in the fireplace, it will acquire dust from air currents created by the heat. It is important to keep your heating outlets clean so they do not circulate dust that will settle on walls, draperies, and home furnishings.

Do's

- Dust units with a soft cloth or the brush attachment on a vacuum when the rest of the room is cleaned.
- Use a crevice tool to get into hard-to-reach places.
- For really trickly spots on radiators, use the blower end of the vacuum and blow the dust out onto some strategically-placed wet newspapers or cloth.
- Periodically remove grids covering vents and returns to vacuum the backs and inside the duct as far as possible.
- Wash the surfaces of baseboard units and radiators with an all-purpose cleaner at least annually.
- Use a long-handled, narrow brush to get between radiator fins for a thorough cleaning.

Fastest and Cheapest

Using a vacuum cleaner with dust brushes and a crevice tool is the fastest way to remove dust from heating units. When a more thorough job is called for, mix a solution of ½ cup vinegar, 1 cup ammonia, and ¼ cup baking soda in a gallon of hot water. **Caution:** Wear rubber gloves and work in a well-ventilated area when using this powerful solution. Place newspapers under the radiator or other heating unit to protect the floor from water, and apply the solution with a sponge or cloth. Use a long-handled brush to clean the fins of standing radiators; a ruler draped with the cleaning cloth will also work. Rinse with clear water.

Best

Mex Multi-Purpose Cleaner (United Gilsonite Laboratories), a phosphate-free powder, is first-rate for removing soil. Dissolve ¼ cup in 1 gallon hot water and apply using the brush or ruler method. Rinse with clear water to complete the job.

Walls

Light, routine cleaning of your walls will keep them looking fresh, and keep strenuous, major cleaning to perhaps once a year.

Do's

- Dust weekly.
- Dust behind pictures and mirrors regularly to prevent wall marks.
- Brush cobwebs monthly.
- Lift cobwebs rather than press them against the wall.
- Use an all-purpose cleaner for general cleaning on washable walls.
- Test walls for washability in an inconspicuous place.
- Wash ceilings before walls.
- Wash from the bottom of the wall to the top, overlapping the cleaned areas to prevent streaks.
- Remove finger smudges quickly.

Don'ts

- **Do not** neglect dusting in humid weather.
- **Do not** use synthetic scouring pads or abrasive cleansers.
- **Do not** use excessive pressure when scrubbing.

Brick

A wall made of brick requires little attention. A solution of hot water and all-purpose cleaner (see Recommended Basic Products) can be used to clean up accumulated dirt and stains from the surface. If the mortar between the bricks is especially dirty, a chlorine bleach added to the solution will help lighten it. Wet the area below a smoke stain first so any runoff won't set in the lower tier of bricks. Also see Fireplaces—Firebox.

Fastest

Smoke stains just above a fireplace opening are quickly removed with **Ajax Cleanser** (Colgate-Palmolive Company). Scrub the powder into the premoistened brick surface and then rinse with clear water to make sure no white residue remains.

Best

If the brick wall is especially dirty, use ½ cup of **Mex Multi-Purpose Cleaner** (United Gilsonite Laboratories), a phosphate-free powder that dissolves quickly in warm water. Use a stiff brush to help scrub the bricks clean. Rinse with clean hot water and wipe dry. **Caution:** Wear rubber gloves when using a strong solution and keep out of the reach of children.

Ceramic Tile

Ceramic tiles are made of baked clay and come glazed or unglazed. An all-purpose cleaner solution (see Recommended Basic Products) is a good method of cleaning these tiles. A toothbrush or nailbrush is a handy implement for grout cleaning. Take care not to scratch the tile. After cleaning, a clear water rinse is recommended.

Fastest

Tile 'n Grout Magic (Magic American Chemical Corp.) cleans ceramic tile fast and works especially well on tile in the shower area. Shake the can well; hold it two inches from the wall and spray the foam on both the tiles and the grout. A handy plastic brush is built on the can top, which makes it very convenient to scrub off the soap film and hard water stains. Concentrate on the grout between tiles. Rinse the tiles with a sponge dampened in clear water and wipe dry.

Walls

Cheapest

The following recipe makes an inexpensive, good cleaner for ceramic tile. Mix ½ cup vinegar, 1 cup clear ammonia (see Recommended Basic Products), ¼ cup baking soda (see Recommended Basic Products), and 1 gallon warm water. **Caution:** This solution is powerful. Wear rubber gloves to protect your hands and work in a well-ventilated area. Applied to the wall with a sponge, the solution does a wonderful job of cutting grease and banishing soil and soap film. Rinse with clear water.

Darkened grout can be cheaply cleaned with a solution of ¼ cup liquid chlorine bleach and 1 quart water. Scrub this cleaner into the grout with a toothbrush and rinse with clear water.

Another inexpensive grout cleaner is a paste made from three parts baking soda and one part water. Apply to the grout with a damp cloth, scrub with a toothbrush, and rinse with clear water.

Best

For cleaning ceramic tiles, the superior cleaner is **20 Mule Power Industrial Strength Bathroom Cleaner** (United States Borax & Chemical Corporation). Spray the liquid directly on the tile and grout, and use a synthetic scouring pad (see Tools of the Trade) to loosen soil. Rinse with clear water. **Caution:** Because this is a powerful cleaner, use plastic gloves to avoid skin contact, and don't breathe in the mist when spraying the tile.

Other Products Tested

Lysol Basin/Tub/Tile Cleaner (Lehn & Fink Products Division of Sterling Drug Inc.)—very good spray cleaner; allow time to penetrate and scrub to remove soap film; moderate odor.
X-14 Instant Mildew Stain Remover (White Laboratories)—spray-on cleaner designed to remove mildew stains and soil from grout; no rinsing required.
Dow Disinfectant Bathroom Cleaner (The Dow Chemical Co.)—moderately good spray cleaner for tile; must be scrubbed to remove soap film; pleasant pine odor.
Afta Tile Cleaner (Afta Solvents Corporation)—moderately good cleaner with spray coming out of handy built-in brush head; moderate odor.

Decorator Tile

Self-sticking decorator tiles, often vinyl-coated, are grease and stain resistant. A quick wipe with a sponge dipped in an all-purpose cleaner solution (see Recommended Basic Products) is usually all that is needed to keep them fresh and bright. Excessive moisture should be avoided, since it might seep between the seams and loosen the backing.

Metal Tile

Metal tile generally can be wiped clean with a cloth dampened in an all-purpose cleaner solution (see Recommended Basic Products) and then buffed dry with a soft cloth to avoid streaking.

Mirror Tile

These wall tiles, either clear or with some design, are cleaned the same as wall mirrors. (See Mirrors.)

Painted

Wall paint is of two types. The most frequently used is *latex,* which is easy to wash after it has "cured" or set for a period of time. The other kind, *alkyd* or oil base, is durable and washable, but stains and soil are harder to remove from the surface. Both types come in three finishes—flat (for walls and ceilings), semi-gloss, and gloss (most often used for woodwork, kitchens, and bathrooms because of easy cleaning).

Fastest

For a fast touch-up, spray **Formula 409 All Purpose Cleaner** (The Clorox Company) to remove dark marks, grime, and smudges. Wipe with a dry cloth to make the painted surface clean and new. Avoid spraying on varnished surfaces.

Cheapest

The following recipe makes a good and inexpensive cleaner for painted walls: ½ cup vinegar, 1 cup clear ammonia (see Recommended Basic Products), ¼ cup baking soda (see Recommended Basic Products), and 1 gallon warm water. **Caution:** Wear rubber gloves and work in a well-ventilated area when using this powerful solution. Apply to the wall with a sponge and rinse with clear water.

Best

Painted walls can be easily freed of soil and stains when cleaned with **Oakite All Purpose Cleaner** (Oakite Products, Inc.). Dissolve ⅓ cup of this phosphate-free powder in a pail of warm water and apply the solution to the wall with a sponge or cloth. Rinse the wall with clear water.

Paper

Paper wall coverings are considered nonwashable and require special cleaning techniques.

Fastest and Best

Absorene (Absorene Manufacturing Co., Inc.), a pink substance that resembles modeling clay, is both the fastest and best way to clean paper wall coverings. Knead a small, manageable piece until soft and pliant, squeeze into an oblong shape, and apply to the wall with light, even strokes in one direction only. After five or six strokes fold the cleaner to absorb the soil. Use until it is entirely dirty and then continue with a fresh piece.

Read manufacturer's cautions and warnings before using any product.

Walls

Cheapest

Although nonwashable wall coverings present some unique cleaning problems, you can successfully and inexpensively remove smudges, finger marks, and pencil marks from the surface by very gently rubbing the spots with an artgum eraser. Other general soil comes off when a piece of rye bread is wadded up and used like the eraser. To clean a grease spot, blot it with paper toweling and sprinkle cornstarch on the stain. After it absorbs the grease, rub it off gently.

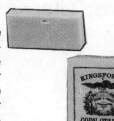

Vinyl

Many wall coverings today are washable vinyl. Some manufacturers caution against using ammonia-based cleaners, so check the instructions before cleaning or do a washability test.

Fastest

A solution of an all-purpose cleaner (see Recommended Basic Products) and water does an effective job of removing dirt and grime from vinyl wall coverings. Apply with a sponge or cloth and rinse with clean water.

Cheapest

Mix ½ cup vinegar to 1 quart water and gently apply to the surface with a sponge. Don't use too much moisture, as it could seep under the seams and loosen the backing.

Best

Vinyl wall coverings can be cleaned very well with the "dry detergent" method and a minimum of moisture. To make this cleaner, mix ¼ cup **Lux Dishwashing Liquid** (Lever Brothers Company) with 1 cup warm water in a mixing bowl and beat to a stiff foam with an eggbeater. Working in a small area, dip a sponge into the foam and apply to loosen the dirt. Rinse off the detergent with a sponge dipped in clear water and squeezed dry.

Wood Paneling

Wood paneling can have a plain, stained, oiled, or waxed finish. Routine care only requires occasional dusting with a soft cloth or a brush attachment on the vacuum. When paneling looks dull, one of the recommended products will restore its vitality.

Don't

- **Do not** use water to clean wood paneling.

Fastest, Oil Finish

As a quick rejuvenator for paneling, nothing beats **Weiman Panel Bright** (The Herbert Stanley Company). After shaking the aerosol can well, spray foam over a three-foot area and rub immediately to a warm polish with a dry piece of terry cloth.

Cheapest, Oil Finish

The least expensive, make-it-yourself polish is one of the best products for restoring the beauty of wood paneling with an oiled finish. Pour equal parts of turpentine and boiled linseed oil into a jar, tighten the lid, and shake the liquid to blend it thoroughly. Pour a small amount of the mix onto a soft cloth and rub up and down with the grain of the wood. The wood surface will appear oily, but within an hour the polish will be completely absorbed, leaving a lovely soft sheen on the wood.

Best, Oil Finish

To clean a soil build-up from wood paneling with an oil finish, apply **Formby's Furniture Cleaner** (Formby's Inc.) with a soft cloth in the direction of the grain. Allow it to penetrate the wood for 45 minutes and repeat the procedure if necessary. However, if the finish is badly damaged, test on an inconspicuous place first. Finish the task with **Formby's Lemon Oil Furniture Treatment** (Formby's Inc.), which reconditions the wood, replaces its natural oils, and leaves a pleasing mellow tone.

Other Products Tested

WOOD CLEANERS. **Weiman Wood Furniture Soap** (The Herbert Stanley Company)—aerosol spray; very good cleaner; pleasant odor.
Stanhome Panel & Cabinet Cleaner (Stanley Home Products, Inc.)—aerosol spray; very good cleaner; pleasant odor.
Cabinet Magic (Magic American Chemical Corp.)—aerosol spray; very good cleaner; moderate petroleum odor; combustible.
Panel Magic (Magic American Chemical Corp.)—aerosol spray; very good cleaner; moderate petroleum odor; combustible.

POLISHES FOR OIL FINISH. **Parker's Perfect Polish** (C. W. Parker Company)—cream; very good cleaner leaving a warm finish to the wood; moderate odor.
FINIS High Gloss Furniture Polish (Scott's Liquid Gold-Inc.)—aerosol spray; very good cleaner, leaving a warm soft finish to the wood; moderate odor; flammable.

Fastest, Wax Finish

As a quick rejuvenator for paneling, nothing beats **Weiman Panel Bright** (The Herbert Stanley Company). After shaking the aerosol can well, spray foam over a three-foot area and rub immediately to a warm polish with a dry piece of terry cloth.

Best, Wax Finish

Restoring the beauty to wax-finish paneling is a cinch with the top-rated preparation, **Amway Buff Up** (Amway Corp.). This easy-to-use aerosol spray polish brings up a moderately high gloss when polished with a soft cloth.

Other Products Tested

WOOD CLEANERS. **Weiman Wood Furniture Soap** (The Herbert Stanley Company)—aerosol spray; very good cleaner; pleasant odor.
Stanhome Panel & Cabinet Cleaner (Stanley Home Products, Inc.)—aerosol spray; very good cleaner; pleasant odor.
Cabinet Magic (Magic American Chemical Corp.)—aerosol spray; very good cleaner; moderate petroleum odor; combustible.
Panel Magic (Magic American Chemical Corp.)—aerosol spray; very good cleaner; moderate petroleum odor; combustible.

Windows

Windows look best if they are cleaned on a regular basis. Home recipes work just as well, or better, than the many commercial products for washing windows.

Do's
- Wash the inside and outside of window panes twice a year.
- Touch up smudges and dirt as needed on readily accessible windows.
- Use a squeegee on a long handle, or a sponge/squeegee combination, to prevent streaks on large windows.
- Wash from the top down to prevent drips on sections you've already washed.
- Use a soft toothbrush or cotton swab to clean corners.
- Clean one side of a pane with horizontal strokes and the other with vertical strokes so you can track down streaks.
- Add 2 tablespoons rubbing alcohol or glycerin to the cleaning solution when the air temperature dips below freezing to keep the pane from icing up.

Don'ts
- **Do not** use soap for cleaning window panes; soap leaves smudges and requires rinsing.
- **Do not** use abrasive cleansers or steel wool that can scratch the glass.
- **Do not** wash windows on a hot or sunny day or windows will streak.
- **Do not** allow drips to fall on the window sill as they can harm the paint or varnish.

Fastest

A home recipe—ammonia and water—is the quickest method of washing windows. Add ⅓ cup clear ammonia to a gallon of warm water. Apply with a sponge/squeegee or pour the solution into a spray container and spray directly onto the glass. Buff the pane dry with a lint-free cloth or paper toweling. Vinegar may be substituted for the ammonia for equally fast results.

Cheapest

Another simple home recipe uses only plain white vinegar and old newspaper. Pour the vinegar into a shallow bowl or pan, crumple up a sheet of newspaper, dip it in the vinegar, and apply to the window. Wipe the glass several times with the same newsprint until the pane is almost dry, then shine the glass with a clean, soft cloth or dry newsprint.

Best

Sparkle Glass Cleaner (A. J. Funk & Co.) works as well as the vinegar and newspaper approach. Spray the liquid onto the window panes and quickly wipe off with paper toweling for a streak-free finish.

Other Products Tested

Window Spray Cleaner (Stanley Home Products, Inc.)—aerosol; very good ammonia cleaner; nonstreaking; strong odor.
Easy-Off Window Cleaner (Boyle-Midway Inc.)—spray with ammonia; moderate to good performance; weak odor.
Glass Plus (Texize Chemicals Company)—spray; moderate to good performance; moderate odor.
Glass Wax (Gold Seal Co.)—creamy liquid; good performance but time-consuming to use; residual powder from dried solution must be continuously shaken from cloth; weak odor.
Windex Glass Cleaner (The Drackett Company)—spray; moderate performance; some streaking; moderate odor.

Woodwork

Woodwork is either painted or left natural with an oiled or varnished finish. Like walls, it benefits from a regular cleaning routine that keeps the job easy and quick.

Do's

- Dust on a regular basis.
- Keep a small bottle of matching paint or stain handy to touch up nicks and scratches.
- Wash from the bottom up on door and window frames.
- Use an all-purpose cleaner on painted surfaces to remove smudges and fingerprints.
- Clean stained and natural finished woodwork with wood cleaner/polishes.
- Dust the tops of door jambs, window frames, cornices, ledges, and baseboards.

Read manufacturer's cautions and warnings before using any product.

Woodwork

Don'ts

- **Do not** use water on stained or natural finished woodwork except for light touch-ups that you buff dry quickly.
- **Do not** spray aerosol cleaner/polishes directly on the woodwork; spray on the cloth instead to prevent staining adjoining surfaces.
- **Do not** use synthetic scouring pads or abrasive cleansers—they will dull the finish.

Fastest, Oiled Finish

Wood Preen (Kiwi Polish Company Pty. Ltd) saves much time by cleaning and waxing woodwork in one operation. Rub a thin coat on a small area at a time and then immediately buff with a soft cloth. **Caution:** This is a combustible mixture and should be used only in a well-ventilated area.

Cheapest, Oiled Finish

A make-it-yourself polish is an inexpensive way to clean and polish woodwork with an oiled finish. Mix equal parts of turpentine and boiled linseed oil (available at hardware or paint stores) in a jar, tighten the lid, and shake until the liquid is blended thoroughly. Pour a small amount of the mix onto a soft cloth and rub into the woodwork with the grain of the wood. The surface will at first look oily, but within an hour the polish will be completely absorbed, leaving a lovely, soft shine.

Best, Oiled Finish

To rid soil build-up from woodwork with an oiled finish, apply **Formby's Furniture Cleaner** (Formby's Inc.) with a soft cloth and allow it to penetrate the wood for 45 minutes. If the surface is badly damaged, test an inconspicuous spot before using on the entire surface. Finish the task with **Formby's Lemon Oil Furniture Treatment** (Formby's Inc.), which reconditions the wood, replaces natural oils, and leaves a pleasing mellow tone.

Other Products Tested

WOOD CLEANERS. **Weiman Wood Furniture Soap** (The Herbert Stanley Company)—aerosol spray; very good cleaner; pleasant odor.
Stanhome Panel & Cabinet Cleaner (Stanley Home Products, Inc.)—aerosol spray; very good cleaner; pleasant odor.
Cabinet Magic (Magic American Chemical Corp.)—aerosol spray; very good cleaner; moderate petroleum odor; combustible.
Panel Magic (Magic American Chemical Corp.)—aerosol spray; very good cleaner; moderate petroleum odor; combustible.

POLISHES FOR OIL FINISH. **Parker's Perfect Polish** (C. W. Parker Company)—cream; very good cleaner leaving a warm finish to the wood; moderate odor.
FINIS High Gloss Furniture Polish (Scott's Liquid Gold-Inc.)—aerosol spray; very good cleaner, leaving a warm soft finish to the wood; moderate odor; flammable.

Fastest, Waxed Finish

Wood Preen (Kiwi Polish Company Pty. Ltd) saves much time by cleaning and waxing woodwork in one operation. Rub a thin coat on a small area at a time and then immediately buff with a soft cloth. **Caution:** This is a combustible mixture and should be used only in a well-ventilated area.

Best, Waxed Finish

Amway Buff Up (Amway Corp.) is a top-rated product for woodwork with a waxed finish. This easy-to-use spray polish in an aerosol can brings up a moderately high gloss when polished with a soft cloth.

Other Products Tested

WOOD CLEANERS.   Weiman Wood Furniture Soap (The Herbert Stanley Company)—aerosol spray; very good cleaner; pleasant odor.
Stanhome Panel & Cabinet Cleaner (Stanley Home Products, Inc.)—aerosol spray; very good cleaner; pleasant odor.
Cabinet Magic (Magic American Chemical Corp.)—aerosol spray; very good cleaner; moderate petroleum odor; combustible.
Panel Magic (Magic American Chemical Corp.)—aerosol spray; very good cleaner; moderate petroleum odor; combustible.

POLISHES FOR WAXED FINISH.   Lemon Behold Furniture Polish (The Drackett Company)—aerosol spray; very good cleaning performance; medium gloss; flammable.
Lemon Pledge (S. C. Johnson & Son, Inc.)—aerosol spray; good cleaning performance; medium gloss.

Home Furnishings

Bedding

All types of bedding should be cleaned on a regular basis. The key to successful cleaning is to do it before the soil is heavy and to know the fabrics involved in order to use the right cleaning products and procedures. Keeping a file of manufacturer's care labels will be a real help when cleaning is necessary. Also see Laundry for cleaning products to use—sheets, pillowcases, and mattress pads should be cleaned according to the instructions for their fabrics. Also see Cotton, Polyester, and Acetate.

Bedspread

Bedspreads are made from many different types of fabrics. Many are washable.

Do's

- Pretreat any spots or stains with a spray prewash product or a liquid detergent.
- Dip a corner of the bedspread in a detergent solution to check for colorfastness before washing. If the color bleeds, have the bedspread dry-cleaned.
- Use a large, commercial washer for oversize bedspreads for best results.
- Dry bedspreads on a clothesline or in the dryer.

Don'ts

- **Do not** allow bedspreads to get heavily soiled before cleaning.
- **Do not** overcrowd the washing machine.

Cheapest and Best

Speed is not a factor when washing bedspreads, since they are usually done in a washing machine. Use a soap or an all-purpose detergent (see Laundry) that is suited to your water conditions. The water temperature will depend on the fabric. The cheapest soap or detergent will be the one least expensive in your area.

Blanket

Although blankets are now made of many different fibers and blends, most of them are washable by hand or machine. Some wool blankets can be machine washed. Check the care label and follow the manufacturer's instructions, and also consult the Natural Fabrics and Synthetic Fabrics sections for cleaning procedures to clean the fabric in your blanket.

Do's

- Mend or replace bindings if necessary before cleaning.
- Brush or vacuum blankets occasionally to remove dust and lint.
- Air blankets on the clothesline periodically to refresh them.
- Treat spots and stains according to the fabric before washing.
- Shake or vacuum blankets to remove loose dirt and lint before washing.
- Use a large commercial washer to wash large blankets.
- Hand or machine wash an electric blanket.
- Use cold water and cold water detergents when washing wool blankets.
- Fill the clothes washer with water and add the detergent so it can completely dissolve before adding the blanket.
- Soak the blanket for about 10 minutes before starting it through a short agitating cycle.
- Use a gentle or delicate clothes washer cycle if possible.
- Use fabric softener to increase fluffiness and reduce static electricity.

Don'ts

- **Do not** store blankets unless they have just been cleaned.
- **Do not** use cleaning solvents or mothproofing solutions on electric blankets—they will damage the wiring.
- **Do not** use soap on washable wool blankets.
- **Do not** overcrowd the machine.
- **Do not** agitate blankets for long periods to prevent matting of fibers.
- **Do not** dry-clean an electric blanket.

Fastest, Cheapest, and Best

Use **Machine Wash Woolite** (Boyle-Midway Inc.) when washing wool blankets. It works well in cold water, reducing the chance of shrinkage.

Yes (Texize Chemicals Company) is the fastest, cheapest, and best product for cleaning other washable blankets. Use ¼ cup of the blue liquid detergent to wash any full-size blanket, with warm water for washing and cold water for rinsing. Yes is also good for pretreating spots and stains—rub the undiluted liquid directly on the soil before putting the blanket in the machine. Since Yes has a built-in fabric softener, it eliminates the need for a separate product, thus saving money.

If Yes is unavailable in your area, **Bold 3** (Procter & Gamble) may be substituted. This low-sudsing powder detergent contains a fabric softener, but is not as cost-efficient as Yes.

Other Products Tested

Arm & Hammer Laundry Detergent (Church & Dwight Co., Inc.)—granular; phosphate-free; excellent performance; high-sudsing action; contains a deodorizing agent.
Rain Barrel Fabric Softener (S. C. Johnson & Son, Inc.)—liquid; added to water along with detergent; very good performance.

Comforter and Quilt, Down-Filled

Down filling in comforters and quilts is held in place by tufts of yarn or by stitched through patterns. Most down-filled comforters and quilts are washable, but some older ones are too fragile to be cleaned at home.

Do's

- Follow the manufacturer's care instructions whenever available.
- Test older comforters/quilts for colorfastness before washing by wetting an inconspicuous spot with detergent solution and blotting the area with a white blotter.
- Clean patchwork quilts with the method used for the most delicate fabric in the quilt.
- Machine wash and dry comforters/quilts only if they are in good condition.
- Hand wash older or fragile comforters/quilts that can withstand gentle washing, using the bathtub or a deep laundry tub.
- Machine wash comforters/quilts that are in good condition in a large-capacity washer, using a cold wash and rinse water and an all-purpose detergent; down-filled articles also may be dry-cleaned.
- Make sure all detergent is rinsed out of the down.
- Drape over several clotheslines to allow excess moisture to drip out; reposition several times; place in a preheated clothes dryer at a low temperature setting and include a pair of clean, dry sneakers to help fluff the down, or set dryer at air dry (no heat) and fluff dry.
- Air before storing and don't compress the down.
- Store in a cool, dry place.

Don'ts

- **Do not** machine wash old quilts.
- **Do not** wash down quilts with wool coverings unless the care label recommends washing.
- **Do not** store just-washed quilts/comforters until they are absolutely dry to prevent mildew.
- **Do not** wash silk- or velvet-covered down quilts/comforters.

Cheapest

For other than washable wool-covered down quilts/comforters, select an all-purpose laundry detergent (see Laundry) that can be used in cold water. The cheapest product will be the one most economical in your area.

Fastest and Best

For washable wool-covered down quilts/comforters, use **Machine Wash Woolite** (Boyle-Midway Inc.), whether you machine or hand wash the article. This product cleans well in cold water and reduces the possibility of shrinkage.

Yes (Texize Chemicals Company) is excellent for other washable down comforters/quilts. This blue liquid contains a built-in fabric softener, which makes it both a time and money saver. Use cold water, making sure the detergent is well-dissolved before adding the quilt.

If Yes is not available in your area, substitute **Bold 3** (Procter & Gamble). This low-sudsing powder detergent softens well but is not as cost-efficient as Yes.

Comforter and Quilt, Wool-, Cotton-, and Synthetic-Filled

Padded bed coverings may be filled with wool, cotton batting, or polyester fiber-fill. The filling is held in place by tufts of yarn or by stitched-through patterns. Most cotton- or polyester-filled comforters/quilts are washable, but some older ones are too delicate to be cleaned at home. Some newer wool-filled or wool-covered comforters/quilts can be washed at home.

Do's

- Follow the manufacturer's care instructions whenever available.
- Use the home washing machine for small- to medium-size quilts/comforters.
- Use a large commercial washer for cleaning larger quilts/comforters.
- Test old quilts/comforters of undetermined fiber for colorfastness before attempting to wash them by wetting a small spot with detergent solution and blotting with a white blotter.
- Clean patchwork quilts with the method used for the most delicate fabric in the quilt.
- Machine wash and dry only quilts/comforters in good condition.
- Hand wash and line dry old or fragile quilts that can withstand washing.
- Hand wash quilts with cotton batting—machine washing is too harsh and can cause bunching of the batting.
- Use the bathtub or deep laundry tub for hand washing quilts/comforters.
- Add soap or detergent to the wash water and allow it to dissolve before adding the quilt/comforter.
- Let a machine-washable quilt/comforter soak in the machine for about 10 minutes before starting it through a short, gentle washing cycle.

Don'ts

- **Do not** machine wash quilts/comforters with cotton batting.
- **Do not** machine wash old quilts/comforters.
- **Do not** wash quilts/comforters with wool batting or coverings unless marked washable.
- **Do not** wash silk- or velvet-covered quilts/comforters.

Bedding

Cheapest

For other than washable wool or wool-filled quilts, select an all-purpose laundry detergent (see Laundry) that can be used in cold water. The cheapest product will be the one most economical in your area.

Fastest and Best

For washable wool or wool-filled comforters/quilts, use **Machine Wash Woolite** (Boyle-Midway Inc.) whether you machine or hand wash the quilt, since this product works well in cold water and reduces the possibility of shrinkage.

Yes (Texize Chemicals Company) is excellent for other washable quilts. This blue liquid contains a built-in fabric softener, which makes it both a time and money saver. Use warm water, making sure the detergent is well-dissolved before adding the quilt.

If Yes is unavailable in your area, substitute **Bold 3** (Procter & Gamble). This low-sudsing powder detergent also contains a fabric softener but is not as cost-efficient as Yes.

Mattress and Box Spring

Modern mattresses are made of foam or springs and casing; older mattresses can be made of hair. All mattresses benefit from routine care.

Do's

- Turn innerspring mattresses over and around end to end once a month to insure even wear.
- Turn foam and hair mattresses less frequently.
- Cover mattresses with a special quilted or rubberized cover to prevent soiling.
- Vacuum or briskly brush the mattress and box springs at least once a month.
- Remove the mattress cover when changing bedding to air the mattress for a short time.
- Remove spots and stains from the mattress promptly.

Don'ts

- **Do not** allow the mattress to become excessively wet when spot treating or cleaning.
- **Do not** make the bed until the mattress is completely dry.

Fastest

The most rapid way to remove dust and blanket fluff from a mattress and box spring is by vacuuming it. Use the upholstery attachment and work around any buttons carefully, using a whisk broom to remove dust and fluff from around the button area and along the edges so the vacuum can reach the dirt easily.

Cheapest

Use a solution of ¼ cup **Lux Dishwashing Liquid** (Lever Brothers Company) and 1 cup warm water, whipped into a high foam with an eggbeater, to clean soiled mattresses or box springs. Apply only the foam with a moderately stiff-bristled brush, making sure that excess water is shaken off. Work on a small section at a time, brushing the foam into the surface fabric. When the entire surface is treated, go over it again with a damp sponge to remove any soap residue. Allow one side to dry thoroughly before turning and cleaning the other side. Using an electric fan to circulate air around the mattress speeds the drying process.

Best

Glamorene Upholstery Shampoo (Airwick Industries, Inc.) is the best product for cleaning mattresses and box springs. Spray the foam over the surface and scrub it in with the attached brush head. Wipe off excess moisture with a clean terry towel, and allow the mattress to dry completely before turning it over to clean the reverse side.

Other Products Tested

Woolite Upholstery Cleaner (Boyle-Midway Inc.)—aerosol foam; vacuum before and after application; excellent performance.
Bissell Upholstery Shampoo for Home & Auto (Bissell Inc.)—aerosol foam with brush head; very good performance; easy to apply.
Stanhome Upholstery and Rug Shampoo (Stanley Home Products, Inc.)—liquid; very good performance; less easy to use than the others.

Pillow

Pillowcases are routinely replaced when soiled bed linens are changed, but little thought is given to the care of the pillow itself. In many cases the pillow is neglected until the ticking is so stained it has to be replaced. Know the pillow filling—down, feathers, foam, polyester, or kapok—so that you use the appropriate cleaning method. For polyester-filled pillows, read hang tags with the manufacturer's care instructions; some polyester-filled pillows are washable, but some are not. Kapok is the silky covering of seeds from the ceiba tree; pillows with this stuffing need frequent airing, but cannot be washed.

Bedding

Do's

- Protect each pillow with a zip-on cotton or polyester cover that you wash regularly.
- Refresh pillows once a month by airing them near an open window or hanging them on a clothesline.
- Make sure pillows are rinsed well after each washing.
- Use a short, delicate cycle when machine washing pillows.
- Wash two pillows at a time or add a couple of bath towels to balance the load in a top-loading washing machine.
- Use a large commercial washing machine if necessary to prevent overcrowding.
- Line dry any type of pillow if desired, changing the hanging position hourly to dry the filling evenly.
- Fluff up feather and down pillows daily to get rid of accumulated dust and redistribute the filling.
- Machine or hand wash feather and down-filled pillows in cool water with a cold water light duty detergent when dirty.
- Make sure there are no holes or ripped seams when washing down or feather pillows.
- Wash feathers and ticking separately if the fabric is worn or the pillow is heavily stuffed. Secure the feathers in a large muslin bag and stitch the opening closed.
- Dry down or feather pillows in the dryer on a low heat setting.
- Add a pair of clean tennis shoes to the dryer with down or feather pillows to help distribute the down as it dries.
- Hand wash and line dry foam pillows.
- Wash polyester-filled pillows in a tumble-type rather than a top-loading machine.
- Machine or hand wash polyester-filled pillows in warm water with an all-purpose detergent when dirty.
- Dry polyester-filled pillows in the dryer on a moderate heat setting.

Don'ts

- **Do not** overcrowd pillows in the washing machine.
- **Do not** dry pillows on the clothesline overnight.
- **Do not** place foam pillows in a dryer.
- **Do not** twist polyester-filled pillows when washing.
- **Do not** wash kapok-filled pillows.

Fastest

Fluff up pillows to remove dust quickly and give them a once-over-lightly with the upholstery attachment of a vacuum.

Cheapest

Choose a liquid dishwashing detergent (see Recommended Basic Products) when hand washing pillows. For machine washing, select the least expensive laundry detergent (see Laundry).

Best

Lux Dishwashing Liquid (Lever Brothers Company) is the best detergent for hand-washable pillows. Take care not to twist or wring them excessively, and make sure the pillows are well-rinsed. The bathtub is a good place to wash pillows.

  Arm & Hammer Laundry Detergent (Church & Dwight Co., Inc.) is the best detergent for machine-washable pillows. This high-sudsing, granular, phosphate-free detergent has a de-odorizing agent so the pillows smell as clean as they look.

Sleeping Bag

Sleeping bags not only are practical for camping out, but serve as excellent beds for the overnight visitor. The most common fillings are polyester fiber or natural down. Both will have a long life if given the proper care.

Do's

- Wash the sleeping bag after each outdoor use.
- Pretreat spots and stains on the bag cover with liquid detergent.
- Follow the manufacturer's washing instructions closely.
- Wash down-filled sleeping bags in cool water with a cold water, mild detergent.
- Wash polyester-filled sleeping bags in warm water with an all-purpose detergent.
- Unzip a sleeping bag to air dry on a clothesline.
- If your sleeping bag can be machine dried, throw in a clean, dry tennis shoe to prevent matting, and a clean, dry towel to absorb excess moisture.

Don'ts

- **Do not** put sleeping bags in the clothes dryer unless specifically recommended by the manufacturer.
- **Do not** store sleeping bags until they dry completely.
- **Do not** put cloth sleeping bags directly on the ground. Use only those especially treated for outdoor use.
- **Do not** wring or twist sleeping bags when washing them.

Fastest, Cheapest, and Best

Machine wash your sleeping bag on a gentle cycle with a mild laundry or cold water detergent. Wash it by itself. Some brands cannot be spin dried, and some cannot be machine dried. Pretreat spots by spraying with **Shout Laundry Soil & Stain Remover** (S. C. Johnson & Son, Inc.) directly on the spot. Spray just enough to cover the spot. Don't saturate the fabric. Let it set a minute and wash.

Other Products Tested

Formula 409 All Purpose Cleaner (The Clorox Company)—pump spray; can be used for treating spots; may not remove difficult stains.
Fantastik Multi-Surface Spray Cleaner (Texize Chemicals Company)—pump spray; can

---

Read manufacturer's cautions and warnings before using any product.

be used for treating spots; may not remove set-in grease stains.
Grease Relief (Texize Chemicals Company)—pump spray; will remove most bad stains, but may leave a spot ring.

Carpets and Rugs

You can remove light soil from carpets and large rugs with one of the spray-foam carpet cleaners. Use a steam cleaning device or carpet shampooer that you can rent at hardware or food stores for heavy soil. Small area rugs, except for wool or fur rugs, usually are machine washable with a good all-purpose detergent (see Laundry). There are three types of products designed for cleaning carpets and rugs: dry cleaners, spray-foam, and self-cleaning for light soil; sponge-in cleaners for moderate soil; and for heavily soiled carpets, cleaning solutions used with rug-cleaning appliances. All three types of cleaners are suitable for all colorfast carpet and rug fibers; the type you choose depends on the amount of soil and your personal preference.

Do's

- Vacuum regularly with an upright, beater-bar vacuum to remove loose soil and dirt, stroking small sections in different directions.
- Clean up spots and spills at once.
- Clean carpets and rugs when vacuuming can no longer restore a clean appearance, at least once a year.
- Shampoo rugs during dry periods of the year to aid drying.
- Before cleaning, test for colorfastness by moistening a white cloth with the cleaning solution and applying to an obscure corner.
- Remove as much furniture from the room as possible before cleaning carpets.
- Place foil or plastic film under legs and bases of remaining furniture to prevent stains.
- Carefully read directions and safety precautions before using any cleaning or spot treatment product.
- Vacuum thoroughly, spot clean, or pretreat any stains before cleaning.
- Follow the instructions printed on a rented rug cleaner to the letter, using single strokes over the carpet surface.
- Wipe cleaner solutions and foam from furniture legs and woodwork immediately to prevent damage to the wood or upholstery.
- Fluff damp fibers against the nap after shampooing to aid drying and prevent matting.
- Make sure the room is well-ventilated after cleaning to speed drying.
- Treat hooked rugs carefully so you don't loosen the loops.
- Vacuum the surface and underneath fiber, sisal, and grass rugs regularly; remove surface dirt and restore moisture with a damp cloth.
- Clean wool area rugs with any of the rug shampoos.
- Clean fur rugs by working multiple applications of cornmeal through the pile until the cornmeal shakes out clean. Then brush or lightly vacuum the remaining granules away.
- Wipe a fur rug with a damp cloth, but don't get the pelt wet.
- Air dry round or oval throw rugs flat to retain their shape.

Don'ts

- **Do not** rely on an electric broom or light-duty canister vacuum for deep cleaning of carpets and large rugs.
- **Do not** rush when vacuuming.
- **Do not** soak carpets/rugs when cleaning—excess moisture can damage the carpet backing, cause shrinkage, or create new stains.
- **Do not** walk on wet carpets and rugs.
- **Do not** use solvent-based spot cleaners on foam or rubber-backed carpets and rugs—solvents deteriorate these materials.
- **Do not** machine-dry throw rugs with foam or rubber backs unless the directions so state to prevent damage to the backing.
- **Do not** hang round or oval throw rugs over the clothesline.
- **Do not** apply heavy pressure with a machine.

Fastest

For a lightly soiled surface, use **Carbona 1 Hour Rug Cleaner** (Carbona Products Company), a no-rub, no-scrub product for the entire carpet. Shake the aerosol can vigorously and spray an even layer of foam, holding the can upside down and about two feet from the surface. The foam dries into a white residue in about 1¼ hours. Vacuum the residue to remove all the dirt and soil.

To clean a moderately soiled carpet, mix one part **Bissell Wall To Wall Rug Shampoo** (Bissell Inc.) with eight parts cool soft water. The solution can be applied by hand or any applicator. It is made to clean the entire rug, or just spot cleaning.

To clean a heavily soiled carpet, rent a **Carpet Magic "Steam" Machine** (Carpet Magic, A Division of Hartz Mountain), a rug-cleaning appliance available at most drug, department, and grocery stores. Assemble the equipment according to the manufacturer's directions, paying close attention to the ratio of shampoo to water. Too little shampoo won't clean, and too much creates excess suds. This machine sprays a stream of hot solution directly in front of the suction head, which draws the water out of the carpet. Allow the carpet to dry thoroughly before you walk on it.

Cheapest

Mix one part **K mart Rug Shampoo** (K mart Corporation) with eight parts cool water. This can be applied by hand or with a commercial shampooer. It contains a deodorizer and has a pleasant odor.

Read manufacturer's cautions and warnings before using any product.

Carpets and Rugs

Best

To remove light soil, **Glamorene Spray 'N Vac** (Airwick Industries, Inc.) is the best spray-on rug shampoo for home use. This no-scrub product with color brighteners is easy to use and cleans beautifully. After vacuuming, spray the foam over the carpet with a side to side motion and allow to dry. After 1½ hours the loosened dirt can be lifted with the dry foam by vacuuming.

For use by hand or commercial machine on moderately soiled carpets, dilute 8 ounces **Bac-Tex Bacteriostatic Rug Shampoo Concentrate** (Airwick Industries, Inc.) with 1 gallon water. It leaves a very pleasant odor, and will remove pet odors. It will also remove pet stains that have not been allowed to set for an extended length of time.

For heavy soil, rent a **Vibra Vac** (Rug Doctor, Inc.), a steam machine with a beater-bar in the head. It cleans carpets thoroughly, but takes more time because it is heavier than other steam carpet cleaners. The bar works solution into the carpet and loosens dirt before the suction removes the water. It is available at hardware, department, and grocery stores. Follow equipment assembly directions exactly. Drying time can be as short as 6 hours, but it is preferable to let it dry overnight.

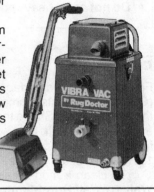

Other Products Tested

LIGHT SOIL.   **Woolite Self Cleaning Rug Cleaner** (Boyle-Midway Inc.)—no-scrub spray foam; moderately high foam; moderate cleaner; dries in approximately 30 minutes.
Lestoil Deodorizing Rug Shampoo (Noxell Corporation)—no-scrub spray foam; medium foam; moderately good soil lifter; dries in approximately 30 minutes.

MODERATE SOIL.   **Glory Professional Strength Rug Cleaner** (S. C. Johnson & Son, Inc.)—scrub-in spray foam; very good cleaner; 4-hour drying time.
Carbona Spray Foam Rug Shampoo (Carbona Products Company)—scrub-in spray foam, very good dirt lifter; medium foam; dries in 2 to 4 hours.
Bissell Foam Rug Cleaner with Resoil-Fighter Additive (Bissell Inc.)—scrub-in spray foam with soil retardant; medium foam; quite good soil lifter; dries in 2 to 4 hours.
Amway Rug & Upholstery Shampoo (Amway Corp.)—apply one part shampoo to ten parts water with sponge or commercial machine; may take several applications to remove difficult stains; mild odor.
Stanley Foam Rug Shampoo (Stanley Home Products, Inc.)—scrub-in spray foam; medium foam; very good soil lifter; dries in approximately 4 hours.
Plush (Airwick Industries, Inc.)—granular dry cleaner and conditioner; scrub in with damp sponge mop; low foam; moderately good soil lifter; dries in approximately 30 minutes.

HEAVY SOIL.   **Kirby Vacuum with a Rug Renovator** (The Kirby Company)—attachment with rotating brush that scrubs the carpet; will use most brands of carpet shampoo; must own the vacuum to use attachment for shampooing.
Rug Doctor Steam Detergent (Rug Doctor, Inc.)—for use with Vibra Vac machine or for occasional spot removal; not effective on heavy stains; mild odor.
Carpet Magic "Steam" Cleaning Cleaner (Carpet Magic, A Division of Hartz Mountain)—for use with the Carpet Magic "Steam" Machine; suitable for lightly soiled carpets; mild odor.

Furniture

Whether your furniture is made with natural or synthetic fabrics, plastic, or metal, is solid or veneered wood, all pieces will have longer lives when cleaned regularly. Furniture uphol- . stery is made from many different materials: fabric, leather, or vinyl. Wood furniture can be natural, stained, or bleached; then a finish or polish is applied using varnish, lacquer, oil, wax, paint, or polyurethane. You must know the type of covering your furniture has in order to select the proper cleaning and polishing products.

Do's

- Read all product labels carefully to learn safety precautions and whether the cleaner suits the surface.
- Test new products on an inconspicuous place before using on the entire piece.
- Protect the finish of furniture by making sure that all lamps and decorative objects have protective pads on their bases.
- Read labels or ask the dealer to determine materials and whether you can clean the furniture and file the manufacturer's care instructions for reference.
- Remove dust regularly with a whisk broom or vacuum attachment.
- Remove cushions of upholstered pieces when dusting and brush or vacuum the crevices and along the trim.
- Treat spots and spills immediately before they become stains, taking care to choose the appropriate spot remover for the type of padding in upholstered pieces.
- Shampoo or deep clean upholstered furniture when vacuuming no longer does the job.
- Speed dusting of wood furniture by spraying **Endust** (The Drackett Company) on the dust cloth.
- Choose a product that will give a high gloss or a satin finish, as desired.
- Use paste wax on wood antiques and other pieces where a hard, durable finish is desired.
- Wipe with the grain of the wood when dusting or cleaning/polishing.

Don'ts

- **Do not** throw away the manufacturer's care instructions.
- **Do not** vacuum down-filled cushions unless you are sure they are protected with a down-proof cover.
- **Do not** use solvent-based spot removers on cushions filled with foam rubber—solvents deteriorate foam rubber.
- **Do not** over-wet the padding and cushion filler when spot and deep cleaning.
- **Do not** use cleaned furniture until it dries completely.
- **Do not** use a wax or polish every time you dust—the wax build-up will dull the finish.
- **Do not** let spray waxes and polishes get on upholstery or wall surfaces.
- **Do not** use heavily oiled cloths to dust furniture with a waxed finish.
- **Do not** leave a cloth moistened with water or furniture polish on a wood surface.

Metal

This furniture should be dusted regularly and cleaned according to the basic metal. Usually, sponging with an all-purpose cleaner solution (see Recommended Basic Products) will keep metal furniture free of dirt. Also see general **Do's** and **Don'ts** under Furniture, and Chromium, Iron, Aluminum, and Outdoor Furniture.

Plastic

Some plastic furniture is made with veneers of plastic laminate, usually in wood grain patterns but sometimes in colors as well. Often, plastic laminate is applied only to the top instead of to the entire piece. Other pieces of plastic furniture are made from solid plastic in clear acrylic or bright colors. Also see Countertops—Plastic Laminate for cleaning products and procedures.

Do's

- See general **Do's** and **Don'ts** under Furniture.
- Care for plastic laminate furniture the same way as plastic laminate countertops.
- Regularly dust plastic furniture with a soft cloth.
- Occasionally wipe with a sponge or cloth dipped in an all-purpose cleaner solution and buff dry to prevent streaks.
- Apply a liquid detergent directly to stubborn spots, rub, rinse well, and buff dry.

Don'ts

- **Do not** use abrasive cleaners or steel wool pads to clean plastic furniture.
- **Do not** use ammonia or alcohol-based products on solid color or clear plastic furniture—they can cloud the surface.

Upholstery, Fabric

Most furniture upholstered in fabric can be shampooed safely at home, except for fabric marked "dry-clean only." You can spot clean this type of fabric with a solvent-based cleaner. Also see general **Do's** and **Don'ts** under Furniture.

Fastest

One of the foam aerosol upholstery shampoos is the fastest way to deep clean upholstered furniture: **Woolite Upholstery Cleaner** (Boyle-Midway Inc.) does a very good job. Spread the foam with a damp sponge, using circular overlapping strokes; let the fabric dry; then vacuum the soil away with a brush attachment.

Cheapest

Making your own shampoo from ordinary liquid dishwashing detergent is the cheapest method. **Lux Dishwashing Liquid** (Lever Brothers Company) gives the greatest volume of suds when ¼ cup is mixed with 1 cup warm water and whipped with an eggbeater. Apply the foam to the upholstery a small section at a time with a clean soft-bristled brush. Shake off any excess water. Rinse the upholstery by gently rubbing the fabric with a moist, clean cloth; rinse the cloth as necessary.

Best

Glamorene Upholstery Shampoo (Airwick Industries, Inc.) is the best cleaner. The aerosol foam is dispensed through a handy brush head attached to the can that you use to rub the foam into the fabric. Wipe the area with a damp sponge to remove excess foam, then wipe again with a dry, clean towel for beautiful results.

Other Products Tested

Stanhome Upholstery and Rug Shampoo (Stanley Home Products, Inc.)—liquid to mix with water and work into a foam; very good cleaner.
Stanhome Foam Upholstery Cleaner (Stanley Home Products, Inc.)—aerosol, good to very good cleaner; easy to apply.
Bissell Upholstery Shampoo for Home & Auto (Bissell Inc.)—aerosol with brush head; good to very good cleaner; easy to apply.

Upholstery, Leather

Leather is used to cover chairs and couches and is also inset into table and desk tops for decoration and utility. Leather must be cleaned with pure soap products only (no detergents) and benefits from applying conditioner occasionally to restore moisture and bring up the sheen. Also see general **Do's** and **Don'ts** under Furniture.

Fastest

The Tannery (Missouri Hickory Corp.), an aerosol foam, is the fastest product for cleaning leather upholstery. It also restores vital moisture and leaves the leather soft and glowing.

Cheapest and Best

A sudsy solution of **Ivory Snow** (Procter & Gamble) and warm water is the cheapest and one of the best ways to clean leather upholstery. Apply the suds only, scrubbing gently with a soft-bristled brush; wipe clean with a damp sponge.

Other Products Tested

Plastic & Leather Cleaner (Stanley Home Products, Inc.)—aerosol foam; very good cleaner and conditioner.
The Leather Works (Knomark Inc.)—aerosol foam; very good cleaner and conditioner.
Action Neatsfoot Oil Compound (Ecological & Speciality Products, Inc.)—good conditioning oil; will darken light-colored leather.
Fiebing's Saddle Soap (Fiebing Chemical Company)—paste soap; cleaner/conditioner; best for firm leather surfaces.
Turtle Wax Instant Saddle Soap (Turtle Wax, Inc.)—aerosol foam; good cleaner/conditioner; easy to use.

Upholstery, Vinyl

Vinyl upholstery is sometimes difficult to tell from real leather. It can be cleaned with the same products and techniques given for leather, or with **Vinyl Magic** (Magic American Chemical Corp.), an aerosol foam with brush-type head; it cleans very well. Also see general **Do's** and **Don'ts** under Furniture.

Wood, Oiled

Oiled wood surfaces have a warm, soft glow and require only an occasional application of furniture oil to keep them looking nice.

Do

- See general **Do's** and **Don'ts** under Furniture.

Don't

- **Do not** use wax products on oil finishes.

Fastest

FINIS High Gloss Furniture Polish (Scott's Liquid Gold-Inc.) is the fastest product for renewing oil-finished wood. Applied with a soft cloth, it buffs easily to a soft glow.

Cheapest and Best

A home recipe of equal parts turpentine and boiled linseed oil (available at hardware or paint stores) can be mixed in a jar and shaken until well-blended. Working on a small area at a time, apply the liquid to the furniture surface with a soft cloth, stroking gently with the direction of the grain. The surface will appear darker and oily when you finish, but in an hour the oil will be completely absorbed, leaving a lovely soft sheen.

Other Products Tested

Furniture Cream (Stanley Home Products, Inc.)—liquid cream; work into wood with soft cloth; satin finish.
Wilbert Dri-Finish Lemon Oil (Wilbert Products Co., Inc.)—oil; dampen soft cloth, pour small amount on cloth, rub in, buff; soft sheen.
Kleen Guard Furniture Polish with Lemon Oil (Alberto-Culver Company)—aerosol; soft sheen.
Parker's Perfect Polish (C. W. Parker Company)—cream; wipe on with dampened cloth, wipe dry immediately; good performance.

Wood, Painted

For painted wood furniture the best care is probably the least, since some polishes and waxes can damage the color and decoration. Also see Wood, Polished.

Do's

- See general **Do's** and **Don'ts** under Furniture.
- Dust such furniture with a soft cloth and wipe occasionally with a damp sponge, buffing dry immediately to remove smudges and finger marks.
- If you must wax, use a hard paste wax only once a year.

Wood, Polished

This type of wood furniture is finished with a varnish, lacquer, or wax. Also see general **Do's** and **Don'ts** under Furniture.

Fastest

Any of the aerosol polishing/waxing products listed here is the fastest way to clean and polish wood surfaces. Considerations that affect your choice are: the type of finish the product gives—high gloss or satin—and the availability of the products in your area.

Cheapest

Kleen Guard Furniture Polish with Lemon Oil (Alberto-Culver Company) is the cheapest product for polished wood. This excellent cleaner/polish removes wax build-up, leaving a low-gloss shine.

Best

Goddard's Cabinet Makers Polish With Lemon Beeswax (S. C. Johnson & Son, Inc.) is the best aerosol; it's easy to apply and buffs to a high gloss.

Paste waxes give a harder, longer lasting finish than spray or liquid polishes, and they are especially recommended for antiques. **Goddard's Cabinet Makers Wax** (S. C. Johnson & Son, Inc.) is the finest; though it takes a bit of "elbow grease," the beautiful results are worth the effort.

Other Products Tested

Amway Buff Up (Amway Corp.)—aerosol; very good cleaner/polish.
Favor (S. C. Johnson & Son, Inc.)—aerosol; very good cleaner/polish.
Klean 'n Shine (S. C. Johnson & Son, Inc.)—aerosol foam; cleaner/polish.
Old English Lemon Creme Furniture Polish (Boyle-Midway Inc.)—spray; moisturizes as well as cleans/polishes.

Read manufacturer's cautions and warnings before using any product.

Pledge (S. C. Johnson & Son, Inc.)—spray foam; natural wood scent.
Wood Crafter Lemon Furniture Polish (Colgate-Palmolive Company)—aerosol; good gloss.
Butcher's Bowling Alley Paste Wax (The Butcher Polish Co.)—paste; buffs to hard, high-gloss finish.
Formby's Furniture Cleaner (Formby's Inc.)—liquid; wood cleaner only, to be used with other paste or polish; good performance.
Formby's Lemon Oil Furniture Treatment (Formby's Inc.)—liquid; good performance.
Guardsman Furniture Polish (Guardsman Chemicals, Inc.)—concentrated liquid; good performance.
Old English Furniture Polish Lemon Oil (Boyle-Midway Inc.)—oil; good performance.

Wood, Specialty

The specialty woods used for furniture are wicker, rattan, bamboo, cane, and rush. They usually have a natural finish, but some pieces may have a varnish or shellac coating.

Do's

- See general **Do's** and **Don'ts** under Furniture.
- Dust regularly with a soft-bristled brush or the brush attachment of your vacuum.
- Wet down woods, except rush, occasionally outdoors with the garden hose or in a shower to restore moisture to the fibers and keep them soft.
- Clean with an all-purpose cleaner solution if the furniture is really dirty. Rinse well and air dry before using again.
- Tighten cane seats by wetting them down and allowing them to dry naturally.

Don't

- **Do not** "wet down" rush chair seats. Moisture damages the fibers.

Lampshades

Lampshades are made of many different materials; some are washable and some are not. Keep all hang tags so you know the proper cleaning procedure. Also see Spots and Stains for methods of spot cleaning nonwashable shades.

Do's

- Dry-clean shades that are glued to the frame.
- Dust shades regularly with an untreated cloth, feather duster, or brush attachment on a vacuum.
- Wash silk, nylon, and rayon shades only if they are sewn onto the frame.
- Use the bathtub or laundry sink for washing lampshades.
- Remove spots from nonwashable fabric shades with a spot remover.
- Wipe plastic and fiberglass shades occasionally with a damp cloth to remove soil.
- Dry shades quickly after washing to prevent rusting of the frame—an electric fan helps here.

Don'ts

- **Do not** wash shades that are glued to the frame.
- **Do not** wash linen, cotton, or hand-painted shades, or ones that have glued-on trim.
- **Do not** dry silk shades in the sun.

Fastest, Cheapest, and Best, Washable

For washable lampshades that are sewn onto their frames, the simplest method is also the fastest, cheapest, and best. Use one of the liquid dishwashing detergents (see Recommended Basic Products) to make a sudsy warm water solution in the bathtub or laundry sink. Dip the shade in and out, make sure all areas are covered, and then rinse in lukewarm water following the same procedure. Rinse until the water is clear. Take the shade outside and swing it vigorously in a circle to get rid of excess moisture, and then dry quickly in the sun or with an electric fan or hair dryer.

If the shade is washable but has glued-on trim that prevents immersing it in water, use the following method for cleaning. Mix ¼ cup **Lux Dishwashing Liquid** (Lever Brothers Company) with 1 cup warm water and whip with an eggbeater until it makes a stiff foam. Apply the foam to the shade with a sponge, being careful not to wet the trim. Rinse by going over the shade with a clean cloth wrung out in clear water. Allow the shade to dry.

Fastest and Cheapest, Nonwashable

Like Magic All Purpose Cleaner (Sterling Products, Inc.) cleans nonwashable parchment shades quickly. Apply the pink paste to the shade with a damp cloth and then immediately wipe it away with another clean, dry cloth.

Best, Nonwashable

An excellent way to clean nonwashable lampshades is with a product designed to clean wallpaper. This substance, which resembles modeling clay and does not crumble, is **Absorene** (Absorene Manufacturing Co., Inc.). Break off a manageable portion about the size of a ping pong ball, knead it until soft and pliant, squeeze it into an oblong shape, and then rub it over the shade in light, even, one-way strokes. After five or six strokes, reknead the cleaner to absorb the dirt and continue cleaning the shade.

Mirrors

Mirrors, whether antique or modern, should be kept spotless for shining reflections. If a liquid cleaner collects along the edges or corners of mirrors, the glue holding the frame can loosen and the silver backing on the glass can peel, crack, or discolor.

Do's

- Quickly remove spots and spatters from bathroom mirrors with a damp facial tissue; polish with a dry one.
- Use a chamois, soft absorbent lint-free cloth, or paper toweling to polish mirrors.
- Dust ornamental mirrors and frames regularly between cleanings.
- Keep cleaners away from frames by holding a blotter or towel against the frame.

Don'ts

- **Do not** use soap—it will streak and leave a film.
- **Do not** allow cleaning products to get on the frame.

Fastest, Cheapest, and Best

Since mirrors are another form of glass, the same techniques and products used for cleaning windows can successfully be used for mirrors too, if you avoid letting moisture seep behind the frame. (See Windows.)

Objets d'Art

Objets d'art add to the interest of a room and often become treasured family heirlooms. Some things can be safely cleaned at home, especially if frequent dusting or a quick dip in warm soapsuds is all that is necessary for cleaning.

Alabaster

Bearing a marked resemblance to marble, alabaster is made into vases, statues, lamp bases, and other ornamental objects around the house. Although it comes in several colors and sometimes has a dark streak or band of color, the best quality is pure white and translucent. It is fine-grained, but soft enough to be scratched with a fingernail and hence, easily carved. Alabaster is also easily broken, soiled, and weathered, so handle with care. See Marble for care and cleaning instructions.

Bone

Bone is used for many art objects, including sword or knife handles and miniature carvings. It is similar to ivory in composition since it is also an animal product. (See Ivory.)

Candlesticks

Candlesticks range from very simple, utilitarian models to very ornate and elaborate designs. They can be made of a number of materials including crystal, porcelain, silver, gold, brass, copper, pewter, or wood. The care of a particular candlestick depends on the material from which it was made, although routine cleaning usually is best done by a regular dusting and an occasional wipe with a damp sponge. Also see Glassware, Dinnerware, Silver, Gold, Brass, Copper, and Pewter for specific care and cleaning instructions.

Fastest, Cheapest, and Best

One soil problem common to all candlesticks is caused by dripped wax. Remove a hardened drip by gently pushing it off with the balls of your fingers or by using a fingernail that has been covered with a thin cloth to prevent scratching the surface. If the wax stubbornly resists these methods, dip the candlestick in warm water to soften the wax for removal, or if the candlestick is not immersible, the wax can be softened with warm air from a hair dryer.

Silver candlesticks that have wax dripped on them can be cleaned unharmed if you put them in the freezer first. After the wax freezes, it will peel off easily.

Fabric Flowers

Many fabric flowers so authentically copy real ones that it's hard to tell them apart—except that when cut flowers begin to wilt, fabric flowers continue to beautify their surroundings. Unfortunately, delicate fabric blossoms collect dust and eventually look dingy unless you clean them.

Do's

- Read and follow the manufacturer's instructions for care of fabric flowers—some are washable, many aren't.
- Remove dust with a blow dryer or vacuum cleaner set at a very low suction.
- Remove stubborn dust by gently wiping each petal with a soft toothbrush.
- Wipe silk flowers with a damp—not wet—sponge or cloth.
- Dip washable flowers into a mild solution of dishwashing detergent only when nothing less drastic works. Hang by the stems to dry or use a blow dryer on the gentle setting.
- Store cleaned fabric flowers in a strong box to prevent crushing their shapes permanently.
- Perk up any slightly wilted flower with steam from a teakettle or steam iron.

Objets d'Art

Don'ts

- **Do not** wash silk flowers.
- **Do not** swish fabric flowers harshly or the fabric and shape will be damaged.
- **Do not** wash any fabric flowers frequently.
- **Do not** store soiled fabric flowers—soil will become uncleanable over time and moths will be attracted.

Fastest, Cheapest, and Best

Some sturdy fabric flowers may be freshened when shaken in a paper bag with dry cut oats, cornmeal, or salt. For more delicate blossoms, see the chapter on the fabric from which they are made.

Ivory

Ivory, an animal dentine taken from elephants, hippos, and walruses and other sea creatures, is used extensively for ornamental objects. It was once the only material used for piano keys. (Also see Pianos.)

Do's

- Dust regularly with a soft cloth.
- Occasionally wash objects other than piano keys in mild soapsuds, rinse, and buff dry.
- Keep ivory objects where light will reach them—continual darkness causes ivory to yellow.

Don'ts

- **Do not** allow ivory objects that are cemented together to soak in water or the adhesive will loosen.
- **Do not** wash ivory-handled cutlery in the dishwasher.

Fastest, Cheapest, and Best

When ivory begins to yellow, treat it with a lemon/salt mixture. Cut a lemon in half, dip it in salt, and rub it over the ivory surface. Let dry, wipe with a damp cloth, and buff dry for a brighter finish.

Jade

Jade is a beautiful stone that may appear in the home as an exquisite lamp base, vase, valuable carved ornament, or piece of jewelry. Jade is hard, heavy, and fine-grained, usually available in colors from pure white to dark green, with occasional tints of brown, mauve, blue, yellow, red, gray, or black.

Fastest, Cheapest, and Best

Because jade is so hard and nonporous, very little care is required. Dust it on a regular basis, and buff with a soft cloth or chamois if it begins to look dull. If the article becomes soiled or sticky, a quick wipe with a damp cloth and buffing with another dry cloth is all that is necessary to restore it.

Marble

Marble, a beautiful form of limestone, is used for tabletops, floors, countertops, walls, steps, fireplace facings, window and door sills, and statuary and building material. It comes in various colors and has either a polished or matte finish.

Do's

- Seal marble used for floors, tabletops, countertops, steps, and window and door sills with a special stone sealer to reduce its porosity.
- Protect marble tabletops with coasters to prevent staining.
- Wipe up wine, fruit juice, or other acid foods immediately to prevent permanent surface etching.
- Dust frequently with a soft, untreated dust cloth.
- Wipe with a damp sponge to remove light soil and buff dry.

Don'ts

- **Do not** use abrasive or caustic cleaners on marble—they will mar the surface.
- **Do not** use oil polish or soft waxes—they discolor marble.
- **Do not** allow oily food substances to remain on marble surfaces—they will cause permanent stains.

Fastest

Mar-Glo Marble Polish (Golden Star Polish Mfg. Co.) is the fastest way to both clean and polish marble surfaces. Apply sparingly, using the same cloth to rub the polish on and buff it to a high gloss. The polish also has an added feature of giving the marble a protective coating. **Caution:** Work in a well-ventilated area to avoid breathing fumes; avoid using while smoking or near open flames as the product is flammable.

Cheapest

An effective, inexpensive way to clean marble is with **20 Mule Team Borax** (United States Borax & Chemical Corporation), which is mild enough not to scratch the surface. Dip a moistened cloth into a small amount of the dry borax and rub it on the marble. Rinse with warm water and buff dry with a soft cloth. The results are admirable, and this technique also brightens light-colored marble.

Read manufacturer's cautions and warnings before using any product.

Objets d'Art

Best

Marble Magic (Magic American Chemical Corp.) is an aerosol spray that cleans and polishes marble surfaces with highly satisfactory results. Spray it on, rub with a clean cloth, and then buff with a dry cloth for a beautiful finish that has a protective coating.

Other Products Tested

Goddards Marble Polish (S. C. Johnson & Son, Inc.)—paste; moderately easy to apply; use with a brush on carved surfaces; wax finish with a low gloss; pleasant odor.

Paintings

Paintings, whether oil, acrylic, or watercolor, require a minimum amount of care. However, if the painting does become damaged, it should not be repaired or cleaned at home.

Do's
- Dust paintings with an untreated, soft cloth or feather duster.
- If the painting is covered by glass, such as a watercolor, clean the glass without allowing any moisture to get behind the glass.

Don't
- **Do not** spray any furniture polish directly on picture frames—spray it on a cloth and then carefully apply it to the frame, making sure that it doesn't get on the painting.

Porcelain

Porcelain and other types of clay are fashioned into many types of art objects, including vases, lamp bases, candlesticks, and statuary.

Do's
- Handle gently—porcelain objects are fragile.
- Dust regularly with a soft cloth.
- Wash in a mild soapsuds solution when dirty, using warm, not hot, water.
- Pad the bottom of the sink with a towel and wrap another one around the faucet to prevent breakage when washing delicate objects in the sink.

Don'ts
- **Do not** subject porcelain objects to sudden extremes of temperature.
- **Do not** use harsh abrasives or steel wool pads on porcelain.
- **Do not** expose porcelain to high heat—it can cause the glaze to craze.
- **Do not** rinse with scalding water—use warm water only.
- **Do not** wash in the dishwasher.

Fastest, Cheapest, and Best

Select a liquid dishwashing detergent (see Recommended Basic Products) and make a warm soapsuds solution for cleaning porcelain objects. If some stubborn soil persists, try dipping a damp cloth in some baking soda (see Recommended Basic Products) and rubbing the spot with this non-abrasive powder.

Pianos

A piano is a valuable instrument, made with expert craftsmanship, and should be treated with respect and care. Whether it is being played much or not, have it tuned and regulated by a competent piano tuner approximately four times the first year for a new piano, semi-annually for an older model, and whenever it is moved from one location to another.

Do's

- Dust the piano case regularly with a soft cloth.
- Dust the interior of a piano occasionally by carefully using the dust brush attachment of a vacuum or a paintbrush.
- Close the top of grand pianos when not in use to keep dust out.
- Cover the keyboard when not in use if the keys are plastic.
- Check with a piano tuner about mothproofing the felts and hammers.
- Use a nonsilicone furniture polish or wax on the cases of pianos that have a varnish or lacquer finish.
- Clean pianos that have the high-gloss, polyester epoxy finish with a damp cloth or chamois and buff dry.
- Remove stubborn stains from ivory or plastic keys with a damp cloth dipped in baking soda, being careful not to let the soda fall between the keys; wipe off with another cloth; buff dry.
- Brighten ivory keys by rubbing very fine sandpaper (400 or 600) along the length of each key with the grain, then buff.

Don'ts

- **Do not** subject a piano to changes of temperature, drafts, or humidity.
- **Do not** place a piano where the sun will shine on it.
- **Do not** use any abrasives on plastic piano keys.
- **Do not** spray aerosols or any polish containing silicone directly onto the case.
- **Do not** cover the keyboard if the keys are made of ivory, or they will yellow over time.
- **Do not** allow anything to seep between the keys, including cleaning substances or moisture.
- **Do not** use furniture polish on a polyester epoxy case.

Read manufacturer's cautions and warnings before using any product.

Pianos

Fastest

The most rapid cleanup for any piano is a thorough dusting of the case and keyboard using a chamois or soft cloth. Spray **Endust** (The Drackett Company) on the dust cloth and watch it work like a dust magnet, eliminating the tendency to move the dust from one place to another. Wrap the cloth around the eraser end of a pencil to get between the keys. Some smudges on the keys can also be eliminated by rubbing them with a pencil eraser. If smudges remain, remove them with a moistened cloth.

Cheapest

For a piano with the high-gloss polyester epoxy coating, a piece of cheesecloth wrung out in warm water can be used to go over the case and plastic keys when they develop a film of soil. Buff dry the case.

The least expensive method for quick cleanups on a lacquered piano case that has been polished over the years is with an application of **Kleen Guard Furniture Polish with Lemon Oil** (Alberto-Culver Company). It serves as both a cleaner and polish, removing soil and the last coat of polish. Spray this pleasant-smelling aerosol foam on a cloth and wipe with the grain of the wood. Buff with a soft cloth to bring up a beautiful shine.

Best

Dusting and an occasional damp cleaning are the quickest and best ways to maintain the polyester epoxy case on some newer pianos. To make an older, lacquer-finished piano look its best, use **Furniture Cream** (Stanley Home Products, Inc.). Shake the bottle well and spread a small amount on a clean cloth. Rub the case lightly, then buff with a clean, dry cloth to a fine gloss.

Slipcovers

Slipcovers usually are washable. Keep the manufacturer's care instructions or the fabric care label for cleaning information. Also see Laundry for cleaning products for your slipcovers and the chapter on the fabric from which they are made for cleaning procedures.

Do's
- Brush or vacuum away lint and dust before removing for cleaning.
- Mend any ripped seams and close all zippers and fasteners before washing.
- Pretreat heavy soil and spots.
- Machine wash slipcovers whenever possible. Hand washing is suitable only for small covers.
- Select water temperature and cycle on the washing machine according to the fabric.
- Press pleats or ruffles if necessary before refitting on the furniture.
- Put slipcovers back on furniture while still slightly damp for a smooth fit.

Don'ts
- **Do not** wash in hot water if there is any possibility of shrinkage or fading.
- **Do not** overcrowd the washing machine.
- **Do not** dry until bone-dry.

Fastest, Cheapest, and Best

For general washing, select an all-purpose laundry detergent (see Laundry) when you wash slipcovers. Speed is determined by the cycle length of the machine; cost depends on the product least expensive in your area. All products listed in the category perform well.

When pretreating heavily soiled areas and spots **Magic Pre-Wash** (Armour-Dial Inc.) is the fastest and best product. Spray this aerosol cleaner on the soiled areas, allow to set a few minutes, and then put in the washer. Results are excellent for both soil and grease stains.

Fels-Naptha Heavy Duty Laundry Bar Soap (Purex Corporation) costs pennies and is a good product to use on heavily soiled areas or spots. Dip the end of the bar in water, rub over the soiled area, and wash as usual for excellent results.

Other Products Tested

Shout Laundry Soil & Stain Remover (S. C. Johnson & Son, Inc.)—aerosol prewash; good soil and spot lifter.

Television Sets

Portable televisions sets usually are made of a durable plastic in either a solid color or wood grain. The cabinets of larger sets and home entertainment centers often are made of wood and should be treated as any other fine wood furniture. (Also see Furniture—Wood, Oiled, Wood, Polished.)

Do's
- Dust the screen and cabinet regularly with a soft cloth.
- Remove film on the screen with a sponge dampened in a dishwashing detergent solution, rinse, and buff dry.
- Wash or apply a cleaner with a sponge or soft cloth to prevent scratches on the screen or cabinet.
- Wipe off plastic cabinets with a damp sponge.
- Use a recommended furniture polish for wood cabinets.
- Use little moisture when washing the screen and cabinet to prevent seepage behind the screen or into the crevices around the controls.

Don'ts
- **Do not** use abrasive cleaners on the screen or cabinet.
- **Do not** use furniture polish on the screen.
- **Do not** allow liquid to seep inside the set.

Fastest

Magic Plastic Window Cleaner (Magic American Chemical Corp.) is a very quick way to give the screen a sparkling finish. Spray it on and wipe it off with a soft cloth to remove dust, film, and fingerprints.

Like Magic All Purpose Cleaner (Sterling Products) not only cleans the black plastic exterior of portable TVs but also the walnut grain as well. Apply the pink paste with a dampened sponge and watch the smudges and marks quickly disappear. To finish, just wipe with a dry cloth and buff up a good shine.

Cheapest

Both the screen and plastic cabinet of TVs can be cleaned inexpensively with a cloth moistened with rubbing alcohol.

Best

To give the wood-grained plastic cabinet of a set an excellent shine there is no better product than **Mica-Lustre** (Multi-Care Corporation). This liquid has silicone in its formula and is easy to apply with a soft cloth. Buff dry with another soft cloth for an excellent shine.

Window Coverings

Blinds

Blinds are made from narrow slats of wood, metal, or plastic, held in place by tapes, cords, or colored yarns and ribbons. All can be adjusted up and down, while venetian blinds can adjust the angle of their slats for light control. Blinds are made with horizontally or vertically placed slats.

Do's

- Dust regularly with a soft cloth or the brush attachment of a vacuum.
- Close adjustable slats when dusting so you can reach more of their surface—remember to dust the headings, too.
- Remove finger marks with a damp sponge.
- Immerse plastic, metal, and painted wood blinds in water if desired for a thorough cleaning.
- Touch up old white tapes on venetian blinds with white shoe polish.
- Wash blinds outdoors (hang them on the clothesline) or in the bathtub.

Don't

- **Do not** immerse natural wood blinds or blinds made with decorative yarn and tapes in water.

Fastest

Dust venetian blinds by wearing a pair of absorbent cotton gloves. Spray the gloves with **Endust** (The Drackett Company) and clean the blinds by wiping both sides of each slat at one time with your gloved hands.

Cheapest and Best

The cheapest and best way to thoroughly clean washable blinds is by giving them a bath in the tub, or taking them outside and hanging them on the clothesline for a scrubbing. **Oakite All Purpose Cleaner** (Oakite Products, Inc.) is an excellent cleaner for either of these procedures. Pour it directly into a tub filled with warm water, or mix a solution of ½ cup Oakite in 1 gallon warm water for outdoor cleaning, and apply with a brush. Rinse well with clean water; allow the blinds to drip dry either on the clothesline or hang the blinds on the shower rod, placing towels underneath to catch the drips. Rehang the blinds on the window when the dripping has stopped, stretching the tapes or cords full length to prevent shrinkage. Leave the slats in the open position until completely dry. *(continued on next page)*

Read manufacturer's cautions and warnings before using any product.

Cheapest and Best (continued)

Klean 'n Shine (S. C. Johnson & Son, Inc.) is an excellent solution to the problem of cleaning natural wood blinds. Dust the blind, open it to its full length, and close the slats. Spray with Klean 'n Shine, reverse the slats, and spray again. Open the blind and wipe each slat with a soft cloth or wear absorbent cotton gloves for the same purpose.

Other Products Tested

METAL OR PLASTIC. Like Magic All Purpose Cleaner (Sterling Products)—paste; excellent cleaner; pleasant odor.
Formula 409 All Purpose Cleaner (The Clorox Company)—spray; very good cleaner; pleasant odor.
Fantastik Multi-Surface Spray Cleaner (Texize Chemicals Company)—spray; very good cleaner; moderate odor.
Soilax (Economics Laboratory, Inc.)—nonsudsing powder; very good cleaner.
Spic and Span (Procter & Gamble)—low-sudsing powder; very good cleaner; moderate odor.

NATURAL WOOD. Lemon Behold Furniture Polish (The Drackett Company)—aerosol; very good cleaner; medium gloss.
Amway Buff Up (Amway Corp.)—aerosol; good cleaner; medium to high gloss.

Curtains

Do's
- Read all care labels carefully and follow the manufacturer's instructions for cleaning.
- Shake out or vacuum excess dust before washing.
- Use bleaches with caution—the resins in certain fabric finishes can be damaged by chlorine bleaches.
- Rinse the washing machine thoroughly after washing fiberglass curtains to ensure that no fine glass filaments remain.
- Wear rubber gloves when hand washing fiberglass curtains.
- Handle cotton curtains gently if they have been hung in a sunny window—sunlight may have weakened the fabric.
- Wash sheers or open weave curtains in a mesh bag or hand wash so the delicate fabric doesn't stretch or tear.
- Tumble or drip-dry curtains according to their instructions.
- Use curtain stretchers for drying old lace or net curtains.
- Iron curtains that must be pressed before they are completely dry.

Don'ts
- **Do not** leave curtain rings or clips in place when cleaning unless they are permanently attached.
- **Do not** overcrowd the washing machine.
- **Do not** dry-clean fiberglass curtains.

Fastest

Put the upholstery attachment on the vacuum and go over all the curtain panels for a quick cleaning. This is almost all that needs to be done to fiberglass curtains, since the fabric sheds dirt almost as easily as it sheds water.

Cheapest

For hand washing lightly soiled curtains, the cheapest product is a light duty detergent (see Laundry). Make a warm soapsuds solution in the bathtub or laundry sink and gently squeeze the suds through the curtain panels. Rinse in lukewarm water until it runs clear, being careful to squeeze rather than twist or wring the fabric. Dry in the dryer or hang on the clothesline to drip-dry according to the manufacturer's instructions.

An all-purpose laundry detergent (see Laundry) is the cheapest detergent for machine washing curtains. A high-sudsing, nonphosphate product does a good job on all fabrics. A gentle wash cycle is recommended unless the curtains are heavily soiled or of a very durable fabric.

Best

Lux Dishwashing Liquid (Lever Brothers Company) is the best product for hand washing curtains of all types because of its high sudsing action. Follow the instructions given for hand washing.

Arm & Hammer Laundry Detergent (Church & Dwight Co., Inc.) is the best product for machine washing curtains. This high-sudsing phosphate-free detergent performs well on all washable fabric types.

Draperies

Draperies are often lined and are usually made of fabrics much heavier than those used for curtains, so it is usually best to dry-clean draperies. Some drapery fabrics are washable, however; check the care label for this information.

Do's

- Dust draperies weekly with the upholstery attachment on the vacuum.
- Use a gentle cycle when washing draperies.
- Shake or vacuum away excess dust before washing or cleaning.
- Remove all hooks and pins unless they are permanently attached before washing or cleaning draperies.
- Test a corner of the fabric in a bowl of warm water and detergent to see if it bleeds.
- Air draperies on a clothesline occasionally on a breezy day to refresh them between cleanings.

Window Coverings

Don'ts

- **Do not** forget to dust the tops of the drapes, the valances, and the drapery hardware.
- **Do not** overcrowd the washing machine if washing draperies; use a large commercial washer if necessary.
- **Do not** wash draperies if the fabric is not colorfast.

Fastest, Cheapest, and Best

The same techniques and products listed for Curtains can be used if the draperies are washable.

Shades, Window

Light-diffusing or opaque shades usually are made of fabric that is washable and also sometimes have a protective vinyl coating that makes them easy to clean. Some shades are not washable and must be dry-cleaned.

Do's

- Dust regularly with a cloth or brush attachment on a vacuum.
- Lower shades completely before dusting to clean the full length.
- Remove finger marks with a damp sponge or a quick spritz of an all-purpose spray cleaner.
- Remove shades from the window and spread out on a flat surface for cleaning.
- Test a small corner of colored shades with a detergent solution to see if the color bleeds.

Don'ts

- **Do not** forget to dust the top of shades.
- **Do not** wash noncolorfast shades.
- **Do not** roll up shades until they are completely dry.
- **Do not** use water on nonwashable shades.

Fastest, Nonwashable

Some spotting can be eliminated from nonwashable shades with an artgum eraser, used as though you are erasing a pencil mark.

Cheapest, Nonwashable

The least expensive method to clean a nonwashable shade thoroughly is to rub the surface with a rough, absorbent cloth dipped in cornmeal. The secret of this treatment is that the abrasiveness and absorption of the cloth and cornmeal pick up soil and grease. Terry cloth is good for this job but an old sweatshirt turned inside out is even better. Substituting dry kitchen flour for the cornmeal works just as well.

Best, Nonwashable

A product for cleaning wallpaper is just as outstanding for a window shade that won't tolerate water. **Absorene** (Absorene Manufacturing Co., Inc.) is a noncrumbling substance that resembles modeling clay. Break a small portion of this pink material from the block and knead it until it is soft and pliant. Squeeze it into an oblong shape and apply it to the rolled-out shade in long, one-way strokes. After a dozen or more strokes, reknead the material to absorb the soil and continue cleaning. Discard a dirty piece for a fresh one when necessary.

Fastest, Washable

Big Wally (S. C. Johnson & Son, Inc.) is the fastest product for removing soil from window shades. Spread the shade out full length on a table and spray a section with the cleaning foam. Wipe with a damp sponge and repeat the procedure until both sides of the shade have been cleaned. Rehang and make sure it is completely dry before rolling it up.

Cheapest, Washable

Make a mild soapsuds solution using a liquid dishwashing detergent (see Recommended Basic Products) and apply it to a rolled out shade with a sponge. Rinse with a clean sponge dipped in clear water and allow it to dry before rerolling.

Best, Washable

A first-rate procedure for removing dirt from a washable shade is by the "dry detergent" method, which requires little moisture. Mix ¼ cup **Lux Dishwashing Liquid** (Lever Brothers Company) with 1 cup warm water in a deep bowl and whip with an eggbeater to a stiff foam. With the shade stretched out full length, apply the foam with a sponge working in a circular motion in small overlapping areas. Rinse the suds and dirt away with another sponge frequently wrung out in clear water. Turn the shade over and do the other side, allowing it to dry completely before rolling it up.

Other Products Tested

Formula 409 All Purpose Cleaner (The Clorox Company)—spray; very good cleaner; moderate odor.
Fantastik Multi-Surface Spray Cleaner (Texize Chemicals Company)—spray; very good cleaner; moderate odor.
Soilax (Economics Laboratory, Inc.)—nonsudsing powder; very good cleaner.
Spic and Span (Procter & Gamble)—low-sudsing powder; very good cleaner; moderate pine odor.
Top Job (Procter & Gamble)—sudsing liquid with ammonia; very good cleaner; moderate ammonia odor.

Read manufacturer's cautions and warnings before using any product.

Shutters

Painted or stained shutters are the most common, but more people are leaving the natural, light wood exposed on their shutters, covered only with a sealer or varnish. Also see Furniture—Wood, Polished and Walls—Painted.

Do's

- Use warm, soapy water with a damp cloth to wash painted shutters.
- Wash each louver separately on both sides.

Don'ts

- **Do not** use abrasive cleansers on your shutters.
- **Do not** spray any cleaner directly onto the shutters—it can seep into the dowels and clog the louvers.

Fastest

To clean stained shutters quickly, spray **Complete All Purpose Polishing Cleaner** (S. C. Johnson & Son, Inc.) on a clean, dry, soft cloth. Wipe on shutters, and wipe off immediately with a clean, soft cloth, turning to the dry part of the cloth as you wipe.

Cheapest

Spray **Lemon Behold Furniture Polish** (The Drackett Company) onto a cloth and wipe evenly onto stained shutters. Wipe off immediately with a soft, clean cloth for a clean and shiny surface.

Best

Apply **Formby's Furniture Cleaner** (Formby's Inc.) to a clean, dry, soft cloth and rub into the stained wood. If desired, this can be followed with an application of **Formby's Lemon Oil Furniture Treatment** (Formby's Inc.) for added protection.

Other Products Tested

STAINED WOOD.   Lemon Pledge (S. C. Johnson & Son, Inc.)—aerosol; spray on cloth and wipe; pleasant odor; easily smudged.
Old English Furniture Polish Lemon Oil (Boyle-Midway Inc.)—aerosol or pump spray; apply to cloth and wipe; pleasant odor; can leave an oily film.

Bathrooms

Bathtubs and Washbasins

The washbasin and bathtub usually are made of porcelain. If the fixtures are older, chances are the material is porcelain-on-cast iron, and they may not be as acid- and alkaline-resistant as the newer porcelain-on-steel tubs and basins. Cultured marble is also used for washbasins, and sometimes is molded into the countertop for an all-in-one look. Fiberglass tubs are now popular in new home construction and remodeling, but they are not nearly as durable as porcelain-coated steel, and need special care to avoid scratching. For methods and products for cleaning the drains in your sink and tub, also see Drains.

Do's
- Clean tubs and basins at least once a week—more often if the bathroom is subject to high traffic.
- Clean the hair from basin and tub drains after use to prevent clogged drains.
- Add bubble bath or a bit of detergent to bathwater to prevent a bathtub ring.
- Use a synthetic scouring pad for stubborn soil.
- Clean a heavily discolored tub with a paste made of hydrogen peroxide and cream of tartar. Scrub in with a brush and rinse well.
- Clean lighter stains with a paste of lemon juice and borax powder.

Don't
- **Do not** use harsh abrasive cleaners—they can scratch delicate surfaces.

Fastest

Bon Ami Deluxe Polishing Cleanser (Faultless Starch/Bon Ami Company) is the fastest product for cleaning porcelain tubs and basins. Sprinkle a bit of this mild abrasive powder on a damp sponge and apply to the tub and basin. Rinse with clear water and admire the sparkling results achieved without scratching the surface.

When cleaning cultured marble or fiberglass tubs and basins use **Gr-reat 'n Easy** (Fiberglass Cleaning Products, Inc.). Shake the can well, spray over the surface, lightly scrub with a damp sponge, and rinse with clear water. Being non-abrasive, Gr-reat 'n Easy will never scratch the surface of these less durable basins and tubs.

Read manufacturer's cautions and warnings before using any product.

Bathtubs and Washbasins

Cheapest

The cheapest cleaning solution for porcelain as well as cultured marble and fiberglass fixtures is a home recipe consisting of ½ cup vinegar, 1 cup ammonia, and ¼ cup baking soda mixed in 1 gallon hot water. **Caution:** Wear rubber gloves and work in a well-ventilated area when using this powerful solution. Apply this solution to the fixtures with a sponge, scrubbing a bit if necessary, and rinse well with clear water.

Best

One of the spray-on products, **20 Mule Power Industrial Strength Bathroom Cleaner** (United States Borax & Chemical Corporation) is the best cleaner for porcelain tubs and basins. Spray the cleaner over the surface, allow to penetrate, and scrub with a sponge, or use a synthetic scouring pad (see Tools of the Trade) for stubborn dirt. Rinse with clear water. Wipe dry to prevent waterspots. **Caution:** Wear rubber gloves to avoid skin contact with this powerful cleaner; be sure your work area is well-ventilated so you don't breathe the mist as you spray.

Soft Scrub Cleanser (The Clorox Company) is the best product to use on cultured marble or fiberglass basins and tubs. This mild, creamy liquid does a good job of cleaning but will never scratch these delicate surfaces. Apply with a sponge, scrubbing where necessary, and rinse well with clear water.

Rust stains can be removed from around a bathtub drain with **Bar Keepers Friend Cleanser & Polish** (SerVaas Laboratories, Inc.), an all-purpose cleanser that also acts as a rust remover. Rub a small amount of the powder onto the wet tub surface with a damp cloth until the discoloration disappears, and then rinse well to stop the acid action of the cleanser.

Other Products Tested

Lysol Basin/Tub/Tile Cleaner (Lehn & Fink Products Division of Sterling Drug Inc.)— spray; very good cleaner; must be scrubbed; moderate odor.

Bon Ami Cleaning Powder (Faultless Starch/Bon Ami Company)—powder; very good cleaner with little abrasion; moderate odor.

Comet Cleanser (Procter & Gamble)—powder; very good cleaner with chlorine for removing stains; slightly abrasive; moderate odor.

Ajax Cleanser (Colgate-Palmolive Company)—powder; very good cleaner with chlorine for removing stains; slightly abrasive; moderate odor.

Formula 409 All Purpose Cleaner (The Clorox Company)—spray; very good cleaner; pleasant odor.

Pine Sol (American Cyanamid Company)—liquid; very good cleaner; pleasant pine odor.

Lysol Deodorizing Cleaner II (Lehn & Fink Products Division of Sterling Drug Inc.)—liquid; very good cleaner; moderate odor.

Breath O' Pine Multi-Purpose Cleaner (Brondow Incorporated)—liquid; moderately good cleaner; heavy pine odor.

Dow Disinfectant Bathroom Cleaner (The Dow Chemical Co.)—aerosol; moderately good cleaner; pleasant pine odor.

Countertops

The materials used for bathroom countertops are generally ceramic tile, plastic laminate, and cultured marble; all are easy to clean.

Do's

- Use a toothbrush or nail brush to help clean tile grout or hard-to-reach places.
- Apply an appliance wax or light polish to plastic laminate countertops to brighten dull surfaces.

Don'ts

- **Do not** allow a cigarette to rest on plastic laminate or cultured marble—it will leave a burn mark.
- **Do not** drop heavy objects on the tile—they can cause chipping or cracks.
- **Do not** use abrasive cleaners—they mar the surfaces.

Fastest, Ceramic Tile

For ceramic tile, **Tile 'n Grout Magic** (Magic American Chemical Corp.) cleans both the tile and grout quickly. Scrub the aerosol foam onto the tile with the handy plastic brush top, rinse clean with a damp sponge, and wipe dry. (Also see Countertops—Ceramic Tile in the Inside the House section for additional methods of cleaning grout.)

Cheapest, Ceramic Tile

To clean this surface inexpensively, combine ½ cup vinegar, 1 cup clear ammonia, and ¼ cup baking soda (see Recommended Basic Products) with 1 gallon warm water and apply to the countertop with a sponge. **Caution:** Wear rubber gloves and work in a well-ventilated area when using this powerful solution. Rinse with clear water and wipe dry to prevent waterspots.

Best, Ceramic Tile

The best ceramic tile cleaner is **20 Mule Power Industrial Strength Bathroom Cleaner** (United States Borax & Chemical Corporation). Spray this liquid on the surface, allow it to penetrate, and use a synthetic scouring pad (see Tools of the Trade) to loosen dirt. Rinse with clear water and wipe dry to prevent waterspots. **Caution:** Wear rubber gloves to avoid skin contact with this powerful cleaner; be sure your work area is well-ventilated so you don't breathe the mist as you spray the tile.

Other Products Tested

Lysol Basin/Tub/Tile Cleaner (Lehn & Fink Products Division of Sterling Drug Inc.)—

Read manufacturer's cautions and warnings before using any product.

Countertops

pump spray cleaner; very good performance; moderate odor.

X-14 Instant Mildew Stain Remover (White Laboratories)—spray cleaner designed to remove mildew stains and soil from grout; no scrub; no rinse; good performance.

Arm & Hammer Baking Soda (Church & Dwight Co., Inc.)—powder mixed with water and used as a paste; good cleaner.

Clorox Bleach (The Clorox Company)—liquid; mild solution cleans grout when scrubbed with a toothbrush; strong odor.

Dow Disinfectant Bathroom Cleaner (The Dow Chemical Co.)—aerosol; moderately good performance; pleasant pine odor.

Afta Tile Cleaner (Afta Solvents Corporation)—moderately good cleaner; built-in spray brush head; moderate odor.

Fastest, Cultured Marble

Cultured marble countertops in the bathroom clean up fast with **Bon Ami Deluxe Polishing Cleanser** (Faultless Starch/Bon Ami Company). Apply the powder directly onto a wet countertop and wipe off dirt and soap film without damage to the synthetic surface.

Cheapest, Cultured Marble

To clean this surface inexpensively, combine ½ cup vinegar, 1 cup clear ammonia, and ¼ cup baking soda (see Recommended Basic Products) with 1 gallon warm water and apply to the countertop with a sponge. **Caution:** Wear rubber gloves and work in a well-ventilated area when using this powerful solution. Rinse with clear water and wipe dry to prevent waterspots.

Best, Cultured Marble

This countertop surface responds best to non-abrasive **Soft Scrub Cleanser** (The Clorox Company). Squeeze this mild cleanser onto a sponge or directly onto the surface, rinse, and wipe dry for a clean finish.

Other Products Tested

Lysol Basin/Tub/Tile Cleaner (Lehn & Fink Products Division of Sterling Drug Inc.)—pump spray; very good cleaner; moderate odor.

Dow Disinfectant Bathroom Cleaner (The Dow Chemical Co.)—aerosol; moderately good cleaner; pleasant pine odor.

Fastest, Plastic Laminate

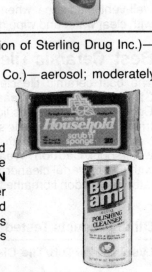

Plastic laminate countertops (such as the Formica brand) should be wiped regularly with a damp cloth or sponge. For more thorough cleaning, use **Scotch-Brite Household Scrub 'N Sponge** (3M). Moisten the pad slightly with water, use the fiber side to loosen soil and smears, then turn the scrubber over and wipe the surface with the sponge side to remove the soil. If stains persist, use **Bon Ami Deluxe Polishing Cleanser** (Faultless Starch/Bon Ami Company) to clean this surface also.

Cheapest, Plastic Laminate

Plain baking soda (see Recommended Basic Products) rids plastic laminate countertops of stains inexpensively. Sprinkle the soda on the stain, rub with a damp cloth or sponge, rinse, and wipe dry. This multipurpose cleaner even removes the dye left by price stamps on packages.

Best, Plastic Laminate

This countertop surface responds best to non-abrasive **Soft Scrub Cleanser** (The Clorox Company). Squeeze this mild cleanser onto a sponge or directly onto the surface, rinse, and wipe dry for a clean finish.

Other Products Tested

Formula 409 All Purpose Household Cleaner (The Clorox Company)—spray liquid; no rinsing; wipe off with dry cloth.
Glass Plus (Texize Chemicals Company)—spray liquid; very good cleaner; moderate odor.
Parsons' Clear Detergent Ammonia (Armour-Dial Inc.)—liquid; dilute ½ cup in 1 gallon warm water; good grease cutter; strong odor.
Amway Zoom Spray Cleaner Concentrate (Amway Corp.)—spray concentrate mixed with equal part water; good on grease; eye irritant.
Mica-Lustre (Multi-Care Corporation)—green liquid with silicone; expensive; good dressing that cleans and polishes; pleasant odor; reduces static electricity.
Countertop Magic (Magic American Chemical Corp.)—aerosol foam; moderately good cleaner; moderate odor.

Hardware

Bathroom hardware consists of the faucets, taps, and drain fixtures; shower heads and rods; soap and toothbrush holders; and towel racks. Faucets, taps, drain fixtures, shower heads and rods usually are made of chromium or stainless steel. Soap dishes and toothbrush holders can be made of ceramic, metal, or plastic. Towel racks can be made of plastic, metal, ceramic, and wood.

Do
- Wipe sink and tub hardware dry after each use to prevent waterspots.

Don't
- **Do not** use abrasive cleaners on any of these items.

Read manufacturer's cautions and warnings before using any product.

Fastest, Cheapest, and Best

A quick wipe with a sponge or cloth saturated with the cleaning product you use to clean the tub and basin (see Bathtubs and Washbasins) is the fastest, cheapest, and best way to clean bathroom hardware. Rinse well with clear water and buff to a high shine with a dry cloth. If the fixture is made of metal and begins to lose some of its shine, see the chapter describing ways to clean that particular metal for special cleaning techniques and products. Treat wooden towel racks with an occasional application of furniture polish to bring up the shine and give a protective coating. (See Furniture.)

Shower Curtains

Shower curtains need to be cleaned on a regular basis to remove built-up soap scum and water deposits. Of course all shower curtains are washable; fabric curtains and some plastic ones can be washed in the machine. However, hand washing does a better job on plastic curtains and leaves fewer wrinkles. Check the care label for the manufacturer's recommendations.

Do's

- Back fabric curtains with a plastic liner to preserve their good looks.
- Wash curtains before they get heavily soiled and spotted to keep the job easy.
- Eliminate mildew by spraying just-cleaned curtains with a disinfectant.
- Use your regular laundry detergent when washing fabric curtains in the washing machine.
- Use a gentle cycle when machine washing plastic shower curtains.
- Shake excess water off shower curtains after each use, and spread out almost the full width of the rod to dry.

Fastest and Best

Partially fill a bathtub with warm water and add ½ cup **Oakite All Purpose Cleaner** (Oakite Products, Inc.). Submerge the curtain and allow it to soak for 10 minutes. Scrub off heavy soil with a brush while holding a section of the curtain against the side of the tub. Rinse well with clean water, shake off the excess, and hang to drip-dry. The curtain will be almost wrinkle-free and the tub will be clean too! For mildew problems, after cleaning the curtain, spray with **Lysol Disinfectant Spray** (Lehn & Fink Products Division of Sterling Drug Inc.) and wipe the curtain free of mildew.

Cheapest

Mix ½ cup vinegar, 1 cup ammonia, ¼ cup baking soda, and 1 gallon hot water, and apply to the shower curtain with a sponge while it is flat in the tub. **Caution:** Wear rubber gloves and work in a well-ventilated area when using this powerful solution. Let stand a few minutes to loosen the scum and then scrub with a sponge or brush, adding more cleaner if necessary. Rinse well in warm water, shake off excess water, and hang to drip-dry.

Plain baking soda is also a cheap helper when there are stubborn stains on a plastic curtain. Scrub it over the soiled area with a damp sponge and then rinse well with clear water.

Other Products Tested

Gr-reat 'n Easy (Fiberglass Cleaning Products, Inc.)—aerosol; very good cleaner; rinse well; pleasant odor.

20 Mule Power Industrial Strength Bathroom Cleaner (United States Borax & Chemical Corporation)—spray; rubber gloves and good ventilation needed; very good cleaner; rinse well; moderately strong odor.

Showers and Shower Stalls

Made of tile, glass, plastic laminate, fiberglass, or cultured marble, showers are housed in a separate stall or are used in the bathtub. The special cleaning problem they present is the removal of soap scum and mineral deposits from the sides of the shower enclosure. Also see Walls—Ceramic Tile and Countertops.

Do's

- Clean shower stalls on a regular basis to keep the job manageable.
- Remove hard water deposits with a solution of white vinegar and water.
- Use an old toothbrush or nail brush to clean the grout of ceramic tile shower stalls.
- If the shower area is subject to mildew, spray it periodically with a mildew inhibitor and disinfectant.
- Remove mildew with an ammonia/water solution, scrubbing with a small brush.
- Remove water spots on metal frames around shower doors and enclosures with lemon oil.

Don'ts

- **Do not** close shower doors completely, as the lack of circulating air will promote mildew growth.
- **Do not** allow the caulking or grout to break away where the walls join the tub or shower floor—recaulk when necessary to prevent water damage.

Read manufacturer's cautions and warnings before using any product.

Showers and Shower Stalls

Fastest

Tile 'n Grout Magic (Magic American Chemical Corp.) cleans shower enclosures quickly. Scrub the aerosol foam onto the surface with the handy plastic brush built into the top of the can, rinse well with clear water, and wipe dry to prevent waterspots.

Cheapest

A home recipe makes a good and inexpensive cleaning solution for shower enclosures. Mix ½ cup vinegar, 1 cup ammonia, ¼ cup baking soda, and 1 gallon hot water. **Caution:** Wear rubber gloves and work in a well-ventilated area when using this powerful solution. Apply to the walls with a sponge, scrubbing with a brush if necessary to remove all the scum. Rinse well with clear water and wipe dry.

Best

The best product for removing soap scum and film from showers is **20 Mule Power Industrial Strength Bathroom Cleaner** (United States Borax & Chemical Corporation). Spray this strong liquid over the surface and wipe with a sponge or scrub with a synthetic scouring pad (see Tools of the Trade) according to the degree of soil. Rinse well with clear water. **Caution:** Wear rubber gloves to prevent skin contact and work in a well-ventilated area to avoid breathing the mist of this powerful cleaner.

Other Products Tested

Gr-reat 'n Easy (Fiberglass Cleaning Products, Inc.)—aerosol; very good cleaner; pleasant odor.

Lysol Basin/Tub/Tile Cleaner (Lehn & Fink Products Division of Sterling Drug Inc.)—pump spray; very good cleaner; no rinsing; moderate odor.

Lime A-Way (Economics Laboratory, Inc.)—liquid to be diluted with water; caustic; test before using; very good cleaner; moderate odor.

X-14 Instant Mildew Stain Remover (White Laboratories)—spray; cleaner designed to remove mildew stains from tile and grout; no scrub; no rinse; good performance.

Fantastik Multi-Surface Spray Cleaner (Texize Chemicals Company)—pump spray; good cleaner; moderate odor.

Amway Zoom Spray Cleaner Concentrate (Amway Corp.)—spray; good cleaner; pleasant odor.

Big Wally (S. C. Johnson & Son, Inc.)—aerosol; moderately good cleaner; moderate odor.

Dow Disinfectant Bathroom Cleaner (The Dow Chemical Co.)—aerosol; moderately good cleaner; pleasant pine odor.

Afta Tile Cleaner (Afta Solvents Corporation)—spray; moderately good cleaner; handy built-on brush head; moderate odor.

Toilets

Toilet bowls and tanks usually are made of vitreous china. Many toilet bowl cleaners and deodorizers are available to help make the cleaning job easier. Some products are placed in the tank and are dispersed each time the toilet is flushed. Most of them color the water a pleasant blue, and while they do clean the bowl a little better than plain water, they are not a substitute for a regular scrubbing using products you apply with a bit of elbow grease. Read labels carefully to know exactly which type of product you are buying.

Do's

- Keep a long-handled brush for cleaning only toilet bowls.
- Clean the exterior of toilets with the same products used for tubs and basins.
- Wipe the toilet seat, tank, around the rim, and around the base when cleaning.
- Protect your hands with plastic or rubber gloves when using strong toilet bowl cleaners.

Don'ts

- **Do not** combine toilet bowl cleaners with bleach—the mix can release toxic gases.
- **Do not** allow bowl cleaners to remain in the toilet—flush it immediately after scrubbing.
- **Do not** use toilet bowl cleaners for the tub or basin—they are too harsh.
- **Do not** set the container of toilet bowl cleaner on any other bathroom surfaces—it can damage these surfaces.

Fastest

Sno Bol Toilet Bowl Cleaner (A. E. Staley Mfg. Co.) is a fast-acting cleaner for the toilet bowl. The handy, directional spout allows you to aim the liquid under the rim for thorough coverage. Scrub with a toilet brush for best results and then flush the toilet immediately to rinse the cleaner away. **Caution:** Wear rubber gloves to prevent skin contact; work in a well-ventilated area to avoid breathing fumes. Do not mix with other chemicals.

Cheapest

The toilet bowl can be cleaned and disinfected quite cheaply with ½ cup chlorine bleach. Pour it into the bowl, let it stand for 10 minutes, and then scrub with the toilet brush and flush. **Caution:** Do not mix chlorine bleach with any other cleaner.

Best

Of the commercial toilet bowl cleaners tested, the most effective is **Lysol Liquid Disinfectant Toilet Bowl Cleaner** (Lehn & Fink Products Division of Sterling Drug Inc.). Squirt the liquid into the bowl and around the rim, scrub with a long-handled brush, and flush for a sparkling bowl. **Caution:** Wear rubber gloves to prevent skin contact; work in a well-ventilated area to avoid breathing fumes. Do not mix with other chemicals.

Read manufacturer's cautions and warnings before using any product.

Toilets

Other Products Tested

Lysol Deodorizing Cleaner II (Lehn & Fink Products Division of Sterling Drug Inc.)—liquid; very good cleaner when used full strength; moderate odor.

Sani-Flush (Boyle-Midway Inc.)—granular; caustic; rubber gloves needed; very good cleaner; peppermint odor.

Vanish Automatic Toilet Bowl Cleaner (The Drackett Company)—in-tank liquid; moderately good cleaner; blue or green dye; moderate odor.

Norsan Blue Automatic Toilet Bowl Cleaner (Gold Seal Co.)—in-tank solid; moderately good cleaner; blue dye; moderate odor.

Ty-D-Bol (Knomark Inc.)—in-tank liquid; moderately good cleaner; blue dye; lemon odor.

Vanish Bowl Freshener (The Drackett Company)—cylinder that fits under the rim; water activated; moderately good cleaner; pleasant odor.

Befresh (S. C. Johnson & Son, Inc.)—cylinder that fits under the rim; water activated; moderately good cleaner; pleasant odor.

Kitchenware

Cookware

Cookware will give many years of service if it is made from a durable material and is given the proper care. Stovetop and oven cookware is made from many different materials; the following procedures and products will help keep your particular cookware in top condition.

Do's

- Read the manufacturer's instructions.
- Wash all pots and pans thoroughly inside and out soon after use.
- Clean a seasoned omelet pan by wiping with a paper towel.
- Keep gas flames low so they cannot lick up the side of pots and pans to cause heat stains.
- Clean scorched pans by bringing 1 teaspoon baking soda and 1 cup water to a boil in the pan. Allow to cool, and wash.
- Substitute vinegar for baking soda in the above procedure when cleaning scorched aluminum pans.
- Use **Lime A-Way** (Economics Laboratory, Inc.) to remove mineral deposits from tea-kettles.

Don'ts

- **Do not** subject cookware to sudden temperature changes. Allow it to cool before washing or soaking.
- **Do not** bang or drop cookware.
- **Do not** expose plastic or wood handles to direct heat.
- **Do not** put pots and pans in a hot oven unless the handles and knobs are heat resistant.

Aluminum

Two types of aluminum are made into cookware; cast aluminum, which is a heavy gauge, and sheet aluminum, which is a lighter gauge that is made in varying thicknesses. There are different finishes too—polished, satin, and anodized, to which decorator colors are added.

Cookware

Do's

- See general **Do's** and **Don'ts** under Cookware.
- Use a steel wool soap pad to remove burned-on food on cast aluminum cookware.
- Remove interior discoloration by filling the pan with water, adding 1 tablespoon cream of tartar or 1 tablespoon lemon juice per quart of water, and simmering until the discoloration is gone. Complete the task by scouring with a steel wool pad.

Don'ts

- **Do not** wash aluminum cookware in an automatic dishwasher. The strong detergent can discolor polished or satin finishes and remove the color from an anodized finish.
- **Do not** soak in soapy water for long periods—the metal will discolor.
- **Do not** allow food to stand or be stored in aluminum cookware—it can discolor and pit the metal.

Fastest

Brillo Steel Wool Soap Pads (Purex Corporation) take the least time to clean and polish an aluminum pan. Moisten the pad to activate the soap, briskly rub the inside and outside of the pan, rinse in hot water, and polish with a towel. This operation takes less than a minute and although the steel wool is slightly abrasive, the scratches are so tiny that they will blend in with the pan's finish.

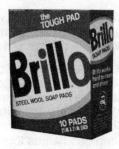

Cheapest

The least expensive method for cleaning aluminum cookware is with baking soda. After rinsing the pot, don't dry it, just sprinkle 1 tablespoon baking soda (see Recommended Basic Products) on the wet surface to make a paste. Use a synthetic scouring pad (see Tools of the Trade) to spread the paste and clean off any stains. A rinse and quick polish will give a bright finish.

Best

Soft Scrub Cleanser (The Clorox Company) is the most efficient product for removing stains, cleaning, and polishing aluminum to a mint-bright shine. This mild abrasive doesn't require vigorous or prolonged scrubbing to do the job when used with a synthetic scouring pad (see Tools of the Trade).

Other Products Tested

Nevr-Dull Magic Wadding Polish (The George Basch Co.)—premoistened, batting-like substance that quickly brings up a good shine.
Bon Ami Cleaning Powder (Faultless Starch/Bon Ami Company)—mild abrasive powder; removes stains well and shines the surface.
Cameo Aluminum and Stainless Steel Cleaner (Purex Corporation)—mild abrasive powder; pleasant odor; produces a high sheen.
Rubin-Brite Metal Polish (David Rubin)—unique cream cleaner; gives a mirror finish.

Noxon Liquid 7 Metal Polish (Boyle-Midway Inc.)—very good liquid cleaner; leaves little shine; moderate odor.
Duro Aluminum Jelly (Woodhill Permatex)—liquid jelly; very good cleaner, but leaves a dull, lifeless sheen; strong odor.
Glass Plus (Texize Chemicals Company)—spray liquid; moderate cleaner; good shine; moderate odor.

Cast Iron

Cast iron cookware is heavy and has a tendency to rust. It also needs to be kept properly seasoned for best performance. Most new cast iron cooking utensils come from the factory already seasoned, but should be washed in mild soap and water before their first use.

Do's
- See general **Do's** and **Don'ts** under Cookware.
- Dry cast iron cookware thoroughly after washing and store in a dry place.
- Occasionally scour, then wipe the inside of pots and pans with oil, place in a warm oven for 2 hours, and wipe off excess oil to maintain the cookware's seasoning.
- Watch out for rust spots—if they appear, rub them with steel wool, wash, dry, and reseason immediately.

Don'ts
- **Do not** store cast iron pots and pans with lids in place—this can promote rust.
- **Do not** wash in the dishwasher—this will remove the seasoning and also cause rust.

Fastest, Cheapest, and Best

The same technique and products fill all three categories for cast iron cookware. Wash in hot sudsy water using a dishwashing liquid (see Recommended Basic Products). Use **Brillo Steel Wool Soap Pads** (Purex Corporation) for hard-to-clean spots. Rinse, dry thoroughly, and reseason before storing.

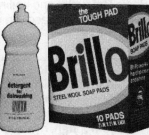

Clay

Soak new clay cookware in water for about ½ hour before using it the first time. Soak both top and bottom and then scrub well with a stiff brush to remove any clay dust.

Do's
- See general **Do's** and **Don'ts** under Cookware.
- Line the cooker with baking parchment paper to prevent the porous surface from absorbing food stains and strong flavors.
- Wash clay cookware immediately after it cools to prevent crusting of food. Dry before storing to prevent mold.
- Fill the cooker with water and 1 to 4 tablespoons baking soda overnight to remove stubborn soil or pungent odors.

Read manufacturer's cautions and warnings before using any product.

Cookware

Don'ts

- **Do not** place a hot clay cooker on a cold surface—it might crack.
- **Do not** wash in a dishwasher.
- **Do not** store with the lid in place or mold can result.
- **Do not** use steel wool soap pads for cleaning.

Fastest, Cheapest, and Best

Soak the cooker for a short time in warm, clear water until the food loosens up. Use a dishwashing liquid (see Recommended Basic Products) and warm water and a stiff brush or synthetic scouring pad (see Tools of the Trade) to finish the job.

If mold spots appear on a clay cooker, brush the surface with a paste made of equal parts baking soda (see Recommended Basic Products) and water. Let stand 30 minutes, preferably in strong sunlight; brush the paste away, rinse well in clear water, and dry thoroughly in a well-ventilated location.

Copper

Copper darkens with use and exposure to air, but you can clean and polish it easily. Copper cookware is lined with some other metal to prevent harmful chemical reactions with food. The lining is usually tin or stainless steel. Tin linings can wear thin and have to be retinned before the copper layer shows through. Sometimes copper cookware comes with a protective lacquer coating that must be removed before the utensil is heated. Follow the manufacturer's instructions or place the utensil in a solution of baking soda (see Recommended Basic Products) and boiling water (1 cup soda to 2 gallons water), let stand until the water is cool, peel off the lacquer, wash, rinse, and dry.

Do's

- See general **Do's** and **Don'ts** under Cookware.
- Clean and polish copper pots and pans regularly to prevent a build-up of tarnish.
- Be sure there is always liquid or fat in a copper pan before placing it over heat to prevent scorching.
- Use wooden, nylon, or nonstick-coated spoons for stirring to prevent surface damage.
- When melting butter, swirl it around the bottom of the pan and up the sides to prevent scorching the pan.

Don'ts

- **Do not** use harsh abrasives to clean copper—they can scratch the surface.
- **Do not** use high heat for long periods; lower the heat when the contents reach a boiling point.

Fastest

Vigilant's Copper and Brass Polishing Cloth (Vigilant Products Co., Inc.) is a fast way to wipe away copper dullness. This is a specially treated cloth that comes in an airtight plastic bag. With only gentle rubbing on a discolored surface tarnish disappears; shine it with a soft, untreated cloth for a nice glow. Never wash the polishing cloth; simply fold and return it to its container for another day.

Cheapest

Vinegar is the featured ingredient in two of the least expensive copper cleaners. Apply a paste consisting of 1 tablespoon salt, 1 tablespoon white vinegar, and 1 tablespoon flour to clean a discolored skillet. Because the vinegar is acid, wash the skillet in hot soapy water and rinse it before completing the job with some vigorous buffing for shiny results. You'll have the same success with a paste made of 2 tablespoons vinegar and 1 tablespoon salt.

Best

Revere Ware Instant Copper Cleaner (Revere Copper & Brass, Incorporated) is a rapid cleaner/polish that is rated best. Pour a small amount of the liquid onto the bottom of a copper pan, wipe with a sponge, and immerse the pan in hot soapsuds. Polishing yields an admirable shine. The cleaner contains a tarnish retardant and also has a very pleasant peppermint odor.

Other Products Tested

Soft Scrub Cleanser (The Clorox Company)—mild liquid abrasive; eliminates heat discoloration marks.

Twinkle Copper Cleaner Kit (The Drackett Company)—easy-to-use paste; pleasant smell; good shine; rinse off in hot water only, not detergent, after cleaning.

Bar Keepers Friend Cleanser & Polish (SerVaas Laboratories, Inc.)—powder; apply to a wet copper surface, then rub with a damp sponge for a high shine.

Wright's Brass Cleaner & Polish (J. A. Wright & Co.)—liquid polish that requires a fair amount of elbow grease to remove discoloration and film; gives a warm, almost antique luster; moderately strong odor.

Noxon Liquid 7 Metal Polish (Boyle-Midway Inc.) —very good liquid cleaner, but hard to polish after drying; medium bright shine; moderate odor.

Cameo Copper Cleaner (Purex Corporation)—powder with a tarnish retardant; moderately good cleaner—can fail to remove some stains; bright shine; almost no odor.

Tarn-X (Jelmar Co.)—liquid instant cleaner; works fast but can stain if not rinsed off promptly; bright shine; heavy odor.

Copper Glo (American Cyanamid Company)—powder with tarnish retardant; moderately good cleaner; medium bright shine; almost no odor.

Hagerty Heavy-Duty Copper Brass & Metal Polish (W. J. Hagerty & Sons, Ltd., Inc.)—liquid polish; moderate cleaner; medium bright shine; moderate odor.

Goddard's Long Shine Brass & Copper Polish (S. C. Johnson & Son, Inc.)—liquid; moderate cleaner; medium shine; strong odor.

Brasso (The R. T. French Co.)—liquid; moderate cleaner; dull shine; strong odor.

Read manufacturer's cautions and warnings before using any product.

Cookware

Enamelware

Do's
- See general **Do's** and **Don'ts** under Cookware.
- Let cool before washing and presoak to loosen cooked-on foods.
- Use a synthetic scouring pad if necessary.
- Wash in the dishwasher if desired.

Don'ts
- **Do not** subject to rapid changes of temperature—the enamel coating can crack.
- **Do not** use abrasive cleaners or steel wool to avoid scratching the surface.

Fastest

A small quantity of dishwashing detergent (see Recommended Basic Products) in hot water is the quickest way to clean enamel cookware. If the food is burned on, a synthetic scouring pad (see Tools of the Trade) helps to whisk it away.

Cheapest

For stains and encrusted food that a detergent doesn't remove, sprinkle baking soda (see Recommended Basic Products) on the wet surface to make a paste. Let sit for an hour, and then scrub the spot and stain away with a synthetic scouring pad (see Tools of the Trade). Rinse well and dry.

Best

Soft Scrub Cleanser (The Clorox Company) applied with a synthetic scouring pad (see Tools of the Trade) works best for cleaning enamelware with encrusted food or stains. This mild liquid abrasive quickly dissolves the dirt and the pad whisks it away without leaving a scratch on the enamel surface.

Other Products Tested

20 Mule Team Borax (United States Borax & Chemical Corporation)—powder; very good, non-abrasive cleaner.

Glass and Ceramic-Glass

Most heat-resistant glass and ceramic-glass cookware is designed for oven use only, although there are some that can be used on rangetops, too. Read the manufacturer's instructions carefully to make sure which kind you have. Both these types of cookware are dishwasher safe or can be quickly washed by hand.

Do's
- See general **Do's** and **Don'ts** under Cookware.
- Remove mineral deposits from coffee pots and teapots by boiling full strength cider vinegar in the container for 15 minutes.

Don't
- **Do not** allow glass rangetop cooking vessels to boil dry—they might shatter.

Fastest, Cheapest, and Best

The same technique and product fill each category. Wash glass or ceramic cookware in hot sudsy water using dishwashing liquid (see Recommended Basic Products). Use a synthetic scouring pad (see Tools of the Trade) for hard-to-clean spots. Rinse and dry.

Nonstick-Coated

Many types of cookware have special nonstick finishes or coatings that prevent foods from sticking. These coatings are relatively thin, and care must be used to prevent surface damage. Some of the familiar names for these coatings are Teflon, Fluon, Hallon, and Silver-Stone.

Do's
- See general **Do's** and **Don'ts** under Cookware.
- Wash new pans before using, coat the inside surface with cooking oil, and wipe off the excess.
- Wash in the dishwasher if desired.
- Reseason with cooking oil after each washing in the dishwasher or after treating for stains.
- Use wooden, nylon, or specially coated spoons or spatulas to prevent surface damage.

Don'ts
- **Do not** cut food in these pans to prevent scratches in the surface.
- **Do not** use steel wool, metal scouring pads, or abrasive scouring powders for cleaning—they will damage the surface.
- **Do not** soak coated pans in soapy water—the coating can retain a soap flavor.

Fastest and Cheapest

When stains need to be removed from nonstick-coated cookware, the fastest and cheapest way of doing it is to mix 2 tablespoons baking soda with 1 cup water and ½ cup liquid bleach. Boil the solution in the pan for several minutes until the stains disappear. After washing the pan, wipe the inner surface with cooking oil to reseason it.

Read manufacturer's cautions and warnings before using any product.

Cookware

Best

Bon Ami Cleaning Powder and **Bon Ami Deluxe Polishing Cleanser** (Faultless Starch/Bon Ami Company) are excellent mild cleaners, used immediately after burned-on spots occur. They will not scratch the coated surface. Reseason the nonstick coating after cleaning.

Stainless Steel

Do's
- See general **Do's** and **Don'ts** under Cookware.
- Store pots and pans separately, not stacked, to prevent surface scratches.
- Make sure cookware sits evenly on the heating unit.
- Dry cookware promptly to prevent waterspots.

Don't
- **Do not** let a pot boil with a high heat setting or allow a flame to lick up the sides of the pan—this will cause discoloration marks.

Fastest

The fastest method for polishing a stainless steel cooking utensil is to use **Nevr-Dull Magic Wadding Polish** (The George Basch Co.). A small piece of this wadding that is premoistened with a cleaner brings back a pan's natural beauty. Rub the wadding over the surface and then finish the job by polishing with a soft cloth. The wadding is also economical because you store it in the can and use it another time.

Cheapest

Sprinkle baking soda (see Recommended Basic Products) on the wet surface of a pan and scrub the metal with a synthetic scouring pad (see Tools of the Trade). After rinsing and drying, the pan will be as bright as new.

Best

The best preparation to give a bright finish to stainless steel is **Cameo Aluminum and Stainless Steel Cleaner** (Purex Corporation). This pleasant-smelling powder is sprinkled on the wet surface to form a paste and then rubbed gently with a damp sponge to allow the silica polishing agents in the cleaner to bring up the luster. After washing in hot soapsuds, rinse and buff the pan to a high shine.

Other Products Tested

Window Spray Cleaner (Stanley Home Products, Inc.)—aerosol spray that buffs up to a nice shine; ammonia odor.

Bon Ami Cleaning Powder (Faultless Starch/Bon Ami Company)—mild abrasive cleaning powder that gives a good shine.

Brillo Steel Wool Soap Pads (Purex Corporation)—soap-filled steel wool pad; good for burned and crusted food; moderate shine.

Soft Scrub Cleanser (The Clorox Company)—mild liquid abrasive; cleans and polishes; pleasant odor.

Rubin-Brite Metal Polish (David Rubin)—cream to be used with ordinary kitchen flour; high sheen.

Gorham Silver Polish (Gorham Division of Textron Inc.)—paste; good to very good performance; medium shine; moderately pleasant odor.

Revere Ware Instant Copper Cleaner (Revere Copper & Brass, Incorporated)—liquid; good to very good performance; medium shine; pleasant odor.

Copper Glo (American Cyanamid Company)—powder; good to very good performance; moderate shine; almost no odor.

Zud (Boyle-Midway Inc.)—strong abrasive powder; control the heavy duty action by making a paste with water instead of applying the powder directly to the pan's surface; good cleaner; nice shine.

Brasso (The R. T. French Co.)—liquid; moderate cleaner; medium shine; strong odor.

Noxon Liquid 7 Metal Polish (Boyle-Midway Inc.)—liquid; moderate cleaner; medium shine; moderate odor.

Hagerty Heavy-Duty Copper Brass & Metal Polish (W. J. Hagerty & Sons, Ltd., Inc.)—liquid; moderate cleaner; medium shine; moderate odor.

Sparkle Glass Cleaner (A. J. Funk & Co.)—liquid spray; moderate cleaner; medium shine; pleasant odor.

Glass Plus (Texize Chemicals Company)—liquid spray; moderate cleaner; medium shine; moderate odor.

Dinnerware

The word *dinnerware* refers to the dishes used on the table; they can be made from simple, inexpensive materials such as plastic or glass, as well as from expensive and delicate china.

Do's

- Follow the manufacturer's recommended cleaning procedures.
- Remove food residue as soon as possible.
- Scrape dishes with a rubber scraper or plastic brush.
- Rinse out coffee and tea cups before the residues have a chance to stain.
- Loosen leftover egg and cheese residues by soaking in cool water.
- Handle glass and china dinnerware carefully to avoid chips and breakage.
- Use a plastic dishpan or plastic sink mat, or pad the bottom of the sink with a towel to help prevent chipping fine dinnerware when you hand wash it.
- Avoid extremes and abrupt changes of temperature when using and washing fine china.
- Load dishwasher-safe dinnerware so it will not rattle against other pieces during the washing cycle.

Dinnerware

Don'ts

- **Do not** allow acid foods to remain on glazed dinnerware.
- **Do not** use harsh abrasive cleaners or steel wool pads on any dinnerware.
- **Do not** use knives or other sharp objects to removed hardened food—such utensils scratch the surface.
- **Do not** stack fine china unless a napkin or cloth protector is placed between the dishes to prevent scratching.
- **Do not** wash especially delicate, hand-painted, gold- or silver-trimmed, or antique dinnerware in the dishwasher.
- **Do not** soak metal-trimmed china for long periods of time—this will damage the trim.
- **Do not** warm plates in an oven unless they are heatproof.
- **Do not** overcrowd the dishpan or sink when washing dinnerware.
- **Do not** rinse glazed dinnerware with boiling-hot water—this will cause the glaze to craze, or develop minute cracks.
- **Do not** stack dinnerware for storing until it is cool.

Fastest, Cheapest, and Best

Speed is not a factor when washing dinnerware. For hand washing, use one of the liquid dishwashing detergents (see Recommended Basic Products)—the cheapest will be the one most economical in your area.

Calgonite Automatic Dishwashing Detergent (Beecham Products Division of Beecham Inc.) is best for washing dinnerware in the dishwasher. It performs very well, leaving the dishes clean and shining.

Other Products Tested

HAND WASHING. **Degreaser** (Stanley Home Products, Inc.)—liquid; contains grease-cutting additive; good performance; not for automatic dishwashers.
Dip-It Coffee Pot Destainer (Economics Laboratory, Inc.)—powder; stain remover for heat-resistant plastic dinnerware; good performance; not for automatic dishwashers.

FOR DISHWASHERS. **Dishwasher All** (Lever Brothers Company)—powder; very good to excellent performance; leaves few spots or streaks; pleasant fresh odor.
Cascade Automatic Dishwashing Detergent (Procter & Gamble)—powder; very good to excellent performance; leaves few spots or streaks; moderate odor.
Electrasol (Economics Laboratory, Inc.)—powder; good to very good performance; leaves few spots; slightly unpleasant odor.
Finish (Economics Laboratory, Inc.)—powder; good to very good performance; leaves few spots; moderate odor.

Flatware and Cutlery

The knives and forks we use at mealtimes can be made of stainless steel, pewter, silver, or gold-plated silver. Cutlery (knives and other cutting instruments) can be handled the same way as fine flatware, but observe the manufacturer's instructions to ensure that the cutlery is dishwasher safe.

Do's

- Wash all fine flatware by hand and buff dry to bring up the shine and prevent water-spots.
- Rinse salt, sulphur, and acidic foods off flatware as soon as possible to avoid stains.
- Use silver often—it tarnishes less and grows more beautiful with use.
- Store silver and gold flatware in special rolls, bags, or cases to prevent tarnishing or scratching.
- Sharpen fine cutlery, except serrated knives, on a carving steel or sharpening stone.

Don'ts

- **Do not** wash pewter, sterling silver, silver plate, or gold-plated silver in the dishwasher.
- **Do not** soak flatware or cutlery with bone, ivory, or wooden handles, and do not wash in the dishwasher.
- **Do not** use abrasive cleaners or steel wool pads to clean flatware.
- **Do not** allow knives with a two-piece handle and blade to soak—water loosens the cement.
- **Do not** allow stainless steel flatware to touch anything silver in the dishwasher. It will set up an electrolytic action that pits the stainless steel.
- **Do not** sharpen knives with serrated edges.

Fastest, Cheapest, and Best

The fastest, cheapest, and best way to clean flatware and cutlery is with one of the liquid dishwashing detergents (see Recommended Basic Products). Fill the sink with hot water, add the detergent, and wash the flatware using a soft cloth or sponge to wipe away the soil. Avoid overcrowding the sink to prevent scratching, rinse with hot water, and buff dry with a soft towel to bring up the shine.

When flatware and cutlery begin to look dull, polish them with one of the products listed in the chapter on the metal from which they are made—see Gold, Pewter, Stainless Steel, and Silver.

Glassware

Do's

- Handle glass carefully.
- Wash most glassware in the dishwasher.
- Wash gilt- and silver-trimmed glass, delicate crystal, and most ornamental glass by hand.
- Wash all glassware by hand if your water is soft, as the soft water/dishwasher detergent combination etches and dulls glassware.
- Cushion the bottom of the sink with a towel or rubber mat when washing to insure against breakage.
- Wash glassware first, before cutlery or dinnerware.
- Slip delicate stemware into the wash water edgewise—not bottom first—to prevent cracking.
- Add a little vinegar to the warm rinse water for more sparkle.
- Drip dry upside down or polish with a soft, lint-free cloth.
- Use a soft brush to get dirt out of crevices of cut glassware.
- Remove stains from crystal by rubbing with a cut lemon or washing in a vinegar solution.
- Clean stained decanters by filling with water, adding 1 cup ammonia or vinegar, and soaking overnight.
- Use two packs of powdered denture cleaner dissolved in water if the above solution is not strong enough.
- Rub baking soda into stubborn food spots to help dissolve them.
- Wash greasy glassware in an ammonia solution.

Don'ts

- **Do not** subject glassware to sudden changes of temperature.
- **Do not** allow dirty glasses to stand—rinse them out immediately.
- **Do not** wash milk glass in the dishwasher—it will yellow.
- **Do not** crowd glassware when washing.
- **Do not** handle delicate stemware by the bowl when washing.
- **Do not** allow glassware objects to touch each other in the dishwasher.
- **Do not** use abrasive cleaners or steel wool pads on delicate glassware.
- **Do not** "dry dust" crystal vases or displayed glassware—wipe them with a soft cloth dampened in an ammonia solution to avoid surface scratches.

Fastest, Cheapest, and Best

A liquid dishwashing detergent (see Recommended Basic Products) will do an excellent job for hand washing glassware. Speed is not a factor here, especially when washing delicate glassware; the cheapest will be the detergent that is least expensive in your area.

For dishwashers, the cheapest and best is **Calgonite Automatic Dishwashing Detergent** (Beecham Products Division of Beecham Inc.). As a cleaning agent, it performs beautifully: Table glasses, dinnerware, and cookware come out spotless. It has a perfumed odor.

Other Products Tested

FOR AUTOMATIC DISHWASHERS. **Dishwasher All** (Lever Brothers Company)—powder; very good to excellent; leaves few spots or streaks; pleasant fresh odor.
Cascade Automatic Dishwashing Detergent (Procter & Gamble)—powder; very good to excellent; leaves few spots or streaks; moderate odor.
Electrasol (Economics Laboratory, Inc.)—powder; good to very good; slightly unpleasant odor.
Finish (Economics Laboratory, Inc.)—powder; good to very good; no streaking; moderate odor.

Preparation, Storing, and Serving Utensils

Food storage containers and serving utensils commonly are made of plastic, rubber, metal, and wood. Metal gives few cleaning problems since it is easily washed and does not retain food odors, or deteriorate in water like wood. The other materials, while relatively easy-care, do need some special treatment.

Metal

Widely used for utensils such as pancake turners, potato mashers, and cooking forks, metals like stainless steel can be cleaned using the methods and products recommended in the chapter on that metal. These utensils usually become greasy when used on fried or broiled foods, so pick a liquid dishwashing detergent that cuts grease well (see Recommended Basic Products). Never soak metal utensils with glued-on handles, or the adhesive will weaken. Also see Cookware—Aluminum, Stainless Steel.

Plastic and Rubberware

Plastic utensils and containers used for food preparation, serving, and storage require much the same care as rubber food scrapers, drain boards, and sink pads. Much of the plastic and rubberware used in the kitchen should not be exposed to high heat. Some plastics will melt and warp. Heat and sunlight can cause rubber products to crack unless they are specially treated to withstand it.

Do's
- Check the manufacturer's instructions to see if an item is dishwasher safe.
- Wash utensils in warm liquid detergent solutions and dry thoroughly before storing.

Don'ts
- **Do not** use solvents to remove stains.
- **Do not** cut on plastic or rubber surfaces with a knife or other sharp object.
- **Do not** use harsh abrasives or scouring pads, especially on plastics.

Read manufacturer's cautions and warnings before using any product.

Preparation, Storing, and Serving Utensils

Fastest and Cheapest

A paste made of baking soda (see Recommended Basic Products) and water is very effective in removing stubborn soil and stains from plastic and rubber utensils and deodorizes them at the same time. Apply the paste with a synthetic scouring pad (see Tools of the Trade) and watch the stains disappear.

Another good way to remove odor from plastic containers without spending a cent is to crumple a piece of newspaper into the container, secure the lid tightly, and leave it until morning. It takes the odor away.

Best

Soft Scrub Cleanser (The Clorox Company) is an excellent product for removing soil and stains from both rubber and plastic utensils. This very mild liquid abrasive is applied with a synthetic scouring pad (see Tools of the Trade) and banishes ground-in soil and stains without scratching the plastic or rubber surfaces.

Woodenware

Wooden bowls, trays, rolling pins, spoons, salad utensils, and cutting boards all need special care to prevent warping and cracking. Because wood is porous, it absorbs moisture. After drying out, it becomes rough. Cutting boards need to be cleaned and oiled periodically to restore their smooth surface and give them protection from moisture. Some salad bowls are finished with a waterproof varnish, but many people prefer to keep their bowls untreated to absorb the seasonings that gourmets feel enhance the flavor of the salad.

Do's

- Wipe woodenware immediately after using it with a sponge or paper towel moistened in cold water.
- Remove stains from woodenware with a mild chlorine bleach solution (¼ cup bleach to 1 quart warm water). Rinse and dry before coating with oil again.
- Wash wooden items one at a time, quickly; rinse immediately; dry thoroughly.
- Get rid of odors by rubbing the surface with the cut side of a lemon.
- Air woodenware before storing.

Don'ts

- **Do not** soak woodenware in water.
- **Do not** put woodenware articles in the dishwasher.
- **Do not** use harsh soaps or detergents to clean woodenware.
- **Do not** heat or chill woodenware.
- **Do not** stack wooden salad bowls before or after washing until they have dried completely.

Fastest and Cheapest

Baking soda (see Recommended Basic Products) cleans and deodorizes wooden surfaces. Mix ½ cup baking soda with 1 quart warm water and rub it on the wood surface. Use a synthetic scouring pad (see Tools of the Trade) if cleaning a cutting board to scour away the gummy residue on the edges. Rinse with clear water, blot up the moisture with a towel, and air dry completely. Bring back the natural wood finish by giving it a coat of boiled linseed oil (salad oil can be used in a pinch), rubbed in with a fine steel wool pad. Apply two more thin coats of oil 24 hours apart, wiping off the excess between each application.

Best

An excellent protector is **Martens Wood Preservative** (Martens Mfg., Inc., A Div. of Foley Mfg. Co.). Clean the wooden article following the instructions given for baking soda. Set the plastic bottle of preservative in a pan of hot tap water for a few minutes to make sure the contents are completely liquified. Pour a small amount of the preservative on the wood surface, and rub with a lint-free cloth. Allow the liquid to penetrate for ½ hour and then wipe off any excess preservative. Notice how the mellow finish of the wood has been restored.

Large Appliances

Automatic Dishwashers

If your dishwasher has a wooden chopping block top, also see the methods and products in Countertops—Wooden.

Do's

- Wipe off the exterior of the dishwasher daily.
- Use a synthetic scouring pad to help remove stubborn soil.
- Leave the dishwasher door open occasionally to air out any odors the liner retains.
- When needed, clean butcher block tops by saturating a cloth or fine steel wool pad with vegetable oil, rubbing it into the wood, and allowing the oil to soak in overnight. Wipe up any excess oil the next day.
- Use a spray glass cleaner to clean and polish chromium trim.
- Clean plastic trim with a damp cloth—buff dry.
- Remove hard water and mineral deposits from the interiors of porcelain tanks by placing a glass bowl containing ¾ cup bleach on the lower rack. Load the dishwasher with glasses and china only and run it through the wash and rinse cycle. Then put 1 cup vinegar in the bowl and run it through a complete cycle.

Don'ts

- **Do not** use harsh abrasives or steel wool to clean either the interior or exterior of the dishwasher.
- **Do not** let appliance wax get on the plastic parts.
- **Do not** remove deposits on plastic-lined tanks with bleach or vinegar.

Fastest

Use **Bon Ami Deluxe Polishing Cleanser** (Faultless Starch/Bon Ami Company) to clean stains from the dishwasher liner. It is strong enough to remove the stain but will not scratch the relatively delicate surface. Dip a damp sponge in the powder and apply to the liner with a gentle scrubbing action. Rinse well with clear water to make sure all of the cleanser is gone.

Use **Jubilee Kitchen Wax** (S. C. Johnson & Son, Inc.) to clean the exterior of the dishwasher. This spray wax cleans and polishes, leaving a thin protective wax coat. Spray it on the surface and wipe dry with a soft cloth.

Cheapest

Baking soda (see Recommended Basic Products) comes in handy when the dishwasher needs cleaning inside and out. Dip a damp cloth into the soda and use it to clean smudges and fingerprints from the exterior as well as stains from the liner.

If the interior retains odors, sprinkle 3 tablespoons baking soda in the bottom of the machine and allow it to sit overnight. The odors will be washed away with the baking soda during the next wash cycle.

Best

Klean 'n Shine (S. C. Johnson & Son, Inc.) is the best product tested for cleaning the exterior of dishwashers, including those faced with plastic laminate. This pleasant-smelling aerosol is easy to spray over the surface, and buffs off quickly for a beautiful shine, leaving a protective coating.

Other Products Tested

EXTERIOR. **Soft Scrub Cleanser** (The Clorox Company)—mild abrasive liquid; excellent cleaner for stubborn soil; does not scratch; pleasant odor.
Kitchen Magic (Magic American Chemical Corp.)—aerosol; excellent cleaner; gives silicone coating on enamel surfaces; pleasant odor.
Formula 409 All Purpose Cleaner (The Clorox Company)—pump spray; very good to excellent spot, grease, and smudge remover; no rinsing; not for use on varnished surfaces; pleasant odor.
Fantastik Multi-Surface Spray Cleaner (Texize Chemicals Company)—pump spray; very good to excellent spot, smudge, and grease remover; moderate odor.
Glass Wax (Gold Seal Co.)—creamy liquid; very good cleaner for enamel; somewhat messy to use; pleasant odor.
Oakite All Purpose Cleaner (Oakite Products, Inc.)—low-sudsing powder; very good cleaner.
Spic and Span (Procter & Gamble)—low-sudsing powder; very good cleaner.
Lestoil Heavy Duty Cleaner (Noxell Corporation)—sudsing liquid; very good cleaner; heavy pine odor.
Sparkle Glass Cleaner (A. J. Funk & Co.)—pump spray; good to very good cleaner for enamel and chromium trim; pleasant odor.
Comet Cleanser (Procter & Gamble)—powder; good cleaner for removing stains and mineral deposits from porcelain, enamel, and plastic liners; too harsh to use on baked enamel.
Windex Glass Cleaner (The Drackett Company)—pump spray; not for use on finished wood surfaces; moderate cleaner for enamel and chromium trim.

Clothes Washers and Dryers

The clothes washer and dryer have very similar surface materials to be cleaned. The top of each unit generally is made of porcelain enamel because of the needed durability, while the sides usually are finished with baked enamel that gives the same look but is less durable. Other parts are made from metal, plastic, and metal-coated plastic. For more information about the specific methods to use on your washer's and dryer's surfaces, also see the chapters that cover the materials used in your machines.

Do's

- Read the manufacturer's instruction booklet carefully for cleaning information.
- Check the manufacturer's recommendations for cleaning the dryer filter and the washing machine filter if it is not self-cleaning.
- Rinse the basket of the washing machine well after using it for dyeing fabrics or washing particularly linty fabrics.
- Clean the exterior surfaces on a weekly basis.
- To clean the interior and hoses, pour 1 gallon white vinegar in the washer tub and run the washer through a normal cycle at the highest water level.
- Use a spray glass cleaner to clean and polish chromium trim.
- Clean plastic trim with a damp cloth—buff dry.
- Wipe off the exterior with a damp cloth, using a synthetic scouring pad for stubborn soil.

Don'ts

- **Do not** let appliance wax get on the plastic parts.
- **Do not** use harsh abrasives or steel wool to clean the enamel surfaces.
- **Do not** put plastic articles in the dryer on the high heat setting—they can melt and stick to the dryer drum.
- **Do not** put fabrics that have been cleaned with a solvent in the dryer until all traces of the solvent are gone.

Fastest

A quick way to clean and protect enamel finishes in one operation is with **Jubilee Kitchen Wax** (S. C. Johnson & Son, Inc.). Shake the can vigorously; holding it six inches from the surface, spray on this creamy wax; buff dry with a soft cloth.

Cheapest

Baking soda (see Recommended Basic Products) is the cheapest way to clean enamel surfaces. Dip a damp sponge in the soda and rub over the soiled area. Because the soda is non-abrasive, it does not scratch the enamel but works as well as scouring powder. Rinse well with clear water and buff dry with a soft absorbent cloth for a shiny-clean surface.

Best

A first rate product to clean exterior enamel surfaces is **Klean 'n Shine** (S. C. Johnson & Son, Inc.). Spray this pleasant-smelling aerosol over the surface, wipe with a clean cloth, and notice the shine. It also leaves a protective coating.

Other Products Tested

Soft Scrub Cleanser (The Clorox Company)—mild liquid abrasive; excellent cleaner for stubborn soil; does not scratch.

Kitchen Magic (Magic American Chemical Corp.)—aerosol; excellent cleaner and wax for enamel surfaces.

Formula 409 All Purpose Cleaner (The Clorox Company)—pump spray; very good to excellent spot, grease, and smudge remover; pleasant odor.

Fantastik Multi-Surface Spray Cleaner (Texize Chemicals Company)—pump spray; very good to excellent spot, smudge, and grease remover; moderate odor.

Oakite All Purpose Cleaner (Oakite Products, Inc.)—low-sudsing powder; very good cleaner.

Spic and Span (Procter & Gamble)—low-sudsing powder; very good cleaner.

Lestoil Heavy Duty Cleaner (Noxell Corporation)—sudsing liquid; very good cleaner; heavy pine odor.

Sparkle Glass Cleaner (A. J. Funk & Co.)—pump spray; good to very good cleaner for both enamel and chromium trim.

Freezers

Freezers require little care other than wiping off smudges and fingerprints and defrosting.

Do's

- Wipe off the outside of the freezer when it becomes dirty.
- Use a synthetic scouring pad for stubborn soil.
- Defrost when frost gets to be over ½ inch thick.
- Turn the freezer controls off when defrosting.
- Remove all the food and put it in a large ice chest, wrap in layers of newspaper, or store it in the refrigerator while defrosting the freezer.
- Open the door and allow the ice to partially melt before scraping it away with a wooden or plastic scraper.
- Speed the melting by setting shallow pans of hot water on the shelves.
- Vacuum up dust from behind the grill at the bottom of the freezer at least annually or whenever defrosting, using the brush attachment.
- Place an open box of baking soda on the back of a shelf every other month to control freezer odors.

Freezers

Don'ts

- **Do not** use harsh abrasives or steel wool on the interior or exterior of the freezer.
- **Do not** use sharp implements to chip ice off the sides and shelves.
- **Do not** put food back into the freezer until you have wiped off any condensation and the freezer has been running for at least ½ hour.

Fastest

Jubilee Kitchen Wax (S. C. Johnson & Son, Inc.) provides a quick way of cleaning the exterior of a freezer. Spray it on and wipe with a soft cloth to remove dirt and smudges and leave a protective wax coating.

The fastest, cheapest, and best way to wash the interior of the freezer is to make a solution of 1 tablespoon baking soda (see Recommended Basic Products) and 1 quart warm water. Dry the interior with a soft cloth before turning the freezer back on. The baking soda solution does a good job of cleaning and also deodorizing.

Cheapest

Dip a damp cloth in some baking soda (see Recommended Basic Products) and rub on the exterior of the freezer to inexpensively clean dirt and smudges. It acts like a scouring powder but will not scratch the enamel surface. Rinse well and wipe dry with a soft cloth.

Best

The best product for cleaning the exterior of a freezer is **Klean 'n Shine** (S. C. Johnson & Son, Inc.). This pleasant-smelling aerosol foam is easy to spray on the surface and then buff off to leave a spotless finish and a protective coating.

Other Products Tested

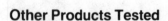

EXTERIOR. **Soft Scrub Cleanser** (The Clorox Company)—mild abrasive liquid; excellent cleaner for stubborn soil; does not scratch.
Kitchen Magic (Magic American Chemical Corp.)—aerosol; excellent cleaner; gives silicone coating on enamel surfaces.
Formula 409 All Purpose Cleaner (The Clorox Company)—pump spray; very good to excellent spot, grease, and smudge remover; pleasant odor.
Fantastik Multi-Surface Spray Cleaner (Texize Chemicals Company)—pump spray; very good to excellent spot, smudge, and grease remover; moderate odor.
Glass Wax (Gold Seal Co.)—creamy liquid; very good cleaner for enamel; somewhat messy to use.
Oakite All Purpose Cleaner (Oakite Products, Inc.)—low-sudsing powder; very good cleaner.
Spic and Span (Procter & Gamble)—low-sudsing powder; very good cleaner.
Lestoil Heavy Duty Cleaner (Noxell Corporation)—sudsing liquid; very good cleaner; heavy pine odor.

Sparkle Glass Cleaner (A. J. Funk & Co.)—pump spray; good to very good cleaner for enamel and chromium trim.
Windex Glass Cleaner (The Drackett Company)—pump spray; moderate cleaner for enamel and chromium trim.

Microwave Ovens

Do's
- Wipe off the exterior of the oven daily.
- Wipe out the interior of the oven after each use.
- Wash the glass tray in the sink or dishwasher when it is heavily soiled.
- Keep the filter free of soil and grease.
- Use a synthetic scouring pad to remove stubborn soil.
- Follow the manufacturer's instructions for suitable utensils for use in the oven.

Don'ts
- **Do not** use harsh abrasive cleaners or steel wool on either the exterior or interior of your microwave.
- **Do not** use a commercial oven cleaner in a microwave oven.

Fastest

Wipe off the interior and exterior of the microwave oven with a cloth or sponge wrung out in a mild dishwashing detergent solution (see Recommended Basic Products). Rinse well and buff dry with a soft cloth.

Cheapest

For stubborn soil, dip a moistened cloth into some baking soda (see Recommended Basic Products) and apply to the spot with a gentle scrubbing action. Rinse well and buff dry for a clean, scratch-free surface.

Best

Sparkle Glass Cleaner (A. J. Funk & Co.) is one of the best products to use when cleaning a microwave oven. It does a good job on the baked enamel exterior and interior, the glass, and any metal surfaces, too. Just spray on and immediately buff dry with a paper towel.

Read manufacturer's cautions and warnings before using any product.

Other Products Tested

EXTERIOR. Soft Scrub Cleanser (The Clorox Company)—mild abrasive liquid; excellent cleaner for stubborn soil; does not scratch.
Jubilee Kitchen Wax (S. C. Johnson & Son, Inc.)—aerosol; excellent cleaner and wax for enamel surfaces.
Kitchen Magic (Magic American Chemical Corp.)—aerosol; excellent cleaner and wax for enamel surfaces.
Klean 'n Shine (S. C. Johnson & Son, Inc.)—aerosol; excellent cleaner for enamel surfaces.
Formula 409 All Purpose Cleaner (The Clorox Company)—pump spray; very good to excellent spot, grease, and smudge remover; pleasant odor.
Fantastik Multi-Surface Spray Cleaner (Texize Chemicals Company)—pump spray; very good to excellent spot, smudge, and grease remover; moderate odor.
Windex Glass Cleaner (The Drackett Company)—pump spray; moderate performance cleaning glass, stainless steel, and chromium trim.

Rangehoods

Most modern stoves have separate or built-in rangehoods above their cooking surfaces. Rangehoods usually are vented to the outside and remove grease, steam, and cooking odors from the kitchen. However, some hoods do not have outside vents, relying on special, replaceable filters to filter smoke and odors and recycle the purified air. Both kinds of hoods need regular cleaning to keep them grease free and efficient. Both vented and nonvented rangehoods have fans to draw up air and smoke from the cooking area.

Do's
- Wipe off the exterior and interior of rangehoods on a weekly basis or after cooking especially greasy foods.
- Remove the filter cover and wash in soapy water. Allow to dry before replacing.
- Wipe the blades of the fan in place.
- Clean the metal mesh filter monthly or when dirty.
- Replace the special filters on nonvented rangehoods every 6 to 9 months or as the manufacturer recommends.

Don'ts
- **Do not** disassemble the fan to clean it.
- **Do not** allow grease to build up on the metal mesh filter.
- **Do not** wash the charcoal filter in a nonvented hood, as this shortens the filter life and reduces its effectiveness.
- **Do not** use an abrasive cleanser on any part of the hood.

Fastest and Best

Degreaser (Stanley Home Products) added to a hot water dish-washing detergent solution (see Recommended Basic Products) is a fast and excellent way to soak and clean rangehood mesh filters as well as wipe off the exterior. The degreaser helps cut the accumulated grease quickly and leaves a film-free surface. Rinse the filter well in hot water and blot dry before replacing.

An excellent alternate product for general cleaning of the interior and exterior is **Fantastik Multi-Surface Spray Cleaner** (Texize Chemicals Company) applied with a damp cloth or sponge. To shine the enamel, spray on **Windex Glass Cleaner** (The Drackett Company) and wipe off with a clean, dry cloth.

Cheapest

Add ½ cup ammonia to a sink partially full of a hot water detergent solution (see Recommended Basic Products) and soak the filter for about 5 minutes to remove the accumulated grease. Rinse well in hot water and blot dry before replacing in the hood. A fresh ammonia solution of ¼ cup in 1 gallon warm water also may be used to wipe off the exterior.

Other Products Tested

Mex Multi-Purpose Cleaner (United Gilsonite Laboratories)—powder; excellent grease cutter and cleaner.

Grease Relief (Texize Chemicals Company)—liquid; excellent grease cutter; moderate odor.

Formula 409 All Purpose Cleaner (The Clorox Company)—pump spray; very good to excellent cleaner and grease remover; pleasant odor.

Lestoil Heavy Duty Cleaner (Noxell Corporation)—liquid; very good cleaner and grease remover; heavy pine odor.

Spic and Span (Procter & Gamble)—low-sudsing powder; very good cleaner; moderate odor.

Mr. Clean All-Purpose Cleaner (Procter & Gamble)—liquid; good to very good cleaner; pleasant odor.

Refrigerators

Refrigerator exteriors should be wiped off regularly, while interiors should be cleaned as soon as stains and odors occur.

Do's

- Use a synthetic scouring pad to remove stubborn soil from the exterior or interior.
- Wipe up spills from the interior immediately before they harden and become difficult to remove.
- Wipe out the interior on a weekly basis.
- Thoroughly clean a frost-free refrigerator every 4 to 6 months.
- Thoroughly clean a manual-defrost refrigerator when the frost gets to be ½ inch thick in the freezer section.
- Turn off the controls when giving the refrigerator a thorough cleaning.
- Remove all food from the refrigerator and freezer compartment, wrapping it in newspapers or putting it in an ice chest to protect perishables.
- Remove all shelves, bins, racks, and trays and wash them in a mild soapsuds solution—dry thoroughly.
- Wipe out the interior of the refrigerator to prevent puddles in the bottom or freezer compartment.
- Speed up defrosting in a manual-defrost refrigerator by placing shallow pans full of hot water on the shelves.
- Warm the freezer area with a hair dryer to speed up defrosting in a manual-defrost refrigerator.
- Make sure frozen food packages are wiped dry of condensation before returning them to the freezer.
- Vacuum the dust away from the area behind the bottom grill at least once every 6 months.
- Clean soiled condenser coiled tubes with the crevice tool of your vacuum.
- Wash the drip pan in warm soapsuds after the automatic-defrost refrigerator has been thoroughly cleaned.
- Clean the drip pan from a manual-defrost refrigerator after the freezer has been defrosted completely.
- Control refrigerator odors by placing an open box of baking soda on the back of a shelf—replace the box every other month.

Don'ts

- **Do not** use harsh abrasives or steel wool to clean either the interior or exterior of refrigerators.
- **Do not** allow spoiled food to remain in the refrigerator—it will cause odors and can spoil other foods.
- **Do not** unplug a refrigerator while the compressor is running.
- **Do not** wash ice trays in a detergent solution—this can remove the special nonstick coating that some of them have.
- **Do not** wash refrigerator parts in the dishwasher.
- **Do not** remove the drip pan from a manual-defrost refrigerator while cleaning, or melting frost will drip.
- **Do not** use sharp tools to scrape frost and ice from the freezer area.

Fastest

Jubilee Kitchen Wax (S. C. Johnson & Son, Inc.) provides a quick way of cleaning the exterior of a refrigerator. Spray it on and wipe with a soft cloth to remove dirt and smudges and leave a protective wax coating.

The fastest, cheapest, and best way to clean the interior of your refrigerator is to mix a solution of 1 tablespoon baking soda (see Recommended Basic Products) in 1 quart warm water. Wipe out the interior of the refrigerator and freezer compartments with a sponge dipped in the solution. If stubborn soil persists, dip a moistened cloth in dry baking soda and apply to the soil with a scouring action. Rinse well for a clean, odor-free refrigerator.

Cheapest

Dip a damp cloth in some baking soda (see Recommended Basic Products) and rub on the exterior of the refrigerator to wipe off dirt and smudges inexpensively. It acts like a scouring powder but will not scratch the enamel surface. Rinse well and wipe dry with a soft cloth.

Best

The best product for cleaning the exterior of a refrigerator is **Klean 'n Shine** (S. C. Johnson & Son, Inc.). This pleasant-smelling aerosol foam is easy to spray on the surface and then buff off to leave a spotless finish and protective coating.

Other Products Tested

EXTERIOR. **Soft Scrub Cleanser** (The Clorox Company)—mild liquid abrasive; excellent cleaner for stubborn soil; does not scratch.
Kitchen Magic (Magic American Chemical Corp.)—aerosol; excellent cleaner and wax for enamel surfaces.
Formula 409 All Purpose Spray Cleaner (The Clorox Company)—pump spray; very good to excellent spot, grease, and smudge remover; pleasant odor.
Fantastik Multi-Surface Spray Cleaner (Texize Chemicals Company)—pump spray; very good to excellent spot, smudge, and grease remover; moderate odor.
Oakite All Purpose Cleaner (Oakite Products, Inc.)—low-sudsing powder; very good cleaner.
Spic and Span (Procter & Gamble)—low-sudsing powder; very good cleaner.
Lestoil Heavy Duty Cleaner (Noxell Corporation)—sudsing liquid; very good cleaner; heavy pine odor.
Sparkle Glass Cleaner (A. J. Funk & Co.)—pump spray; good to very good cleaner for enamel and chromium trim.

Read manufacturer's cautions and warnings before using any product.

Stoves

Three general types of rangetops are available on stoves: gas, electric, and ceramic-glass. The best way to care for all parts of a stove is to clean them continually—never allow spilled food or grease spatters to become baked on. If you wipe up every spill as soon as the stove is cool, it will not bake onto the surface and cleaning will stay simple.

Ceramic Cooktops

The ceramic cooktop is a variation of the electric range, with electric elements hidden under the marked surface areas. While the smoothtop range appears easy to clean, special care must be taken to avoid damaging or discoloring the ceramic surface. A ceramic cooktop comes with a glossy or matte finish.

Do's
- Wait until the top cools to wipe up any spills.
- Follow the manufacturer's cleaning procedures.
- Always treat the ceramic surface with extra care.

Don'ts
- **Do not** set soiled pots or pans on the surface—they can mar the surface.
- **Do not** use abrasive cleaning products on ceramic cooktops.
- **Do not** use a wet sponge or cloth on a hot panel.

Fastest, Cheapest, and Best

Bon Ami Deluxe Polishing Cleanser (Faultless Starch/Bon Ami Company) is the fastest, cheapest, and best way to clean ceramic cooktops. Sprinkle the powder over the surface, rubbing it in with a sponge or synthetic scouring pad (see Tools of the Trade). Rinse well with clean water and buff dry with a soft cloth for a clean finish.

Other Products Tested

Delete Polishing Cleanser (The Drackett Company)—powder; excellent cleaner.

Ovens

There are many strong cleaning products designed to work in standard ovens. **Caution:** Many oven cleaners are dangerous when they come in contact with your skin or eyes. Wear rubber gloves and protect your eyes while cleaning. Don't breathe the spray mist. Avoid dripping the cleaner on any nearby surface.

Newer stoves often are equipped with self-cleaning or continuous-cleaning oven systems. A self-cleaning oven uses a pyrolytic, or high heat, system to incinerate all oven grime, creating a powdery ash. A continuous-cleaning or catalytic system eliminates small splatters through the porous porcelain enamel finish on the oven liner that absorbs and spreads soil to promote cleaning at normal temperature settings; large spills must be wiped up.

For cleaning procedures to use with microwave ovens, also see Microwave Ovens.

Do's

- Follow the manufacturer's instructions when using the cleaning cycle of a self-cleaning oven.
- Follow the manufacturer's instructions for the recommended care of a continuous-cleaning oven.
- Clean the broiler pan and rack after each use, or clean the broiler unit if it is separate from the oven.
- Wipe out the oven after each use to avoid a real build-up of baked-on spills.
- Protect your hands and eyes when cleaning a standard oven with one of the commercial oven cleaners.
- Clean noncoated parts of a continuous-cleaning oven, such as the door and racks, with a steel wool soap pad.

Don'ts

- **Do not** use commercial oven cleaners, abrasives, or powdered cleaners on a continuous-cleaning oven—they can damage the surface.
- **Do not** allow a commercial oven cleaner to get on heating elements, oven wiring, or the thermostat—cover them with strips of aluminum foil.
- **Do not** breathe the fumes from strong oven cleaning products.

Fastest

Easy-Off Oven Cleaner (Boyle-Midway Inc.) makes cleaning a conventional oven a quick job. Heat the oven to 200° F., shake the can, and spray on the oven walls, top, bottom, and door. Allow to soak for about 10 minutes, and then rinse well with a sponge and clear water.

Cheapest

A cheap and effective way to clean a soiled oven is with ordinary household ammonia (see Recommended Basic Products). Pour 1 cup ammonia in a glass or ceramic bowl, place it in a cold oven, and allow it to set in the closed oven overnight. The next morning, pour the ammonia into a pail of warm water and use this solution and a sponge to wipe out the loosened soil. The fumes are strong at first, but they soon dissipate.

Best

Oven Cleaner (Stanley Home Products, Inc.) sprayed onto the surfaces of a cold oven and left overnight is the best way to clean a dirty standard oven. Protect the floor with newspapers or paper towels in case any of the cleaner leaks out during the night. Rinse the oven clean the next morning with a sponge for sparkling results.

Read manufacturer's cautions and warnings before using any product.

Stoves

Other Products Tested

Dow Oven Cleaner (The Dow Chemical Co.)—aerosol; good warm-oven cleaner; very good overnight oven cleaner; caustic; harsh odor.
Arm & Hammer Oven Cleaner (Church & Dwight Co., Inc.)—aerosol to be used on cool oven; good to very good cleaner; less harsh fumes and odor; not caustic.
Mr. Muscle Overnight Oven Cleaner (The Drackett Company)—pump spray; must penetrate for at least 6 to 8 hours; good to very good cleaner; harsh odor; caustic.

Stovetops and Exteriors

Other than the recently marketed ceramic cooktop surface, ranges have gas or electric surface heating units with many components that require cleaning regularly. The exteriors of most ranges are baked-on porcelain enamel; trim is usually chrome (also see Chromium for cleaning procedures and products), with durable plastic control knobs.

Do's

- Wipe off the surface around the heating units after each use.
- Use a synthetic scouring pad for stubborn soil.
- Wash reflector bowls or drip pans and grids in warm soapsuds whenever food or grease is spilled on them.
- Wipe up spills from the surface under the heating units—many stovetops can be raised for access to this area.
- Occasionally remove gas burners and wash them thoroughly—clean the holes with a fine wire cleaner or pipe cleaner.
- Quickly dry just-washed gas burners in a warm oven.
- Remove all knobs when cleaning the stove exterior to make the job easier.
- Turn off power to an electric range at the service panel before cleaning the elements.

Don'ts

- **Do not** use harsh abrasives or steel wool on the stove enamel.
- **Do not** submerge electrical burners in water—they are self-cleaning.
- **Do not** clean the holes of a gas burner with a toothpick—it can break off and clog the hole.
- **Do not** clean racks, drip pans, and other stove parts of a self-cleaning oven unless the manufacturer specifically recommends this procedure.
- **Do not** allow reflector bowls to become blackened and dull—this lessens the heating efficiency.
- **Do not** allow the oven vent to become clogged with spillovers.

Fastest

Jubilee Kitchen Wax (S. C. Johnson & Son, Inc.) provides a quick way of cleaning the exterior of a stove. Shake the can well; holding it six inches from the surface, spray it on and wipe with a soft cloth to remove dirt and smudges. It leaves a protective wax coating.

Cheapest

Dip a damp cloth in some baking soda (see Recommended Basic Products) and rub on the exterior of the stove to get rid of soil and grease inexpensively. It acts like a scouring powder but will not scratch the enamel surface. Rinse well and wipe dry with a soft cloth.

Best

The best product for cleaning the exteriors of stoves is **Klean 'n Shine** (S. C. Johnson & Son, Inc.). This pleasant-smelling aerosol foam is easy to spray on the surface; then buff it off to leave a spotless finish and protective coating.

Other Products Tested

Soft Scrub Cleanser (The Clorox Company)—mild abrasive liquid; excellent cleaner for stubborn soil; does not scratch.
Kitchen Magic (Magic American Chemical Corp.)—aerosol; excellent cleaner and wax for enamel surfaces.
Formula 409 All Purpose Cleaner (The Clorox Company)—pump spray; very good to excellent spot, grease, and smudge remover; pleasant odor.
Fantastik Multi-Surface Spray Cleaner (Texize Chemicals Company)—pump spray; very good to excellent spot, smudge, and grease remover; moderate odor.
Oakite All Purpose Cleaner (Oakite Products, Inc.)—low-sudsing powder; very good cleaner.
Spic and Span (Procter & Gamble)—low-sudsing powder; very good cleaner.
Lestoil Heavy Duty Cleaner (Noxell Corporation)—sudsing liquid; very good cleaner; heavy pine odor.
Sparkle Glass Cleaner (A. J. Funk & Co.)—pump spray; good to very good cleaner for enamel and chromium trim.

Trash Compactors

Do's

- Refer to the manufacturer's cleaning instructions for the trash compactor interior.
- Wipe off the exterior routinely to remove smudges and fingerprints.
- Use bags specially made for trash compactors for best results.
- Wash the interior when necessary.
- Watch out for small glass particles that may be left by the trash when cleaning the interior.

Don't

- **Do not** put wet garbage in the trash compactor unless a deodorant spray is used or the trash is emptied frequently.

Read manufacturer's cautions and warnings before using any product.

Trash Compactors

Fastest

Use **Jubilee Kitchen Wax** (S. C. Johnson & Son, Inc.) to clean the exterior of the trash compactor quickly. Shake the can; holding it about six inches from the surface, spray on this cleaner/wax, and wipe off with a soft cloth for a clean finish with a protective coat of wax.

The fastest, cheapest, and best way to clean the interior of trash compactors is with a homemade recipe. One tablespoon baking soda (see Recommended Basic Products) dissolved in 1 quart warm water makes an excellent and cheap cleaning solution for the interior of a trash compactor. Apply with a sponge, dipping the sponge in some dry soda to remove any stubborn soil. Not only does this simple solution clean well, it also deodorizes the interior.

Cheapest

Dip a damp sponge in some baking soda (see Recommended Basic Products) and rub on the exterior of the trash compactor for an inexpensive way to get rid of soil. It acts like a scouring powder but will not scratch the enamel or plastic laminate surface. Rinse well and wipe dry with a soft cloth.

Best

The best product for cleaning the exterior of a trash compactor is **Klean 'n Shine** (S. C. Johnson & Son, Inc.). This pleasant-smelling aerosol foam is easy to spray on the surface and then buff off to leave a spotless finish and protective coating.

Other Products Tested

EXTERIOR.   Soft Scrub Cleanser (The Clorox Company)—mild abrasive liquid; excellent cleaner for stubborn soil; does not scratch.
Kitchen Magic (Magic American Chemical Corp.)—aerosol; excellent cleaner and wax for enamel surfaces.
Formula 409 All Purpose Cleaner (The Clorox Company)—pump spray; very good to excellent spot, grease, and smudge remover; pleasant odor.
Fantastik Multi-Surface Spray Cleaner (Texize Chemicals Company)—pump spray; very good to excellent spot, smudge, and grease remover; moderate odor.
Oakite All Purpose Cleaner (Oakite Products, Inc.)—low-sudsing powder; very good cleaner.
Spic and Span (Procter & Gamble)—low-sudsing powder; very good cleaner.
Lestoil Heavy Duty Cleaner (Noxell Corporation)—sudsing liquid; very good cleaner; heavy pine odor.
Sparkle Glass Cleaner (A. J. Funk & Co.)—pump spray; good to very good cleaner for enamel and chromium trim.

Small Appliances

Blenders and Food Processors

For products and procedures to use on the stainless steel and chrome surfaces of your blender or food processor, also see Stainless Steel and Chromium.

Do's
- Follow the manufacturer's cleaning instructions.
- Wipe the base clean after each use.
- Use a synthetic scouring pad to remove stubborn soil.
- Clean the blender jar by filling it with a warm water detergent solution and running it for about 15 seconds on high speed. Rinse well and dry.
- Wash the food processor's container, cover, pusher, blades, and discs in warm soapy water or in the automatic dishwasher.

Don'ts
- **Do not** use harsh abrasives or steel wool on the base or the jar.
- **Do not** put the blender's jar assembly in the dishwasher—the detergent chemicals may affect the blades over time.

Fastest

A mild detergent solution made from a liquid dishwashing detergent (see Recommended Basic Products) is the fastest way to clean all parts of a blender or food processor. Apply with a sponge or cloth, rinse, and buff dry with another dry cloth.

Cheapest

Dissolve 1 tablespoon baking soda (see Recommended Basic Products) in 1 quart warm water and wipe off the base for a cheap cleanup. If stubborn soil persists, dip a moistened cloth into the dry soda and apply with a gentle scrubbing action. The soda quickly loosens soil, yet doesn't scratch the surface.

BAKING SODA
BICARBONATE OF SODA U.S.P.

Read manufacturer's cautions and warnings before using any product.

Best

Sparkle Glass Cleaner (A. J. Funk & Co.) is excellent for cleaning stainless steel blender or food processor bases and trim.
Simply spray it on and buff dry immediately with a soft cloth.

Coffeemakers

Coffee is made in either a percolator, brewer, or drip-type coffeemaker. Drip coffeemakers
are easy to clean, requiring a new filter, a wash of the pot in a detergent solution, and a quick
wipe with a damp cloth for the base. Percolators need a more thorough cleaning occasionally
to get rid of oil build-up on the stem, basket, and walls that can affect the taste of the coffee.
To clean metal surfaces of the coffeemaker, also see Chromium, Stainless Steel, and
Aluminum.

Do's

- Read and follow the manufacturer's cleaning instructions.
- Allow the heated coffeemaker to cool before cleaning.
- Use a synthetic scouring pad to help remove stubborn soil.
- Wash all percolator parts in a warm detergent solution after each use.
- Sweeten a plastic basket by rubbing it with a paste of baking soda and water.
- Wipe off the exterior with a damp cloth and buff dry if the coffeemaker is not immersible.
- Clean the spout and tubes of a percolator at least weekly with a special percolator
  brush and warm dishwashing detergent solution.

Don'ts

- **Do not** use harsh abrasives or steel wool to clean coffeemakers.
- **Do not** put coffee grounds down the sink.
- **Do not** immerse the heating section of an electric percolator in water unless the unit is
  designated safe to immerse.

Fastest and Cheapest

Use baking soda (see Recommended Basic Products) to rid an
electric coffeemaker of the built-up oil deposits that can give
coffee a bitter taste. With the stem and basket in place, fill the
percolator to the limit with cold water and add 6 tablespoons of
baking soda. Plug it in and allow the coffeemaker to run through
the complete cycle. Wait for 15 minutes, unplug, and empty the
solution. Wash in a mild detergent, rinse, and dry. Also, ¼ cup
vinegar in a potful of water works when allowed to run through the
brewing cycle.

Best

Dip-It Coffee Pot Destainer (Economics Laboratory, Inc.) is an excellent way to remove stains and rancid oils from percolators. It can be done by just soaking, or by running the cleaner through a complete heating cycle. Either way is very effective, and after a thorough rinsing the rancid oil taste is gone.

Electric Can Openers

Your can opener needs light but regular care. Also see Chromium for products and procedures to use on the chrome surfaces.

Do's

- Always unplug the can opener before cleaning it.
- Wipe off the can opener after each use to remove food spills or drips.
- Periodically, remove the cutting wheel and lid holder and soak them in a jar of hot sudsy water. Scrub caked-on food with an old toothbrush, rinse, dry, and replace the parts.

Don'ts

- **Do not** use harsh abrasives or steel wool to clean the case.
- **Do not** immerse the case in water.

Fastest, Cheapest, and Best

A warm soapsuds solution made from one of the liquid dishwashing detergents (see Recommended Basic Products) is the best way to clean an electric can opener. Wipe off all surfaces with a dampened sponge and buff dry. For stubborn soil, moisten the spot and let soak for a few minutes.

Read manufacturer's cautions and warnings before using any product.

Electric Irons

A good steam iron makes ironing easier, but only if the iron is clean so that it can operate efficiently.

Soleplate

Do's
- Make sure the steam vents are not clogged by mineral deposits or improperly applied cleaning products.
- Remove cleaning product residues from vent areas with a cotton swab or pipe cleaner.

Don'ts
- **Do not** iron over sharp objects or buttons—this can damage the soleplate.
- **Do not** use a sharp knife or other tool to remove deposits from the soleplate.

Fastest

Remove starch build-up and other soil from the soleplate of an iron by applying **Bon Ami Deluxe Polishing Cleanser** (Faultless Starch/Bon Ami Company) with a fine piece of steel wool. Scour until the residue is gone and then rinse away all traces of the cleanser with a damp cloth, paying particular attention to the vent areas.

Cheapest

Using a damp cloth, apply baking soda (see Recommended Basic Products) to the soleplate of a slightly warm iron, scrubbing it over the residue until gone. Rinse well with another damp cloth, paying particular attention to the vent areas.

Best

Faultless Hot-iron Cleaner (Faultless Starch/Bon Ami Company) is an excellent product for cleaning dirty soleplates when the iron is hot. Empty all water from the iron and apply the jelly-like paste to the bottom of the iron with a very thick pad made of eight layers of folded-over cloth, and then finish the job by rubbing the iron back and forth over another clean cloth to remove all traces of the cleaner. Check the steam vents and remove all residue with a cotton swab if any of the cleaner remains in them.

Water Reservoir

Do's

- Use tap water in steam irons only if the manufacturer recommends it and if your tap water is soft.
- Use melted frost from the freezer in place of distilled water for steam irons if desired.

Don't

- **Do not** use hard water in a steam iron even if the manufacturer recommends tap water—use distilled water instead.

Fastest and Cheapest

Remove mineral deposits from the water reservoir when the steam action begins to decrease by pouring a solution containing ⅓ cup white vinegar and ⅓ cup water into the iron reservoir. Heat the iron and let it steam for about 3 minutes. Unplug the iron and position it, soleplate down, on a small glass dish that has been placed in a larger shallow pan. Allow the water to drain from the vents for about an hour. Drain away any remaining solution and flush the reservoir with clear water before using the iron.

Best

Iron Klean (Sunbeam Appliance Service Co.) is excellent for removing mineral deposits from the water reservoir and vents of a steam iron. Mix 5 capfuls of this liquid with about ¾ cup water and pour it into the iron. Heat the iron and let it steam for 3 minutes, then unplug it and position it, soleplate down, on a small glass bowl set in a larger shallow pan. Allow the reservoir to drain for about 30 minutes. Pour out any remaining cleaner, flush the reservoir with clear water, and the iron will be free of mineral deposits.

Garbage Disposers

Whether it is a batch-feed or continuous-feed model, the disposer unit is designed to be self-cleaning, but occasionally you have to deal with unpleasant odors.

Do's

- Operate the disposer with a full stream of running cold water and the lid lightly in place.
- Flush the disposer for a few seconds after turning it off to ensure all debris is washed away.

Read manufacturer's cautions and warnings before using any product.

Don'ts
- **Do not** let metal, wood, glass, paper, or plastic objects fall into the disposer.
- **Do not** reach into the disposer while it is operating.
- **Do not** put fibrous items such as artichoke leaves or corn husks down the disposer.
- **Do not** use caustic drain cleaners in the disposer.

Fastest, Cheapest, and Best

If an odor begins to come from the disposer, eliminate it by tearing up the peels of some citrus fruits and putting them into the disposer. Grind away with a stream of cold running water and enjoy the fresh smell. Another excellent method is to sprinkle baking soda (see Recommended Basic Products) over several ice cubes and grind them in the disposer.

Hot Trays

A quick wipe with a damp sponge usually is sufficient to clean hot trays. However, if spilled food gets baked on, stronger measures are needed. For special procedures and products to use on ceramic hot tray surfaces, also see Stoves—Ceramic Cooktop.

Do's
- Allow the heated tray to cool before cleaning.
- Use a synthetic scouring pad to help get rid of stubborn soil.

Don't
- **Do not** immerse a hot tray in water.

Fastest

Soft Scrub Cleanser (The Clorox Company) applied with a synthetic scouring pad (see Tools of the Trade) will quickly remove almost any soil from a hot tray. Rinse well with clear water and buff dry with a soft cloth.

Cheapest

Baking soda (see Recommended Basic Products) applied with a damp cloth is the cheapest method to clean stains and soil from the surface of a hot tray. Use a synthetic scouring pad (see Tools of the Trade) instead of the cloth for especially stubborn soil and rinse well with clear water.

Best

The stained surface of a hot tray is efficiently cleaned with an application of **Easy-Off Oven Cleaner** (Boyle-Midway Inc.). Heat the tray first to a warm temperature and carefully spray the foam so it doesn't touch the outer perimeter of the tray or seep into the crevice between the frame and tray surface. Allow the foam to soak for 10 minutes and then remove with a clean wet sponge. **Caution:** Follow the manufacturer's warnings for proper use of this product.

Toaster Ovens and Broilers

It is important for you to clean your toaster oven/broiler regularly to prevent spatters and grease from becoming baked on. For products and procedures to use on the metal surfaces, also see Aluminum, Chromium, and Stainless Steel.

Do's

- Wipe off the exterior of the oven regularly.
- Shake off or wash the crumb tray regularly.
- Wipe out the interior with a warm dishwashing detergent solution after cooking greasy foods.
- Use a synthetic scouring pad to remove stubborn soil from the tray or racks.
- Clean the plastic parts of the oven with a warm detergent solution and buff the surface dry.

Don'ts

- **Do not** clean the oven until it is cool and the cord has been disconnected.
- **Do not** use harsh abrasives or steel wool to clean the oven.
- **Do not** use a commercial oven cleaner on the interior of the oven.
- **Do not** immerse the oven in water.

Fastest and Cheapest

Toaster ovens/broilers usually have a polished-metal surface. The fastest way to clean them is to dip a dry cloth in some baking soda (see Recommended Basic Products) or flour and rub it over the oven. For stubborn soil, moisten the cloth first and apply only baking soda with a gentle scrubbing action. Dust off any soda residue and enjoy the shiny, scratch-free finish.

Best

Stainless Steel Magic (Magic American Chemical Corp.) is a pump spray that cleans and polishes the surface of a toaster oven/broiler beautifully. Just spray the liquid onto the surface from a distance of five inches. After 3 to 4 minutes, wipe the exterior with a soft cloth to give a sparkling finish.

Read manufacturer's cautions and warnings before using any product.

Toasters

All toasters need regular attention to keep them clean, shiny, and crumb-free.

Do's

- Unplug the toaster before cleaning it.
- Wipe off the exterior of the toaster regularly.
- Remove the crumb tray at the base of the toaster and shake out accumulated crumbs—wash the tray in warm soapsuds.
- If the toaster has no crumb tray, turn it upside down and shake it over the sink or large garbage can.
- Use a thin, soft brush to remove crumbs from the interior.

Don'ts

- **Do not** use harsh abrasives or steel wool to clean a toaster.
- **Do not** clean the toaster until it is cool and has been disconnected.
- **Do not** wash the inside of the toaster with water or immerse the whole unit in water.
- **Do not** clean the interior of the toaster with a metal utensil.

Fastest and Cheapest

Most toasters have a polished-metal finish that needs to be cleaned regularly to remove smudges and fingerprints. The fastest way to clean the metal surface is to dip a dry cloth into some baking soda (see Recommended Basic Products) or flour and rub it over the surface. This removes those annoying marks quickly, requires no rinsing or wiping, and will not scratch the surface. If there is a baked-on spill, moisten the cloth first and apply only baking soda with a gentle scrubbing action.

Best

Stainless Steel Magic (Magic American Chemical Corp.), a pump spray, is the best product for bringing up the shine on metal toasters. Shake the can well; holding it five inches from the toaster, spray a light coating over the surface. After 3 to 4 minutes, buff with a soft cloth for a beautiful shine.

Waffle Irons

Waffle irons need little care. The grids are made from seasoned cast iron or a nonstick surface and generally don't require washing after ordinary use. Also see Chromium and Stainless Steel for products and procedures to use on these surfaces.

Do's
- Wipe off the exterior of the waffle iron after each use, cleaning up any batter spills.
- Wipe off the grids with a paper towel after use.
- If necessary, remove the grids and wash them in warm soapsuds, using a plastic brush to remove any food debris. Season the surface with a light brushing of vegetable oil.

Don'ts
- **Do not** clean the waffle iron until it has been unplugged and is cool.
- **Do not** use harsh abrasives or steel wool for cleaning.
- **Do not** immerse the waffle iron in water.

Baked Enamel

Fastest, Cheapest, and Best

Wipe off the exterior surfaces of the waffle iron with a sponge dipped in a warm soapsuds solution made with a liquid dishwashing detergent (see Recommended Basic Products). For stubborn soil use a synthetic scouring pad (see Tools of the Trade). Rinse and buff dry with a soft cloth.

Metal

Fastest and Cheapest

Rub baking soda (see Recommended Basic Products) or flour onto the surface with a dry cloth to remove light soil and smudges. If a spot persists, moisten the cloth first and apply only baking soda with a gentle scouring action. Dust off any remaining baking soda for a bright, scratch-free finish.

Best

An excellent commercial product for cleaning bright metal surfaces is **Stainless Steel Magic** (Magic American Chemical Corp.). Holding the can five inches away, spray over the surface. After 3 to 4 minutes, buff dry with a soft cloth for a clean and polished finish.

Read manufacturer's cautions and warnings before using any product.

Natural Fabrics

Cotton

Cotton fabric is strong, long wearing, and absorbent. It will shrink and wrinkle unless given special treatment and finishes, and often is blended with other fibers to give it more wrinkle resistance. It is available in a wide variety of weights and textures, from denim or corduroy to percale.

Do's

- Machine wash and tumble dry using a water temperature ranging from cold to hot, depending on the manufacturer's care instructions, and an all-purpose detergent.
- Use a chlorine bleach on white and colorfast fabrics, unless a fabric finish has been applied.
- Pretreat oil-based spots and stains with a prewash.
- Preshrink cotton fabrics before using them for home sewing.
- Use a fabric softener to improve softness and to reduce wrinkling.
- Use **Easy-On Speed Starch** (Boyle-Midway Inc.) when ironing cotton garments to restore their crisp appearance.
- Iron with a hot iron for best results.

Don'ts

- **Do not** use more than the recommended amount of bleach—this can damage the fibers.
- **Do not** use soap on 100% cotton flame retardant items—soap reacts to cover up the flame retardant properties.
- **Do not** use nonphosphate detergents containing sodium carbonate as a builder on 100% cotton flame retardant items—this builder reacts to cover up the flame retardant properties.
- **Do not** use a fabric softener frequently on cotton towels and washcloths—the softener can reduce absorbency.

See Laundry for recommended cleaning products.

Linen

Pure linen fabric wrinkles easily, so many manufacturers now make linen blends or add wrinkle-resistant finishes to combat this problem. Lint is not a problem with linen; it is absorbent and comfortable to wear, but can crack or show wear at seamlines and along creases or finished edges of the garment.

Do's

- Machine wash and tumble dry using an all-purpose detergent.
- Use a chlorine bleach only on white linen.
- Dry-clean linen if desired.
- Iron when still slightly damp with a hot iron for best results.

Don'ts

- **Do not** use more than the recommended amount of bleach on white linen—it can weaken the fibers.

See Laundry for recommended cleaning products.

Silk

Silk, the most lustrous of natural fibers, is a delight to wear but does require special care. Most silk garments are marked "dry-clean only." However, some silk can be washed by hand, especially if it is a piece of silk fabric that you are going to make into a garment.

Do's

- Check a corner of the fabric for colorfastness before washing the whole piece, as some dyed silk will bleed.
- Use hair shampoo containing protein and warm or cold water for hand washing—the protein in the shampoo feeds the protein in the silk.
- Hang out of sunlight to drip dry.
- Press while still damp with a warm iron (below 275° F.) or use steam.
- Use only oxygen bleach or mix one part 3% hydrogen peroxide to eight parts water to bleach washable white silk.
- Handle washable silk gently during washing.

Don'ts

- **Do not** twist or wring washable silk.
- **Do not** use chlorine bleach.
- **Do not** dry silk in sunlight, as it weakens the fabric.

See Laundry for recommended cleaning products.

Read manufacturer's cautions and warnings before using any product.

Wool

Wool fabric is highly resilient, absorbent, and sheds wrinkles well; but wool also will shrink and mat if exposed to heat and rubbing. Popular in both knit and woven fabrics, wools range from fine wool crepe and jersey to felt and mohair.

Do's

- Treat spots and stains with solvent-based spot removers.
- Dry-clean only unless specifically marked "washable."
- Clean felt by wiping with a dry sponge; for more thorough treatment, hold the material over steam from a teakettle, brush lightly with a dry sponge or lint-free cloth to smooth the surface.
- Use only a light duty detergent to wash wool.
- Use cold water to clean washable woolens.
- Allow the wool article to soak in a light duty laundry detergent solution for a few minutes before starting the washing process.
- Handle woolens carefully when wet to avoid stretching.
- Wash by machine only if the care label so directs, and then use cold water and a gentle cycle.
- Remove excess moisture by rolling woolens in a towel, then block to shape and dry on a flat surface.
- Dry woolens in a dryer only if the manufacturer's instructions recommend it.
- Press wool with a hot iron with lots of steam, covering the article with a damp cloth or chemically treated press cloth, then allow to dry before storing the garment.

Don'ts

- **Do not** over-wet felt to avoid shrinkage.
- **Do not** bleach wool.
- **Do not** rub, twist, or wring during the washing process.
- **Do not** wash woolens in hot water—it shrinks the fabric and makes white wool yellow.
- **Do not** hang to dry—this can stretch the wool out of shape.
- **Do not** dry wool in direct heat.
- **Do not** use the automatic dryer unless specifically marked "machine dryable."
- **Do not** store wool items unless they have been cleaned and mothproofed.

See Laundry for recommended cleaning products.

Synthetic Fabrics

Acetate

Acetate is made from cellulose and has a silk-like appearance. Closely related to rayon, it has good body and drapes well. Taffeta, satin, crepe, brocade, and double knits often contain acetate. It is not very absorbent or colorfast and loses strength when wet.

Do's
- Hand wash carefully using a light duty detergent if the care label specifies that the article is washable—otherwise, have it dry-cleaned.
- Use only a light duty soap or detergent and wash in warm water.
- Add a liquid fabric softener if desired.
- Line dry away from heat or direct sunlight.
- Iron at the coolest setting, on the wrong side, while the article is damp.
- Use a press cloth for right side pressing.

Don'ts
- **Do not** soak colored items or wash them with white articles.
- **Do not** soak, wring, or twist acetates when washing.
- **Do not** allow nail polish remover or perfumes to touch acetate—they damage the fabric.

Trademarked names for acetate include: Avisco, Celanese, Celara, and Estron. See Laundry for recommended cleaning products.

Acrylic

Many acrylic weaves resemble wool's softness, bulk, and fluffiness. Acrylics are wrinkle resistant and usually are machine washable. Quite often acrylic fibers are blended with wool or polyester fibers to combine the best qualities of each. Acrylic's biggest drawback is its tendency to pill. Blends will do this less than pure acrylic.

Acrylic/Fiberglass

Do's

- Dry-clean if desired.
- Pretreat oil-based stains before washing.
- Turn garments inside out before laundering to reduce pilling.
- Wash delicate items by hand in warm water, gently squeezing out water.
- Machine wash sturdy articles with an all-purpose detergent and tumble dry at low temperatures.
- Use either a chlorine or oxygen bleach if the fabric is colorfast.
- Add a fabric softener every third or fourth time the article is washed to reduce static electricity.
- Press at a moderate temperature setting using steam.

Trademarked names used for acrylic include: Acrilan, Creslan, Orlon, and Zefran. See Laundry for recommended cleaning procedures.

Fiberglass

Fiberglass fabrics are very wrinkle and soil resistant, but they have poor abrasion resistance. They are not absorbent and stand up well to sun and weather, making them ideal for curtains and draperies. Fiberglass never is made into wearing apparel because it sheds small glass fibers.

Do's

- Dust periodically with the upholstery attachment of the vacuum.
- Hand wash for best results, using an all-purpose detergent.
- Wear rubber or plastic gloves to protect your hands from the small glass fibers.
- Rinse out the machine tub if used to wash the newer, machine-washable fiberglass fabrics.
- Drip dry only.

Don'ts

- **Do not** spin dry, twist, or wring fiberglass items.
- **Do not** dry-clean.
- **Do not** wash anything else with fiberglass.
- **Do not** iron—it is not necessary.

Trademarked names for fiberglass include: Beta Glass, Fiberglas, P.P.G., and Vitron. See Laundry for recommended cleaning products and Window Coverings—Curtains and Draperies for more specific washing techniques.

Modacrylic

Modacrylic is a fiber often used in fake furs, fleece robes, blankets, stuffed toys, and wigs. It is resilient, soft, and warm and resists moths, mildew, sunlight damage, and wrinkling.

Do's

- Hand wash delicate items such as wigs.
- Machine wash sturdy items in warm water with a gentle cycle and a light duty detergent.
- Use a fabric softener to reduce static electricity.
- Use a low-heat setting on the dryer and remove articles as soon as tumbling stops.
- Use a cool iron if pressing is needed.
- Dry-clean deep pile coats.

Trademarked names used for modacrylic include: Dynel and Verel. See Laundry for recommended cleaning products, Bedding—Blanket, and Wigs and Hairpieces.

Nylon

Nylon fabrics are extremely strong, lightweight, smooth, and lustrous. They are also non-absorbent and have excellent abrasion and wrinkle resistance. Nylon is used extensively for delicate and sheer undergarments. Often combined with spandex, nylon knits are very stretchy, with excellent recoverability. Available in many textures, nylon often is used to make everything from lingerie, carpets, and rainwear, to tents.

Do's

- Follow the manufacturer's cleaning instructions.
- Pretreat oil-based stains before washing.
- Machine wash sturdy articles in warm water with an all-purpose detergent.
- Hand wash fine lingerie and hosiery, using warm water and a light duty laundry detergent, or machine wash in a mesh bag to prevent stretching or tearing.
- Use a chlorine bleach only if the article is colorfast.
- Use a fabric softener to reduce static electricity.
- Tumble dry at a low temperature setting.
- Iron at a low temperature setting.

Don't

- **Do not** launder white nylon with any other colored fabric.

Trademarked names used for nylon include: Antron, Enkalon, Cantrece, Nyloft, Caprolan, and Qiana. See Laundry for recommended cleaning products and Rainwear for cleaning information for nylon rainwear.

Read manufacturer's cautions and warnings before using any product.

Polyester

Polyester fabrics are strong, resilient, wrinkle resistant, colorfast, crisp, and hold pleats and creases well. But they are also nonabsorbent, attract and hold oil-based stains, may pill when rubbed, and may yellow with age. Besides polyester's popularity for clothing and filling, many bed linens and towels are made from polyester blends. It can be dry-cleaned if desired.

Do's

- Pretreat oil-based stains with a prewash or all-purpose liquid detergent before washing.
- Turn polyester knits inside out before washing to prevent snags.
- Machine wash in warm water using an all-purpose detergent and tumble dry at a low-temperature setting.
- Use a chlorine bleach if necessary.
- Use a fabric softener to reduce static electricity.
- Iron at a moderate temperature setting or use steam.

Don't

- **Do not** over-dry—this will cause gradual shrinkage.

Trademarked names used for polyester include: Dacron, Fortrel, Kodel, and Trevira. See Laundry for recommended cleaning products; Bedding and Outerwear—Polyester Fiber-Filled.

Rayon

Rayon is a strong, absorbent fabric, but it tends to lose strength when wet. It commonly is used for drapery and upholstery fabrics, as well as for clothing.

Do's

- Dry-clean if desired.
- Wash by hand in lukewarm water with a light duty detergent for best results.
- Machine wash in warm water on a gentle cycle with a light duty detergent only if marked "machine washable."
- Squeeze moisture out gently when washing by hand.
- Use a chlorine bleach unless the fabric has been treated with a resin finish.
- Drip dry for best results.
- Press on the wrong side with a medium temperature setting while the fabric is damp.

Don'ts

- **Do not** wring or twist when washing by hand.
- **Do not** use chlorine bleach on resin-finished rayon—the fabric may discolor.

Trademarked names used for rayon include: Fibro, Xena, Celanese, Avril, Avron, Suprenka, and Zantrel. See Laundry for suitable cleaning products.

Spandex

Spandex is a lightweight fiber resembling rubber in durability. It has good stretch and recovery, and is resistant to sunlight damage, abrasion, and oils. Always blended with other fibers, spandex provides the stretch in waistbands, foundation garments, swimwear, and dancewear.

Do's

- Pretreat oil-based stains before washing.
- Hand or machine wash in warm water using an all-purpose detergent.
- Use only an oxygen or sodium perborate bleach.
- Rinse thoroughly.
- Line dry or tumble dry at a low temperature setting.
- Press rapidly, if needed, at a low temperature setting.

Don'ts

- **Do not** wash white spandex with other color fabrics.
- **Do not** use chlorine bleach.

Trademarked names used for spandex include: Glospan, Lycra, and Spandelle. See Laundry for recommended cleaning products.

Triacetate

Triacetate resembles acetate but is less sensitive to heat, which allows it to be creased and crisply pleated. Often it is a component in jersey, textured knits, and taffeta.

Do's

- Hand wash pleated garments if desired.
- Machine wash pleated garments in cold water at gentle speed for 3 minutes.
- Machine wash most triacetate articles with an all-purpose detergent in hot or warm water.
- Tumble dry or line dry.
- Air dry in the dryer or drip dry permanently pleated garments.
- Press if necessary, using a hot temperature setting.

Trademarked names for triacetate include: Arnel. See Laundry for recommended cleaning products.

Wearing Apparel

Diapers

With the drastic changes in cleaning agents and laundry equipment during the last 20 years, diaper washing is no longer the chore it once was. For listings of soaps, detergents, presoaks, detergent boosters, bleaches, and fabric softeners not described here, also see Laundry.

Do's

- Use a large plastic pail with a tight-fitting lid for a diaper pail.
- Flush out heavily soiled diapers as soon as possible and soak immediately in a diaper pail that contains a laundry detergent or presoak solution.
- Before laundering, spin out the soaking water in the machine or wring out each diaper by hand.
- Machine wash diapers in water that is as hot as possible.
- Use the normal cycle of the washer—diapers are not delicate!
- Use liquid bleach to whiten, disinfect, and remove stains.
- Rinse *thoroughly,* using warm or cold water.
- Add 1 cup white vinegar or ½ cup borax to the final rinse water to remove all detergent and alkaline residue.
- Add ⅓ cup baking soda to the beginning of the wash cycle to whiten diapers, using less bleach.
- Add bleach 5 minutes after the wash cycle has begun or use the automatic bleach dispenser.
- Dry diapers in the dryer or on the clothesline.
- Always rinse the diaper pail well before adding fresh presoak solution.

Don'ts

- **Do not** wash diapers with any other dirty clothes.
- **Do not** overcrowd the machine.
- **Do not** use a fabric softener for each washing—too much softness reduces absorbency.
- **Do not** iron diapers—this will decrease their fluffiness and absorbency.

148

Cheapest

20 Mule Team Borax (United States Borax & Chemical Corporation) is less expensive to use to presoak diapers than any other product. Add ½ cup to 1 gallon warm water in a clean diaper pail and swish around until dissolved. Use a laundry detergent (see Laundry) after presoaking.

Yes (Texize Chemicals Company) is the most economical detergent to use for washing diapers. Only ¼ cup of this blue liquid is needed for a washer load, and it includes a built-in fabric softener that saves you the expense of using an extra product.

If Yes is not available in your area, substitute **Bold 3** (Procter & Gamble), a low-sudsing powder detergent that contains a fabric softener but is not as cost-efficient as Yes.

Best

Biz (Procter & Gamble) works in a dual capacity as a presoak and detergent booster. Very little is needed in the presoak capacity: Only 2 tablespoons of this granular product in 1 gallon warm water in the diaper pail works very well. Along with the enzymes that lift out difficult stains, Biz contains oxygen bleach, a fabric whitener, and blueing, which boost the detergent in the wash cycle.

Although **Ivory Snow** (Procter & Gamble) is considered a light duty soap, it performs beautifully on diapers, and the mildness gives them a softness and fluffiness without adding other products. Pour 1 cup into the machine before adding diapers to give this pure soap time to dissolve, and the diapers will be soft and clean.

If you are using a nonphosphate detergent, **Calgon Water Softener** (Beecham Products Division of Beecham Inc.) will supplement the effectiveness of the detergent because it ties up the minerals that cause water hardness instead of combining with them so no chalky alkaline residue can cause irritation.

Clorox Bleach (The Clorox Company) is the best chlorine bleach for whitening diapers that have yellowed and for disinfecting them at the same time. Dilute 1 cup bleach in 1 quart warm water and add to the wash load 5 minutes after the cycle has begun, or use an automatic bleach dispenser if your machine has one.

Rain Barrel Fabric Softener (S. C. Johnson & Son, Inc.) is an excellent and convenient product to use for softening diapers. Pour this blue liquid directly into the machine at the beginning of the wash cycle. With no further attention it softens the diapers and leaves them static free.

For automatic dryers, **Purex Toss 'n Soft** (Purex Corporation) is the most effective of all the convenient fabric softener sheets. It works well when placed on the wet diapers in the dryer and also can be tossed into the final rinse cycle of the washer.

Read manufacturer's cautions and warnings before using any product.

Gloves

Gloves can be woven or knitted fabric; leather from any of a wide variety of animal skins; vinyl; or a combination of leather/vinyl and fabric, like driving gloves. Many gloves—including some leather—are washable, but the care label should be the guide. White or light-colored gloves usually can be washed by hand or by machine with other laundry. Unless they are definitely colorfast, it is safer to wash dark-colored gloves by hand.

Do's

- Lightly apply a soft-bristled brush to areas with stubborn soil.
- Hand wash leather gloves in soap while wearing them, without rubbing; rinse well and dry flat.
- Run a stream of water into leather gloves to help remove them from the hand after washing.
- Blow into leather gloves to help reshape the fingers before drying.
- When leather gloves are almost dry, carefully put them on and flex the fingers so the gloves will not be stiff. Carefully remove the gloves and allow them to dry completely.
- Handle doeskin and chamois gloves carefully—they can tear and stretch easily when wet.
- Hand or machine wash fabric gloves, roll in a towel to remove excess moisture, and dry flat.

Don'ts

- **Do not** wash leather gloves in detergent.
- **Do not** dry leather gloves in the sun, direct heat, or the clothes dryer.
- **Do not** wash leather gloves once they have been dry-cleaned.
- **Do not** dry fabric gloves in the clothes dryer.

Fastest, Cheapest, and Best

Ivory Snow (Procter & Gamble) is the fastest, cheapest, and best product for hand washing leather and fabric gloves. Dissolve the powder in a basin of warm water, swish your hand through to create suds, and wash the gloves using the method described for their material. Rinse well, blot out excess moisture, and dry flat.

For machine washing gloves, use an all-purpose detergent (see Laundry).

Outerwear

Outerwear is the coats and jackets we wear outdoors to protect us from the weather. Whether it is a down-filled coat, a polyester fiber-filled vest, or a water-repellant raincoat (also see Rainwear), outerwear needs periodic cleaning to keep its fresh look and to prolong its life. Also see Acrylic and Nylon.

Down-Filled

Do's

- Follow the manufacturer's instructions for recommended cleaning procedures.
- Close all zipper and self-sticking closures before washing.
- Pretreat spots and stains with liquid detergent or prewash before washing.
- Repair any holes or broken seams before washing or cleaning.
- Hand or machine wash in an all-purpose detergent, using cold water.
- Make sure down-filled garments are rinsed well to remove all traces of soap or detergent.
- Hang the garment on a clothesline or tumble dry at moderate heat, adding a pair of clean sneakers to the dryer to help prevent matting as the down dries.

Fastest, Cheapest, and Best

Choose an all-purpose laundry detergent (also see Laundry) to use for hand or machine washing. Allow it to dissolve in the water before adding the down garment.

Polyester Fiber-Filled

Many outerwear garments are insulated with some form of polyester.

Do's

- Close all zippers and self-sticking closures before washing or cleaning.
- Repair any holes or open seams before washing or cleaning.
- Pretreat any spots and stains with a liquid detergent or prewash.
- Line dry or machine dry at moderate heat.
- Dry-clean the garment if the manufacturer's instructions recommend this procedure.

Don'ts

- **Do not** dry-clean fiber-filled garments insulated with Thinsulate brand, as the insulation deteriorates in the solvent.
- **Do not** twist or wring a fiber-filled garment excessively during the washing process.

Fastest, Cheapest, and Best

Choose an all-purpose laundry detergent (see Laundry), allowing it to dissolve in the washer before adding the garment.

Wool

Most wool coats and jackets must be dry-cleaned, but if the manufacturer's care instructions specify, you can hand wash or spot clean some outerwear. Also see Wool and Sweaters for instructions for cleaning wool garments, and Spots and Stains.

Read manufacturer's cautions and warnings before using any product.

Do's

- Follow the care label's instructions to the letter.
- Cover the dry garment with a damp cloth and press with a warm iron if necessary, shake out steam from the wool, then air well before storing.

Don't

- **Do not** dry woolens in the dryer unless specifically recommended by the manufacturer.

Rainwear

Rainwear, whether vinyl, plastic, or fabric, should provide years of protection against the elements. Proper handling and routine cleaning will not only add years to the garment, but will also prevent mildew and provide the maximum waterproofing effect.

Do's

- Always dry an umbrella open to speed drying and prevent mildew.
- Always hang wet clothing by itself in a well-ventilated area to dry before hanging in the closet.

Don't

- **Do not** fold or hang wet rainwear in the closet.

Cloth

Whether you have an expensive all-weather coat or a nylon windbreaker that you can fold and store in your pocket, care must be taken when cleaning to preserve its water-repellant qualities and resiliency. Most cloth rainwear is washable, but the care tags in the garments list specific instructions for safe washing.

Do's

- Dry-clean the zip-out lining of an all-weather coat.
- Allow dirt and mud stains to dry thoroughly and brush them with a stiff brush.
- Always test spot removers on the inside hem before using them on your coat.
- Pretreat spots before washing.
- Read care labels and follow washing instructions to the letter.
- Apply a commercial water repellant such as **Scotchgard** (3M) to rainwear, like nylon jackets, after each washing.

Don't

- **Do not** wash the zip-out lining of all-weather coats.

Fastest and Cheapest

To remove a spot or stain, treat it with **Amway Remove Fabric Spot Cleaner** (Amway Corp.) according to the label directions. Test first on an inconspicuous spot. Let it dry thoroughly before brushing off.

Best

Treat grease and dirt spots of washable rainwear (see Spots and Stains) and put it in the washing machine with any light duty laundry detergent on a gentle cycle (see Laundry). Rinse at least three times to be sure that all the soap is removed. Do not spin it dry. Then tumble dry in a warm dryer for about 10 minutes. Remove the rainwear while still damp and hang it to dry. A cool iron may be used to touch up wrinkles.

Other Products Tested

K2r Spot-lifter (Texize Chemicals Company)—spray-on spot remover; repeat application is often necessary; mild odor; can leave a ring that is difficult to remove.

Rubber, Plastic, and Vinyl

Plastic and vinyl rainwear requires relatively little care.

Do's
- Turn boots, galoshes, and rubbers upside down to dry.
- Hang garments separately to speed drying.

Don'ts
- **Do not** put plastic or rubber rainwear in the dryer.
- **Do not** use abrasive cleansers on plastic or vinyl—they remove the protective covering, dry out the material, and make it brittle.
- **Do not** use harsh cleaning fluids that can melt the fabric.
- **Do not** dry rainwear near an open flame or heat source, as it can melt.
- **Do not** dry-clean a garment, unless specified by the manufacturer.

Fastest and Cheapest

Mix 1 tablespoon of a mild dishwashing detergent (see Recommended Basic Products) in 1 gallon water. With a damp cloth or sponge, wipe off the garment. Allow it to air dry before putting it away.

Best

Spray the garment with **Formula 409 All Purpose Cleaner** (The Clorox Company), only on the soiled spots. Rinse well with a cloth or sponge dipped in clear water.

Read manufacturer's cautions and warnings before using any product.

Other Products Tested

Fantastik Multi-Surface Spray Cleaner (Texize Chemicals Company)—pump spray; removes all but stubborn stains; must be washed off immediately.

Shoes

For centuries the universal basic material for shoes has been leather, but recently other materials such as fabric, plastic, and straw have gained in popularity. Whatever the upper part of the shoe is made of, the inner and outer soles usually are made from a synthetic or composition material, or wood.

Fabric

Fabric shoes can be made of durable canvas or duck, as in sneakers or casual slip-ons, or more dressy fabrics such as cotton, linen, satin, silk, and nylon. Some fabric shoes are machine washable, some are hand washable, and some may only be spot cleaned.

Do's

- Test shoe uppers for colorfastness in an inconspicuous place before cleaning with water or solvents.
- Treat spots on nonwashable fabric shoes with spot removers.
- Remove dirty smudges from nonwashable shoes with an artgum eraser.
- Lift off a fresh grease spot from a nonwashable fabric shoe by sprinkling the spot with cornstarch; allow it to soak up grease for a few minutes; brush cornstarch away.
- Treat grass stains, oil, or heavily soiled areas with a prewash spot and stain remover, or a bit of liquid laundry detergent on washable fabric shoes.
- Machine wash only sneaker-type shoes with rubber or plastic soles and no leather or suede trim.
- Use a shoe shampoo to clean nonimmersible, washable shoes.

Don'ts

- **Do not** machine dry washable shoes—the heat can damage the soles and wet shoes can shrink.
- **Do not** immerse rope trimmed shoes in water.
- **Do not** immerse shoes that have composition soles or insoles.

Fastest, Cheapest, and Best

Machine-washable shoes are quickly cleaned using an all-purpose detergent (see Laundry). Pretreat any spots or stains and air dry to prevent shrinkage or damage to the soles.

Kiwi Sneaker Shampoo (The Kiwi Polish Company Pty. Ltd.) is an excellent product for cleaning nonimmersible, washable shoes. Shake well, invert the bottle, and apply the foam to the shoe fabric with the sponge applicator on the top of the container, scrubbing in well. Allow to penetrate for a few minutes, blot with a dry, clean cloth, and allow to dry at room temperature. Rinse the applicator with water after each use.

As an all-over cleaner for nonwashable fabric shoes, nothing beats **Absorene** (Absorene Manufacturing Co., Inc.). Knead a small portion of this dough-like substance until it is soft and apply to the shoe surface with light, even strokes, in one direction only. Rework the cleaner periodically to absorb the soil.

Other Products Tested

Premier Sneaker Cleaner (Premier Dye & Polish Co., Inc.)—foam; built-in applicator on bottle top; very good cleaner and stain remover for washable shoes.

Leather and Vinyl

Commonly used leathers for shoe tops include side leather (cowhide), calf, kid, sheep, reptile, horsehide (cordovan), kangaroo, pig, deer, and occasionally ostrich. Sheepskin often is made into slippers and linings. Patent leather is cowhide coated with varnish or enamel for a special finish. Many shoes that appear to be leather today actually are made from synthetic materials such as vinyl.

Do's

- Clean leather shoes and boots regularly to protect and clean the leather.
- Brush off any mud with a stiff brush before cleaning.
- Remove soil from leather shoes with foam made from pure soap or saddle soap. Apply polish after they dry.
- Wipe patent leather shoes with a damp cloth.
- Soften and recondition damaged shoes with saddle soap.
- Rub on a solution of equal parts water and vinegar to remove salt marks from leather—then polish.
- Stuff shoes with paper if they become wet, allow them to dry naturally, redampen with warm water, and apply glycerin with a soft cloth.

Don't

- **Do not** dry wet shoes in direct heat—this will dry out and stiffen the shoes.

Shoes

Fastest

Use **The Tannery** (Missouri Hickory Corp.) for quick cleaning of smooth leather and vinyl shoes and boots of any color. Brush away the surface soil with a stiff brush; check to see the leather is colorfast on the instep of the shoe, then spray the aerosol foam cleaner over the shoe, rubbing in with a damp sponge. When dry, buff the shoes with a soft cloth. Usually no polish is required because the cleaner leaves a good shine.

Esquire Spray Shine (Knomark Inc.), with lanolin, can be purchased to match your shoes' color, and is a quick way to restore the shine to leather and vinyl shoes and boots. After they have been brushed free of soil, place the shoes on a newspaper and spray with the polish. Allow to dry for about 5 minutes. Buff to a high gloss with a soft cloth or shoe brush. Do not use on new, unpolished shoes.

Cheapest

The least expensive saddle soap is the cheapest product for cleaning leather shoes. Apply it with a damp cloth or sponge, create a lather, wipe, and stuff the shoes with paper to dry.

Best

Clean and condition wet or dry leather shoes or boots with **Fiebing's Saddle Soap** (Fiebing Chemical Company). Apply the soap with a damp sponge, working the lather well into the leather. Stuff the shoes with paper to help retain their shape, and dry away from direct heat. The leather will be soft and can be buffed to a beautiful, soft shine.

A very fine dressing for patent leather or high-gloss vinyl shoes of any color is **Kiwi Patent & Vinyl** (The Kiwi Polish Company Pty. Ltd.). Apply the cleaner/polish over the shoe and buff dry with a soft cloth. Available in liquid form with built-on applicator head and as an aerosol foam.

The best product for restoring shine to leather shoes and boots is **Esquire Boot Polish** (Knomark Inc.). Available in many colors, this paste polish contains lanolin and waxes that both soften and restore moisture as well as give a mirror-like shine. Apply with a piece of cloth or polishing applicator, allow to dry, and then buff vigorously for a high shine.

Kiwi Shoe White (The Kiwi Polish Company Pty. Ltd.) is the best polish for white leather shoes. Apply only after the soil has been removed from the leather with a sponge wrung out in a warm soapsuds solution and the shoes are completely dry. Use the built-on applicator head to apply the polish, let dry, and buff to a low gloss with a soft cloth.

Other Products Tested

CLEANERS/CONDITIONERS. Plastic & Leather Cleaner (Stanley Home Products, Inc.)—aerosol; very good cleaner/conditioner; must be worked in with a sponge; works on all colors of leather; soft shine.

The Leather Works (Knomark Inc.)—aerosol foam; very good cleaner/conditioner; must be worked in with sponge; works for all colors of leather; leaves soft shine.
Kiwi Spray Shine (The Kiwi Polish Company Pty. Ltd.)—aerosol; very good cleaner/conditioner; works for all colors of leather; soft shine.
Kiwi Saddle Soap (The Kiwi Polish Company Pty. Ltd.)—paste; very good cleaner/conditioner; works for all colors of leather.
Turtle Wax Instant Saddle Soap (Turtle Wax, Inc.)—aerosol foam; very good cleaner/conditioner; works for all colors of leather.

POLISHES. **Hollywood Sani-White** (Hollywood Shoe Polish, Inc.)—liquid; very good polish for white shoes.
Kiwi Scuff Magic (The Kiwi Polish Company Pty. Ltd.)—liquid; has self-applicator; good polish; available in many colors.
Kiwi Liquid Wax (The Kiwi Polish Company Pty. Ltd.)—liquid; has self-applicator; good polish; available in many colors.

Suide

Suede can be made from calf, kid, cowhide, or pigskin, with the napped finish created by buffing the inner surface.

Do's

- Remove dirt or grit from suede shoes with a fine-wire or short-bristled brush.
- Remove dirty marks from suede shoes with an artgum eraser.
- Restore the nap on suede shoes by rubbing them gently with a piece of fine sandpaper or use a stiff wire brush.
- Give black suede shoes a facelift by applying a sponge slightly moistened with cool, black coffee—rub in gently.
- Stuff suede shoes with paper if they become wet and allow them to dry naturally.

Don't

- **Do not** dry wet shoes in direct heat—this will dry out and stiffen the shoes.

Cheapest

Use an artgum eraser or emery board to clean suede shoes inexpensively.

Best

A new product that is excellent for cleaning suede shoes is **Suede Stone** (Canden Company). This rubber-like bar acts like a gentle pumice to remove stains and spots, and the package also contains a special block for raising the nap. Apply dry for average spots or wet for stubborn spots and rub away the mark without damaging the suede. Suede Stone also is good for suede garments.

Sweaters

With the use of more synthetic fibers and special finishes, these knitted garments have become easier to care for. Sweaters can be knit from a variety of fibers or fiber blends. Natural fibers commonly used are wool, cashmere, angora, cotton, and silk. Synthetic fibers include the acrylics (Orlon and Acrilan are two well-known brand names) and nylon. Wool, cashmere, and angora sweaters usually can be dry-cleaned or hand washed if you use extreme care. Some fabrics have special finishes that make them shrinkproof and moth-proof. Synthetic fiber sweaters can be hand or machine washed. The care label gives specific washing instructions. For other procedures to use on your sweaters, also see the chapters on the fabrics from which they are made; also see Laundry.

Do's

- Before hand washing a wool sweater, trace around it on a large piece of paper to record its dimensions so you can reshape it to the proper measurements as it dries.
- Use cool water and a cold water laundry detergent when washing wool and cashmere sweaters to prevent shrinkage.
- Dissolve the laundry detergent completely in the wash water before adding the sweater.
- Hand wash sweaters of any fabric gently, squeezing the suds through the sweater rather than rubbing or twisting.
- Rinse the sweater thoroughly and gently squeeze out excess water.
- Roll the damp sweater in a bath towel and gently knead out the excess moisture.
- Block the sweater to size, using the paper outline over a dry towel, and let dry, turning the sweater over once.
- Use a cold water detergent in cool water or a liquid dishwashing detergent in warm water when you hand wash synthetic-fiber sweaters.
- Use a light duty or all-purpose detergent for machine-washable sweaters.
- Use a delicate cycle when machine washing sweaters.
- If machine drying, use a delicate or low-heat setting.
- Turn sweaters inside out when machine washing to help prevent fuzz balls.
- Try removing existing fuzz balls by rubbing the sweater with very fine sandpaper, or an emery board, or shave off the balls with an electric shaver.
- Add 2 tablespoons of glycerin to 2½ to 3 gallons lukewarm rinse water when hand washing a wool sweater to make it soft and help eliminate the wool "itch."

Don'ts

- **Do not** use soap to wash wool sweaters—the alkaline content can damage wool fibers.
- **Do not** soak a sweater more than 5 minutes before washing.
- **Do not** lift a sweater with the full weight of the water in it—this can cause stretching.
- **Do not** dry hand-washed sweaters in sunlight or direct heat.
- **Do not** hang sweaters on hangers to dry—this will stretch them out of shape.

Fastest and Best

Any sweater can be laundered more quickly by hand than by machine and **Liquid Woolite** (Boyle-Midway Inc.) does the job fastest and best. Add 2 capfuls of the detergent to 1 gallon cold water, swish it around to dissolve, and then add the sweater, letting it soak about 3 minutes before washing. Do not rub or twist. Rinse well, blot out the excess moisture in a towel, and dry flat, blocking the sweater to size if necessary.

       Machine Wash Woolite (Boyle-Midway Inc.), a granular, cold water detergent, is the best product for machine washing any sweater.

Cheapest

It costs very little to add ½ tablespoon ammonia to a dishwashing detergent solution (see Recommended Basic Products) when hand washing a soiled sweater. The ammonia helps remove the soil without harsh rubbing.

Other Products Tested

HAND OR MACHINE WASH. Carbona Cold Water Wash (Carbona Products Company)—liquid; high suds; cold water only; very good performance; clean smell.
Handle With Care (The Drackett Company)—liquid; high suds; cold or lukewarm water; good performance; clean smell.

HAND WASH ONLY. Dermassage Dishwashing Liquid (Colgate-Palmolive Company)—liquid; high suds; very good in warm water; pleasant almond odor.
Dove Dishwashing Liquid (Lever Brothers Company)—liquid; high suds; very good in warm water; pleasant odor.
Joy (Procter & Gamble)—liquid; high suds; very good in warm water; pleasant odor.
Ajax Dishwashing Liquid (Colgate-Palmolive Company)—liquid; high suds; very good in warm water; pleasant, fresh odor.
Ivory Liquid (Procter & Gamble)—liquid; high suds; very good in warm water; pleasant, fresh odor.
Instant Fels Dishwashing Soap (Purex Corporation)—liquid; high suds; good in warm water; moderate odor.
Gentle Fels (Purex Corporation)—liquid; medium suds; good in warm water; pleasant odor.

Eyeglasses

Lenses are available in glass or plastic. Each has its own particular advantages, but both can be cleaned in much the same manner.

Do's

- Use a specially treated lens tissue to polish lenses when water is not available.
- Handle the frames only.
- Use both hands to put on and take off eyewear to prevent fingerprints on the lenses.
- Keep your eyewear in a case when not in use.
- Clean frames occasionally with a soft brush dipped in soap and water.
- Dry eyeglasses with a soft, lint-free cloth.

Don'ts

- **Do not** use any paper products, such as tissues or paper towels, to clean lenses.
- **Do not** wipe lenses that are dry or dusty.
- **Do not** lay eyewear face down with the lenses touching another surface.
- **Do not** allow eyeglasses to be unprotected in your pocket or purse.

Fastest and Cheapest

Fog the lenses with your breath, or place a few drops of water on each side of the lens. Wipe dry with a soft, lint-free cloth.

Best

For plastic lenses, spray a drop of **Duriklens Plastic Lens Cleaner** (Benson Optical Company) on each side of the lens; use **Sparklens Lens Cleaner** (Benson Optical Company) for glass lenses. Wipe dry with a clean, soft cloth. Both products are antistatic and anti-fogging.

Other Products Tested

Sparkle Glass Cleaner (A. J. Funk & Co.)—pump spray; cleans well; rather cumbersome for cleaning eyewear.

Windex Glass Cleaner (The Drackett Company)—pump spray; cleans, but may leave smudges; awkward for eyewear.

Hairbrushes and Combs

Combs and brushes need to be cleaned to prevent redepositing oily residue and other soil picked up from previous usages on the hair.

Do's

- Clean combs and brushes at least once a week.
- Remove loose hair from combs and brushes after each use and before washing them.
- Soak in the cleaning solution at least 10 minutes, then scrub with a nail brush.
- Comb the brush to remove any soil, then brush the comb to get out any deposits between the teeth.
- Rinse combs and brushes under running water, shake off excess moisture, and dry, turning over occasionally.
- Add 1 tablespoon ammonia to boost effectiveness of a cleaning solution, except for plastic combs and brushes.
- Boil nylon and metal combs and all-nylon brushes to sterilize them if necessary.
- Sanitize combs and brushes made of bone or hard rubber, and hairbrushes with natural bristles, with alcohol or a disinfectant spray.
- Soak combs or brushes in a tall jar when cleaning them.

Don't

- **Do not** add ammonia to a solution used to clean plastic combs and brushes—it can soften the plastic.

Fastest

Soak and clean combs and brushes in a warm soapsuds solution made with a few drops of a liquid dishwashing detergent (see Recommended Basic Products).

Cheapest and Best

Combs and brushes can be cheaply and effectively cleaned with a baking soda solution. Add 3 tablespoons baking soda (see Recommended Basic Products) to 1 quart warm water and let them soak for at least 10 minutes, then rinse. The baking soda loosens oily deposits so they can be easily brushed away; it also leaves a fresh, clean odor.

Read manufacturer's cautions and warnings before using any product.

Jewelry

Some jewelry is made of precious gems and metals, but a great deal of jewelry worn today is costume, fashioned from imitation gems, plastic, wood, and cheaper metals, which can also be plated with more expensive metal.

Do's

- Store jewelry (except pearls) in plastic bags to reduce tarnish and to protect it from dust, lint, and moisture.
- Check the clasps, prongs, and guard chains of jewelry before wearing it.
- Clean pieces that are not immersible—those glued instead of set in prongs—by wiping them with a soft cloth or damp cloth and buffing them dry.
- Clean immersible fine jewelry with a liquid commerical preparation or by giving it a bath in warm soapsuds.
- Add sudsy or clear ammonia to warm soapy solutions when cleaning metal and precious stone jewelry.
- Close or cover drains with a strainer when you clean jewelry at the sink.
- Have expensive jewelry periodically checked by a professional to remove stubborn dirt and to ensure prongs don't weaken so much that stones slip out of their settings.

Don'ts

- **Do not** pile jewelry together in a jewel box—harder stones will scratch softer stones and metals.
- **Do not** allow jewelry to soak for long periods of time in cleaning solutions.
- **Do not** use alcohol- or ammonia-based solutions on pearls or plated jewelry.
- **Do not** immerse jewelry not set in prongs.
- **Do not** immerse turquoise or opals.

Costume

For popular wear, synthetic or manufactured gems outnumber real ones. Glass is used to make transparent "paste" gems such as sapphires, rubies, or diamonds. Simulated pearls are glass beads dipped in a solution of sea scales and lacquer. There are all sorts of "fun" jewelry such as beads, wood carved into pendants, and jewelry made with ceramic glazes on metal. Most costume jewelry requires little cleaning. To find specific methods and products for your pieces, also see the chapters that describe how to clean the materials from which the jewelry is made.

Do's

- See general **Do's** and **Don'ts** under Jewelry.
- Wipe the piece with a damp cloth or scrub paste jewels—but not plastic—with a soft toothbrush dipped in ammonia.
- Wipe electroplated metal carefully to avoid wearing off the plating.
- Polish simulated pearls with a damp cloth.

Don'ts

- **Do not** use ammonia on plastic.
- **Do not** immerse simulated pearls in any liquid.

Pearl

An organic product, a pearl is composed of lime and an animal substance formed around an irritating particle that enters a mussel, oyster, or clam. This same material, mother of pearl, lines the mollusk's shell. Pearls may be white, pink, rose, yellow, cream, golden, blue, or black. *Mother of pearl* is commonly used for buttons, combs, compacts, and handles for tableware. *Cultured pearl* refers to the bead formed when humans place a mother-of-pearl bead inside a pearl oyster; cultured pearls sometimes have thin coatings that can wear through over time.

Do's

- See general **Do's** and **Don'ts** under Jewelry.
- Wear pearls often—air and natural skin oils help maintain the luster.
- Protect pearls from dust, cosmetics, perfume, and perspiration, which can make them dull.
- Occasionally wash real and cultured pearls, but not mother of pearl, in mild, warm soapsuds and carefully dry them.
- Wipe pearls with a soft cloth or dry chamois after each wearing to remove perspiration that can cause pearls to change color or decompose.
- Have a pearl necklace restrung periodically to keep the string from breaking and to keep the pearls from rubbing against each other.

Don'ts

- **Do not** allow sharp objects, heat, or acid to come in contact with pearls.
- **Do not** keep pearls in an airtight container for long periods of time.
- **Do not** immerse mother of pearl.

Fastest, Cheapest, and Best

Give real and cultured pearls an occasional bath in **Ivory Snow** (Procter & Gamble), a natural soap that dissolves in lukewarm water and will not damage pearls. After gently washing the piece, rinse it and carefully dry it with a soft cloth. A dry chamois or all-cotton T-shirt will not scratch the pearls; for necklaces, softly rub the whole surface of each pearl right down to the knot to remove dust and perspiration. Following the bath and buffing, allow the pearls to air dry before storing them so moisture on the string and knots will evaporate.

Precious Metal

Fine jewelry is made of gold, platinum, or silver; often these metals are combined with other metals to form more durable, more tarnish resistant, or less expensive alloys. Solid gold and pure silver are too soft for use in jewelry. Gold is measured in *carats:* 24 carats denotes pure gold, with jewelry created in 18, 14, 12, and 10 carats, copper comprising the remaining parts. Sterling silver is 92½% silver, 7½% copper.

Do's

- See general **Do's** and **Don'ts** under Jewelry.
- Remove light soil and fingerprints from these metals with a damp cloth and buff dry.
- Wash platinum and silver pieces that become greasy or sticky in a mild soap or dishwashing detergent solution and shine with a soft cloth.
- Store silver jewelry in specially treated bags or rolls that help prevent tarnishing, or seal the pieces in plastic bags.
- Wear silver jewelry frequently to help prevent tarnish and to develop a satiny finish over time.
- Use a metal polish on gold when it begins to look dull.
- Clean the back of a ring setting each time you clean the front.
- Buff away the smudges and fingerprints on platinum with a dry chamois or soft cloth; shine platinum with dry baking soda or flour applied with a soft cloth.

Don'ts

- **Do not** rub hard when cleaning or polishing jewelry that is filled or plated with the precious metals—you can wear through the thin coating.
- **Do not** allow gold-filled or -plated objects to remain in contact with perspiration—it can damage the surface.
- **Do not** wear rubber gloves to polish silver pieces—rubber promotes tarnishing—wear plastic gloves instead.
- **Do not** allow gold jewelry to come into contact with mercury, as it damages the metal.
- **Do not** immerse pieces that use cement in their settings rather than prongs—soaking will loosen the adhesive.

Fastest

To clean intricately shaped gold articles or other immersible pieces, use **Hagerty Jewel Clean** (W. J. Hagerty & Sons, Ltd., Inc.). Place the piece into the handy basket provided; lower it into the jar for a few minutes, remove, and drip dry on a soft cloth or buff dry. The results are excellent.

Nevr-Dull Magic Wadding Polish (The George Basch Co.) is the fastest product for cleaning silver. Rub a piece of the chemically treated wadding over the surface to eliminate tarnish. Buff with a soft cloth to bring up a beautiful shine. Return the wadding to the can for future use.

Cheapest

Any immersible piece can be soaked in a solution of 1 tablespoon sudsy ammonia (see Recommended Basic Products) and 1 cup warm water for 5 minutes. Scrub with a soft brush, rinse with warm water, and pat dry.

A cheap way to clean silver is to combine three parts baking soda and one part water to form a paste; rub the paste on the surface gently, rinse, and buff with a soft cloth. Use a soft, dry brush to remove any remnant of the paste.

An inexpensive recipe for cleaning gold is to mix 1 teaspoon of cigarette ashes with enough water to form a paste. Rub the paste onto the gold surface with a soft cloth, rinse, and buff dry with a chamois. If there is no smoker in the house, baking soda also will work.

Best

Stanley Jewelry Cleaner (Stanley Home Products, Inc.) is the best product for cleaning gold. Pour the liquid into a small bowl, submerge the jewelry for about 10 minutes, rinse in clear water, and pat dry.

Goddard's Long Term Silver Polish (S. C. Johnson & Son, Inc.) is the best product for silver jewelry. Shake before applying the liquid with a soft cloth. Rinse off the piece and polish lightly with a soft cloth.

Other Products Tested

Tarni-Shield Silver Cleaner (3M)—liquid; excellent performance; contains tarnish retardant; soft shine; strong odor.
Tarn-X (Jelmar Co.)—liquid; instant tarnish remover; rinse immediately under hot water; little shine; strong odor.
Parsons' Sudsy Detergent Ammonia (Armour-Dial Inc.)—liquid; soak jewelry in full-strength liquid; excellent performance; strong odor.
International Silver Polish (International Silver Company)—liquid; moderate tarnish remover that requires rubbing; high shine; pleasant odor.

Precious Stone

Many stones are set in fine jewelry, from hard crystalline minerals such as diamonds, rubies, jade, and emeralds, to softer, porous substances like coral, opals, and turquoise. How you clean each gem depends on its unique properties, but different general rules apply to crystalline and porous stones.

Jewelry

Do's

- See general **Do's** and **Don'ts** under Jewelry.
- Use a cotton swab dipped in alcohol to clean around the settings of precious stones.
- Clean a piece with more than one kind of stone by following the method you use for the most delicate stone.
- Remove stubborn dirt on crystalline gems with an old, soft toothbrush or mascara brush.
- Clean regularly worn diamond rings at least once a month to remove accumulated grease film.
- Swab diamonds with isopropyl alcohol to remove oil.
- Clean jade pieces by buffing regularly with a soft cloth or quick bath in a cleaning solution.
- Dip a toothpick in olive oil to restore the luster to dried-out emeralds or jade—only use this method if the piece will not be resold, as the stone may darken.

Don'ts

- **Do not** soak porous opals that may have been dyed; the color may bleed in liquids.
- **Do not** immerse turquoise, ivory, porous cameos, mirror-back or foil-back stones.

Fastest and Cheapest

Wipe nonimmersible jewelry with a soft cloth or chamois to remove smudges and restore its shine. A slightly damp cloth can be used on stubborn dirt. Immersible jewelry can be buffed with a cloth or chamois too, but the cheapest way of restoring the gem's sparkle is to add a few drops of sudsy ammonia (see Recommended Basic Products) to warm water in a small cup and soak the jewelry for 5 minutes. Scrub harder finishes with a small, soft brush, rinse clean under warm water, and pat dry for a sparkling clean finish.

Best

Nonimmersible jewelry responds to baking soda rubbed over the surface with a soft cloth. Brush the soda away and buff for a high shine.

Hagerty Jewel Clean (W. J. Hagerty & Sons, Ltd., Inc.) is the best cleaner for immersible jewelry. This liquid comes with its own plastic dipping tray, which makes it convenient as well as quick to use. Using the handy dipping basket, submerge the piece in the jar for a few minutes. No rinsing is required; simply pat dry for a sparkling shine.

Other Products Tested

IMMERSIBLE STONES. Stanley Jewelry Cleaner (Stanley Home Products, Inc.)—liquid; excellent cleaner; no brush or dipping basket; moderate odor.

Wigs and Hairpieces

Two types of wigs are available: human hair and synthetic fiber.

Do's
- Wash your wig or hairpiece after every third or fourth wearing, or more frequently in the summer.
- Gently hand wash synthetic wigs or hairpieces when dirty.
- Remove excess moisture after washing by rolling in a towel and gently kneading. Shake out and allow to dry naturally.
- Allow perspiration to dry before storing a wig or hairpiece.

Don'ts
- **Do not** put a wig in the clothes dryer.
- **Do not** dry a wig on a headform—this may stretch the band.

Human Hair

Human hair wigs and hairpieces are not as resilient as the synthetic ones. Extra care must be given to ensure longevity and restore the wig's or hairpiece's good looks.

Do's
- Remove all tangles from long hair wigs or hairpieces before washing.
- Use only the mildest shampoos—others may ruin the backing.

Don'ts
- **Do not** wash the wig or hairpiece in hot water.
- **Do not** blot a human hair wig or lay it flat to dry.

Fastest and Cheapest

Wash the wig or hairpiece with a mild baby shampoo in cool water. Rinse well by swishing it in cool water. Place it on a propped broom handle or something that will suspend it off any surface—it cannot lie flat to dry. When it's completely dry, return it to the form and comb or brush it out. To restyle, slightly dampen only the strands (not the backing) and set on rollers as you would your own hair.

Best

Squeeze just a dab of **Amino Pon Concentrate Shampoo** (Redken Laboratories, Inc.) onto your hand. Gently work it into the wet wig or hairpiece. Use a very small amount as it is highly concentrated. Run it under cool water, then rinse it well to be sure all of the shampoo is out. Gently press against the hair to remove excess water; set up to dry. When it has dried thoroughly, dampen the strands with a wet comb and style the hair.

Synthetic

Synthetic wigs and hairpieces are easier to care for than your own hair. The style is permanent, so little work is needed to keep them looking their best.

Do's

- Wash the wig or hairpiece in cool water.
- Blot it dry with a towel.
- Place it on a towel or rack to dry.

Don'ts

- **Do not** wear your wig or hairpiece or return it to its form until it is completely dry.
- **Do not** use a harsh shampoo or soap on your wig or hairpiece—it can damage the backing.

Fastest, Cheapest, and Best

Hand wash your synthetic wig or hairpiece in a mild baby shampoo and cool water. Rinse it several times to remove all soap residue. Lightly blot with a towel and gently comb any severe tangles. When it is dry, return it to its form and comb or brush it back into style.

Metals

Aluminum

Aluminum turns up in many places around the house: screens and storm doors; window frames; pails; garden tools; siding; pots, pans, and baking utensils (also see Cookware).

Do's
- Handle carefully—aluminum objects dent or bend rather easily.
- Store aluminum objects in a dry place—moisture can cause white spots to form.
- Wash satin-finish aluminum objects in a detergent solution, using a steel wool soap pad for stubborn dirt.

Don't
- **Do not** allow aluminum objects to stand in sudsy water for long periods—this will cause the metal to discolor.

Fastest

Nevr-Dull Magic Wadding Polish (The George Basch Co.) makes quick work of polishing dull aluminum. A small piece of this batting-like substance, which comes premoistened with a cleaning and polishing agent, is all that is needed to bring up the shine on aluminum surfaces. Rub surface with a small piece of the product and buff with a dry, soft cloth.

Cheapest

Baking soda (see Recommended Basic Products) is the cheapest way to clean and polish aluminum surfaces. Sprinkle some powder on the wet surface, making a paste, and use a synthetic scouring pad (see Tools of the Trade) to spread it. A rinse and quick buffing will give a bright finish.

Best

Cameo Aluminum and Stainless Steel Cleaner (Purex Corporation) produces the highest sheen on polished aluminum. After washing the aluminum product, work this mild abrasive powder into a paste on the wet aluminum surface and rub in with a moist cloth or sponge. Rinse well and buff dry for an incredible shine.

Other Products Tested

Soft Scrub Cleanser (The Clorox Company)—mild liquid abrasive; easily removes stains and brings up a good shine; pleasant odor.

Bon Ami Cleaning Powder (Faultless Starch/Bon Ami Company)—mild abrasive powder; very good cleaner; good shine.

Rubin-Brite Metal Polish (David Rubin)—cream to be used with ordinary flour; very good cleaner/polish.

Noxon Liquid 7 Metal Polish (Boyle-Midway Inc.)—liquid; very good cleaner; little shine; moderate odor.

Duro Aluminum Jelly (Woodhill Permatex)—liquid jelly; very good cleaner; dull, lifeless shine; strong odor.

Glass Plus (Texize Chemicals Company)—spray liquid; moderate cleaner; good shine; moderate odor.

Brass

Brass tarnishes when exposed to air and benefits from a good cleaner/polish. Some ornamental brass objects have a lacquer finish for protection. Also see Fireplaces—Tools for products and procedures to use on brass.

Do's

- Dust lacquered brass regularly and wipe occasionally with a damp sponge.
- Wash brass objects in warm soapsuds before applying a cleaner/polish, scrubbing with a synthetic scouring pad to remove spots and stains.
- Always rewash in warm soapsuds after using an acid-base cleaner to prevent rapid discoloration.
- Wipe brass objects that can't be immersed in water with a specially treated cleaning cloth or wadding polish.
- Strip cracked and peeling lacquer from coated brass objects with a solution of baking soda and boiling water (1 cup soda to 2 gallons water). Let the article stand in the water until it cools and peel off the lacquer. Have the piece relacquered or clean and polish as for other brass.
- Clean fire-stained andirons by dipping fine (00) steel wool in cooking oil and rubbing gently. Apply a polish to bring up the shine.

Don't

- **Do not** use brass cleaners on lacquered brass.

Fastest

Nevr-Dull Magic Wadding Polish (The George Basch Co.) is the fastest method of cleaning and polishing brass objects. A quick rub with the premoistened wadding removes tarnish and brings up an excellent shine.

Cheapest

A paste made of 1 tablespoon each of salt, flour, and vinegar is the most economical method for cleaning brass. Applied with a cloth, the paste is very effective in making tarnish disappear and the shine reappear. Dipping a cut lemon in salt and then rubbing it on the brass surface is another quick and inexpensive way to clean brass. Be sure to wash the brass in warm soapsuds afterward and buff dry to bring up the shine.

Best

Wright's Brass Cleaner & Polish (J. A. Wright & Co.) is the best product for cleaning brass. This liquid cleaner has an ammonia odor but is easy to use and gives excellent results. Apply with a soft cloth, rub, and let dry; polish with a dry cloth.

Other Products Tested

Brasso (The R. T. French Co.)—liquid; excellent cleaner/polish; strong odor.

Noxon Liquid 7 Metal Polish (Boyle-Midway Inc.)—creamy liquid; excellent cleaner/polish; moderate odor.

Rubin-Brite Metal Polish (David Rubin)—cream to be used with flour; excellent cleaner/polish with tarnish retardant; moderate odor.

Twinkle Copper Cleaner Kit (The Drackett Company)—paste; excellent cleaner/polish; pleasant odor.

Bar Keepers Friend Cleanser & Polish (SerVaas Laboratories, Inc.)—powder; excellent cleaner/polish; little odor.

Cameo Copper Cleaner (Purex Corporation)—powder; excellent cleaner with tarnish retardant; little odor.

Revere Ware Instant Copper Cleaner (Revere Copper & Brass, Incorporated)—liquid; excellent cleaner/polish with tarnish retardant; pleasant odor.

Vigilant's Copper and Brass Polishing Cloth (Vigilant Products Co., Inc.)—chemically treated cloth; fast cleaner/polish; very good performance.

Hagerty Heavy-Duty Copper Brass & Metal Polish (W. J. Hagerty & Sons, Ltd., Inc.)—liquid; good cleaner; medium bright shine; moderate odor.

Zud (Boyle-Midway Inc.)—powder; good heavy duty cleaner; medium bright shine; little odor.

Tarni-Shield Copper & Brass Cleaner (3M)—liquid; moderate cleaner with tarnish retardant; medium shine; strong odor.

Copper Glo (American Cyanamid Company)—powder; moderate cleaner with tarnish retardant; medium shine; little odor.

Goddard's Long Shine Brass & Copper Polish (S. C. Johnson & Son, Inc.)—liquid; moderate cleaner; medium shine; strong odor.

Read manufacturer's cautions and warnings before using any product.

Bronze

Bronze is an alloy of copper and tin, possessing qualities of hardness superior to either of those metals. Used for ornamental as well as useful objects, it will sometimes have a protective lacquer finish.

Do's

- Read labels to see if a product can be used on lacquered or antique-finish bronze.
- Wash in a detergent or soap solution to remove dirt and film, dry thoroughly, and buff with a soft cloth.
- Dust lacquered pieces regularly and wipe occasionally with a damp cloth.
- Have a lacquer finish redone by a competent jeweler if it begins to crack or peel.

Don'ts

- **Do not** attempt to clean lacquered objects with a commercial polish.
- **Do not** polish with a heavy hand—some bronze objects are not solid and rubbing can wear through the surface bronze.

Fastest

Of all the cleaners, the fastest and easiest is **Nevr-Dull Magic Wadding Polish** (The George Basch Co.), a chemically treated cotton material that comes in a can. Pull off a small piece of wadding and rub the bronze surface to remove film and grime. Almost instantaneously, the tarnish will be wiped from the surface onto the wadding. A brisk buffing with a soft cloth brings out the natural warm glow of the metal. The wadding can be returned to the can to be used again.

Cheapest

By tapping supplies you have on hand, you can make an excellent cleaner for a fraction of the cost of a commercial product. Making a paste of 1 tablespoon each of flour, vinegar, and salt, apply it to the bronze surface with a soft cloth. It will immediately begin to cut through the film, making the tarnish and grime disappear. Because the cleaner contains some acid, wash the object in warm soapsuds, rinse, and buff to a soft, satiny sheen with a dry cloth.

Best

Noxon Liquid 7 Metal Polish (Boyle-Midway Inc.) is the best bronze cleaner. After shaking the bottle, apply a liberal amount of the liquid to the bronze surface with a soft cloth, remove the discoloration and grimy film with a little rubbing, and leave a clean and bright surface.

Other Products Tested

Rubin-Brite Metal Polish (David Rubin)—cream to be used with flour; excellent cleaner/polish with tarnish retardant; moderate odor.

Wright's Brass Cleaner & Polish (J. A. Wright & Co.)—liquid; very good cleaner with ammonia; medium bright shine; strong odor.

Revere Ware Instant Copper Cleaner (Revere Copper & Brass, Incorporated)—liquid; good to very good cleaner with tarnish retardant; medium bright shine; pleasant odor.

Zud (Boyle-Midway Inc.)—powder; good cleaner for extreme discoloration; use as a paste, rubbing gently to avoid scratching the surface; little odor.

Chromium

Chromium, or chrome as it's commonly called, is an electroplated finish on some other metal. This hard, shiny, nontarnishing plating is used many ways inside and outside the house as well as on cars.

Do's
- Wipe regularly with a damp cloth and buff dry.
- Use a mild detergent solution for heavier soil.
- Use a light hand when polishing—some chrome plating can wear through.
- Rinse salt off as soon as possible to prevent surface damage.
- Remove baked-on spills by rubbing baking soda on the wet surface; rinse; buff dry with a soft cloth.

Don'ts
- **Do not** allow grease and dirt to build up.
- **Do not** use harsh abrasives and steel wool pads—they can scratch through the plating.

Fastest

Cleaning chromium is faster using baking soda (see Recommended Basic Products). Pour some baking soda into a saucer, dip a dry cloth in the soda and rub on the chrome surface. This will remove fingerprints, smudges, and even sticky residue with no further rinsing or wiping.

Cheapest

The least expensive way to clean up greasy film and smudges is to rub the surface with a dry cloth dipped in dry kitchen flour. The results are just as remarkable as with the dry baking soda technique given above.

Read manufacturer's cautions and warnings before using any product.

Best

Stainless Steel Magic (Magic American Chemical Corp.) is the best product for bringing out the sparkle on chrome. Spray this product over the surface, wipe it with the grain of the metal, and then buff dry with a soft cloth. Easy to use, the results are excellent.

Other Products Tested

Nevr-Dull Magic Wadding Polish (The George Basch Co.)—premoistened wadding; excellent cleaner/polish.
Wright's Brass Cleaner & Polish (J. A. Wright & Co.)—liquid; excellent cleaner/polish with ammonia; strong odor.
Klean 'n Shine (S. C. Johnson & Son, Inc.)—aerosol foam; excellent cleaner/polish.
Sparkle Glass Cleaner (A. J. Funk & Co.)—spray liquid; excellent cleaner/polish; pleasant odor.
Window Spray Cleaner (Stanley Home Products, Inc.)—aerosol; excellent cleaner/polish with ammonia; strong odor.
Windex Glass Cleaner (The Drackett Company)—spray liquid; excellent cleaner/polish with ammonia; moderate odor.
Easy-Off Window Cleaner (Boyle-Midway Inc.)—spray liquid; excellent cleaner/polish; moderate odor.
Hagerty Heavy-Duty Copper Brass & Metal Polish (W. J. Hagerty & Sons Ltd., Inc.)—liquid; good to very good cleaner; good shine; moderate odor.
Copper Glo (American Cyanamid Company)—powder; good to very good cleaner; good shine; little odor.
Glass Plus (Texize Chemicals Company)—spray liquid; good to very good cleaner; moderate shine; moderate odor.
Cameo Aluminum and Stainless Steel Cleaner (Purex Corporation)—powder; good cleaner; good shine; pleasant odor.

Copper

Copper is used extensively in homes for decorative and useful objects (also see Cookware—Copper), as well as water pipes and electrical wiring. Available with a bright shine or satin luster, it darkens with use and exposure to air but is easily cleaned and polished.

Do's
- After cleaning articles with an acid-base product, wash them in warm soapsuds to prevent discoloration.
- Use a polish with a tarnish retardant to slow down the tarnishing process.
- Clean and polish copper objects regularly to keep the job easy.
- Dust or wipe lacquered copper with a damp cloth and wipe dry.

Don't
- **Do not** use cleaner/polish products on copper articles covered with protective lacquer.

Fastest

Vigilant's Copper and Brass Polishing Cloth (Vigilant Products Co., Inc.), a chemically treated cloth, is the fastest way of polishing copper objects. Gently rub the tarnished surface with the cloth and then buff to a high shine with another soft, untreated cloth. Never wash the polishing cloth; fold and return it to its plastic bag for another day.

Cheapest

A homemade paste of 1 tablespoon each of salt, vinegar, and flour is an excellent and inexpensive way to clean copper. Rub over the surface, and then wash the object in hot soapy water. Rinse and buff dry for a shiny finish. Also, 2 tablespoons vinegar mixed with 1 tablespoon salt, or a cut lemon dipped in salt and then rubbed over the surface does a good job; just remember to wash, rinse, and buff dry as above.

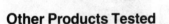

Best

Revere Ware Instant Copper Cleaner (Revere Copper & Brass, Incorporated) rates best as a copper cleaner/polish. Rub on the liquid with a sponge, then wash the object in hot soapy water and buff dry to an admirable shine. This product contains a tarnish retardant and also has a very pleasant peppermint odor.

Other Products Tested

Twinkle Copper Cleaner Kit (The Drackett Company)—paste; excellent cleaner/polish with tarnish retardant; rinse with water only; high shine; pleasant odor.

Bar Keepers Friend Cleanser & Polish (SerVaas Laboratories, Inc.)—powder; excellent cleaner/polish; high shine; little odor.

Wright's Brass Cleaner & Polish (J. A. Wright & Co.)—liquid with ammonia; excellent cleaner/polish; soft shine; moderately strong odor.

Rubin-Brite Metal Polish (David Rubin)—cream to be used with flour; excellent cleaner/polish with tarnish retardant; soft shine; moderate odor.

Zud (Boyle-Midway Inc.)—powder to be sprinkled on wet surface; excellent cleaner/polish; bright shine; little odor.

Noxon Liquid 7 Metal Polish (Boyle-Midway Inc.)—creamy liquid; very good cleaner but hard to polish after drying; medium bright shine; moderate odor.

Tarn-X (Jelmar Co.)—liquid; good fast cleaner; must be rinsed promptly; bright shine; strong odor.

Cameo Copper Cleaner (Purex Corporation)—powder; moderate cleaner with tarnish retardant; bright shine; little odor.

Copper Glo (American Cyanamid Company)—powder; moderately good cleaner with tarnish retardant; medium bright shine; little odor.

Hagerty Heavy-Duty Copper Brass & Metal Polish (W. J. Hagerty & Sons, Ltd., Inc.)—liquid; moderate cleaner; medium bright shine; moderate odor.

Goddard's Long Shine Brass & Copper Polish (S. C. Johnson & Son, Inc.)—liquid; moderate cleaner; medium shine; strong odor.

Tarni-Shield Copper & Brass Cleaner (3M)—liquid; moderate cleaner with tarnish retardant; medium shine; strong odor.

Brasso (The R. T. French Co.)—liquid; moderate cleaner; dull shine; strong odor.

Gold

Gold has a brilliant luster that resists corrosion and tarnish. Usually combined with other metals to add hardness, it is graded by carats; 24 is pure gold, and 18, 14, and 10 carats (also see Jewelry—Precious Metal) are measurements of gold mixed with baser metals like nickel or copper for jewelry. Gold is used in a filled, rolled, or plated finish (also see Flatware and Cutlery), which uses much less gold, is less expensive, but can wear away over a period of time or wear thin from excessive polishing.

Do's

- Remove light soil with a damp cloth—buff dry to restore shine.
- Use a metal polish if the surface begins to look dull.

Don'ts

- **Do not** rub hard when cleaning or polishing gold-filled or -plated objects—you can wear through the thin surface.
- **Do not** allow gold-filled or -plated objects to remain in contact with perspiration and salt—this can damage the surface.

Fastest

Use **Nevr-Dull Magic Wadding Polish** (The George Basch Co.) for quick polishing of larger gold articles. Tear off a small piece of the chemically treated wadding, briskly rub the surface, and complete the task by buffing with a soft cloth.

When cleaning intricately shaped gold articles such as rings or chains, use **Hagerty Jewel Clean** (W. J. Hagerty & Sons, Ltd., Inc.). This product's jar has a dipping basket that lowers into the liquid cleaner; put the jewelry in the basket, submerge for a few minutes, remove, and drip dry on a soft cloth or buff dry. The results are excellent.

Cheapest

If there is a smoker in the house, here is a good way to get rid of ashes and clean gold inexpensively. Place a teaspoon of cigarette ashes in a small bowl, add enough water to make a paste, and using a soft cloth, rub the paste over the gold surface. Rinse and buff dry with a soft cloth or chamois. Baking soda can be substituted for the ashes with equally good results.

Best

Rubin-Brite Metal Polish (David Rubin) is the best product for larger gold surfaces. After applying the cream to the object, remove the dark residue by dipping a cloth in dry kitchen flour and rubbing it over the surface. The job is finished by buffing with a soft cloth to bring up a high shine.

For rings and necklaces or other intricately shaped objects, **Stanley Jewelry Cleaner** (Stanley Home Products, Inc.) is the best. Pour the acidic-smelling liquid into a small bowl, submerge the jewelry for about 10 minutes, rinse in clear water, and pat dry for beautiful results.

Other Products Tested

Hagerty Silver Foam (W. J. Hagerty & Sons, Ltd., Inc.)—paste; excellent cleaner/polish; high shine; moderate odor.

Parsons' Sudsy Detergent Ammonia (Armour-Dial Inc.)—liquid; excellent performance; strong odor. Soak jewelry in equal parts ammonia and lukewarm water for 10 minutes; buff with a soft brush, and let dry.

Iron

Iron is commonly manufactured in two forms, wrought or cast. Wrought iron has a low carbon content, is light gray in color, and is relatively soft. Cast iron is harder and more brittle. Some of the common iron items found around the home include pots and pans (also see Cookware—Cast Iron), grills, lamp bases, furniture, casement window frames, decorative hinges, ornamental objects, and fireplace tools. For additional products and procedures to use on iron objects, also see Fireplaces, Furniture—Metal, and Outdoor Furniture—Wrought Iron.

Do's

- Dust iron surfaces frequently—this is the only routine cleaning required.
- Remove traces of rust by rubbing with an emery cloth or steel wool containing a few drops of turpentine or kerosene.
- Periodically coat unpainted iron surfaces with liquid wax and buff to preserve the highlights of the original finish and prevent rust.
- Remove any rust spots before painting or repainting iron objects.
- Use paint designed especially for iron to protect against further rust.

Don't

- **Do not** allow iron to remain wet or retain moisture, as this causes rust.

Read manufacturer's cautions and warnings before using any product.

Fastest and Cheapest

Most iron objects can be cleaned quickly with a good detergent solution applied with a synthetic scouring pad (see Tools of the Trade) for heavily soiled areas.

Best

Bar Keepers Friend Cleanser & Polish (SerVaas Laboratories, Inc.) is superior in removing rust on iron objects. Sprinkle some of the powder on the rust spot, let stand for half a minute, and then rub with a wet cloth or sponge until the rust or stain disappears. Coat the treated area with liquid wax or iron paint to prevent more rust.

Other Products Tested

Zud (Boyle-Midway Inc.)—powder; similar to Bar Keepers Friend but a bit more abrasive.

Pewter

Pewter is a somewhat soft alloy that comes in either a high-polish finish or a soft satin sheen, both of which do not tarnish readily. For products and procedures to clean pewter flatware, also see Flatware and Cutlery.

Do's

- Wash pewter food containers and flatware immediately after use to prevent stains and pitting.
- Use pewter objects regularly—they will need less polishing.
- Wash frequently with a liquid detergent solution.
- Keep pewter away from hot ranges or extremely hot foods.
- Polish occasionally to restore the shine.

Don'ts

- **Do not** allow acid foods, salt, or salad dressing to linger on pewter.
- **Do not** wash pewter in the dishwasher—it will stain and discolor.
- **Do not** use abrasive cleaners or steel wool pads to clean pewter.

Fastest

Nevr-Dull Magic Wadding Polish (The George Basch Co.) restores the shine quickly on pewter objects. Rub the chemically treated wadding over the surface, then buff with a soft cloth to a beautiful shine.

Cheapest

Save the outer leaves from a head of cabbage and use them to polish pewter. Rub the leaf over the surface of the pewter and then buff with a soft cloth. You'll be amazed at the shine this simple technique gives.

Best

For clean and brightly polished antique pewter, top honors go to **Rubin-Brite Metal Polish** (David Rubin). The cream, with tarnish retardant, is applied with a soft cloth and then wiped off with another cloth dipped in flour. The dark tarnish-laden paste rolls off in tiny balls when the flour mixes with the polish. Finally, a brief buffing will create a beautiful shine.

Other Products Tested

Wright's Brass Cleaner & Polish (J. A. Wright & Co.)—liquid; good cleaner/polish; medium shine; moderately strong odor.

Rainbow Sundry Products Rotten Stone (Empire White Products Co.)—powder to be mixed with cooking oil; good tarnish remover; low luster.

Zud (Boyle-Midway Inc.)—powder; good spot and tarnish remover; with hard rubbing it may scratch the surface; use as a paste.

Gorham Silver Polish (Gorham Division of Textron Inc.)—paste; good cleaner; unable to remove all spots; soft shine.

Brasso (The R. T. French Co.)—liquid; moderately good cleaner; unable to remove all spots; soft shine.

Noxon Liquid 7 Metal Polish (Boyle-Midway Inc.)—liquid; moderately good cleaner; unable to remove all spots; soft shine.

Platinum

One of the most valuable of the precious metals, silvery white platinum is used in jewelry for watch cases, watch fobs, rings, and elegant chains. This heavy, easy-to-work metal resists corrosion and tarnish as well as most acids. Also see Jewelry—Precious Metal.

Do's

- Wipe with a soft cloth to remove smudges and fingerprints.
- Wash in a mild soap or detergent solution if dirty.

Fastest

A dry chamois is the fastest way to buff away smudges and fingerprints on platinum. A soft cloth will also work.

Platinum/Silver

Cheapest

A little dry baking soda (see Recommended Basic Products) on a soft cloth will restore the shiny bright surface of platinum. Substitute ordinary kitchen flour for the soda for equally good results.

Best

When platinum articles become greasy or sticky, wash them in a warm, sudsy solution using a liquid dishwashing detergent (see Recommended Basic Products). Swish around in the suds for a minute, rinse, and buff dry for a beautiful shine.

Other Products Tested

Klean 'n Shine (S. C. Johnson & Son, Inc.)—aerosol; very good cleaner/polish.

Silver

Silver is meant to be used and does not deteriorate with time. When properly cared for, it just gets better as it grows older. With many polishings and much handling, good silver will develop a satiny patina—actually a blending of many tiny scratches that give it an overall luster, sometimes described as a "butler's finish."

Do's

- Take more care when cleaning silver plate—the plating can wear off.
- Use silver objects regularly—this helps reduce tarnish.
- Dust ornamental silver regularly and wash it in a mild soap or detergent.
- Store seldom-used silver in specially treated bags, rolls, chests, or drawers, or seal in plastic wrap to prevent tarnish.
- Wash silver in warm soapsuds, rinse, and dry before using a polish.
- Use an old, soft toothbrush to clean beaded edges and intricate patterns.
- Wash silver after polishing to ensure all of the cleaner is removed.
- Buff with a soft, dry cloth or chamois after polishing and rinsing to bring up the shine.
- Have a jeweler lacquer silver that is used for decorative purposes only, to prevent tarnish.

Don'ts

- **Do not** allow foods containing sulphur (such as eggs), salt, or acid to remain on silver—they will cause stains.
- **Do not** allow silver to touch other objects if washed in the dishwasher.
- **Do not** wear rubber gloves when polishing silver as rubber encourages tarnish; use plastic gloves instead.

Fastest

Nevr-Dull Magic Wadding Polish (The George Basch Co.) is the fastest product for cleaning all types of silver. Rub the chemically treated wadding over the silver surface and watch the tarnish disappear. Buff with a soft cloth to bring up a beautiful shine. The wadding can be returned to the can and used again, which makes this cleaner quite economical.

Cheapest

An easy and inexpensive way to clean silver is with ordinary baking soda (see Recommended Basic Products). Combine three parts soda to one part water to form a paste; using a soft cloth, rub the paste gently on the silver surface. The tarnish disappears rapidly, and after rinsing a quick buff with a soft cloth brings up the shine. The process is quick and easy, there is little mess, no smell, and the results are very good.

Best

Goddard's Long Term Silver Polish (S. C. Johnson & Son, Inc.) is the best product for cleaning silver. Shake well and apply the liquid with a soft cloth. Rinse off ornate pieces or allow to dry on large surfaces. Polish with a soft cloth. The liquid is able to remove heavy tarnish from ornate trays with little effort and leaves a rich, high shine. The polish has a tarnish retardant.

Other Products Tested

Rubin-Brite Metal Polish (David Rubin)—cream to be used with flour; excellent performance; contains tarnish retardant; high shine.
Tarni-Shield Silver Cleaner (3M)—liquid; excellent performance; contains tarnish retardant; high shine; strong odor.
Hagerty Silver Foam (W. J. Hagerty & Sons, Ltd., Inc.)—paste; excellent performance; soft shine; mild odor.
Tarn-X (Jelmar Co.)—liquid; instant tarnish remover; must be rinsed immediately under hot water; little shine; strong odor.
International Silver Polish (International Silver Company)—liquid; moderate tarnish remover that requires rubbing; high shine; pleasant odor.
Gorham Silver Polish (Gorham Division of Textron Inc.)—paste; moderate tarnish remover that requires heavy rubbing; moderate shine; moderately pleasant odor.
Rokeach Silver Polish (I. Rokeach & Sons, Inc.)—paste; good tarnish remover; moderate shine; pleasant odor.
Wright's Silver Cleaner & Polish (J. A. Wright & Co.)—paste; moderately good tarnish remover; moderate shine; little odor.
Twinkle Silver Polish Kit (The Drackett Company)—paste; fair tarnish remover; contains tarnish retardant; enclosed sponge inadequate; moderately high shine; pleasant odor.
Glass Wax (Gold Seal Co.)—creamy liquid; excellent for light tarnish only; moderate shine; pleasant odor.
Afta Silver Dip (Afta Solvents Corporation)—liquid; moderate tarnish remover; strong odor.
Instant-Dip Silver Cleaner (Lewal Industries, Inc.)—liquid; moderate tarnish remover; strong odor.

Read manufacturer's cautions and warnings before using any product.

Stainless Steel

Stainless steel is a beautiful, strong metal alloy that doesn't tarnish, rust, chip, or break, and needs minimum care. It comes with a satin or high-polish finish. Also see Cookware—Stainless Steel for cleaning procedures and products to use on pots and pans, and Flatware and Cutlery.

Do

- Remove spots with a mild scouring powder and synthetic scrubber or sponge.

Don't

- **Do not** expose stainless steel to acids, acid foods, or salt without rinsing immediately after use, as this can cause pitting or staining.

Fastest

Window Spray Cleaner (Stanley Home Products, Inc.) is the fastest way to clean and polish stainless steel surfaces. Spray and buff dry with a soft cloth for a beautiful shine.

Cheapest

Baking soda (see Recommended Basic Products) brings a shine to stainless steel inexpensively. Sprinkle the soda on the wet surface and scrub with a synthetic scouring pad. Rinse and buff dry with a soft cloth for a sparkling bright surface.

Best

Cameo Aluminum and Stainless Steel Cleaner (Purex Corporation) is the best product for cleaning and shining high-polish stainless steel. Sprinkle the pleasant-smelling powder on the wet surface to form a paste and then gently rub in with a damp sponge to allow the silica polishing agents in the cleaner to bring up the shine. Rinse well and buff dry.

Stainless Steel Magic (Magic American Chemical Corp.) is the best product for satin-finish stainless steel. This product is easy to use and has special additives to eliminate water spotting.

Other Products Tested

Soft Scrub Cleanser (The Clorox Company)—mild liquid abrasive; excellent cleaner/polish; pleasant odor.
Rubin-Brite Metal Polish (David Rubin)—cream to be used with flour; excellent cleaner/polish; high shine; moderate odor.
Gorham's Silver Polish (Gorham Division of Textron Inc.)—paste; good to very good performance; medium shine; moderately pleasant odor.
Revere Ware Stainless Steel Cleaner (Revere Copper & Brass, Incorporated)—liquid;

good to very good performance; medium shine; pleasant odor.

Copper Glo (American Cyanamid Company)—powder; good to very good performance; moderate shine; little odor.

Zud (Boyle-Midway Inc.)—abrasive powder; good cleaner/polish.

Nevr-Dull Magic Wadding Polish (The George Basch Co.)—premoistened wadding; good cleaner/polish; moderately strong odor.

Bon Ami Cleaning Powder (Faultless Starch/Bon Ami Company)—mild scouring powder; good cleaner/polish.

Brillo Steel Wool Soap Pads (Purex Corporation)—rust inhibitor; good cleaner/polish.

S.O.S. Steel Wool Soap Pads (Miles Laboratories, Inc.)—moderate cleaner/polish.

Brasso (The R. T. French Co.)—liquid; moderate cleaner; medium shine; strong odor.

Noxon Liquid 7 Metal Polish (Boyle-Midway Inc.)—creamy liquid; moderate cleaner; medium shine; moderate odor.

Hagerty Heavy-Duty Copper Brass & Metal Polish (W. J. Hagerty & Sons, Ltd., Inc.)—liquid; moderate cleaner; medium shine; moderate odor.

Sparkle Glass Cleaner (A. J. Funk & Co.)—liquid spray; moderate cleaner; medium shine; pleasant odor.

Glass Plus (Texize Chemicals Company)—liquid spray; moderate cleaner; medium shine; moderate odor.

Tin

Tin is commonly used as a coating or liner to protect other metals. Often found on cookware, it comes with either a shiny bright finish or is darkly tinted for better heat retention.

Do's

- Handle carefully; tin will dent fairly easily when dropped.
- Remove crusted-on food with a mild cleaner and synthetic scouring pad.
- Wash in a detergent solution for general cleaning.
- Rinse in clear water and dry thoroughly before storing.
- Remove minor rust spots by rubbing with a cut, raw potato dipped in a mild cleansing powder.
- Loosen burnt-on foods by boiling 1 quart water and 2 teaspoons baking soda in the vessel for 5 minutes.

Don'ts

- **Do not** polish tin cookware—polishing impairs its efficiency when heated.
- **Do not** use abrasive cleaners or steel wool—they can wear through the thin tin plating.

Fastest

Bon Ami Deluxe Polishing Cleanser (Faultless Starch/Bon Ami Company) is the fastest product for removing stubborn soil from tinware. Sprinkle a small amount of this mild cleanser on the damp tin surface and rub with a damp plastic scouring pad (see Tools of the Trade) until loose enough to rinse away.

Cheapest

Less expensive but just as effective is baking soda. Use the method described for Bon Ami Deluxe Polishing Cleanser.

Best

Soft Scrub Cleanser (The Clorox Company), a mild liquid abrasive, is the best product for removing stubborn soil without scratching the thin tin surface. Apply with a damp sponge, rinse well, and dry completely to prevent rust.

Zinc

Zinc generally is used as a coating on other metals to prevent corrosion, but it sometimes appears as tops for counters, tables, and dry sinks.

Do's

- Clean regularly with a hot soapy solution, rinse, and buff dry.
- Use a non-abrasive scouring powder and synthetic scouring pad when tarnish becomes objectionable.

Don't

- **Do not** cut on zinc surfaces with a knife—it is soft and can be scratched easily.

Fastest

Use a liquid dishwashing detergent (see Recommended Basic Products) for routine cleaning. **Bon Ami Deluxe Polishing Cleanser** (Faultless Starch/Bon Ami Company) is a good product to use for fast cleanups of dried-on food, stubborn soil, or light tarnish. Rub in with a damp sponge, rinse, and buff dry.

Cheapest

Baking soda (see Recommended Basic Products) rubbed into the surface with a damp sponge works just as well as the scouring powder, but is a lot cheaper. Rinse and buff dry. Another inexpensive way to remove tarnish is to wipe the surface with vinegar, let stand for 2 minutes, rinse with clear water, and buff dry.

Best

Bar Keepers Friend Cleanser & Polish (SerVaas Laboratories, Inc.) is the best product for removing stains and discolorations from zinc. Dampen the surface, sprinkle the powder onto it, and scrub with a synthetic scouring pad (see Tools of the Trade). Rinse well and buff dry.

Other Products Tested

Soft Scrub Cleanser (The Clorox Company)—mild liquid abrasive; excellent cleaner; pleasant odor.

Nevr-Dull Magic Wadding Polish (The George Basch Co.)—premoistened wadding; excellent cleaner.

Outside the House

Awnings

Do's

- Hose down all awnings occasionally to flush off soot, soil, and mild acids from air pollution and to prevent general deterioration.
- Use a long-handled, soft brush to remove dust and old leaves.
- Clean in the direction of the seam, not against it. As fabric awnings age, their seams become weak.
- Lower rolled-up awnings after a storm to allow them to dry.
- Rejuvenate faded canvas awnings with a special paint available from awning dealers or a paint store.

Don'ts

- **Do not** roll awnings up if they are still wet from rain or washing.
- **Do not** use harsh cleaners on any type of awning.

Fastest

Lux Dishwashing Liquid (Lever Brothers Company) is good for quick cleanups of soiled canvas, acrylic, vinyl-coated, and metal awnings. Mix a solution of this mild detergent in a pail of warm water and apply it to the awning with a long-handled brush. Rinse well with the garden hose and allow to dry completely before rolling up.

Cheapest

Fels-Naptha Heavy Duty Laundry Bar Soap (Purex Corporation) is an inexpensive product for cleaning awnings. Rub the soap onto a wet brush and apply it to the awning with a light scrubbing action. Rinse thoroughly, using a garden hose.

Best

Lysol Deodorizing Cleaner II (Lehn & Fink Products Division of Sterling Drug Inc.) not only acts as an excellent general cleaner for cloth awnings but also is a very good product for mildew control. Add ¼ cup of this sudsing liquid to 1 gallon warm water, apply with a long-handled brush, and rinse well with the garden hose.

Other Products Tested

Palmolive Dishwashing Liquid (Colgate-Palmolive Company)—liquid; very good cleaner; high suds; pleasant odor.
Amway Multi-Purpose L.O.C. Cleaner (High Suds) (Amway Corp.)—liquid; very good cleaner; high suds; pleasant odor.
Tide (Procter & Gamble)—granular; very good cleaner; high suds; mild odor.

Barbecue Grills

Do's

- Follow the manufacturer's instructions, especially for electric and gas-fired equipment.
- Wear rubber or plastic gloves when cleaning—this is a messy job.
- Remove the electrical attachment that powers the spit before cleaning if it is a separate unit.
- Clean the grill outside where there is access to a garden hose.
- Remove the grill and scrape off the residue with a stiff wire brush after each use (on all except nonstick surfaces).
- Clean permanent briquettes by removing the grill, closing the lid, opening the vent, and turning the heat to high for about 20 minutes.
- Use only synthetic scouring pads on a nonstick surface.
- Wash the grill, base, and cover with an all-purpose cleaner solution.
- Rinse with a garden hose and dry thoroughly to prevent rusting.
- Empty ashes frequently when using charcoal.
- Spray the grill with vegetable oil to prevent food from sticking.

Don'ts

- **Do not** leave the barbecue grill uncovered and outside in all weather—moisture rusts the metal.
- **Do not** use a wire brush to clean nonstick-coated grill surfaces.

Barbecue Grills

Fastest

Grease Relief (Texize Chemicals Company) cuts through grease build-up in a matter of seconds when sprayed onto the barbecue and wire grill and rubbed briskly with a synthetic scouring pad (see Tools of the Trade). When the grease deposits are loosened, spray the grill with a jet stream from the garden hose to rinse off all of the cleaner.

Cheapest

A solution of ½ cup **Arm & Hammer Washing Soda** (Church & Dwight Co., Inc.) dissolved in ½ gallon hot water is the cheapest way to clean a grill. Apply it by dipping a stiff brush into the liquid and scrubbing the surface, using a synthetic scouring pad (see Tools of the Trade) for stubborn soil. Rinse well and leave in the sun to dry completely.

Best

Gunk Garage Floor, Bar-B-Q and Mower Cleaner (Radiator Specialty Company) is top-rated for removing grease and smoke build-up from the inside and outside of a heavily-soiled barbecue grill. After the encrusted food deposits are all scraped off, spray the solvent on the surface and vigorously scrub all surfaces with a wire brush. Let it soak for 15 minutes, and repeat the procedure if necessary. Flush away the loosened debris with the jet stream from a garden hose and allow to dry. **Caution:** For use on a gas-fired grill, close the main shut-off valve before using. After using, the barbecue should be fired at full flame for 30 minutes before cooking.

Other Products Tested

Mex Multi-Purpose Cleaner (United Gilsonite Laboratories)—powder; rubber gloves needed; excellent grease cutter and cleaner.
Formula 409 All Purpose Cleaner (The Clorox Company)—pump spray; very good cleaner; pleasant odor.
Mr. Clean All-Purpose Cleaner (Procter & Gamble)—liquid; very good cleaner; pleasant odor.

Brick

Generally, brick is so sturdy that it requires little care, but occasional cleaning is needed whenever brick is subjected to adverse weather.

Do's

- Hose brick surfaces periodically to remove soil.
- Preserve the life of brick patio floors with a masonry sealer available at hardware stores.
- Thoroughly saturate a brick surface with clean water before and after cleaning for best results.
- Test strong cleaning products on a small, inconspicuous area first, wait a week, and evaluate the results before doing the complete job. Some cleaners can stain some bricks.
- Work from the top of the wall down, applying the cleaning solution with a long-handled brush.
- Scrub brick walls with a stiff brush and a strong detergent solution; rinse well.
- Use a wooden or nonmetal tool to scrape off stubborn soil.
- Remove paint spots with a paste-type paint remover.
- Even out the brick color after removing spots by rubbing another brick of the same color over the surface.
- Protect painted and metal doors, windows, and house trim when cleaning brick.

Don't

- **Do not** scrape off stubborn soil with a metal tool—this will stain the brick.

Fastest and Cheapest

Make a solution of ½ cup strong household detergent, ½ cup laundry detergent (see Laundry), and 1 gallon warm water. Saturate the area to be cleaned with water and apply the cleaning solution with a stiff brush. Rinse well with clear water.

Best

Use **Mex Multi-Purpose Cleaner** (United Gilsonite Laboratories) for especially dirty walls. First saturate the surface with water, then dissolve ½ cup of the powder in 1 gallon hot water and apply to the brick with a stiff brush. Rinse well with hot water.

 For stubborn smoke stains that appear above a barbecue, use **Ajax Cleanser** (Colgate-Palmolive Company). Scrub the powder into the premoistened brick and rinse well with clear water to make sure no white residue remains.

Garbage Cans

Garbage cans, whether made of metal or plastic, should be cleaned on a regular basis to keep them fresh and sanitary.

Do's

- Line garbage cans with disposable plastic bags to make the cleaning job easy.
- Empty indoor cans often.
- Frequently wash indoor cans with an all-purpose cleaner.
- Keep a long-handled brush handy just for cleaning garbage cans.
- Rinse outdoor cans with the hose after each emptying—dry them in the sun.

Don't

- **Do not** place wet garbage in cans unless it is wrapped in newspapers or the can is plastic-lined.

Fastest

A truly dirty garbage can can be cleaned quickly with **Grease Relief** (Texize Chemicals Company), a concentrated all-purpose cleaner. Spray the cleaner directly on the surface, scrub with a brush, and rinse. A solution of ½ cup Grease Relief in 1 gallon water is also good when left to soak in the garbage can.

Cheapest

A solution of ⅓ cup **20 Mule Team Borax** (United States Borax & Chemical Corporation) dissolved in 1 gallon hot water is a good, inexpensive cleaner. Let it soak for a few minutes and then scrub with a long-handled brush. Drain, rinse, and dry in the sun for a clean and deodorized garbage can.

Best

Lysol Deodorizing Cleaner II (Lehn & Fink Products Division of Sterling Drug Inc.) is the best cleaner for garbage cans. Dissolve ¼ cup of the phosphate-free liquid in 1 gallon warm water in the garbage can. After scrubbing, rinsing, and drying, the can will be clean and odor free.

Other Products Tested

Lestoil Heavy Duty Cleaner (Noxell Corporation)—liquid; excellent cleaner; pine odor.
Spic and Span (Procter & Gamble)—low-sudsing powder; very good cleaner; moderate pine odor.
Pine Forest Ajax All Purpose Cleaner (Colgate-Palmolive Company)—sudsing liquid; very good cleaner; pine odor.

Breath O' Pine Multi-Purpose Cleaner (Brondow Incorporated)—sudsing liquid; good cleaner; heavy pine odor.

West Pine Cleaner Deodorizer (Glenwood Laboratories Inc.)—sudsing liquid; moderately good cleaner; light pine odor.

Outdoor Furniture

Outdoor furniture is made from durable materials such as aluminum, plastic, wood, and wrought iron, some of which can withstand the elements very well. But even the hardiest, rust-resistant materials need proper attention. One of the best things you can do for all types of outdoor furniture is to cover it or store it in the garage or basement after summer to prevent weather damage and to minimize your routine cleaning.

Aluminum, Painted

Do's

- Wash painted aluminum with a mild detergent solution.
- Coat painted aluminum with an automotive paste wax for protection.

Don't

- **Do not** use harsh abrasives or steel wool on painted aluminum.
- **Do not** use a naval aluminum jelly on painted/anodized aluminum.

Fastest

Painted aluminum furniture is quickly cleaned with a warm water solution using a liquid dishwashing detergent (see Recommended Basic Products). Apply it with a sponge; rinse well.

Cheapest

Baking soda (see Recommended Basic Products), either in a warm water solution or straight from the box, cleans and deodorizes painted and unpainted aluminum outdoor furniture cheaply. Use it in solution for general cleaning, applying it with a sponge and then rinsing well. For stubborn soil, dip a moistened cloth in the powder and rub on the spot until it disappears—baking soda will not scratch the finish. Rinse well.

Best

Use **Soft Scrub Cleanser** (The Clorox Company), a mild liquid abrasive, for cleaning painted aluminum outdoor furniture. Apply with a sponge and rinse well with clear water.

Outdoor Furniture

Other Products Tested

Amway Zoom Spray Cleaner Concentrate (Amway Corp.)—spray; very good cleaner; pleasant odor.

Fantastik Multi-Surface Spray Cleaner (Texize Chemicals Company)—pump spray; very good cleaner; moderate odor.

Formula 409 All Purpose Cleaner (The Clorox Company)—pump spray; very good cleaner; not for use on varnished surfaces; pleasant odor.

West Pine Cleaner Deodorizer (Glenwood Laboratories Inc.)—sudsing liquid; very good cleaner and disinfectant agent; pine smell.

Aluminum, Unpainted

Aluminum outdoor furniture is usually left in its natural state with a polished or matte finish. **Caution:** If you use kerosene to clean aluminum furniture, store the kerosene in a cool place. Kerosene is highly flammable and should not be stored in the home in large amounts.

Do's

- Use a jelly aluminum cleaner to remove oxidation from natural finished metal.
- Occasionally spray with a clear lacquer to protect the surface.
- Dip steel wool in kerosene and rub over the unpainted aluminum surface to restore its appearance and give it protection.

Don't

- **Do not** let kerosene touch any webbing or cushion material.

Fastest

Brillo Steel Wool Soap Pads (Purex Corporation) are the fastest product to use for cleaning up unpainted aluminum outdoor furniture. Moisten the pad to activate the soap and then briskly rub the entire surface, rinsing well with clear water; towel dry.

Cheapest

Baking soda (see Recommended Basic Products), either in a warm water solution or straight from the box, cleans and deodorizes painted and unpainted aluminum outdoor furniture cheaply. Use it in solution for general cleaning, applying it with a sponge and then rinsing well. For stubborn soil, dip a moistened cloth in the powder and rub on the spot until it disappears—baking soda will not scratch the finish. Rinse well.

Best

Cameo Aluminum and Stainless Steel Cleaner (Purex Corporation) is an excellent cleaner for unpainted aluminum. Sprinkle the powder on the wet aluminum surface and rub with a damp sponge or cloth to start the polishing agents in action. Wipe the surface with a soapy sponge, rinse well, and towel dry for a brilliant finish.

Other Products Tested

Nevr-Dull Magic Wadding Polish (The George Basch Co.)—premoistened wadding; excellent cleaner for shiny finished aluminum; can be reused.

Bon Ami Cleaning Powder (Faultless Starch/Bon Ami Company)—powder; very mild abrasive; excellent cleaner.

Noxon Liquid 7 Metal Polish (Boyle-Midway Inc.)—liquid; very good cleaner; leaves little shine; moderate odor.

Duro Aluminum Jelly (Woodhill Permatex)—liquid jelly; very good cleaner; leaves surface dull; strong odor.

Formula 409 All Purpose Cleaner (The Clorox Company)—pump spray; very good cleaner; not for use on varnished surfaces; pleasant odor.

Vinyl and Plastic

Do's

- Hose down furniture on a regular basis to remove surface dirt and dust.
- Occasionally wipe with a damp sponge to remove light soil.
- Use a mild dishwashing detergent solution for a more thorough cleaning.
- Dry vinyl cushions in the sun if they become wet to prevent mildew.
- Spray cushions with a disinfectant after they become wet to prevent mildew.
- Close umbrellas before a storm and open immediately after rain ends to facilitate drying and prevent mildew.
- Wash umbrella fringe with a mild dishwashing detergent solution.

Don't

- **Do not** leave cushions in the rain or allow them to get wet.

Fastest

Tuff Stuff Foam Cleaner (Union Carbide Corp.) is a fast, effective cleaner for vinyl and plastic surfaces. Spray the cleaner over the surface, allow it to soak for about half a minute, then rub briskly with a damp sponge to remove soil and stains. Wipe dry with a soft cloth.

Cheapest

Baking soda (see Recommended Basic Products) is an inexpensive way to clean vinyl and plastic outdoor furniture. Dissolve ¼ cup baking soda in 1 quart warm water and apply to the surface with a brush. For more difficult spots, dip a damp cloth into the soda and rub directly on the area. Rinse well with clear water.

Read manufacturer's cautions and warnings before using any product.

Outdoor Furniture

Best

Vinyl Magic (Magic American Chemical Corp.), an aerosol spray, is an excellent product for cleaning vinyl and plastic. With a brushlike plastic applicator on the can top, it is easy to apply and does a beautiful cleaning job. Shake the can well, spray on the surface, brush with the plastic applicator to loosen dirt, and wipe clean with a damp cloth.

Other Products Tested

Mr. Clean All-Purpose Cleaner (Procter & Gamble)—liquid; excellent performance; pleasant odor.

Lysol Disinfectant Spray (Lehn & Fink Products Division of Sterling Drug Inc.)—aerosol; excellent for mildew control.

Formula 409 All Purpose Cleaner (The Clorox Company)—pump spray; very good to excellent cleaner; not for use on varnished surfaces; pleasant odor.

West Pine Cleaner Deodorizer (Glenwood Laboratories Inc.)—liquid; very good to excellent cleaner; pine odor.

Amway Zoom Spray Cleaner Concentrate (Amway Corp.)—spray; very good cleaner; pleasant odor.

Fantastik Multi-Surface Spray Cleaner (Texize Chemicals Company)—pump spray; very good cleaner; moderate odor.

Wood

Do's

- Bring painted or varnished pieces indoors or store under a shelter at night.
- Wipe painted or varnished wood furniture with a clean, damp cloth.
- Read the manufacturer's label to see if your redwood furniture has been given a protective wax coat.
- Treat uncoated redwood with one or two coats of preservative to extend its life.
- Hose or wipe off redwood furniture to keep it clean.
- Remove soot and grease stains from redwood with a mixture of 1 cup strong granular detergent, 1 cup liquid bleach, and 1 gallon warm water. Scrub in and rinse well.

Don't

- **Do not** hose painted or varnished wood furniture.

Fastest, Cheapest, and Best

Make a solution of warm water and an all-purpose cleaner (see Recommended Basic Products) and apply it to the wooden surface with a sponge. Rinse well and blot up the excess moisture with an old terry towel, and then allow the furniture to dry in the sun.

Wrought Iron

Frames for many styles of outdoor furniture are created with wrought iron. It is available in a painted or unpainted finish.

Do's

- Remove rust immediately, repainting the furniture if necessary.
- Keep it clean with an occasional hosing—use a mild detergent solution for heavier soil and be sure to dry the furniture quickly.
- Use a stiff toothbrush to clean intricate ornamental work.
- Repaint when necessary with a rust-resistant paint intended for use on wrought iron.

Don't

- **Do not** paint with ordinary paint.

Fastest and Best

A quick hosing or wash with a detergent solution is the normal procedure for cleaning wrought iron furniture, but stopping the spread of rust is the real problem. The fastest and best way to remove a rust spot is to use **Zud** (Boyle-Midway Inc.), a highly abrasive powder. Sprinkle some of the powder on the wet rusty spot, let it sit for about a minute, then rub with a piece of steel wool until the rust disappears. It is important that you remove every trace of the rust, otherwise it will continue to spread. Rinse the surface and wipe dry. Repaint if the furniture is painted.

Cheapest

The cheapest way to remove rust is to rub the spot briskly with a stiff wire brush, then sand with coarse steel wool. If the rust is especially deep, a steel file may be helpful in getting it all out. Repaint if necessary.

Other Products Tested

Bar Keepers Friend Cleanser & Polish (SerVaas Laboratories, Inc.)—powder; very good rust remover.

Window Screens

The wire mesh of window and door screens is a dust collector. When it rains this deposit is transferred easily to closed windows, leaving the glass streaked and dirty. This is less of a problem for inside-mounted screens, but they also acquire dust each season.

Window Screens

Do's

- Dust screens regularly using a hand brush or the brush attachment of the vacuum.
- Give screens a thorough cleaning before rehanging them in the spring.
- Wash screens outdoors in the driveway for less mess.
- If you wash screens in the bathtub, protect the porcelain with old towels.
- Apply an all-purpose cleaner solution with a brush to both sides of the screen.
- Rinse well with a fine spray of clear water.
- Shake off excess moisture and wipe dry with an old cloth.
- Wash windows, window sills, and door frames before putting the screens back.
- Store screens in a dry place when not in use, covering them with newspaper or plastic to keep them clean.

Don'ts

- **Do not** hang screens until they dry completely.
- **Do not** exert too much pressure when washing the mesh—it can be pulled away from the frame.
- **Do not** rinse with a jet stream of water.

Fastest

Tuff Stuff Foam Cleaner (Union Carbide Corp.) is a multi-purpose aerosol foam cleaner and is a rapid way to clean screens and painted wood frames. Spray on the surface, let soak half a minute, then scrub gently with a brush. Follow with a fine spray with the hose.

Cheapest

An inexpensive but effective way to clean aluminum screens outdoors and keep them from pitting is with kerosene. Dip a rag in the kerosene and rub both sides of the mesh as well as the frames. Wipe off the excess. This is a good rust inhibitor for older screens too. **Caution:** Kerosene is highly flammable and should not be stored in the home in large amounts. Store kerosene in a cool place.

Best

Mr. Clean All-Purpose Cleaner (Procter & Gamble) performs very well cleaning older screens as well as the new fiberglass mesh screens. Pour ¼ cup of the liquid cleaner into 1 gallon water and apply with a soft-bristled brush to both mesh and frames. Rinse with a fine spray of clear water and dry.

Other Products Tested

West Pine Cleaner Deodorizer (Glenwood Laboratories Inc.)—liquid; very good cleaner; pine odor.

Amway Multi-Purpose L.O.C. Cleaner (Regular) (Amway Corp.)—liquid; very good cleaner; pleasant odor.

Big Wally (S. C. Johnson & Son, Inc.)—aerosol; good cleaner; easy to use; moderate odor.

Automobiles

Carpets

Automobile carpeting is difficult to keep fresh and clean looking. Although mats are a great help, dirt and grime that vacuuming won't remove inevitably accumulate in the carpet fibers. Also see Carpets and Rugs for cleaning products and procedures.

Do's
- Use either rubber or fiber mats to preserve the life of your car's carpet.
- Vacuum the carpet periodically to remove grit and soil that can break down the fibers and cause unnecessary wear.
- Wipe up spills as soon as they occur.
- Keep a whisk broom in the glove compartment for quick brushouts.

Don't
- **Do not** let rain or water leaks soak the carpet. It is difficult to dry thoroughly, and mildew can set in quickly.

Fastest

Vacuum the carpet thoroughly, then spray **Woolite Self Cleaning Rug Cleaner** (Boyle-Midway Inc.) onto the carpet. Vacuum again when dry. This should remove most stains.

Cheapest

After vacuuming the carpet, spray **Glory Professional Strength Rug Cleaner** (S. C. Johnson & Son, Inc.) on the carpet. Gently work the foam in with a damp sponge. Vacuum again when dry.

Salt residues can be removed cheaply from carpets with a solution made of equal parts vinegar and water. Apply the liquid with a sponge, but do not over-wet the carpeting. Allow to dry thoroughly, then vacuum.

Best

Turtle Wax Auto & Van Carpet Cleaner (Turtle Wax, Inc.) is a spray-on foam that loosens and lifts ground-in dirt and grime from auto carpets. Scrub in with a damp sponge and vacuum when dry. This product also contains a special silicone shield that repels dirt and grime so that your carpet will stay cleaner longer.

Other Products Tested

Westley's Automotive Rug & Carpet Cleaner (Westley Industries, Inc.)—aerosol foam; must be worked in with a damp sponge; no rinsing; requires vacuuming.
Bac-Tex Bacteriostatic Rug Shampoo Concentrate (Airwick Industries, Inc.)—use diluted or full strength; very good for removing odors from car sickness and most dirt, but not highly effective on routine grime.
J/Wax Vinyl Top & Interior Cleaner (S. C. Johnson & Son, Inc.)—aerosol; must be thoroughly rinsed; removes slight stains.

Chrome

Shiny chrome adds sparkle to a car's appearance and should be cleaned and polished regularly to prevent rust and corrosion. For additional procedures to use on chrome surfaces, also see Chromium.

Do's

- Polish chrome after the car has been washed.
- Remove rust spots with a steel wool pad or a piece of crumpled aluminum foil.
- Hose off salt residues before they pit the metal.
- Wax chrome when you wax the car's body with a cleaner/wax—use different cloths for the body and chrome.

Fastest

Garry's Knight's Armor Chrome Cleaner & Polish (Garry Laboratories Inc., Division of Northeast Chemical Co.) makes quick work of dirty and dull chrome. Apply this creamy liquid with a soft cloth, allow to dry, and buff off with a clean cloth for a shiny bright finish.

Cheapest

For a quick and cheap way to clean chrome, dip a moistened sponge into baking soda (see Recommended Basic Products) and rub onto the chrome surface. Let set for a minute, then rinse off and buff dry with a soft cloth. Use a synthetic scouring pad (see Tools of the Trade) with the soda for particularly stubborn spots.

Best

Simoniz Chrome Cleaner (Union Carbide Corp.) is an excellent way to clean rust and stains from car chrome. Shake the can well and apply the liquid to the chrome with a soft cloth. Let sit for 7 minutes and wipe away the corrosion and stains with another soft cloth, buffing up to a beautiful shine.

Other Products Tested

J/Wax Chrome Cleaner-Polish (S. C. Johnson & Son, Inc.)—liquid; very good cleaner/polish; cleaning fluid odor.

Floor Mats

The use of rubber floor mats will help protect your automobile's carpet from extensive wear and tear. Also see Tires for a product to protect and add shine to rubber.

Do's

- Clean the mats every time you wash your car.
- Use a stiff-bristled brush to clean the mats.
- Apply a good rubber protectant after washing with detergent to restore the shine.
- Clean mats often in winter, because they accumulate salt and sand more in snowy weather.

Don'ts

- **Do not** use harsh chemicals or solvents to clean the mats.
- **Do not** use steel wool scouring pads—they can scratch the rubber.

Fastest and Cheapest

Mix 3 tablespoons of a mild dishwashing detergent (see Recommended Basic Products) in 1 gallon warm water. Gently scrub the mats until all the dirt and grime have been removed. Allow to dry thoroughly on both sides before replacing the mats.

Best

Wet the mats with water. Squirt **Turtle Wax Whitewall Tire & Mat Cleaner** (Turtle Wax, Inc.) onto the floor mats and work in with a stiff-bristled brush. Thoroughly rinse off the mats with clear water.

Read manufacturer's cautions and warnings before using any product.

Other Products Tested

Classic Whitewall Tire Cleaner (Classic Chemical)—pump spray; can be used for deep scuff marks; caustic—rubber gloves required; avoid contact with magnesium or aluminum wheels and painted surfaces.
Armor All Cleaner (Armor All Products)—pump spray; scrubbing not required on lightly soiled mats; rinse thoroughly.

Paint

Drive-through car washes may be convenient, but they are not good in the long run for a car's finish because they use strong detergents, scratchy brushes, and high water pressures. Take time to wash, dry, and wax your car by hand. Fiberglass and paint-over-metal finishes may be cleaned the same way, although fiberglass bodies are not subject to rust.

Do's

- Close all windows tightly before starting to wash the car.
- Thoroughly hose off the dust and loose dirt before scrubbing.
- Spray the wheels, hubcaps, undersurface of the fenders (avoid wetting the engine compartment), bumpers, and as far under the chassis as possible with a jet stream of water to remove dirt, mud, and salt.
- Use a cleaner, automotive rubbing compound, or cleaner/wax on older cars to help remove the oxidized layer.
- Remove any tar deposits with a special tar remover.
- Apply the cleaning solution with a large sponge, mitt, or soft cloth, scrubbing lightly where necessary.
- Work from the top down, washing one area at a time and rinsing well before the suds dry (especially important on hot days and in dry climates).
- Rinse the entire car again after scrubbing and dry with soft absorbent terry cloths or a chamois to help prevent waterspotting.
- Apply a wax or polish when water no longer beads up on the car's surface, following the manufacturer's instructions.
- After wax has dried, sprinkle baking soda or cornstarch on the surface. Either one will pick up the wax and help bring out surface luster.

Don'ts

- **Do not** wash or wax a car in the hot sun or if the surface is hot—this may cause streaking and damage the finish.
- **Do not** use paper towels to dry a car—they can scratch the finish.
- **Do not** brush dust off with a cloth or your hand—this can leave small scratches in the finish.
- **Do not** wax a car unless it has just been washed.
- **Do not** use cleaner/waxes on vinyl, wood grain trim, or on new or newly painted cars—a new paint finish should not be polished for at least 90 days.
- **Do not** use one of the liquid dishwashing detergents or all-purpose cleaners to wash an automobile—they can dull the finish.

Fastest

Turtle Wax Zip Wax Car Wash (Turtle Wax, Inc.) washes and lightly waxes the car in one quick operation. Pour 2 tablespoons into a pail and add 2 gallons warm water to make a good cloud of suds. Apply with a large sponge, scrubbing lightly where necessary. Rinse well and dry with a soft cloth or chamois for a clean, bright finish.

After washing the car, apply **J/Wax Sprint No-Buff Car Wax** (S. C. Johnson & Son, Inc.), an excellent non-abrasive liquid wax that brings up a high shine on paint without buffing. Just apply it with a clean, dry cloth and wipe it off immediately for beautiful results.

Best

Top marks are given to **Du Pont Car Wash Concentrate** (E. I. Du Pont de Nemours & Co., Inc.) for its performance. Pour ½ capful into a bucket and add warm water to make generous suds. Apply with a large sponge and rinse well. Dry with soft cloths.

An excellent wax to apply after the finish has been cleaned is **Classic Car Wax** (Classic Chemical), a hard paste wax that contains carnauba wax. Apply a thin film of this paste with a soft, damp cloth to a small section at a time. Rub firmly to form a seal, wipe away the residue, and buff vigorously with a buffer or soft cloth.

Other Products Tested

CLEANERS. Garry's Black Knight Tar and Bug Remover (Garry Laboratories Inc., Division of Northeast Chemical Co.)—liquid; excellent cleaner; moderate odor.
Garry's Prince Regent Concentrated Car Wash (Garry Laboratories Inc., Division of Northeast Chemical Co.)—liquid; good cleaner; moderate odor.
Westley's Hi-Lustre Car Wash (Westley Industries, Inc.)—powder; good cleaner.

LIQUID WAXES. Garry's Royal Satin (Garry Laboratories Inc., Division of Northeast Chemical Co.)—liquid; excellent cleaner and polish.
J/Wax Car-Plate (S. C. Johnson & Son, Inc.)—creamy liquid; very good to excellent performance; removes oxidation; high shine.
Du Pont Rain Dance Car Wax (E. I. Du Pont de Nemours & Co., Inc.)—creamy liquid; very good to excellent performance; removes film; leaves high shine.
Star Brite Car Polish (Star Brite Inc.)—creamy liquid; very good to excellent performance; cleans away oxidation; leaves high shine.
Simoniz No Buff Car Wax (Union Carbide Corp.)—creamy liquid; very good to excellent polish; high shine; no haze.

PASTE WAXES. Du Pont Rally Cream Wax (E. I. Du Pont de Nemours & Co., Inc.)—soft paste; very good to excellent performance; very good on chrome; high shine; relatively easy to apply and buff.
J/Wax Kit (S. C. Johnson & Son, Inc.)—presoftened paste wax; very good to excellent performance; good on chrome; high shine; relatively easy to apply and buff.
Turtle Wax Turtle Extra (Turtle Wax, Inc.)—soft paste; very good performance; high shine; relatively easy to apply; requires vigorous buffing.

Read manufacturer's cautions and warnings before using any product.

Simoniz Shines Like the Sun (Union Carbide Corp.)—soft paste wax; very good performance; high shine; relatively easy to apply; needs vigorous buffing to remove all residue.

Tires

Clean tires and white sidewalls can help give your car an almost new look.

Do's
- Wash tires and hubcaps after the rest of the car has been washed, wetting them to remove loose dirt before scrubbing.
- Use a special tire brush or large sponge to help remove soil and pebbles from the tires and spokes of the hubcaps.
- Use a synthetic scouring pad to help remove black scuff marks from whitewalls.
- Wipe alloy hubcaps gently, as the surface can be damaged easily.
- Give cleaned tires a coating of special rubber protectant to help maintain a shiny appearance and minimize rubber deterioration.

Fastest

Formula 409 All Purpose Cleaner (The Clorox Company) cleans whitewalls and removes grease from hubcaps quickly. Spray it on, let it sit a minute or two, and wipe off with a damp sponge. For difficult marks, add more cleaner, and scrub with a synthetic scouring pad (see Tools of the Trade).

Cheapest

Brillo Steel Wool Soap Pads (Purex Corporation) cleans white sidewall tires inexpensively. Moisten the pad in water first, then scrub away to remove even the most stubborn marks. Rinse well with a stream of water from a hose.

Best

Garry's Really White Whitewall Speed Kleener (Garry Laboratories Inc., Division of Northeast Chemical Co.) is an excellent cleaner for tires with white sidewalls. Spray all around the tire, wait 2 or 3 minutes, and then lightly scrub with a synthetic scouring pad (see Tools of the Trade) to remove the soil. Rinse well with the hose to remove all the cleaner.

Armor All Protectant (Armor All Products) provides an excellent protective coating for rubber tires. Spray on, allow to penetrate for a minute, and then wipe with a soft cloth. This restores the new look to tires and is also excellent for other areas of the car such as rubber bumpers, bumper guards, floor mats, and body side moldings.

Other Products Tested

Fantastik Multi-Surface Spray Cleaner (Texize Chemicals Company)—pump spray; very good cleaner; moderate odor.
Big Wally (S. C. Johnson & Son, Inc.)—aerosol; good cleaner; moderate odor.
Armor All Cleaner (Armor All Products)—spray; moderate cleaner.

Upholstery, Cloth

Care should be taken to avoid spots and spills on cloth upholstery because it is not quite as cleanable as vinyl upholstery. Also see Furniture—Upholstery, Fabric for additional products and procedures to use on your car's cloth interior.

Do's
- Vacuum cloth upholstery at least once a month.
- Brush off the upholstery with a whisk broom or clothes brush regularly.
- Mop up all spills immediately and spot treat them to avoid stains.

Fastest and Best

Glamorene Upholstery Shampoo (Airwick Industries, Inc.) is a quick and excellent cleaner for cloth upholstery. Shake the can well and apply the aerosol foam with the attached brush head, working it into one small area at a time. Wipe with a sponge wrung out in clear water to remove the loosened soil. Finish by going over the upholstery with a dry towel, then allow the fabric to dry completely.

Cheapest

Make a stiff foam by mixing ¼ cup **Lux Dishwashing Liquid** (Lever Brothers Company) in 1 cup warm water and beating the liquid with an eggbeater. Spread only the foam over the upholstery with a sponge, using circular, overlapping strokes. Let dry, then vacuum the soil away.

Other Products Tested

Bissell Upholstery Shampoo for Home & Auto (Bissell Inc.)—aerosol foam; good to very good cleaner with brush head.

Upholstery, Vinyl and Leather

Vinyl is used extensively for car upholstery because it is very easy to care for and quite durable. Luxury cars often have real leather upholstery. The care for both kinds of upholstery is identical.

Do's

- Vacuum the creases and crevices of the upholstery as part of routine, general car cleaning, but avoid scratching with sharp-edged attachments.
- Use a whisk broom to remove loose soil or debris.
- Use a leather or vinyl conditioner periodically to prevent cracking, drying out, and fading.

Don'ts

- **Do not** allow sharp objects to come into contact with these upholstery materials, because they can be easily cut.
- **Do not** use harsh chemicals as these may fade color.

Fastest

Use **Garry's VLP Vinyl-Leather-Plastic Cleaner and Conditioner** (Garry Laboratories, Inc., Division of Northeast Chemical Co.) to clean vinyl and leather upholstery quickly. Lightly rub in the spray with a soft brush, allow to penetrate for 3 minutes, and then wipe dry with a soft cloth.

Cheapest

Make a warm soapy solution using **Ivory Snow** (Procter & Gamble) and water; apply just the suds to the upholstery with a soft-bristled brush, working the cleaner into the grain gently. Wipe clean with a damp sponge and buff dry with a soft cloth.

Best

An excellent cleaner/conditioner for leather and vinyl upholstery is **The Tannery** (Missori Hickory Corp.). Shake the can well, spray the foam over the surface, and rub with a soft-bristled brush to loosen embedded soil. Wipe clean with a damp sponge and buff dry with a soft cloth.

Other Products Tested

Vinyl Magic (Magic American Chemical Corp.)—aerosol foam with attached plastic brush; excellent cleaner.

Plastic & Leather Cleaner (Stanley Home Products, Inc.)—aerosol foam; very good cleaner; moderate odor.

The Leather Works (Knomark Inc.)—aerosol foam; very good cleaner; pleasant odor.

J/Wax Vinyl Top & Interior Cleaner (S. C. Johnson & Son, Inc.)—aerosol foam; very good cleaner; pleasant odor.

Tuff Stuff Foam Cleaner (Union Carbide Corp.)—aerosol foam; very good cleaner; pleasant odor.

Vinyl Tops

Many cars have decorative vinyl tops that need special cleaning products to help keep their good looks and lengthen their lives.

Do's

- Scrub the cleaner in with a soft-bristled brush to get soil out of the grain.
- Apply a protective vinyl coating to protect from sun, pollutants, and extreme weather.

Don't

- **Do not** use ordinary car wax or harsh chemicals.

Fastest

Vinyl Magic (Magic American Chemical Corp.) is a quick way to clean vinyl car tops. Spray the foam over the surface and scrub in with the plastic brush attached to the cap; wipe away the foam with a damp sponge.

Cheapest

Pour ⅛ cup liquid dishwashing detergent (see Recommended Basic Products) into a pail and add a jet stream of 1 gallon warm water to make lots of suds. Apply the solution with a sponge and scrub with a brush. Rinse well, wipe dry, and apply a vinyl dressing for protection.

Best

The Tannery (Missouri Hickory Corp.) is an excellent product to use on vinyl car tops. Shake the can well and spray over the surface. Spread and scrub in with a soft-bristled brush to loosen embedded soil, then wipe off with a damp sponge.

Once a vinyl car top has been cleaned, it's a good idea to spray it with **STP Son of a Gun** (STP Corp.) to give it a protective coating against harsh weather and sun. Spray on, allow to penetrate for 2 hours, and then buff to a bright sheen with a soft cloth.

Other Products Tested

Garry's VLP Vinyl-Leather-Plastic Cleaner and Conditioner (Garry Laboratories Inc.,

Division of Northeast Chemical Co.)—pump spray; very good cleaner.
Plastic & Leather Cleaner (Stanley Home Products, Inc.)—aerosol foam; very good cleaner; moderate odor.
The Leather Works (Knomark, Inc.)—aerosol foam; very good cleaner; pleasant odor.
J/Wax Vinyl Top & Interior Cleaner (S. C. Johnson & Son, Inc.)—aerosol foam; very good cleaner; pleasant odor.
Tuff Stuff Foam Cleaner (Union Carbide Corp.)—aerosol foam; very good cleaner; pleasant odor.
Armor All Cleaner (Armor All Products)—pump spray; moderate cleaner.

Windows and Windshields— Glass and Plastic

A clean windshield is crucial to safe driving. Street grime and bugs can be difficult to remove if allowed to set on the glass. Plastic convertible windows can be kept clean and clear with the proper care. Dirty headlights and filmed-over taillights also can be hazardous.

Do's

- Clean all exterior glass and plastic each time you wash the car. Use a synthetic scouring pad to remove stubborn dirt.
- Clean windshields and other car windows each time you refuel.
- Make sure any cloth used for wiping the windshield is free of any grit that can scratch.
- Use only a mild detergent in warm water to clean plastic windshields.
- If possible, wipe the windshield with only a full-skin, clean chamois. It won't streak and is unlikely to scratch.
- Clean the inside windows with strokes in one direction and the outside with strokes in the opposite direction so you can pinpoint where streaks originate.
- Use specially formulated windshield washer fluid; keep the washer reservoir filled with the proper mix of water and fluid.
- Keep windshield washer jets clear so they will operate properly; adjust so jets spray onto windshields properly.
- Replace windshield wiper rubber when it's "dead"—when wipers smear or skip on the windshield.
- Wet the windshield surface before using the wipers.

Don'ts

- **Do not** use any abrasive cleaners or solvents on plastic surfaces, as these products can scratch or fog up the plastic.
- **Do not** use your wipers on a dry windshield.

Fastest

Spray **Sparkle Glass Cleaner** (A. J. Funk & Co.) directly onto the windshield. Wipe with a clean, dry cloth. This is also very effective for removing smoke residue from the inside of the windows.

Cheapest

Mix ¼ cup vinegar in 1 gallon warm water. Wipe the windows inside and out with a cloth dipped in the solution. Rinse and wipe with a clean, dry cloth. This also works for plastic windshields.

Best

Use **Wipe-R Clean** (Interstate Oil Co., Inc.) in the windshield washer reservoir under the hood of your car. This is very effective for removing almost all the bugs and grime that can accumulate on the front windshield. A trigger-spray bottle can be used for the other windows. However, since this is a combustible poison, it is not recommended for use on the inside of the car.

Other Products Tested

Garry's Foaming Glass Cleaner (Garry Laboratories Inc., Division of Northeast Chemical Co.)—pump spray; excellent cleaner; contains ammonia; also effective vinyl and chrome cleaner; pleasant odor.

"500"-XL Windshield Washer Anti-Freeze & Solvent (Barton Chemical Corp.)—for use in the windshield washer reservoir; combustible, poison; effective de-icer and defogger for winter driving.

Windex Glass Cleaner (The Drackett Company)—pump spray; works best on inside of car; leaves streaks.

Classic Finish Restorer (Classic Chemical)—paste; apply with a soft cloth; used for plexiglass and plastic; can be used on plastic windshields, but may cause fogging if used over an extended period of time.

Wood-Grain Trim

Most wood-grain trim—both interior and exterior—is actually plastic, rather than real wood. Clean this the same as interior vinyl upholstery. For the chrome trim that surrounds the wood-grain area, also see Chromium and Chrome.

Books

Do's

- Leave dust jackets on as long as they remain in reasonable condition to protect the book covers from dust and dirt.
- Arrange books on the front of the shelves to allow for air circulation.
- Protect books from excessive heat and moisture.
- Dust weekly with a soft cloth or the brush attachment of the vacuum.
- Yearly, remove all books from the shelves and wipe them gently with a barely dampened cloth.
- Periodically treat leather-covered books with a light oil.
- Wash vinyl- and imitation leather-covered books with a mild detergent. Treat with a light coating of petroleum jelly or a vinyl dressing.

Don'ts

- **Do not** allow books to lean against each other or slump on the shelf.
- **Do not** squeeze books tightly together on the shelf.
- **Do not** allow the sun to shine directly on books—it can fade and deteriorate the book covers.
- **Do not** reassemble just-cleaned books until they are completely dry.

Fastest

The fastest way to clean books is with the brush attachment on your vacuum. Tilt each book back one at a time on the shelf so you can remove the dust from the binding and book edges. Another rapid approach is to wipe books lightly with a clean, unused paint brush. This is a very good way to handle book edges trimmed in gold leaf.

Cheapest

For books bound with imitation leather, wipe the surface clean with a damp cloth, dry with a soft towel, and then coat the bindings with a very thin coating of petroleum jelly. Leather-bound books will benefit from a light application of **Action Neatsfoot Oil Compound** (Ecological & Specialty Products, Inc.) during the yearly cleaning. **Caution:** This product is highly flammable and can be fatal if swallowed. Pour a small amount of the oil onto a pad made of several folded layers of cheesecloth or absorbent cloth and rub gently into the leather, being careful not to touch any paper part of the book. Keep the book separated until the oil has been completely absorbed, approximately 2 hours. Wipe dry. Note: Action Neatsfoot Oil Compound will cause some darkening of leather.

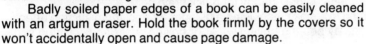

Badly soiled paper edges of a book can be easily cleaned with an artgum eraser. Hold the book firmly by the covers so it won't accidentally open and cause page damage.

Best

Leather and vinyl book covers can be both cleaned and conditioned effectively with **The Tannery** (Missouri Hickory Corp.). Carefully cover the book pages and spray this cleaner on the covers. Spread it with a damp sponge, allow it to set for a minute or two, and then buff with a soft cloth. Use a soft-bristled brush on grained surfaces to help get the dirt out of the creases.

Other Products Tested

Plastic & Leather Cleaner (Stanley Home Products, Inc.)—aerosol; excellent cleaner.
The Leather Works (Knomark Inc.)—aerosol foam; excellent cleaner.

Drains

All that some clogged drains need is to have the lint trap cleaned of hair and soap curds. Others require stronger measures. Commercial drain cleaners are sold in liquid, granular, and pressurized form. Granular products rely on lye to do the job; liquid cleaners use lye and other chemicals; and pressurized drain cleaners work by a chlorofluorocarbon propellant and pressure.

Do's

- Treat slow-running drains when the flow begins to slow down.
- Clean the lint trap of bathroom drains regularly to prevent clogging.
- Keep a plunger or "plumber's helper" handy for quick drain help.
- Plug the overflow opening in a sink when using a plunger for maximum suction effect.
- Dissolve grease deposits by pouring boiling water or boiling water and washing soda down the drain.
- Use a chemical drain cleaner when all else fails.
- Use chemical drain openers carefully—most are caustic, harmful to skin and eyes, and should be used in a well-ventilated area.
- Remove standing water from the sink when using granular drain cleaners—this is not necessary with liquid cleaners.

Don'ts

- **Do not** wait until no water drains to treat drains.
- **Do not** pour greasy substances down drains.
- **Do not** empty coffee grounds down the drain.
- **Do not** allow chemical drain cleaners to remain on porcelain enamel—they can damage the finish.
- **Do not** combine ammonia and other household cleaners with drain cleaners—hazardous gases can result.
- **Do not** mix two different drain cleaners.
- **Do not** use one cleaner after another unless the initial cleaner has been flushed away with gallons of water.
- **Do not** use a plunger or pressurized drain cleaner after a chemical cleaner has been used—this may cause chemical splash-back.
- **Do not** neglect to inform the plumber if you have used a chemical drain cleaner.

Fastest

A pressurized drain cleaner, **Drain Power** (Airwick Industries, Inc.), is the fastest. Apply the product to the drain according to the manufacturer's directions. The drain should be cleared instantly. Flush away the remainder of the clog with a flush of full-force water for 2 minutes, and your drain should be fast running again. **Caution:** Read the manufacturer's warnings, especially if you have tried a lye or acid drain opener first.

Cheapest

Moderately clogged drains usually can be unclogged by pouring ½ cup baking soda, followed by ½ cup vinegar down the drain. **Caution:** The two ingredients interact with foaming and fumes, so replace the drain cover loosely. Flush the drain after about three hours.

Greasy drains usually respond to having ½ cup of both salt and baking soda poured down the drain followed by a teakettle-full of boiling water. Allow to sit overnight if possible.

Best

The most effective drain cleaner for clogs is **Heavy Duty Mister Plumber Drain Opener** (Cromwell Products, Inc.). Pour ½ bottle of the liquid down the drain, according to instructions, and allow to stand 30 minutes. Flush drain with warm water. Repeat if necessary; this liquid may be poured through standing water. For regular preventive use, ¼ bottle is sufficient.

Other Products Tested

Liquid Drano Drain Opener (The Drackett Company)—liquid; very good to excellent for dissolving hair; very good on sluggish drains; moderate odor.
Crystal Drano Drain Opener (The Drackett Company)—granular; very good on sluggish drains; good for dissolving hair; slight odor.
Liquid-plumr Drain Opener (The Clorox Company)—liquid; moderately good for dissolving hair; good on sluggish drains; chlorine odor.

Paintbrushes and Paint Rollers

The best brush that money can buy may not last beyond the first job if it is neglected. A brush will give years of service, however, if it is treated properly. Cleaning a paintbrush shouldn't take long if you do it promptly after each use.

Do's

- Work in a well-ventilated area.
- Before cleaning, rid the brush of excess paint by tapping it against the inside rim of the can and then vigorously stroking the brush back and forth on newspapers several layers thick until very little paint comes off.
- Clean all brushes immediately after the painting job is completed.
- Clean brushes used for shellac in denatured alcohol, then wash in a detergent solution.
- Clean brushes used for lacquer in lacquer thinner or acetone and then wash in a detergent solution.
- Clean brushes used for oil-based paints and varnishes in turpentine or paint thinner and then wash in a detergent solution.
- Clean brushes used for latex-based paints in water and then wash in a detergent solution.
- Rinse all brushes well after washing and shake vigorously to remove excess water.
- Wrap brushes that you will use again after a short period of time in aluminum foil or plastic wrap to keep them soft.
- Make sure there is enough cleaner in a jar to completely cover the bristles of the brush.
- Comb the bristles with a wire brush after cleaning to straighten them for storage.
- Always allow paintbrushes to dry completely after cleaning them.
- After brushes are completely dry, wrap them in brown paper to help hold their shape and store flat or hang in a rack.
- Reuse a commercial brush cleaner after pouring the liquid through an old cloth to strain out the old paint residue.
- Treat sable or artists' brushes gently and carefully reshape bristles after each use—they are easily damaged.
- Treat paint rollers the same as brushes—according to the type of paint used.

Don'ts

- **Do not** use paint-removing products near an open flame.
- **Do not** breathe in the fumes when using solvent-based brush cleaners.
- **Do not** rest a brush in a jar of cleaner so that the bristles touch the bottom—always suspend the brush in the cleaner.
- **Do not** soak brushes for long periods of time in water—this can loosen the bristles.
- **Do not** comb the bristles of a sable or fine artists' brush.

Fastest, Cheapest, and Best, Latex-Based

A solution of one part **Mr. Clean All-Purpose Cleaner** (Procter & Gamble) in five parts hot water is the fastest, cheapest, and best way to clean latex-based paint from brushes and rollers. Soak overnight, rinse well under a stream of clear hot water, then submerge in the cleaning solution and work back and forth to remove all traces of paint. Rinse again in clear water, shake vigorously to remove excess water, comb the bristles, and lay the brush flat or hang to dry.

Fastest, Oil-Based

Epic Brush & Roller Cleaner (Enterprise Paint Co.) is a quick way to clean brushes used for oil-based paint or varnish. Place the brush in an old coffee or juice can and add enough liquid to cover the bristles. Work the brush back and forth to make sure the cleaner reaches the inner bristles. Rinse the brush in clear water, shake vigorously to remove excess water, comb the bristles (except sable brushes), and lay on a paper towel or hang to dry. This is also a good cleaner for rollers.

Cheapest, Oil-Based

Odorless Paint Thinner (Nankee Aluminum Paint Co.) cleans oil-based paint from brushes quite cheaply. Follow the same procedure as with Epic Brush & Roller Cleaner except repeat it once to make sure all the paint is removed.

Best, Oil-Based

Kwikeeze Water Rinsing Brush Cleaner (The Savogran Co.) is the best product for cleaning oil-based paint, lacquers, and varnishes from brushes. Follow the procedure for Epic Brush & Roller Cleaner, but eliminate washing in detergent as the cleaner contains its own detergent. Just rinse well in clear water.

Read manufacturer's cautions and warnings before using any product.

Records

Even the most expensive sound system can't correct the sound of static and dust on your recordings. Cleaning your albums will not only improve their sound quality, but will add to their life and to the life of your stereo cartridge or needle.

Do's

- Replace worn or dirty needles. They damage records quickly.
- Clean your records before you play them.
- Clean lightly soiled records on the turntable. Heavily smudged albums should be placed on a soft cloth for cleaning.
- Clean records with a circular motion, following the grooves.
- Use at least three revolutions to clean properly.
- Always store albums in their protective jackets.
- Handle records around the edge.
- Keep the dust cover lowered while you play your records.
- Remove dust accumulation from around the stylus or needle with an artists' brush dipped in isopropyl alcohol.

Don'ts

- **Do not** clean across the grooves. This will leave a build-up of dust and can damage the playing surface.
- **Do not** store your records flat. This can warp them.
- **Do not** use paper products to clean your records.
- **Do not** touch the playing surface of your records.
- **Do not** rub your album against anything. No record cleaner can remove scratches.

Fastest

Hold a **Pickwick Record Cleaning Cloth** (Pickwick Int'l.) lightly against the grooves. Use a rolling motion to lift the cloth so the cleanest portion leaves the record last. Always store in its plastic bag to prevent the antistatic chemicals from drying out.

To clean your albums continuously as you play them, attach **The Dust Bug** (Empire Scientific Corp., Distributor for C. E. Watts), a cleaning pad containing an antistatic agent. It is mounted on the turntable unit plate, and its fibers clean the record grooves before the tone arm stylus reaches them.

Cheapest

Mix a few drops of a mild dishwashing detergent (see Recommended Basic Products) in lukewarm water. Swish each record in the solution, then rinse in distilled water. Air dry each record vertically in your dishrack. Never put records in an automatic dishwasher.

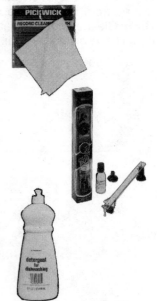

Best

For the optimum sound quality available from your records, the **Discwasher Record Cleaning System**(Discwasher, Inc.) is the best. The kit includes a solution and pad that removes almost all dust and static. Apply a few drops of the solution to the pad. Following only the direction of the grooves (never across), rub the record. This will remove most static and dust. For best results, use a light touch; let the fluid dry a few moments and then rub lightly around the record to pick up any remaining moisture or dust.

Other Products Tested

Pickwick Pro Care Deluxe Record Maintenance System (Pickwick Int'l.)—solution applied to brush; removes almost all dust and static; difference between Discwasher and Pickwick Pro Care not noticeable on moderately-priced equipment, only on expensive sound systems.

Manual Parastat Model MKIIA (Empire Scientific Corp., Distributor for C. E. Watts)—brush and antistatic fluid; applied before record is played.

Clean-Sweep Record Purifier (Horian Engineering, Inc.)—cloth-covered tool; removes dust, lint, and dirt, but not static.

Tools

Tools used for gardening, car or machine repairs, and for all jobs around the house should be cleaned after each use and stored properly to prevent damage. Setting aside places in the garage for garden tools keeps them organized and easy to find when next needed. Cleaning is a simple matter—the biggest problem with tools is rust.

Do's

- Wear gloves to protect your hands when cleaning tools—it is a messy job.
- Hose mud and dirt off tools after each use. Dry thoroughly.
- Periodically wipe the metal parts of each tool with a cloth moistened with lubricating or olive oil.
- Remove any rust spots immediately with a steel wool pad dipped in oil.
- Fill a bucket with sand soaked with motor oil, and thrust the heads of small tools into it for cleaning and rust protection.
- Periodically treat the wooden handles of tools with linseed oil.
- Store tools in a box containing oil-soaked sand if moisture is a problem.

Don'ts

- **Do not** store tools in humid locations.
- **Do not** let tools air dry—this can promote rust.

Tools

Fastest

A very good rust remover and preventive is the aerosol **Magic Handycan** (Magic American Chemical Corp.). Spray a heavy coating on the tool, allow it to penetrate the rust for a minute or two, then scour the metal with a steel wool pad. Wipe off the residue with old newspaper and respray the surface lightly to give it a protective coating.

Cheapest

Pour a small amount of kerosene onto the metal part of a tool and rub vigorously with **Brillo Steel Wool Soap Pads** (Purex Corporation). Then wad a piece of aluminum foil into a ball and rub the wad on the surface. Wipe the residue away with old newspaper and coat the tool lightly with olive oil before storing. **Caution:** Store kerosene in a cool place. Kerosene is extremely flammable and never should be stored in large amounts in the home.

Best

Zud (Boyle-Midway Inc.) removes rust from tools best. Make a thick paste from the powder and spread it on the surface to be cleaned. Allow a few minutes for the paste to penetrate the rust, then scrub vigorously with steel wool. Rinse well with water, dry thoroughly, and give the tool a light coating of olive oil.

Other Products Tested

Duro Naval Jelly (Woodhill Permatex)—brush-on liquid jelly; allow to penetrate; excellent rust and stain remover; caustic.
Mr. Rust (Lewis Research Labs. Co. Inc.)—pump spray; good to very good for removing rust on tools.
Formula 409 All Purpose Cleaner (The Clorox Company)—pump spray; removes grass and plant stains; much scouring required.

Tools of the Trade

Here's a list of the cleaning tools needed for most cleaning procedures and ways to clean the tools. Brand names are given for products that proved outstanding in tests by CONSUMER GUIDE®.

Brooms: for sweeping dirt off the floor.

Do's

- When dirty, wash brooms in warm, sudsy water. Rinse and shake off excess moisture.
- Wipe the broom handle with a sudsy sponge or cloth. Rinse with a damp cloth, then wipe it dry.
- Hang the broom, head down, until completely dry.

Recommended Product

O-CEDAR Angler Broom (The Drackett Company)—with flare-tip bristles made of fibers that hold loose dust; the angle cut helps reach into corners.

Brushes: soft-, medium-, or stiff-bristled for removing dust or embedded soil.

Do's

- Wash dirty brushes in a strong all-purpose cleaner solution in warm water.
- Wash two brushes at a time, scrubbing each one clean with the other.
- Run a coarse-toothed comb through brush bristles to help remove stubborn debris and soil.
- Always dry brushes with the bristles down.

Recommended Products

Empire Dust-R-Magic Brush (Empire Brushes, Inc.)—long handle and soft, flexible bristles; excellent for dusting curved surfaces and hard-to-reach places.

Empire Handled Hand & Nail Brush (Empire Brushes, Inc.)—with nylon bristles; good for cleaning tile grout and brushing off dried spot cleaners.

Read manufacturer's cautions and warnings before using any product.

Tools

Oxco Tile & Grout Brush (Vistron/Pro Brush)—narrow, stiff nylon bristle brush for cleaning grout and tile; curved plastic handle.

Oxco Perc Brush (Vistron/Pro Brush)—long-handled, thin nylon-bristle brush for cleaning spouts and tubes of coffee percolators.

Handle Scrub Brush w/Scraper (Suburbanite Industries)—stiff-bristled; arc-shaped for easy handling with rounded slot for fingertip or to hang on side of scrub pail.

Rubbermaid Toilet Bowl Brush Set (Rubbermaid Incorporated)—with small vinyl bristles; comes with hide-away caddy.

Stanhome Upholstery Brush (Stanley Home Products, Inc.)—triangular hand brush with foam rubber center surrounded by rows of bristles; used to work shampoo foam into upholstery.

Bar-B-Q and Oven Grill Brush (Brushtech, Inc.)—double steel brush for cleaning barbecue and oven grills.

Carpet Sweepers: handy for quick cleaning of carpets.

Do's
- Empty carpet sweeper dustpans over several large sheets of newspaper.
- Pick off any lint, thread, and string from the brushes each time the dust is emptied.
- Occasionally wash the brushes of a sweeper, if accessible, in a dishwashing detergent solution and hang the brushes to dry before replacing.
- Periodically wipe out the dustpan, exterior, and handle of sweepers with a damp cloth.

Cloths: for dusting, cleaning, dishwashing, and other cleaning jobs.

Do's
- Remove all buttons, snaps, hooks and eyes, and zippers when cutting up old clothing for cleaning cloths.
- Use all-white or light-colored cotton, linen, or wool fabrics for cleaning cloths.
- Wash a chamois in natural soap, not detergent.
- Handle a chamois carefully when washing, rinse well, stretch to original size, and dry away from direct heat.

Don'ts
- **Do not** use synthetic fabrics for cleaning cloths—synthetics are non-absorbent and create static electricity.
- **Do not** store oily rags, especially those that have been used with solvents. They are potential fire hazards.

Recommended Products

CONSUMER GUIDE® found that when a soft cloth is required for a procedure, no purchased material or packaged cloth can beat the effectiveness of an old **cotton T-shirt, birdseye diaper, retired sheet, pillowcase,** or **lint-free linen dish towel.** Old **terry bath towels** are excellent for drying patio furniture, cars, and awnings.

Chamois cloth

One-Wipe Dust Cloth (Guardsman Chemicals, Inc.)—grease-less, lintless, heavy but soft treated cloth for dusting furniture, automobile interiors, shoes, records, and equipment; can be washed at least 20 times without losing the chemical treatment.

Black Wonder Dusting Cloth (John Ritzenthaler Co.)—lint-free cloth for ebony-finished furniture.

Handi Wipes (Colgate-Palmolive Company)—reusable mesh cloth that can be washed many times; good for dishwashing, dusting, polishing, scrubbing, and wiping up spills.

Dishpans: plastic is best; choose a round or square model that fits your sink.

Dustmops

Do's
- Slip a large paper bag over the head of a dustmop, secure the top, and shake so the dust falls into the bag.
- Machine wash dustmop heads with other dirty articles.

Don'ts
- **Do not** shake a dustmop from an open window—the dust will only float back in.
- **Do not** store an oily dustmop.

Recommended Product

O-CEDAR Every-Which-Way (The Drackett Company)—mop with a washable cotton head that can swivel completely around.

Dustpans: plastic or metal; a dustpan with partial cover over the lower pan allows you to tilt the pan to hold dirt securely.

Floor Scrubbers/Polishers/Rug Shampooers:
can be rented at a hardware store or supermarket.

Tools

Gloves: for protecting hands from harsh cleaning agents and to help keep hands clean during gardening and other dirty chores.

Do's
- Lay rubber or plastic gloves flat to dry; blow in the fingers occasionally to promote drying.
- Sprinkle talcum or baby powder inside unlined rubber or plastic gloves to help them slide on easily.

Don't
- **Do not** dry in direct heat or lay on ovens or radiators.

Recommended Products

Playtex Handsaver Gloves (International Playtex, Inc.)—made of natural latex and synthetic neoprene to resist household solvents and grease; flock-lined; palms have anti-slip patterns.

Disposable plastic gloves are very handy for light-duty cleaning or painting chores.

Mitts: sometimes more convenient than using a cloth.

Recommended Products

CONSUMER GUIDE® found that worn out **cotton sweat socks,** especially those with terry-lined feet, make excellent dusting mitts.

Stanhome Cleaning Mitt (Stanley Home Products, Inc.)—made of fleecy polyester for dusting, cleaning, and polishing; washable.

Mops

Do's
- Wash the heads of string and sponge mops in a pan or tub with a warm water all-purpose cleaner solution and rinse well.
- Remove the sponge from the mop for easy cleaning.

Don't
- **Do not** store oily mops, especially those that have been used with solvents—they are potential fire hazards.

Recommended Products

Squeez-a-Matic Sponge Mop (Suburbanite Industries)—sponge mop; two rollers on either side of a removable sponge squeeze out the water when a lever on the handle is pressed.

Quickie Automatic Wet Mop (Quickie Manufacturing Corp.)—string mop; push rod on the handle operates a ring that slides down over the yarn head to extract water into the pail.

Pails: plastic or metal pails are most useful in either round or square shapes. Some pails are available with a double compartment to give one side for cleaning solution and another for rinse water. Pails with pour spouts are also extra handy.

Paper Towels

Recommended Products

Teri Towels (Kimberly-Clark Corporation)—strongest paper towels available; can be used for scrubbing; will hold up to wringing out.

Viva paper towels (Scott Paper Company)—one of the most absorbent towels available; excellent wet strength.

Bounty Designer Towels (Procter & Gamble)—excellent absorption, very good wet strength.

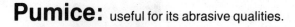

Pumice: useful for its abrasive qualities.

Recommended Products

Pumie Scouring Stick (United States Pumice Company)—pumice bar; removes corrosion, stains, and built-up soil from the toilet bowl, bathroom fixtures, garden tools, ceramic tile, swimming pools, ovens, barbecues, pots, pans, and griddles.
Suede Stone (Canden Company)—rubberlike bar for removing marks from suede garments and shoes, walls and wallpaper, and heel marks from floors.

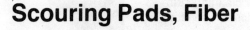

Scouring Pads, Fiber

Recommended Products

Bathroom Scrubber (3M)—thick fiber scouring pad glued to plastic handle; good for scrubbing very dirty bathroom fixtures, ceramic tile, countertops, and painted walls; not for use with solvents.

Scotch-Brite Cookware Scrub 'N Sponge (3M)—two-sided scrubbing pad with white fiber on one side and a pink sponge on the other; will not scratch nonstick finishes.

Tools

Reusable Sponge Towel (American Sponge and Chamois Company, Inc.)—cleaning towel made of natural cellulose, with fiber mesh on one side, sponge on the reverse; will not scratch nonstick finishes.

Scouring Pads, Steel

Recommended Products

Brillo Steel Wool Soap Pads (Purex Corporation)—soap-filled steel wool pad; better cleaner and longer lasting than others.

Supreme Steel Wool Balls (Purex Corporation)—plain steel wool ball without soap.

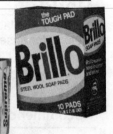

Scouring Pads, Synthetic

Recommended Products

Dobie Cleaning Pad (Purex Corporation)—synthetic sponge encased in polyester netting; good when considerable moisture is needed for scrubbing.

Nylon Clean 'n Sweet (John Ritzenthaler Co.)—all-nylon, reusable scouring cloth for washing dishes, pots, and pans; fabric will not absorb water or grease; will not scratch nonstick surfaces.

Scotch-Brite Scouring Pad (3M)—thin, harsh-plastic scouring pad without a sponge layer; not for nonstick surfaces, highly polished finishes, or porcelain.

Tuffy Scouring Pad (Miles Laboratories, Inc.)—durable plastic scouring pad; will not scratch.

Scrapers: to remove food residue from nonstick surfaces.

Recommended Product

Flambeau Nylon Pan Scraper (Flambeau Products Corporation)—square, hard nylon scraper to be used for cleaning stubborn food residue from pots and pans; will not scratch nonstick finishes.

Sponges: a good selection of various sizes is handy.

Do's

- Soak cellulose sponges before using, because they are brittle when dry.
- Clean very dirty natural sponges by adding 1 tablespoon ammonia per quart of sudsy water to the cleaning solution.
- Squeeze dishwashing detergent water through sponges and rinse well in clean water for a thorough cleaning.
- Soak very dirty cellulose sponges briefly in a mild solution of chlorine bleach; rinse thoroughly.
- Boil cellulose sponges to sanitize them, if necessary.
- Remove odors from sponges by soaking in a baking soda solution overnight.

Recommended Products

The Grabber (American Sponge and Chamois Company, Inc.)—large sponge made of cellulose and shaped to grasp easily around the middle.

Nylonge Super Surface Sponge (Sponge, Inc.)—smaller cellulose sponges, four to a package; a waffle-textured side for scrubbing and a terry side for wiping.

Stepladders or Step Stools: choose a sturdy model that is tall enough so you can easily reach everything you clean. See the chapters covering the materials from which your stepladder or stool is made for cleaning products and procedures.

Vacuum Cleaners and Attachments

Do's

- Empty vacuum cleaner bags over several large sheets of newspaper.
- Pick off any lint, thread, and string from the brushes each time the vacuum is emptied.
- Occasionally wash the brushes of a vacuum, if accessible, and hang to dry before replacing.
- Periodically wipe off the exterior of a vacuum with a damp cloth.
- Keep brushes and vacuum attachments free of lint and dust.
- Check the filter of a canister vacuum when changing the bag to see if it needs cleaning or replacing.
- Clean the clogged hose of a vacuum by sticking a mop handle down it or attaching it to the blower end of the vacuum.

Don't

- **Do not** allow vacuum cleaner bags to become overly full before emptying—a full bag reduces suction power.

Read manufacturer's cautions and warnings before using any product.

Tools

Window Cleaners: a rubber squeegee or squeegee/sponge combination is a great help. Long-handled brushes are also available that attach to a garden hose and dispense detergent for cleaning high windows from the outside.

Recommended Product

Superwasher (The Atlas Textiles Division of the Ohio Wiping Cloth Mfg. Co.)—combination window cleaning tool with a plastic head that holds a sponge covered by netting on one side and a squeegee on the other; head is attached to a 12-ounce squeeze bottle, which holds window washing fluid or water.

Recommended Basic Products

CONSUMER GUIDE® tested a few types of products for which no one particular brand outperformed the others. Differences in performance were quite minor for all-purpose cleaners and dishwashing liquids within each rank—"excellent," "very good," and "good." Occasionally one of these products will be designated in a chapter of the book as a "fastest," "cheapest," or "best," because it does an outstanding job for a particular cleaning task.

Also, many household ingredients can be mixed or used alone for many cleaning tasks, and they often are less expensive and just as effective as commercial products. Many of the Recommended Basic Products are available in inexpensive, generic packages. The common household products described in this section are items that work well for many cleaning problems. When the cleaning procedures call for "flour," for instance, use the brand you have on hand for an inexpensive cleanup.

All-Purpose Cleaners

Like Magic All Purpose Cleaner (Sterling Products)—pink paste; excellent cleaner, especially for surfaces that shouldn't get wet.

Mex Multi-Purpose Cleaner (United Gilsonite Laboratories)—phosphate-free powder; excellent cleaner and grease cutter.

Mr. Clean All-Purpose Cleaner (Procter & Gamble)—sudsing liquid; excellent performance; pleasant odor.

Fantastik Multi-Suface Spray Cleaner (Texize Chemicals Company)—pump spray; very good to excellent cleaner; moderate odor.

Formula 409 All Purpose Cleaner (The Clorox Company)—pump spray; very good to excellent cleaner; pleasant odor.

Amway Multi-Purpose L.O.C. Cleaner (Amway Corp.)—liquid; regular and high suds formulas; very good cleaner; pleasant odor.

Amway Zoom Spray Cleaner Concentrate (Amway Corp.)—spray; very good cleaner; pleasant odor.

Lestoil Heavy Duty Cleaner (Noxell Corporation)—sudsing liquid; very good cleaner; cuts grease; pine odor.

Lysol Deodorizing Cleaner II (Lehn & Fink Products Division of Sterling Drug Inc.)—sudsing liquid; phosphate-free; very good cleaner and disinfectant; moderate odor.

Read manufacturer's cautions and warnings before using any product.

Recommended Basic Products

Oakite All Purpose Cleaner (Oakite Products, Inc.)—low-sudsing powder; phosphate-free; very good cleaner.

Pine Forest Ajax All Purpose Cleaner (Colgate-Palmolive Company)—sudsing liquid; very good cleaner; clean pine odor.

Spic and Span (Procter & Gamble)—low-sudsing powder; very good cleaner; moderate pine odor.

Soilax (Economics Laboratory, Inc.)—nonsudsing powder; very good cleaner.

Top Job (Procter & Gamble)—sudsing liquid with ammonia; very good cleaner; moderate ammonia odor.

West Pine Cleaner Deodorizer (Glenwood Laboratories Inc.)—sudsing liquid; very good cleaner and deodorizer; pleasant pine odor.

Big Wally (S. C. Johnson & Son, Inc.)—aerosol foam; good cleaner; easy to use; moderate odor.

Breath O' Pine Multi-Purpose Cleaner (Brondow Incorporated)—sudsing liquid; good cleaner; heavy pine odor.

Janitor In A Drum (Texize Chemicals Company)—sudsing liquid; good cleaner; moderate odor.

Sea Mist All-Purpose Pine Oil Cleaner (Trager Mfg. Co., Inc.)—sudsing liquid; good cleaner; strong pine odor.

Liquid Dishwashing Detergents

Joy (Procter & Gamble)—high suds; excellent performance; fresh odor.

Lux Dishwashing Liquid (Lever Brothers Company)—very high suds; excellent performance; fresh odor.

Ajax Dishwashing Liquid (Colgate-Palmolive Company)—high suds; very good to excellent performance; clean odor.

Dove Dishwashing Liquid (Lever Brothers Company)—moderately high suds; very good to excellent performance; pleasant odor.

Dawn (Procter & Gamble)—high suds; very good performance; fresh odor.

Dermassage Dishwashing Liquid (Colgate-Palmolive Company)—high suds; very good performance; pleasant almond odor.

Ivory Liquid (Procter & Gamble)—high suds; very good performance; fresh odor.

Instant Fels Dishwashing Soap (Purex Corporation)—moderately high suds; good to very good performance; moderate odor.

Palmolive Dishwashing Liquid (Colgate-Palmolive Company)—high suds; good to very good performance; pleasant odor.

Dazzle (J. L. Prescott Co.)—moderate suds; good performance; pleasant odor.

Gentle Fels (Purex Corporation)—medium suds; good performance; pleasant odor.

Common Household Products

Ammonia: available in clear or sudsy forms, ammonia is an excellent cleaner or cleaning booster for many household surfaces. It is a good grease cutter, wax stripper, window cleaner, and general soil remover. No brand outperformed all others in tests by CONSUMER GUIDE®. If you object to ammonia's strong odor, buy one of the pleasantly scented products.

Baking Soda: this common household ingredient is one of the most versatile cleaning products available. Used by itself in dry form, it acts as a very mild scouring powder that won't scratch even the most delicate surfaces. Add a bit of water to make a paste and it scours even better. Combined with other ingredients, it makes a very good cleaning solution that also deodorizes. No brand outperformed all others in tests by CONSUMER GUIDE®.

Flour: ordinary kitchen flour is useful for some cleaning tasks. Always use flour in dry form as it creates a messy paste when water is added.

Lemon Juice: bottled lemon juice or juice squeezed from a cut lemon provides the key ingredient for many do-it-yourself cleaning products. Either way, the juice provides the mild acid reaction needed for many cleaning solutions.

Vinegar: vinegar can many times be substituted cheaply for lemon juice, and it is often listed as one of the main ingredients on homemade cleaning solutions. Usually white vinegar is preferred to clean fabrics, but cider vinegar is perfectly adequate for other applications. No brand outperformed all others in tests by CONSUMER GUIDE®.

Laundry

Proper laundry procedures should be used to keep garments clean and preserve their good looks. Other washable fabric items around the house consist of draperies, curtains, linens, bedding, small rugs, upholstery, and slipcovers. Specific cleaning procedures for many of these articles are given in other sections of this book. Also see Window Coverings—Draperies, Curtains; Bedding; Slipcovers; Furniture—Upholstery, Fabric; and Carpets and Rugs.

A clean wash is the result of careful attention to the proper sorting, pretreating, water temperature, machine cycle, and laundry products for the given fabrics. This chapter describes how to follow the proper procedures for laundering and lists products to use in the order of their performance.

Sorting

Properly sorting the laundry is the first step to a clean wash and helps to keep your clothes and household linens looking their best through repeated washings.

COLOR.   First sort the laundry by color. Put all the white or predominantly white articles in one pile, the light colors and pastels in another pile, and the bright and dark-colored items into a third. Then, separate the bright and dark pile into two piles, one for colorfast items and one for noncolorfast items.

DEGREE OF SOIL.   Separate each pile into three smaller piles: lightly soiled, moderately soiled, and heavily soiled.

FABRIC TYPE AND CONSTRUCTION.   Now you have up to 12 various-sized piles of laundry. Sort through them until you come up with a reasonable number of compatible, washer-sized loads.

Do's

- Combine white and light-colored items that have similar degrees of soil into the same pile.
- Combine noncolorfast items with similarly colored, colorfast items with the same degree of soil.
- Create a separate pile for delicate items that must be hand washed.
- Separate white synthetic articles and only wash them with other white fabrics.
- Separate synthetics, blends, and permanent-press fabrics from natural fiber fabrics without special finishes.

228

Don'ts

- **Do not** combine white synthetic articles with any colored fabrics.
- **Do not** combine delicate articles with heavy duty fabrics and garments.
- **Do not** combine lint-giving fabrics, such as chenille robes and bath towels, with lint-taking fabrics, such as corduroy, knits, synthetics, and permanent press.
- **Do not** wash dark-colored lint-givers with light-colored lint-givers.

Preparing the Wash

Check all items to be laundered for the following to minimize damage to the articles and to help clean them thoroughly.

Do's

- Know of any special finishes and the fiber content so you can select the proper water temperature and cleaning products.
- Save the care information so you can follow the recommended cleaning procedures.
- Close all zippers, hook all hooks, and button all buttons.
- Turn pockets inside out to get rid of debris.
- Turn down cuffs at the bottom of sleeves and pants and brush away the loose soil.
- Remove any nonwashable trim or decorations, and pins or buckles that might make holes or snag other articles in the wash.
- Tie and buckle all belts and sashes to prevent tangling.
- Mend seams, tears, holes, or loose hems to prevent further damage during the wash cycle.
- Turn sweaters and corduroy garments inside out to prevent pilling and their tendency to collect lint.
- Pretreat spots, stains, and heavily soiled items with either a prewash spot and stain remover, liquid detergent, paste made from granular soap or detergent, bar soap, or a presoak.

Prewash Spot and Stain Removers

While soaps and detergents can be worked directly into spots and heavily soiled areas before putting the laundry into the washer, a special product designed just for removing spots and stains is more convenient to use. Called prewash spot and stain removers, these aerosols or pump sprays are excellent for spot treating stubborn soil and stains, especially grease marks on synthetic fabrics.

Do's

- Treat the stain while it is still fresh.
- Saturate the soiled area completely, then lightly rub the fabric together to work the product into the fibers.

Don'ts

- **Do not** expect to remove spots and stains completely once the fabric has been washed and dried or pressed.
- **Do not** spray prewash products near the washer or dryer—some may damage the exterior finish.

Read manufacturer's cautions and warnings before using any product.

Laundry

Recommended Products

Magic Pre-Wash (Armour-Dial Inc.)—aerosol; excellent spot and stain remover.

Shout Laundry Soil & Stain Remover (S. C. Johnson & Son, Inc.)—aerosol; excellent spot and stain remover.

Spray 'n Wash (Texize Chemicals Company)—pump spray or aerosol; very good spot and stain remover.

Miracle White Laundry Soil & Stain Remover (The Drackett Company)—pump spray; good spot and stain remover.

Presoaks

Granular presoak products containing enzymes can break down stubborn stains such as milk, blood, baby formula, chocolate, gravy, some fruits and vegetables, and grass. They are not effective on rust, ballpoint ink, oil, or grease. Following the manufacturer's directions, mix a solution in a large sink or the washer and add the soiled laundry, soaking for the recommended length of time. You also can use a presoak for solutions in diaper pails and as a detergent booster.

Do's
- Dissolve the presoak thoroughly in the water before adding the laundry.
- Soak articles overnight in a presoak solution whenever they look dull and dingy.
- Wash the laundry as usual after using a presoak.

Don't
- **Do not** soak dark- and light-colored fabrics together for a long period—this can cause colors to run.

Recommended Products

Axion (Colgate-Palmolive Company)—granular; excellent stain remover and detergent booster; not for use on wool or silk; not for use with chlorine bleach.

Biz (Procter & Gamble)—granular; very good stain remover; contains oxygen bleach, fabric whitener, and blueing; good detergent booster; can be used on undyed silk or wool.

Laundry Products

Most commercial laundry preparations are designed to be used in washing machines, but some can be used for hand and machine washing. Read the label carefully before purchasing any product to make sure it is the right one for the job. When you use a laundry product, follow the directions precisely and measure accurately.

Water Conditioners

Water can be hard or soft—depending on the amounts and types of chemicals and minerals dissolved in it. This influences the effectiveness of laundry products: The softer the water, the more effective for cleaning. Determine the hardness of your water so you will know if extra steps must be taken to condition it for effective cleaning. Hard water leaves a residue on articles you launder, known as *washing film.* To soften water, the hardness minerals must be removed or locked up. Water that measures under four grains hardness per gallon will probably clean effectively, especially if a detergent rather than soap is used. You can soften harder water with a mechanical water softener that attaches to your home's water tank, or by adding a water conditioning product to the wash and rinse water.

The two types of water conditioning products are nonprecipitating, which can be used with soaps or detergents in both the wash and rinse water and are the best choice for really hard water, and precipitating, which should be used only in the wash water and are not very effective with soaps or phosphate-free detergents.

Do's

- Follow directions on water conditioning product labels precisely.
- Remove light hard-water washing film from from diapers, towels, or fabrics by soaking them in a solution of 1 cup white vinegar and 1 gallon water in a plastic container.
- Wash flame retardant items only in soft water.
- Thoroughly rinse off residues of precipitating water softeners from fabrics to prevent skin irritation, fabric yellowing, or loss of softness.
- Use a nonprecipitating conditioner to remove previously formed washing film or soap/detergent build-up.
- Use a nonprecipitating conditioner if you use soap in hard water or if you use a phosphate-free detergent.

Don't

- **Do not** use a precipitating water conditioner with a phosphate-free detergent.

Recommended Products

NONPRECIPITATING. Calgon Water Softener (Beecham Products Division of Beecham Inc.)—powder; excellent for use with soaps and phosphate or phosphate-free detergents.

PRECIPITATING. Arm & Hammer Washing Soda (Church & Dwight Co., Inc.)—granular; excellent conditioner for detergents containing phosphates.

20 Mule Team Borax (United States Borax & Chemical Corporation)—powder; very good conditioner for detergents containing phosphates.

Detergents and Soaps

Soap is a mixture of alkalies and fats that is a good cleaner in soft water, breaks down beautifully in city sewer systems, and does not harm the environment. Soap is less effective in hard water, however, because it reacts with the high mineral content to form a soap curd that leaves a gray scum on clothing. Detergents are synthetic washing aids derived from petroleum or other nonfatty materials, are less affected by hard water, and have excellent cleaning power. They contain wetting agents that lift off dirt and builders that help to inactivate hard water minerals, eliminating scum. Most detergents contain phosphates, while some products now are phosphate free. Some states and municipalities have banned detergents containing phosphates, which are believed harmful to the environment because they promote overgrowth of algae in water. The cleaning ability of phosphate-free detergents is not as effective in hard-water areas and in cold-water washes, and these detergents

Laundry

cause excessive wear on many fabrics. Some companies make the same detergent in phosphate and phosphate-free versions.

Do's

- Always follow the manufacturer's instructions for the amount to use, proper wash cycle, and recommended water temperature.
- Measure laundry products to prevent waste from overuse and inadequate cleaning from underuse.
- Use liquid detergents in cold water washes for best results, or predissolve powder or granular detergents in some hot water, then add the solution to the cold wash water.
- Increase the amount of detergent for extra heavy and/or greasy soil, larger loads, warm or cold water washes, hard water, and when using phosphate-free detergent.
- Use a nonprecipitating water conditioner when using a soap or phosphate-free detergent to boost its cleaning power, especially if you have hard water.
- Avoid phosphate-free detergent build-up in the washer tub by using ½ cup nonprecipitating water conditioner in the wash at least once for every six to eight loads.
- Dissolve soap or detergent in the wash water before adding the clothes to distribute the product more evenly.
- Add 1 cup ammonia to the wash water to boost detergent effectiveness for heavily soiled or greasy wash loads.

ALL-PURPOSE DETERGENTS. All-purpose detergents (also referred to as heavy duty and/or concentrated) are suitable for heavily soiled clothes and sturdy natural and synthetic fabrics. Many can now be used in all water temperatures—hot, warm, or cold; a few brands are for use in cold water. However, all detergents perform better in warmer water. Detergents also are classified by suds produced—high, medium, or low. Front-loading machines and washer/dryer combinations use only low-sudsing products; medium- and low-sudsing detergents should be used only for laundry, not other cleaning jobs.

Recommended Products

Yes (Texize Chemicals Company)—liquid that contains fabric softener; excellent performance in all water temperatures; fresh odor.

Bold 3 (Procter & Gamble)—powder; low suds; contains fabric softener; excellent performance in all water temperatures; fresh odor.

Arm & Hammer Laundry Detergent (Church & Dwight Co., Inc.)—granular; high suds; excellent performance in all water temperatures; deodorizing agent; fresh odor.

Rinso (Lever Brothers Company)—granular; high suds; excellent performance in all water temperatures; fresh odor.

Cold Power XE (Colgate-Palmolive Company)—granular; high suds; very good performance in cold water; good in warm and hot water; fresh odor.

All Temperature Cheer (Procter & Gamble)—granular; high suds; very good performance in all water temperatures; fresh odor.

Era (Procter & Gamble)—liquid; high suds; very good performance in all water temperatures; fresh odor.

Fab All Temperature Laundry Detergent (Colgate-Palmolive Company)—granular; high suds; very good performance in all water temperatures; fresh odor.

Oxydol (Procter & Gamble)—granular; high suds; very good performance in hot or warm water; contains oxygen bleach; moderate odor.

All Temperature Punch (Colgate-Palmolive Company)—granular; medium suds; very good performance in all water temperatures; fresh odor.

Tide (Procter & Gamble)—granular; high suds; very good performance in warm or hot water; moderate odor.

Trend Heavy Duty Laundry Detergent (Purex Corporation)—granular; high suds; very good performance in warm and hot water; little odor.

Concentrated All Detergent (Lever Brothers Company)—granular; low to medium suds; good performance in all water temperatures; fresh odor.

Dynamo (Colgate-Palmolive Company)—liquid; high suds; good performance in all water temperatures; fresh odor.

Dash (Procter & Gamble)—granular; low suds; good performance in all water temperatures; fresh odor.

Gain (Procter & Gamble)—granular; low to medium suds; good performance in all water temperatures; fresh odor.

Wisk Laundry Detergent (Lever Brothers Company)—liquid; high suds; good performance in all water temperatures; fresh odor.

LIGHT DUTY DETERGENTS. Light duty detergents are used for delicate, lightly soiled fabrics. The liquid dishwashing detergents also belong in this group, but they should be used only for hand washing as they make too many suds if used in the machine (see Recommended Basic Products for a list of these detergents).

Recommended Products

Liquid Woolite (Boyle-Midway Inc.)—liquid; for use in cold water; high suds; excellent performance; pleasant odor.

Carbona Cold Water Wash (Carbona Products Company)—liquid; high suds; for use in cold water by hand or in machine; very good performance; fresh odor.

Handle With Care (The Drackett Company)—liquid; high suds; hand or machine wash; very good performance in warm or cold water; fresh odor.

Machine Wash Woolite (Boyle-Midway Inc.)—granular; high suds; for cold water machine wash; very good performance; fresh odor.

LIGHT DUTY SOAP. Light duty soaps are designed for delicate, lightly soiled fabrics and are available in powder or bar form. Bar soaps are good for pretreating stains and for hand washing, but do not perform well in the washing machine.

Recommended Products

Ivory Snow (Procter & Gamble)—powder; high suds; very good performance in warm and hot water.

Fels-Naptha Heavy Duty Laundry Bar Soap (Purex Corporation)—bar; very good for pretreating spots and stains.

Kirkman Borax Soap (Colgate-Palmolive Company)—bar; moderate suds; very good for pretreating spots and stains; moderate odor.

Octagon (Colgate-Palmolive Company)—bar; medium suds; very good for pretreating spots and stains; pleasant odor.

Laundry

Bleach

Bleach works with detergent or soap to remove stains and soil, whiten white items, and brighten colors. It acts as a mild disinfectant. The two basic types of laundry bleach are chlorine and oxygen. Common liquid chlorine bleach is the most effective and least expensive, but cannot be used on all fabrics. Oxygen bleach is safer for all washable fabrics, resin-finished fibers, and most washable colors, but is less strong than chlorine bleach.

Do's

- Always give colored fabrics a colorfastness test before using any bleach by mixing 1 tablespoon chlorine bleach with ¼ cup water or 1 tablespoon oxygen bleach with 2 quarts hot water; apply to an inconspicuous place; wait a few minutes and check for a color change. If the color does not bleed, use the bleach according to the manufacturer's directions.
- Bleach clothes only in the wash cycle so the bleach can be completely removed during the rinse cycle.
- Use one part 3% hydrogen peroxide mixed in eight parts water to safely bleach delicate fabrics like silk.
- Add diluted chlorine bleach to the wash water about 5 minutes after the wash cycle has begun or use an automatic bleach dispenser.
- Use bleach according to the fabric type and care recommendations.
- Use chlorine bleach only on white and colorfast fabrics.
- Use oxygen bleach on delicate fabrics or when chlorine bleach cannot be used.
- Use the hottest water possible when using a bleach, as this improves its performance.

Don'ts

- **Do not** bleach just a stain—bleach the whole item.
- **Do not** use ammonia and bleach together—the combination can create hazardous fumes.
- **Do not** pour any type of bleach directly onto fabrics—dilute the bleach in water first.
- **Do not** use chlorine bleach on wool, silk, spandex, or acetate.
- **Do not** use chlorine bleach on flame-retardant and permanent-press finishes unless the hang tag or label recommends it.
- **Do not** use bleach in the rinse water.

Recommended Products

CHLORINE. **Clorox Bleach** (The Clorox Company)—liquid; excellent performance.

Purex Liquid Bleach (Purex Corporation)—liquid; very good to excellent performance.

OXYGEN. **Clorox 2 All Fabric Bleach** (The Clorox Company)—powder; excellent performance.

Snowy Bleach (Gold Seal Co.)—powder; very good performance.

Fabric Softeners

Fabric softeners add softness and fluffiness, reduce static electricity on synthetics so they will not cling, help decrease linting, and make ironing easier. They are available in liquid, sheet, or solid form. Liquid fabric softeners are added to the wash or rinse cycle; sheet and solid products are inserted in the dryer.

Do's

- Read fabric softener instructions carefully to determine at what time in the laundering cycle to add them—with the detergent, in the rinse water, or in the dryer.
- Dilute liquid fabric softeners before adding to the automatic dispenser or the rinse.
- To prevent build-up, use a fabric softener every third time you wash towels and diapers or other fabrics you wish to remain absorbent.
- Remove stains caused by fabric softeners by rubbing the area with a liquid detergent or prewash spot and stain remover and then rewashing the article.

Don'ts

- **Do not** pour or spray fabric softeners directly onto clothes—this can cause temporary staining.
- **Do not** use any other laundry product, such as a water conditioner, in the rinse water with a fabric softener—this can cause stains.
- **Do not** use sheet fabric softeners in the dryer when drying delicate polyester articles—the softener can stain the fabric temporarily.
- **Do not** overuse fabric softeners, especially on towels and diapers—excess softener can "waterproof" them.

Recommended Products

LIQUID.   Final Touch Concentrated Fabric Softener (Lever Brothers Company)—liquid with blueing; very good softener and static eliminator; add to final rinse; heavily scented.

Rain Barrel Fabric Softener (S. C. Johnson & Son, Inc.)—liquid; add just before detergent in wash cycle; very good softener and static eliminator.

Sta-Puf Fabric Softener (A. E. Staley Mfg. Co.)—liquid with blueing; very good softener, good static eliminator; add to the final rinse; heavily scented.

Downy Fabric Softener (Procter & Gamble)—liquid with blueing; good softener and static eliminator; add to the final rinse; heavily scented.

SHEET.   Purex Toss 'n Soft (Purex Corporation)—excellent softener and static eliminator.

Bounce (Procter & Gamble)—very good softener and static eliminator.

Cling Free Fabric Softener Sheets (Beecham Products Division of Beecham Inc.)—good softener and static eliminator.

SPRAY.   Cling Free (Beecham Products Divison of Beecham Inc.)—spray; to be sprayed on curved surface of dryer drum; very good static electricity eliminator.

SOLID.   Free 'n Soft (Economics Laboratory, Inc.)—self-stick packet of solid softener to attach to dryer vanes; economical; good softener; good static electricity eliminator.

Using an Automatic Washer

The automatic washer is a great time saver, but for the best results you must know how to combine multiple load capacities, water levels, temperature settings, and cycles properly.

Loading the Machine

Do's

- Read the washer manufacturer's instruction booklet for recommended laundry procedures.
- Mix small and large items in each load for best circulation.
- Distribute the weight and volume evenly around the washbasket.
- Load the washer to capacity if possible to save time and energy.
- Place belts and other small items in a mesh bag to prevent tangling or damage during the wash cycle.

Don'ts

- **Do not** overload the machine—garments should not pile up past the top of the agitator vanes.
- **Do not** wash large loads of permanent press or synthetic fiber knits to keep wrinkling to a minimum.

Water Temperature

Water temperature in the washer varies according to the fabric and amount of soil. Use this chart to help you select the proper wash and rinse settings. **Caution:** Be aware of the actual temperature of the water, since it can vary during the year. If water temperature is below 80° F. it is too cold to do a good job even if you use a cold water detergent; it will also influence the temperature of a "warm water" setting. Adjust the amount of cold water flowing into the machine to get the right temperature range if this is a problem—hot water may be mixed with cold water to adjust the cleaning temperature.

Type of Load	Wash Temperature	Rinse Temperature
White and light-colored cottons and linens Diapers Heavily soiled permanent press and wash and wear All other greasy or heavily soiled wash	130° F.–150° F. (hot)	warm or cold
Dark colors Lightly and moderately soiled permanent press and wash and wear fabrics Some woven or knit synthetic fabrics (see care label) Some washable woolens (see care label) Any other moderately soiled wash	100° F.–110° F. (warm)	cold

Type of Load	Wash Temperature	Rinse Temperature
Noncolorfast fabrics	80° F.–100° F.	cold
Some washable woolens (see care label)	(cold)	
Some woven or knit synthetic fabrics (see care label)		
Fragile items		
Bright colors		
Any lightly soiled wash		

Do's

- Use the hottest water possible that is compatible with the type of laundry for best results.
- Use a cold water detergent when washing in cold water—other detergents will not perform well.

Water Level

Use enough water to provide good circulation, but not so much that you waste water and energy. Most machines have a water-level control and you will save money if it is adjusted for each load. Refer to the manufacturer's instructions for this information.

Machine Cycle

Select the type of cycle and the length of washing time according to the type of load and the degree of soil. Follow these guidelines, using a longer cycle for heavily soiled laundry.

Type of Load	Cycle	Wash Time
Sturdy white and colorfast items	Normal	10–12 minutes
Sturdy noncolorfast items	Normal	6–8 minutes
Sturdy permanent press and wash and wear	Permanent Press	6–8 minutes
Delicate fabrics and knits	Gentle or Delicate	4–6 minutes

Using a Wringer Washer

If you use a wringer washer, follow the same basic procedures as for an automatic washer for sorting, preparing the wash, selecting the water temperature, and laundry products. The difference between the two types of washers is that with a wringer washer, laundry is passed through a wringer into a tub of rinse water.

Do's

- Fill the washer with hot water and dissolve the laundry products in it before adding the laundry.
- Distribute the wash evenly around the washer tub.
- Wash items that need hot water first, items that need warm water second, and cold-water items last.
- Rinse the clothes twice, running them through the wringer each time.
- Start clothes through the wringer flat—keep buttons and other closures folded to the inside.
- Know how to stop, reverse, and open the wringer quickly for safety's sake.

Laundry

Don'ts

- **Do not** use the same wash water for more than two or three loads.
- **Do not** wash lightly or moderately soiled laundry in the same wash water as heavily soiled clothes.
- **Do not** overload the machine.
- **Do not** allow children around the washer—especially the wringer—while it is operating.

Hand Washing

Most washable fabrics can be put into the machine, but some items are marked "hand wash only," and hand washing is quicker and cheaper than using the machine when you have only a few items to clean.

Do's

- Sort by color, putting white and light colors together, dark and noncolorfast items into separate piles.
- Pretreat stains and heavily soiled areas with a prewash spot and stain remover or by rubbing liquid detergent into the area.
- Use a light duty soap or detergent and dissolve it in the wash water before adding the clothes.
- Use cool or warm water.
- Submerge the articles in the water and let soak 3 to 5 minutes.
- Gently squeeze the suds through the fabric, being careful not to rub, twist, or wring excessively.
- Rinse articles thoroughly in cool water until it runs clear.
- Add a few drops of fabric softener to the last rinse if desired.
- Hang blouses, dresses, scarfs, and lingerie to drip dry. The shower is a good place for this.
- Use towels to blot up excess moisture in sweaters, stockings, panties, and bras. Hang to dry only if the weight of the water will not stretch them out of shape—otherwise dry on a towel-covered, flat surface.

Drying Clothes

Most clothes dried in an automatic dryer come out soft and almost wrinkle free. However, you may prefer to dry the laundry on the clothesline on sunny days, reserving the dryer for inclement weather and for your permanent press fabrics.

Machine Drying

Do's

- Read the manufacturer's instruction book to familiarize yourself with the dryer's operating procedures and recommended cycles.
- Shake out each article before placing it in the dryer to speed the drying time and cut down on wrinkles.
- Use a low or delicate heat setting to dry knits or delicate fabrics, especially if you use a sheet fabric softener.
- Dry clothes until they are "almost dry" rather than "bone dry" if you are going to iron them.
- Remove items from the dryer as soon as it stops, and hang or fold all articles to prevent wrinkling.
- Throw in a pair of clean, dry sneakers when drying down-filled articles to help redistribute the down.
- Clean the lint filter after each use.

Don'ts

- **Do not** overload the dryer—this will cause excessive wrinkling and uneven drying.
- **Do not** put plastic or foam rubber items in the dryer.
- **Do not** dry woolen items in the dryer unless given specific instructions to do so.
- **Do not** use a high heat setting when drying lightweight synthetics, especially if you use a sheet fabric softener.
- **Do not** use the dryer for any item cleaned at home with a solvent-based cleaning product.
- **Do not** dry fiberglass items in the dryer.

Line Drying

Do's

- Wash plastic clothespins in mild soap and warm water in the sink or in the automatic clothes washer, using a mesh bag.
- Wash wooden clothespins in a hot dishwashing detergent solution.
- Wipe the clothesline with a damp cloth before using it.
- Attach items to the clothesline by their most sturdy edges.
- Secure clothes to the line with clothespins.
- Smooth clothes as you hang them, running your fingers down seams and along the front and collar and cuff edges.
- Dry white and light-colored items in the sun and bright colored items in the shade.

Don'ts

- **Do not** hang clothes on a dirty clothesline.
- **Do not** allow clothes that need to be ironed to dry completely—a bit of moisture speeds the pressing process.

Solving Washing Problems

Some problems can appear in the laundry from time to time that require special attention.

Brown Stains

Cause: Soap, detergent, or bleach reacting with iron or manganese in the water.
Solution: Install an iron filter on your water system. Do not use chlorine bleach in the wash. Use a nonprecipitating water conditioner in both the wash and rinse water.

Excessive Wear

Cause: Improper use of bleach.
Solution: Always dilute chlorine bleach before adding it to the washer. See the **Do's** and **Don'ts** under Bleach.

Cause: Tears, holes, split seams, and loose hems not mended before washing the articles.
Solution: Make all repairs before washing an item.

Cause: Snags from hooks, pins, or zippers.
Solution: Hook all hooks, close zippers, and remove pins or other sharp objects before putting articles in the washer.

Cause: Clothes not circulating freely during the wash and rinse cycles.
Solution: Reduce the load size or increase the water level.

Gray and Dingy Fabric

Cause: Incorrect sorting.
Solution: Follow the rules listed in Sorting.

Cause: Insufficient detergent.
Solution: Increase the amount of detergent.

Cause: Water temperature too low.
Solution: Increase the temperature, using instructions listed in Water Temperature.

Greasy Spots

Cause: Undiluted, liquid fabric softener coming into contact with fabric.
Solution: Dilute liquid fabric softeners before adding to the rinse or softener dispenser.

Cause: Fabric softener sheets in the dryer with lightweight fabrics.
Solution: Use liquid softener in the washing machine when doing delicate fabrics. These spots can be removed by rubbing in liquid detergent and then washing again. Also use a lower temperature setting on the dryer.

Cause: Hard water.
Solution: Use a water conditioner according to the detergent type or install a water softener.

Cause: Overloaded washer.
Solution: Reduce the load size so the clothes can circulate more freely.

Harsh-Feeling Fabrics

Cause: Spin speed not adequate.
Solution: Increase the spin speed or check to make sure the load is balanced so the spin can reach its maximum speed.

Cause: Hard water.
Solution: Increase the amount of detergent, install a mechanical water softener, or use a water conditioning product.

Cause: Using soap in hard water.
Solution: Switch to a detergent, install a mechanical water softener, or use a water conditioner.

Linting

Cause: Incorrect sorting.
Solution: Follow the rules listed in Sorting.

Cause: Not enough detergent.
Solution: Increase the amount of detergent to help hold lint in suspension so it can be flushed down the drain.

Cause: Overloaded washer.
Solution: Reduce load size or increase the water level so the wash can circulate freely.

Cause: Improper use of fabric softener.
Solution: Do not add softener directly to wash water unless specifically directed to do so.

Cause: Debris in cuffs or pockets.
Solution: Remove any tissues, paper, and loose dirt before washing.

Scorching During Ironing

Cause: Iron temperature setting too high.
Solution: Reduce heat setting on iron.

Cause: Heat of iron reacting with a build-up of laundry products.
Solution: Run clothes through one or two complete washing cycles with 1 cup nonprecipitating water conditioner and no other laundry product, then wash as usual.

Static Electricity

Cause: Synthetic fabrics' natural tendency to produce static electricity.
Solution: Use a fabric softener in the washer or dryer.

Yellowing

Cause: Incomplete removal of soil, especially of body oils.
Solution: Pretreat heavily soiled areas, increase the amount of detergent, use hotter water, and use a bleach.

Cause: Iron in the water.
Solution: Install an iron filter, use extra detergent, and use a nonprecipitating water conditioner.

Cause: Natural aging of some fabrics.
Solution: No solution except the above suggestions for routine washing to slow the aging process.

Read manufacturer's cautions and warnings before using any product.

Spots and Stains

The best way to deal with spots and stains is to take fast action. Dealing with a spot quickly gives you a better chance of removing it. The stain removal method you use depends on what has been spilled, the fiber content of the fabric, its washability, and the dye's stability. Generally, stains are classified as greasy, nongreasy, or a combination of both. Greasy stains can be caused by spills of butter, oil, or machine grease, to name a few. Nongreasy stains include fruit juices, tea, mustard, wine, and others; combination stains result from spills of substances like milk, chocolate, or egg.

This section lists instructions for removing stains from washable and nonwashable surfaces, whether the stained fabric is delicate—like silk—or sturdy—like cotton. To remove stains quickly, first try the commercial stain removing product listed for the stain; if you don't have the commercial product on hand, or if you prefer your own "home recipe" stain removers, follow the step-by-step instructions given for removing the stain.

You may not have to use each step of the stain removing instructions—only follow these steps until the stain is removed. But it is important for you to follow the steps in sequential order until the surface is stain-free.

Do's

- Blot up any spill promptly with paper toweling, white blotting paper, facial tissue, or a soft white cloth.
- Save all care and content labels for cleaning information.
- Carefully read and follow directions on commercial stain-removing preparations.
- Keep all spot and stain removers and other cleaning products out of the reach of children.
- Test all spot and stain removers, including water, in an inconspicuous place on the article to be cleaned to determine if the cleaners will damage or waterspot the fabric.
- Use a hard work surface that is not affected by the chemicals used—such as an inverted glass pie plate—and protect the countertop or table with aluminum foil in case of spills.
- Use the proper stain-removing technique for the type of stain and the type of surface stained. You may not have to use all procedures, but follow the sequence of the steps as listed.
- Carefully scrape off solids with a spoon, spatula, or dull knife.
- Conduct a colorfastness test before using bleach: mix 1 tablespoon bleach in ¼ cup water, apply a drop with a medicine dropper to a hidden part of the fabric, allow to penetrate for 1 minute, blot dry, and examine for color changes.
- Pat lightly when treating stains.
- Use cool water to remove most stains—on washable objects, hot water can set some stains.
- Use a medicine dropper or glass rod to apply cleaner preparations to very small stains to avoid spreading them.
- Work in a well-ventilated area when using a solvent-based product.
- After treating an article, air or rinse out spot and stain-removing products.

Don'ts

- **Do not** wash, iron, or dry-clean an article until the spot or stain has been treated and/or removed.
- **Do not** use hot water or press over stains caused by meat juices, blood, or eggs—this will set them.
- **Do not** allow spot and stain remover products to remain on the fabric after treating the stain.
- **Do not** let cleaning agents come in contact with the skin or eyes.
- **Do not** attempt to remove stains on old or extremely delicate articles.

Stain Removing Agents to Have on Hand

The following items are used to remove various types of stains. Many of them are common household products, while some have limited application and are needed for a particular type of stain.

Abrasive: for removing crayon marks from wallpaper.

Recommended Product

Suede Stone (Canden Company).

Absorbent Powders: cornstarch, fuller's earth, cornmeal, talcum powder, French chalk, salt.

Ammonia: clear household ammonia without added color. When used on silk or wool, dilute with equal parts water.

Recommended Product

Parsons' Clear Detergent Ammonia (Armour-Dial Inc.).

Amyl Acetate: a poisonous chemical available at drug stores that is useful for removing stains such as those caused by nail polish.

Bleaches: chlorine, oxygen-type (containing sodium perborate), and hydrogen peroxide. Use chlorine bleach on white cottons and other colorfast fabrics. However, chlorine bleach can weaken some fibers and damage some dyes and finishes. Do not use a chlorine bleach in a metal container—this may speed up the action and cause fiber damage. Do not use chlorine bleach on fire-resistant finishes, unless the item's care label specifies it as safe. Use an oxygen-type bleach on delicate fabrics, because it has a much milder action. Hydrogen peroxide in a 3% solution (sold in the drug store as a mild antiseptic) is safe for all fibers and colorfast fabrics, acting faster than an oxygen-type bleach.

Spots and Stains

Recommended Products

Clorox Bleach (The Clorox Company)—chlorine bleach.

Clorox 2 All Fabric Bleach (The Clorox Company)—oxygen-type bleach.

Dry Spotter: mix one part coconut oil and eight parts dry cleaning solvent. Keep container tightly capped.

Glycerin: a liquid sold in drug stores used to prepare a "Wet Spotter."

Mildew Remover: disinfectant or mildew stain products that remove the mold.

Recommended Product

X-14 Instant Mildew Stain Remover (White Laboratories)—pump spray.

Rust Removers: powders and liquids formulated to remove rust from metal and fabrics.

Recommended Products

Bar Keepers Friend Cleanser & Polish (SerVaas Laboratories, Inc.)—powder; for use on metals, ceramic, fabrics, and porcelain.

Mr. Rust (Lewis Research Labs. Co. Inc.)—liquid; for use on metals, ceramic, carpets, and porcelain.

RoVer Rust Remover (Hach Chemical Company)—to be added to wash water when laundering fabrics.

Putnam's Color Remover (Putnam Color and Dye Corporation)—to be added to wash water when laundering fabrics.

Whink Rust Stain Remover (Whink Products Co.)—liquid safe for colorfast fabrics and carpets, and for toilet bowls.

Solvents: denatured or rubbing alcohol, turpentine, dry cleaning solvents, and spot lifters.

Recommended Products

Goddard's Dry Clean Spot Remover (S. C. Johnson & Son, Inc.)—aerosol spray; not for use on rainwear, rubberized or foam-backed articles, suede, sheepskin, or washable wallpaper.

K2r Spot-lifter (Texize Chemicals Company)—aerosol with plastic brush on cap, or cream in tube; not for use on rubber, leather, suede, plastic, latex, velvet, or varnished surfaces.

Amway Remove Fabric Spot Cleaner (Amway Corp.)—aerosol with plastic brush on cap; not for use on plastic, vinyl, leather, or leatherette.

Afta Cleaning Fluid (Afta Solvents Corporation)—liquid solvent; not for use on plastic, rubber, or painted surfaces.

Carbona Spot Remover with Applicator Top (Carbona Products Company)—liquid with built-in applicator; not for use on rubberized fabrics or styrene plastic.

Afta Carpet Stain Remover (Afta Solvents Corporation)—liquid.

Stain-X Carpet Stain Remover (Positive Products Laboratories, Inc.)—squeeze bottle with squirt-spout top; safe for all fabrics, leather, and vinyl.

Spot Shot (Sifers Chemicals, Inc.)—aerosol liquid for carpets; designed to remove greasy, nongreasy, and combination stains.

Trewax Up & Out (Trewax Company)—pump spray for carpets; not for use on wool carpets.

Vinegar: white vinegar only—cider or wine vinegar can stain.

Washing Agents: enzyme presoaks, prewash spot and stain removers, all-purpose detergents, light-duty detergents, water conditioners, and baking soda.

Recommended Products

See Laundry.

Wet Spotter: inexpensive preparation made at home of one part glycerin, one part liquid dishwashing detergent (see Recommended Basic Products), and eight parts water. Shake well before each use. Store in plastic squeeze bottle.

Miscellaneous: club soda; foam shaving cream; lemon juice.

Stain Removing Equipment

Other cleaning basics you will need include the following:

glass bowls
clean white cotton rags or
  terrycloth towels
white paper towels and/or
  paper diapers
glass stirring rod
smooth, stainless steel teaspoon

glass measuring cup
white blotting paper
white facial tissue
sponge
medicine dropper
dull knife or spatula
small, stiff brush

Stain Removing Techniques

There are six basic techniques used throughout the "How to Remove Staining Substances" section. When instructions call for absorbing, flushing, freezing, scraping, sponging, or tamping, follow the directions listed here for the technique.

Read manufacturer's cautions and warnings before using any product.

Spots and Stains

Absorbing

Hardened stains sometimes can be loosened by placing a pad dampened with stain remover on top of the stain and allowing it to penetrate for an hour or more. Place a pad under the stain also, and keep the top pad damp by adding more stain remover as needed.

Flushing

Flushing releases the staining substance and removes the chemicals used to treat the stain so they don't damage the fabric later. To flush, place a clean pad under the stain and add small amounts of the cleaning agent to the stain with a medicine dropper, or with a container that allows very slow pouring. Do not add the stain remover faster than the pad underneath can absorb it. As the stain is flushed through the fabric into the pad beneath, change the absorbent pad several times during flushing. Use dry pads to remove any excess moisture as soon as the stain disappears. If water is used for flushing on a washable article, you can dip the stained area up and down in a bowl of warm water; change the water at least twice during this process.

Freezing

Freezing solidifies substances such as candle wax and gum to make removing them easier. To freeze a stain, gently rub an ice cube across the area. To freeze semiliquid substances, like hot candle wax, work quickly to avoid spreading the stain. Once the material has hardened, gently lift or scrape it off the stained surface. Portable items may be wrapped in a plastic bag and placed in the freezer until the stain hardens.

Scraping

An effective way to loosen many stains is by scraping with a teaspoon. Place the stain directly on the work surface and grasp the spoon by the side of the bowl. After adding the stain remover to the stain, move the edge of the spoon's bowl back and forth in short strokes without pressing hard on the spoon. This procedure should not be used on delicate fabrics.

Sponging

When instructions call for sponging, place the stained side down over an absorbent pad. Then dampen another pad with the water or stain remover and blot with a light touch from the center of the stain outward to the edge to minimize the formation of rings. Sponge in an irregular pattern around the outside of the stain. Change the absorbent or sponging pads when there is any sign of the stain transferring to them, so the stain won't be redeposited on the fabric. For ring-prone fabrics, barely touch the stain with the sponging pad, so the stain absorbs the cleaner slowly. When the spot has been lifted, use a dry pad on either side to blot up as much excess moisture as possible.

Tamping

Tamping is a good way to remove stains if the fabric is sturdy enough. The best tamping instrument is a small, dry brush with a handle—an old toothbrush can be used. Place the stain on the work surface without a pad underneath, raise the brush about three inches and bring it down squarely on the fabric, much like using a small hammer. The action should be light, never enough to bend the bristles. Use only the amount of tamping needed to remove the stain.

How to Remove Staining Substances

Here are methods and products for removing common stains from both washable and nonwashable articles. When instructions call for absorbing, flushing, freezing, scraping, sponging, or tamping, be sure to follow instructions for these techniques given in Stain Removing Techniques. To remove stains quickly, try the recommended products; if fast action is required and you don't have the commercial products listed here, follow the step-by-step procedures for removing stains with more common household products.

Alcoholic Beverages

Washable

1. Wipe or blot up excess moisture.
2. Sponge (see Stain Removing Techniques) with cool water and white vinegar (1 tablespoon to 3 tablespoons water) to stop the alcohol from making the fabric dye fade or run.
3. Apply a solution of 1 teaspoon liquid dishwashing detergent (see Recommended Basic Products) in 1 cup water, then rinse.

Nonwashable

1. Sponge (see Stain Removing Techniques) with water.
2. Apply Wet Spotter with a pad that also is moistened with a few drops of white vinegar.
3. Blot up the moisture.
4. Flush (see Stain Removing Techniques) the stain with water.

Alternate Method

1. Sponge (see Stain Removing Techniques) the stain with cold water.
2. Sponge with a mixture of cool water and glycerin.
3. Flush (see Stain Removing Techniques) with white vinegar and water solution.

For Carpets *(Try recommended product first)*

1. Quickly blot up the spill with a white towel.
2. Sponge (see Stain Removing Techniques) with cold water.
3. Sponge with a solution of ½ cup borax dissolved in 1 pint lukewarm water.
4. Wait 30 minutes.
5. Apply a foaming rug shampoo.
6. Let dry and then vacuum dry foam.

Recommended Product

Glory Professional Strength Rug Cleaner (S. C. Johnson & Son, Inc.)—foam to be scrubbed into stain; 4-hour drying time.

Blood

Washable *(Try recommended product first)*

1. Sponge (see Stain Removing Techniques) stain with cold water until much of the stain is removed. Do not use hot water; it will set blood.
2. Soak in an enzyme presoak solution (see Laundry).
3. Launder using an all-purpose detergent (see Laundry).

Alternate Method

1. Apply a solution of 2 tablespoons washing soda (see Laundry) in 1 cup warm water with an absorbent pad.
2. Launder.

Recommended Product

Stain-X Carpet Stain Remover (Positive Products Laboratories, Inc.)—squeeze bottle with squirt-spout; for use on all colorfast fabrics, carpets, and upholstery.

Nonwashable *(Try recommended product first)*

1. Sponge (see Stain Removing Techniques) with cool water.
2. Apply Wet Spotter with a few drops of ammonia sprinkled on an absorbent pad; change the pad as it absorbs the stain.
3. Flush (see Stain Removing Techniques) the area with water to remove the ammonia.
4. If the stain remains, test for colorfastness, then wet the stain with an oxygen bleach in solution of 3% hydrogen peroxide.
5. Add a drop of ammonia and allow it to penetrate for 15 minutes.
6. Flush thoroughly with water.

Recommended Product

Stain-X Carpet Stain Remover (Positive Products Laboratories, Inc.)—squeeze bottle with squirt-spout; for use on all colorfast fabrics, carpets, leather and vinyl, and upholstery.

Butter or Margarine

Washable *(Try one of the recommended products after step 1)*

1. Remove the solids with an absorbent pad under the stain.
2. Apply dry cleaning solvent with another pad, and leave it on the stain to penetrate.
3. Remove the moistened pad every 5 minutes and tamp or scrape (see Stain Removing Techniques).
4. Use a prewash spot and stain remover (see Laundry) before laundering with an all-purpose detergent.

Recommended Products

Goddard's Dry Clean Spot Remover (S. C. Johnson & Son, Inc.)—aerosol liquid that dries to a powder; designed to remove grease and oil stains.

Amway Remove Fabric Spot Cleaner (Amway Corp.)—aerosol liquid with plastic brush lid; dries to a powder; designed to remove grease and oil stains.

Carbona Spot Remover with Applicator Top (Carbona Products Company)—for natural and synthetic fabrics; built-in cloth applicator.

Nonwashable *(Try recommended product first)*

1. Sprinkle with fuller's earth on darker-colored surfaces or cornmeal on lighter items.
2. Allow time to absorb the grease.
3. Brush off.

Recommended Product

K2r Spot-lifter (Texize Chemicals Company)—aerosol with plastic brush lid; dries to a powder; safe for dry cleanable fabrics except acetate and velvet; can be used on carpets, upholstery, and wallpaper.

Candle Wax

Washable and Nonwashable

1. Rub the spot with an ice cube and scrape off excess. Or place the item in plastic wrapping and freeze (see Stain Removing Techniques) until the wax hardens.
2. Place the cloth between two white blotters or folded facial tissues and press with a warm iron.
3. Replace the blotters or facial tissues as they absorb the wax.
4. If wax color remains, use a dry cleaning solvent, or sponge (see Stain Removing Techniques) with a solution of one part alcohol to two parts water.

Recommended Products

Goddard's Dry Clean Spot Remover (S. C. Johnson & Son, Inc.)—aerosol liquid that dries to a powder; designed to remove grease and oil stains.

Amway Remove Fabric Spot Cleaner (Amway Corp.)—aerosol liquid with plastic brush lid; dries to a powder; designed to remove grease and oil stains.

Carbona Spot Remover with Applicator Top (Carbona Products Company)—for natural and synthetic fabrics; built-in cloth applicator.

Catsup

Washable *(Try one of the recommended products first)*

Delicate Fabrics. 1. Sponge (see Stain Removing Techniques) with dry cleaning solvent.
2. Apply Dry Spotter to the stain and cover with an absorbent pad dampened with Dry Spotter.
3. Let stand as long as stain is being removed.
4. Change the pad as it picks up stain.

5. Keep stain and pad moist with Dry Spotter.
6. Flush (see Stain Removing Techniques) with dry cleaning solvent.
7. Repeat Dry Spotter application and flushing with dry cleaning solvent until no more stain can be removed.
8. Allow to dry completely, then sponge with water.
9. Apply a few drops of liquid dishwashing detergent (see Recommended Basic Products) and a few drops of ammonia.
10. Cover with an absorbent pad dampened with water.
11. Let stand as long as any stain is being removed.
12. Change the pad as it picks up the stain.
13. Keep stain and pad moist with detergent and ammonia.
14. Flush with water to remove all ammonia.
15. Soak in a solution of 1 quart warm water and 1 tablespoon enzyme presoak (see Laundry) for 30 minutes.
18. Rinse with water.
17. Launder.

Sturdy Fabrics. 1. Sponge (see Stain Removing Techniques) with dry cleaning solvent.
2. Apply Dry Spotter and tamp or scrape (see Stain Removing Techniques).
3. Keep the stain moist with Dry Spotter and blot occasionally with absorbent material.
4. Repeat application of Dry Spotter and blotting.
5. Flush (see Stain Removing Techniques) with dry cleaning solvent.
6. Repeat Dry Spotter application and flushing with dry cleaning solvent until no more stain can be removed.
7. Allow to dry completely.
8. Sponge with water.
9. Apply a few drops of liquid dishwashing detergent (see Recommended Basic Products) and a few drops of ammonia.
10. Tamp or scrape.
11. Keep stain moist with detergent and ammonia and blot occasionally with absorbent material.
12. Flush with water to remove all ammonia.
13. Soak in a solution of 1 quart warm water and 1 tablespoon enzyme presoak (see Laundry) for 30 minutes.
14. Rinse with water.
15. Launder.
16. If traces of the stain remain, test the article for colorfastness.
17. If color doesn't change, bleach with a solution of 1 teaspoon chlorine bleach to 1 tablespoon water, applying the solution to the stain with a medicine dropper.
18. Allow the solution to remain on the stain for no more than 2 minutes, then flush with water onto clean, absorbent material.
19. Apply 1 teaspoon white vinegar and flush again with water.
20. Make sure all bleach is removed.

Recommended Products

Carbona Spot Remover with Applicator Top (Carbona Products Company)—for natural and synthetic fabrics; built-in cloth applicator.

K2r Spot-lifter (Texize Chemicals Company)—aerosol with plastic brush lid; dries to a powder; safe for dry cleanable fabrics except acetate and velvet.

Nonwashable *(Try recommended product first)*

Delicate Fabrics.   1. Follow the same procedure as for washable fabrics, but do not soak in the enzyme presoak solution or launder.
2. After using the dishwashing liquid solution and ammonia, and rinsing out all the ammonia with water, moisten the stain with a solution of ½ teaspoon enzyme presoak (see Laundry) dissolved in ½ cup warm water.
3. Cover with a clean pad that is moistened in the warm presoak solution and squeezed nearly dry.
4. Let stand for 30 minutes. Add more warm enzyme presoak solution if needed to keep the area warm and moist, but do not let the wet area spread.
5. Flush (see Stain Removing Techniques) with water.

Sturdy Fabrics.   1. Follow steps 1–5 for delicate fabrics.
2. If traces of the stain remain, test the article for colorfastness.
3. If color doesn't change, bleach with a solution of 1 teaspoon chlorine bleach to 1 tablespoon water, applying the solution to the stain with a medicine dropper.
4. Allow the solution to remain on the stain for no more than 2 minutes, then flush (see Stain Removing Techniques) with water onto clean, absorbent material.
5. Apply 1 teaspoon white vinegar and flush again with water.
6. Make sure all bleach is removed.

Recommended Product

K2r Spot-lifter (Texize Chemicals Company)—aerosol with plastic brush lid; dries to a powder; safe for most fabrics, carpets, upholstery, and wallpaper.

Chewing Gum

Washable *(Try one of the recommended products after step 2)*

1. Freeze (see Stain Removing Techniques) the stain with ice cubes or wrap a portable item in plastic and put in the freezer until the gum hardens.
2. Scrape (see Stain Removing Techniques) or roll off as much of the gum as possible.
3. Sponge (see Stain Removing Techniques) with a dry cleaning solvent.
4. If a sugar stain remains, sponge it off with water.

Recommended Products

Carbona Spot Remover with Applicator Top (Carbona Products Company)—for natural and synthetic fabrics; built-in cloth applicator.

Afta Cleaning Fluid (Afta Solvents Corporation)—has no applicator; designed to clean auto interiors, machine parts, or marble.

Nonwashable

1. Sponge (see Stain Removing Techniques) repeatedly with dry cleaning solvent until the gum is removed.
2. If a sugar stain remains, sponge it off with water.

Spots and Stains

Recommended Product

Afta Cleaning Fluid (Afta Solvents Corporation)—for dry cleanable fabrics, upholstery, or furs; has no applicator.

Chocolate

Washable *(Try recommended product first)*

Delicate Fabrics. 1. Flush (see Stain Removing Techniques) with club soda to keep stain from setting, then sponge (see Stain Removing Techniques) with dry cleaning solvent.
  2. Apply Dry Spotter to the stain and cover with an absorbent pad dampened with Dry Spotter.
  3. Let stand as long as stain is being removed.
  4. Change the pad as it picks up stain.
  5. Keep stain and pad moist with Dry Spotter.
  6. Flush with dry cleaning solvent.
  7. Repeat Dry Spotter application and flushing with dry cleaning solvent until no more stain can be removed.
  8. Allow to dry completely, then sponge with water.
  9. Apply a few drops of liquid dishwashing detergent (see Recommended Basic Products) and a few drops of ammonia.
  10. Cover with an absorbent pad dampened with water.
  11. Let stand as long as any stain is being removed.
  12. Change the pad as it picks up the stain.
  13. Keep stain and pad moist with detergent and ammonia.
  14. Flush with water to remove all ammonia.
  15. Soak in a solution of 1 quart warm water and 1 tablespoon enzyme presoak (see Laundry) for 30 minutes.
  16. Rinse with water.
  17. Launder.
  18. If traces of the stain remain, bleach with 3% hydrogen peroxide. Wet the stain with hydrogen peroxide and add a drop or two of ammonia.
  19. Add more hydrogen peroxide and a drop of ammonia as needed to keep the stain moist.
  20. Do not bleach longer than 15 minutes.
  21. Rinse with water.

Sturdy Fabrics. 1. Sponge (see Stain Removing Techniques) with dry cleaning solvent.
  2. Apply Dry Spotter and tamp or scrape (see Stain Removing Techniques).
  3. Keep the stain moist with Dry Spotter and blot occasionally with absorbent material.
  4. Repeat application of Dry Spotter and blotting.
  5. Flush (see Stain Removing Techniques) with dry cleaning solvent.
  6. Repeat Dry Spotter application and flushing with dry cleaning solvent until no more stain can be removed.
  7. Allow to dry completely.
  8. Sponge with water.
  9. Apply a few drops of liquid dishwashing detergent (see Recommended Basic Products) and a few drops of ammonia.
  10. Tamp or scrape.
  11. Keep stain moist with detergent and ammonia and blot occasionally with absorbent material.
  12. Flush with water to remove all ammonia.

13. Soak in a solution of 1 quart warm water and 1 tablespoon enzyme presoak (see Laundry) for 30 minutes.
14. Rinse with water.
15. Launder.
16. If traces of the stain remain, bleach with 3% hydrogen peroxide. Wet the stain with hydrogen peroxide and add a drop or two of ammonia.
17. Add more hydrogen peroxide and a drop of ammonia as needed to keep the stain moist.
18. Do not bleach longer than 15 minutes.
19. Rinse with water.

Recommended Product

Goddard's Dry Clean Spot Remover (S. C. Johnson & Son, Inc.)—aerosol liquid that dries to a powder; designed to remove grease and oil stains.

Nonwashable *(Try recommended product first)*

Delicate Fabrics.   1. Follow the same procedure as for washable fabrics, but do not soak in the enzyme presoak solution or launder.
2. After using the dishwashing liquid solution and ammonia, and rinsing out all the ammonia with water, moisten the stain with a solution of ½ teaspoon enzyme presoak (see Laundry) dissolved in ½ cup warm water.
3. Cover with a clean pad that is moistened in the warm presoak solution and squeezed nearly dry.
4. Let stand for 30 minutes. Add more warm presoak solution if needed to keep the area warm and moist, but do not let the wet area spread.
5. Flush (see Stain Removing Techniques) with water.

Sturdy Fabrics.   1. Follow steps 1–5 for delicate fabrics.
2. If traces of the stain remain, bleach with 3% hydrogen peroxide. Wet the stain with hydrogen peroxide and add a drop or two of ammonia.
3. Add more hydrogen peroxide and a drop of ammonia as needed to keep the stain moist.
4. Do not bleach longer than 15 minutes.
5. Rinse with water.

Recommended Product

Goddard's Dry Clean Spot Remover (S. C. Johnson & Son, Inc.)—aerosol liquid that dries to a powder; designed to remove grease and oil stains.

Coffee and Tea

Washable *(Try one of the recommended products after step 1)*

1. Wipe or blot up excess before it dries.
2. If the beverage contains cream, sponge (see Stain Removing Techniques) the area with a dry cleaning solvent.
3. Flush (see Stain Removing Techniques) with cool water.
4. Launder with an all-purpose detergent (see Laundry) with a warm water temperature setting.

Spots and Stains

Alternate Method

1. Stretch the spot over a bowl and anchor in place with a rubber band.
2. Pour hot water through the stain from a height of two feet, being careful not to splash the scalding water.
3. If any stain remains, treat it with an oxygen bleach in solution or with 3% hydrogen peroxide.
4. Flush (see Stain Removing Techniques) with water.

Recommended Products

Spot Shot (Sifers Chemicals, Inc.)—aerosol liquid; designed to remove greasy, nongreasy, and combination stains from carpets.

Afta Carpet Stain Remover (Afta Solvents Corporation)—liquid in a squeeze bottle; for use on carpets.

Nonwashable *(Try one of the recommended products first)*

1. Sponge (see Stain Removing Techniques) with cool water.
2. Cover with a pad moistened with Wet Spotter and let stand to absorb the stain.
3. Flush (see Stain Removing Techniques) with water.

Recommended Products

Spot Shot (Sifers Chemicals, Inc.)—aerosol liquid; designed to remove greasy, nongreasy, and combination stains from carpets.

Afta Carpet Stain Remover (Afta Solvents Corporation)—liquid in a squeeze bottle; for use on carpets.

Crayon Marks

Washable *(Try recommended product first)*

1. Pretreat the fabric with an enzyme presoak (see Laundry) moistened with water to make a paste.
2. Brush the paste on the marks.
3. Launder with an all-purpose detergent (see Laundry) with a warm temperature setting.

Recommended Product

Afta Cleaning Fluid (Afta Solvents Corporation)—for all fabrics; has no applicator.

Nonwashable

1. Sponge (see Stain Removing Techniques) with dry cleaning solvent.
2. Blot up excess moisture.

For Wallpaper

1. Use a wadding of white paper toweling moistened with dry cleaning solvent to sponge the surface.
2. Carefully blot and lift in a small area to prevent solvent from spreading and discoloring the wallpaper.

Recommended Products

Suede Stone (Canden Company)—removes crayon from walls and wallpaper; test inconspicuous spot first; abrasive.

Afta Cleaning Fluid (Afta Solvents Corporation)—for dry cleanable fabrics, auto interiors, and marble; has no applicator.

Deodorant

Washable

1. If the deodorant has an oily base, sponge (see Stain Removing Techniques) with dry cleaning solvent.
2. Launder with an all-purpose detergent (see Laundry) with a warm water temperature setting.

Recommended Products

Carbona Spot Remover with Applicator Top (Carbona Products Company)—for natural and synthetic fabrics; built-in cloth applicator.

Stain-X Carpet Stain Remover (Positive Products Industries, Inc.)—squeeze bottle with squirt-spout; for use on all colorfast fabrics, carpets, leather and vinyl, and upholstery.

Nonwashable *(Try recommended product first)*

1. Sponge (see Stain Removing Techniques) with water.
2. Apply Wet Spotter with a few drops of ammonia sprinkled on the pad.
3. Let stand until the stain has been removed.
4. Blot with a soft cloth.
5. Flush (see Stain Removing Techniques) with water.
6. Apply Wet Spotter again, adding a few drops of white vinegar.
7. Flush with water.
8. If the deodorant contains aluminum salts, the color possibly may be restored by sponging with ammonia, then rinsing with clear water.
9. Remove the entire stain before pressing the article.

Recommended Product

Carbona Spot Remover with Applicator Top (Carbona Products Company)—for natural and synthetic fabrics; built-in cloth applicator; designed for oil-based deodorant stains.

Egg White

Washable *(Try recommended product first)*

Delicate Fabrics.   1. Soak in a solution of 1 quart warm water, ½ teaspoon liquid dish-washing detergent (see Recommended Basic Products), and 1 teaspoon ammonia for 15 minutes.
2. Blot occasionally with an absorbent pad.
3. Repeat procedure as long as it removes stain.
4. Soak again in the solution for 15 minutes.
5. Rinse thoroughly with water to remove all ammonia.
6. Soak in a solution of 1 quart warm water and 1 tablespoon enzyme presoak (see Laundry) for 30 minutes.
7. Launder.
8. If any stain remains after laundering, soak again in the warm water presoak solution for 30 minutes and relaunder.

Sturdy Fabrics.   1. Soak for 15 minutes in a solution of 1 quart warm water, ½ teaspoon liquid dishwashing detergent (see Recommended Basic Products), and 1 teaspoon ammonia.
2. Tamp or scrape (see Stain Removing Techniques) the stained area.
3. Blot occasionally with an absorbent pad.
4. Repeat procedure as long as it removes stain.
5. Soak again in the solution for 15 minutes.
6. Rinse thoroughly with water to remove all ammonia.
7. Soak in a solution of 1 quart warm water and 1 tablespoon enzyme presoak (see Laundry) for 30 minutes.
8. Launder.
9. If any stain remains after laundering, soak again in the warm water presoak solution for 30 minutes and relaunder.

Recommended Product

Carbona Spot Remover with Applicator Top (Carbona Products Company)—for natural and synthetic fabrics; built-in cloth applicator.

Nonwashable *(Try recommended product first)*

Delicate Fabrics.   1. Sponge (see Stain Removing Techniques) with water.
2. Apply Wet Spotter and a few drops of ammonia.
3. Cover with an absorbent pad dampened with Wet Spotter and let stand as long as stain is being removed.
4. Replace the pad as it picks up the stain and keep both the stain and the pad moist with Wet Spotter and ammonia.
5. Blot occasionally with an absorbent pad.
6. Continue this procedure as long as stain is being removed, then flush (see Stain Removing Techniques) with water to remove all ammonia.
7. Moisten the stain with a solution of ½ teaspoon enzyme presoak (see Laundry) and ½ cup warm water.
8. Cover with a clean pad that has been dipped in the warm presoak solution and squeezed nearly dry.
9. Let stand 30 minutes, adding more warm presoak solution if needed to keep the stain

warm and moist, but avoid letting the wet area spread.
10. Flush with water.
11. Repeat the entire procedure if the stain persists.

Sturdy Fabrics.   1. Sponge (see Stain Removing Techniques) with water.
2. Apply Wet Spotter and a few drops of ammonia.
3. Tamp or scrape (see Stain Removing Techniques).
4. Keep the stain moist with Wet Spotter and ammonia and blot occasionally with an absorbent pad.
5. Continue as long as the stain is being removed, then flush (see Stain Removing Techniques) with water to remove all ammonia.
6. Moisten the stain with a solution of ½ teaspoon enzyme presoak (see Laundry) and ½ cup warm water.
7. Cover with a clean pad that has been dipped in warm presoak solution and squeezed nearly dry.
8. Let stand 30 minutes, adding more warm presoak solution if needed to keep the stain warm and moist, but avoid letting the wet area spread.
9. Flush with water.
10. Repeat the entire procedure if the stain persists.

Recommended Product

Stain-X Carpet Stain Remover (Positive Products Laboratories, Inc.)—squeeze bottle with squirt-spout; for use on all colorfast fabrics, carpets, leather and vinyl, and upholstery.

Egg Yolk

Washable *(Try recommended product first)*

Delicate Fabrics.   1. Sponge (see Stain Removing Techniques) with dry cleaning solvent.
2. Apply Dry Spotter to the stain and cover with an absorbent pad dampened with Dry Spotter.
3. Let stand as long as stain is being removed, changing the pad as it picks up stain.
4. Keep stain and pad moist with Dry Spotter.
5. Flush (see Stain Removing Techniques) with dry cleaning solvent.
6. Repeat Dry Spotter application and flushing with dry cleaning solvent until no more stain can be removed.
7. Allow to dry completely, then sponge with water.
8. Apply a few drops of liquid dishwashing detergent (see Recommended Basic Products) and a few drops of ammonia.
9. Cover with an absorbent pad dampened with water and let stand as long as any stain is being removed.
10. Change the pad as it picks up the stain, keeping the stain and pad moist with detergent and ammonia.
11. Flush with water to remove all ammonia.
12. Soak in a solution of 1 quart warm water and 1 tablespoon enzyme presoak (see Laundry) for 30 minutes.
13. Rinse with water.
14. Launder.

Sturdy Fabrics.   1. Sponge (see Stain Removing Techniques) with dry cleaning solvent.
2. Apply Dry Spotter and tamp or scrape (see Stain Removing Techniques).

Spots and Stains

3. Keep the stain moist with Dry Spotter and blot occasionally with clean, absorbent material, repeating until no more stain can be removed.
4. Flush (see Stain Removing Techniques) with dry cleaning solvent.
5. Repeat Dry Spotter application and flushing with dry cleaning solvent until no more stain can be removed.
6. Allow to dry completely and then sponge with water.
7. Apply a few drops of liquid dishwashing detergent (see Recommended Basic Products) and a few drops of ammonia.
8. Tamp or scrape the stained area.
9. Keep stain moist with detergent and ammonia and blot occasionally with clean, absorbent material.
10. Flush with water to remove all ammonia.
11. Soak in a solution of 1 quart warm water and 1 tablespoon enzyme presoak (see Laundry) for 30 minutes.
12. Rinse with water.
13. Launder.

Recommended Product

Carbona Spot Remover with Applicator Top (Carbona Products Company)—for natural and synthetic fabrics; built-in cloth applicator.

Nonwashable *(Try recommended product first)*

1. Follow the same procedure as for washable fabrics, but do not soak in the enzyme presoak solution or launder.
2. After using the dishwashing liquid solution and ammonia, and rinsing out all the ammonia with water, moisten the stain with a solution of ½ teaspoon enzyme presoak (see Laundry) dissolved in ½ cup warm water.
3. Cover with a clean pad that is moistened in the warm presoak solution and squeezed nearly dry.
4. Let stand for 30 minutes. Add more warm enzyme presoak solution if needed to keep the area warm and moist, but do not let the wet area spread.
5. Flush (see Stain Removing Techniques) with water.

Recommended Product

Carbona Spot Remover with Applicator Top (Carbona Products Company)—for natural and synthetic fabrics; built-in cloth applicator.

Grass

Washable *(Try one of the recommended products first)*

1. Test article for colorfastness.
2. If color doesn't change, sponge (see Stain Removing Techniques) with rubbing or denatured alcohol or use an enzyme presoak (see Laundry) and launder. Dilute alcohol with two parts water to clean acetate.
3. If the stain persists, use an oxygen bleach in solution or 3% hydrogen peroxide.
4. Flush (see Stain Removing Techniques) with water.

Recommended Products

K2r Spot-lifter (Texize Chemicals Company)—cream in tube; removes grease and oil stains from most fabrics.

Stain-X Carpet Stain Remover (Positive Products Laboratories, Inc.)—squeeze bottle with squirt-spout; for use on all colorfast fabrics, carpets, and upholstery.

Nonwashable *(Try one of the recommended products first)*

1. Test article for colorfastness.
2. If color doesn't change, sponge (see Stain Removing Techiques) with rubbing or denatured alcohol. Dilute the alcohol with two parts water to clean acetate.
3. If the stain persists, use an oxygen bleach in solution or 3% hydrogen peroxide.
4. Flush (see Stain Removing Techniques) with water.

Recommended Products

K2r Spot-lifter (Texize Chemicals Company)—cream in tube; removes grease and oil stains from most fabrics.

Stain-X Carpet Stain Remover (Positive Products Laboratories, Inc.)—squeeze bottle with squirt-spout; for use on all colorfast fabrics, carpets, and upholstery.

Grease and Oil, Cooking

Washable and Nonwashable *(Try one of the recommended products first)*

Delicate Fabrics.   1. Place clean, absorbent material under the stain.
2. Apply dry cleaning solvent and cover the stain with an absorbent pad dampened with dry cleaning solvent.
3. Change the absorbent material as it picks up the stain, keeping the pad and stain moist with solvent at all times.
4. Apply Dry Spotter to the stain and cover with a pad dampened with Dry Spotter.
5. Flush (see Stain Removing Techniques) with dry cleaning solvent and allow to dry.

Sturdy Fabrics.   1. Follow steps 1–4 for delicate fabrics.
2. Remove the pad every 5 minutes and tamp or scrape (see Stain Removing Techniques) the stained area.
3. Continue soaking and tamping or scraping until all the stain has been removed.
4. Flush (see Stain Removing Techniques) with dry cleaning solvent and allow to dry.

Recommended Products

Amway Remove Fabric Spot Cleaner (Amway Corp.)—aerosol liquid with plastic brush lid; dries to a powder; designed to remove grease and oil stains; works on wallpaper.

Carbona Spot Remover with Applicator Top (Carbona Products Company)—for natural and synthetic fabrics; built-in cloth applicator.

Afta Cleaning Fluid (Afta Solvents Corporation)—for dry cleanable fabrics, upholstery, or furs; has no applicator.

Read manufacturer's cautions and warnings before using any product.

Grease and Oil, Lubricating and Automotive

Washable and Nonwashable *(Try one of the recommended products first)*

Delicate Fabrics.   1. Sponge (see Stain Removing Techniques) with dry cleaning solvent.
2. Apply Dry Spotter to the stain and cover with an absorbent pad dampened with Dry Spotter.
3. Keep the stain moist with Dry Spotter and blot occasionally with absorbent material.
4. Continue this procedure as long as any stain is being removed.
5. Flush (see Stain Removing Techniques) with dry cleaning solvent.
6. Repeat application of the Dry Spotter and flushing until stain is no longer being removed.
7. Allow to dry completely, then sponge with water.
8. Apply Wet Spotter and a few drops of ammonia.
9. Cover with an absorbent pad dampened with Wet Spotter.
10. Let stand as long as stain is being removed.
11. Change the pad as it picks up stain, keeping both the stain and pad moist with Wet Spotter and ammonia.
12. Flush with water.
13. Continue applying Wet Spotter and ammonia and flushing with water as long as the procedures remove some stain.

Sturdy Fabrics.   1. Sponge (see Stain Removing Techniques) with dry cleaning solvent.
2. Apply Dry Spotter and tamp or scrape (see Stain Removing Techniques).
3. Keep the stain moist with Dry Spotter and blot occasionally with absorbent material.
4. Flush (see Stain Removing Techniques) with dry cleaning solvent.
5. Repeat applying the Dry Spotter and flushing until stain is no longer being removed.
6. Allow to dry completely, then sponge with water.
7. Apply Wet Spotter and a few drops of ammonia.
8. Tamp or scrape.
9. Keep the stain moist with Wet Spotter and ammonia and blot occasionally with absorbent material.
10. Flush with water.
11. Continue using Wet Spotter and ammonia and flushing with water as long as the procedures remove some stain.

Recommended Products

Afta Cleaning Fluid (Afta Solvents Corporation)—for dry cleanable fabrics, auto interiors, and tools.

Carbona Spot Remover with Applicator Top (Carbona Products Company)—for natural and synthetic fabrics; built-in cloth applicator.

Hair Spray

Washable and Nonwashable *(Try recommended product first)*

Delicate Fabrics.   1. Sponge (see Stain Removing Techniques) with dry cleaning solvent.
2. Apply Dry Spotter to the stain and cover with an absorbent pad dampened with Dry Spotter.

3. Keep stain moist with Dry Spotter and blot occasionally with absorbent material.
4. Flush (see Stain Removing Techniques) with dry cleaning solvent.
5. Continue using Dry Spotter and flushing until stain is no longer being removed.
6. Allow to dry completely, then sponge with water.
7. Apply Wet Spotter and a few drops of ammonia.
8. Cover with an absorbent pad dampened with Wet Spotter and let stand as long as stain is being removed.
9. Change the pad as it picks up stain and keep both the stain and pad moist with Wet Spotter and ammonia.
10. Flush with water.
11. Continue using Wet Spotter and ammonia and flushing with water as long as the procedures remove some stain.

Sturdy Fabrics. 1. Sponge (see Stain Removing Techniques) with dry cleaning solvent.
2. Apply Dry Spotter and tamp or scrape (see Stain Removing Techniques).
3. Keep stain moist with Dry Spotter and blot occasionally with absorbent material.
4. Flush (see Stain Removing Techniques) with dry cleaning solvent.
5. Repeat applying Dry Spotter and flushing with dry cleaning solvent until no more stain can be removed.
6. Allow to dry completely, then sponge with water.
7. Apply Wet Spotter and a few drops of ammonia.
8. Tamp or scrape the stained area.
9. Keep the stain moist with Wet Spotter and ammonia and blot occasionally with absorbent material.
10. Flush with water.
11. Continue using Wet Spotter and ammonia and flushing with water as long as the procedures remove some stain.

Recommended Product

Carbona Spot Remover with Applicator Top (Carbona Products Company)—for natural and synthetic fabrics; built-in cloth applicator.

Ice Cream

Washable *(Try recommended product first)*

Delicate Fabrics. 1. Sponge (see Stain Removing Techniques) with dry cleaning solvent.
2. Apply Dry Spotter to the stain and cover with an absorbent pad dampened with Dry Spotter.
3. Let stand as long as stain is being removed, changing the pad as it picks up stain.
4. Keep the stain and pad moist with Dry Spotter.
5. Flush (see Stain Removing Techniques) with dry cleaning solvent.
6. Repeat Dry Spotter application and flushing with dry cleaning solvent until no more stain can be removed.
7. Allow to dry completely, then sponge with water.
8. Apply a few drops of liquid dishwashing detergent (see Recommended Basic Products) and a few drops of ammonia.
9. Cover with an absorbent pad dampened with water and let stand as long as stain is being removed.
10. Change the pad as it picks up the stain, keeping the stain and pad moist with detergent and ammonia.

Spots and Stains

11. Flush with water to remove all ammonia.
12. Soak in a solution of 1 quart warm water and 1 tablespoon enzyme presoak (see Laundry) for 30 minutes.
13. Rinse with water.
14. Launder.

Sturdy Fabrics. 1. Sponge (see Stain Removing Techniques) with dry cleaning solvent.
2. Apply Dry Spotter and tamp or scrape (see Stain Removing Techniques).
3. Keep the stain moist with Dry Spotter and blot occasionally with absorbent material, repeating until no more stain can be removed.
4. Flush (see Stain Removing Techniques) with dry cleaning solvent.
5. Repeat Dry Spotter application and flushing with dry cleaning solvent until no more stain can be removed.
6. Allow to dry completely, then sponge with water.
7. Apply a few drops of liquid dishwashing detergent (see Recommended Basic Products) and a few drops of ammonia.
8. Tamp or scrape the stained area.
9. Keep stain moist with detergent and ammonia and blot occasionally with absorbent material.
10. Flush with water to remove all ammonia.
11. Soak in a solution of 1 quart warm water and 1 tablespoon enzyme presoak (see Laundry) for 30 minutes.
12. Rinse with water.
13. Launder.

Recommended Products

Stain-X Carpet Stain Remover (Positive Products Laboratories, Inc.)—squeeze bottle with squirt-spout; for use on all colorfast fabrics, carpets, and upholstery.

Nonwashable *(Try recommended product first)*

1. Follow the same procedure as for washable fabrics, but do not soak in the enzyme presoak solution or launder.
2. After using the dishwashing liquid solution and ammonia, and rinsing out all the ammonia with water, moisten the stain with a solution of ½ teaspoon enzyme presoak (see Laundry) dissolved in ½ cup warm water.
3. Cover with a clean pad that is moistened in the warm presoak solution and squeezed nearly dry.
4. Let stand for 30 minutes. Add more warm enzyme presoak solution if needed to keep the area warm and moist, but do not let the wet area spread.
5. Flush with water.
6. Chocolate or coffee ice cream stains may require bleaching with 3% hydrogen peroxide. Wet the stain with hydrogen peroxide and a drop or two of ammonia.
7. Add more hydrogen peroxide and a drop of ammonia as needed to keep the stain moist. Do not bleach for more than 15 minutes.
8. Rinse with water.

Recommended Product

Amway Remove Fabric Spot Cleaner (Amway Corp.)—aerosol liquid with plastic brush lid; dries to a powder; designed to remove grease and oil stains.

Ink, Ballpoint

Washable and Nonwashable *(Try recommended product first)*

Delicate Fabrics. 1. Apply lukewarm glycerin, pressing against the stain with a moistened pad.
2. Flush (see Stain Removing Techniques) with water.
3. Apply Wet Spotter by moistening another pad and loosen the stain by scraping (see Stain Removing Techniques) very gently.
4. Add a few drops of ammonia and repeat the Wet Spotter/scraping procedure until the stain is gone.
5. Flush with water.
6. If traces remain, test fabric for colorfastness.
7. If color doesn't change, try rubbing the stain with denatured or rubbing alcohol.
8. Launder washable fabrics.

Sturdy Fabrics. 1. Apply lukewarm glycerin, pressing against the stain with a moistened pad.
2. Flush (see Stain Removing Techniques) with water.
3. Apply Wet Spotter by moistening another pad and loosen the stain by tamping (see Stain Removing Techniques).
4. Add a few drops of ammonia and repeat the Wet Spotter/tamping procedure until the stain is gone.
5. Flush with water.
6. If traces remain, test fabric for colorfastness.
7. If color doesn't change, bleach with a solution of 1 teaspoon chlorine bleach to 1 tablespoon water, applying the solution to the stain with a medicine dropper.
8. Allow the solution to remain on the stain for no more than 2 minutes, then flush with water onto clean, absorbent material.
9. Apply 1 teaspoon white vinegar and flush again with water.
10. Make sure all bleach is removed.
11. On washables, try rubbing the stain with denatured or rubbing alcohol and launder.

Recommended Product

Trewax Up & Out (Trewax Company)—pump spray for carpets other than wool.

Lipstick

Washable and Nonwashable *(Try one of the recommended products first)*

Delicate Fabrics. 1. Apply dry cleaning solvent and Dry Spotter and blot immediately with absorbent material.
2. Repeat this procedure until no more stain can be removed.
3. Allow all the dry cleaning solvent to evaporate, then sponge (see Stain Removing Techniques) with water.
4. Apply a Wet Spotter and a few drops of ammonia, blotting frequently with absorbent material.
5. Flush (see Stain Removing Techniques) with water.
6. Apply a Wet Spotter with a few drops of white vinegar, blotting frequently.

Spots and Stains

7. Flush for water and allow to dry.
8. Test for colorfastness.
9. If color doesn't change, sponge with rubbing or denatured alcohol and allow to dry.

Sturdy Fabrics.   1. Follow steps 1–3 for delicate fabrics.
2. Tamp or scrape (see Stain Removing Techniques) the stained area.
3. Blot frequently with absorbent material.
4. Flush (see Stain Removing Techniques) with water.
5. Apply a Wet Spotter with a few drops of white vinegar.
6. Tamp or scrape the stained area.
7. Blot frequently.
8. Flush with water and allow to dry.
9. Test for colorfastness.
10. Sponge (see Stain Removing Techniques) with rubbing or denatured alcohol and allow to dry.
11. If stain persists, bleach with a solution of 1 teaspoon chlorine bleach to 1 tablespoon water, applying the solution to the stain with a medicine dropper.
12. Allow the solution to remain on the stain for no more than 2 minutes, then flush with water onto clean, absorbent material.
13. Apply 1 teaspoon white vinegar and flush with water again.
14. Make sure all bleach is removed.

Recommended Products

Afta Cleaning Fluid (Afta Solvents Corporation)—for dry cleanable fabrics, furs, upholstery, auto interiors, and marble; has no applicator.

Trewax Up & Out (Trewax Company)—pump spray for carpets other than wool.

K2r Spot-lifter (Texize Chemicals Company)—cream in tube; removes grease and oil stains from most fabrics.

Makeup

Washable and Nonwashable *(Try one of the recommended products first)*

Delicate Fabrics.   1. Sponge (see Stain Removing Techniques) with dry cleaning solvent.
2. Apply Dry Spotter and cover the stain with an absorbent pad dampened with Dry Spotter.
3. Keep the stain moist with Dry Spotter and blot occasionally with absorbent material.
4. Continue this procedure as long as any stain is being removed.
5. Flush (see Stain Removing Techniques) with dry cleaning solvent.
6. Repeat application of the Dry Spotter and flushing until stain is no longer being removed.
7. Allow to dry completely, then sponge with water.
8. Apply Wet Spotter and a few drops of ammonia.
9. Cover with an absorbent pad dampened with Wet Spotter.
10. Let stand as long as stain is being removed.
11. Change the pad as it picks up stain, keeping both the stain and pad moist with Wet Spotter and ammonia.
12. Flush with water.
13. Continue applying Wet Spotter and ammonia and flushing with water as long as the procedures remove some stain.

Sturdy Fabrics.   1. Sponge (see Stain Removing Techniques) with dry cleaning solvent.
2. Apply Dry Spotter and tamp or scrape (see Stain Removing Techniques).
3. Keep the stain moist with Dry Spotter and blot occasionally with absorbent material.
4. Flush (see Stain Removing Techniques) with dry cleaning solvent.
5. Repeat applying the Dry Spotter and flushing until stain is no longer being removed.
6. Allow to dry completely, then sponge with water.
7. Apply Wet Spotter and a few drops of ammonia.
8. Tamp or scrape the stained area.
9. Keep the stain moist with Wet Spotter and ammonia and blot occasionally with absorbent material.
10. Flush with water.
11. Continue using Wet Spotter and ammonia and flushing with water as long as the procedures remove some stain.

Recommended Products

Goddard's Dry Clean Spot Remover (S. C. Johnson & Son, Inc.)—aerosol liquid that dries to a powder; designed to remove grease and oil stains.

Carbona Spot Remover with Applicator Top (Carbona Products Company)—for natural and synthetic fabrics; built-in cloth applicator.

K2r Spot-lifter (Texize Chemicals Company)—cream in tube; removes grease and oil stains from most fabrics.

Meat Juices

Washable *(Try recommended product first)*

Delicate Fabrics.   1. Sponge (see Stain Removing Techniques) with dry cleaning solvent.
2. Apply Dry Spotter and cover the stain with an absorbent pad dampened with Dry Spotter.
3. Let stand as long as stain is being removed, changing the pad as it picks up stain.
4. Keep the stain and pad moist with Dry Spotter.
5. Flush (see Stain Removing Techniques) with dry cleaning solvent.
6. Repeat Dry Spotter application and flushing with dry cleaning solvent until no more stain can be removed.
7. Allow to dry completely, then sponge with water.
8. Apply a few drops of liquid dishwashing detergent (see Recommended Basic Products) and a few drops of ammonia.
9. Cover with an absorbent pad dampened with water and let stand as long as any stain is being removed.
10. Change the pad as it picks up stain, keeping both the stain and pad moist with detergent and ammonia.
11. Flush with water to remove all ammonia.
12. Soak in a solution of 1 quart warm water and 1 tablespoon enzyme presoak (see Laundry) for 30 minutes.
13. Rinse with water.
14. Launder.

Sturdy Fabrics.   1. Sponge (see Stain Removing Techniques) with dry cleaning solvent.
2. Apply Dry Spotter and tamp or scrape (see Stain Removing Techniques).

Spots and Stains

3. Keep the stain moist with Dry Spotter and blot occasionally with absorbent material, repeating until no more stain can be removed.
4. Flush (see Stain Removing Techniques) with dry cleaning solvent.
5. Repeat Dry Spotter application and flushing with dry cleaning solvent until no more stain can be removed.
6. Allow to dry completely, then sponge with water.
7. Apply a few drops of liquid dishwashing detergent (see Recommended Basic Products) and a few drops of ammonia.
8. Tamp or scrape the stained area.
9. Keep stain moist with detergent and ammonia and blot occasionally with absorbent material.
10. Flush with water to remove all ammonia.
11. Soak in a solution of 1 quart warm water and 1 tablespoon enzyme presoak (see Laundry) for 30 minutes.
13. Rinse with water.
14. Launder.

Recommended Product

Stain-X Carpet Stain Remover (Positive Products Laboratories, Inc.)—squeeze bottle with squirt-spout; for use on all colorfast fabrics, carpets, and upholstery.

Nonwashable *(Try recommended product first)*

1. Follow the same procedure as for washable fabrics, but do not soak in the enzyme presoak solution or launder.
2. After using the dishwashing liquid solution and ammonia, and rinsing out all the ammonia with water, moisten the stain with a solution of ½ teaspoon enzyme presoak (see Laundry) dissolved in ½ cup warm water.
3. Cover with a clean pad that is moistened in the warm presoak solution and squeezed nearly dry.
4. Let stand for 30 minutes. Add more warm enzyme presoak solution if needed to keep the area warm and moist, but do not let the wet area spread.
5. Flush (see Stain Removing Techniques) with water.

Recommended Product

Stain-X Carpet Stain Remover (Positive Products Laboratories, Inc.)—squeeze bottle with squirt-spout; for use on all colorfast nonwashable fabrics, carpets, leather and vinyl, or upholstery.

Mildew

Washable and Nonwashable *(Try recommended product first)*

Delicate Fabrics. 1. Brush the excess stain off gently and flush (see Stain Removing Techniques) with dry cleaning solvent.
2. Apply Dry Spotter and amyl acetate.
3. Scrape (see Stain Removing Techniques) very gently with a spoon or pat the stain with an absorbent pad dampened with Dry Spotter.
4. Flush (see Stain Removing Techniques) with dry cleaning solvent and allow to dry.

5. Sponge (see Stain Removing Techniques) with water and apply Wet Spotter and white vinegar.
6. Scrape very gently with a spoon or pat the stain with an absorbent pad.
7. Flush with water and allow to dry.
8. If stain persists, test for colorfastness.
9. If color doesn't change, apply rubbing or denatured alcohol and pat the stain with an absorbent pad dampened with alcohol.
10. Flush with alcohol.
11. Repeat the patting and flushing until no more stain can be removed.
12. Allow to dry.

Sturdy Fabrics.   1. Follow steps 1–12 for delicate fabrics.
2. If the stain persists, bleach with a solution of 1 teaspoon chlorine bleach to 1 tablespoon water, applying the solution to the stain with a medicine dropper.
3. Allow the solution to remain on the stain for no more than 2 minutes, then flush with water onto clean, absorbent material.
4. Apply 1 teaspoon white vinegar and flush again with water.
5. Make sure all bleach is removed.

For Books

1. Wipe off the mold and spread the pages fanlike to dry in the air.
2. Sprinkle damp pages with talcum powder or cornstarch until the moisture is absorbed.
3. Shake or brush the powder away.
4. For leather bindings and covers, wipe off the mold.
5. Wipe the leather surface with a cloth dampened with a solution of one part denatured or rubbing alcohol to one part water.
6. Apply saddle soap or leather conditioner.

For Mattresses

1. Vacuum to remove loose mildew and empty the vacuum bag outside the house to avoid scattering mildew spores in the house.
2. Let dry thoroughly before making the bed.

Recommended Product

X-14 Instant Mildew Stain Remover (White Laboratories)—pump spray designed for use on tile and grout, shower curtains, awnings, and painted surfaces.

Mustard

Washable and Nonwashable *(Try one of the recommended products after step 1)*

Delicate Fabrics.   1. Brush or scrape (see Stain Removing Techniques) away the excess.
2. Flush (see Stain Removing Techniques) with dry cleaning solvent and allow to dry.
3. If the stain persists, sponge (see Stain Removing Techniques) with water and apply a Wet Spotter with a few drops of white vinegar on an absorbent pad.
4. Flush with water.
5. Wet the stain with 3% hydrogen peroxide and a few drops of ammonia, using a medicine dropper.

Read manufacturer's cautions and warnings before using any product.

Spots and Stains

6. Allow to penetrate for 15 minutes and flush with water.

Sturdy Fabrics. 1. Brush or scrape (see Stain Removing Techniques) away the excess.
2. Flush with dry cleaning solvent and tamp (see Stain Removing Techniques) or scrape.
3. Follow steps 2–6 for delicate fabrics.

Recommended Products

Carbona Spot Remover with Applicator Top (Carbona Products Company)—for natural and synthetic fabrics; built-in cloth applicator.

K2r Spot-lifter (Texize Chemicals Company)—aerosol with plastic brush lid; dries to a powder; safe for dry cleanable fabrics except acetate and velvet; can be used on carpets and wallpaper.

Paint, Latex

Washable

1. Sponge (see Stain Removing Techniques) the stain with water before the paint sets (within 2 hours).
2. Launder with an all-purpose detergent (see Laundry) using a warm water temperature setting.
3. If the stain persists or if the paint has dried, sponge the area with turpentine or paint thinner.
4. Launder again.

Nonwashable *(Try recommended product first)*

Delicate Fabrics. 1. Sponge (see Stain Removing Techniques) with turpentine or paint thinner.
2. If stain persists, moisten with dry cleaning solvent and cover the stained area with an absorbent pad moistened with solvent.
3. Keep both the stain and pad moistened with solvent for 30 minutes, changing the pad as it picks up stain.
4. Test for colorfastness.
5. If color doesn't change, flush (see Stain Removing Techniques) with rubbing or denatured alcohol to remove the turpentine. Use one part alcohol to two parts water for acetate.
6. If fabric is not colorfast, sponge with a solution of liquid dishwashing detergent (see Recommended Basic Products) and water, then sponge with clear water.

Sturdy Fabrics. 1. Sponge (see Stain Removing Techniques) with turpentine or paint thinner.
2. If stain persists, moisten with dry cleaning solvent and cover the stained area with an absorbent pad moistened with solvent.
3. Keep both the stain and pad moistened with solvent for 30 minutes, changing the pad as it picks up stain.
4. Apply one drop of liquid dishwashing detergent (see Recommended Basic Products) and tamp or scrape (see Stain Removing Techniques).
5. Continue the solvent and detergent treatment until the stain is gone.
6. Test for colorfastness.

7. If color doesn't change, flush (see Stain Removing Techniques) with rubbing or denatured alcohol to remove the turpentine. Use one part alcohol to two parts water for acetate.
8. If fabric is not colorfast, sponge with a solution of liquid dishwashing detergent and water, then sponge with clear water.

Recommended Product

Afta Cleaning Fluid (Afta Solvents Corporation)—for dry cleanable fabrics, upholstery, auto interiors, and marble; has no applicator.

Perfume

Washable

Delicate Fabrics. 1. Sponge (see Stain Removing Techniques) with water.
2. Apply Wet Spotter, then flush (see Stain Removing Techniques) with water.
3. Test for colorfastness.
4. If color doesn't change, moisten the stain and an absorbent pad with rubbing or denatured alcohol and cover the stain with the pad.
5. Let it stand, keeping the pad and stain moist with alcohol and changing the pad as it picks up stain.
6. Flush with water.
7. Launder.

Sturdy Fabrics. 1. Sponge (see Stain Removing Techniques) with water.
2. Apply Wet Spotter and tamp or scrape (see Stain Removing Techniques).
3. Flush (see Stain Removing Techniques) with water.
4. Test for colorfastness.
5. If color doesn't change, moisten the stain and an absorbent pad with rubbing or denatured alcohol and cover the stain with the pad.
6. Let it stand, keeping the pad and stain moist with alcohol and changing the pad as it picks up stain.
7. Flush with water.
8. Launder.

Nonwashable

1. Sponge (see Stain Removing Techniques) then flush (see Stain Removing Techniques) with water.
2. Test for colorfastness.
3. If color doesn't change, cover the stain with an absorbent pad moistened with rubbing or denatured alcohol.
3. Let the alcohol penetrate, keeping the pad and stain moist with alcohol and changing the pad as it picks up stain.
4. Flush with water.

Perspiration

Washable

1. Presoak the garment in an enzyme presoak (see Laundry).
2. Launder with a detergent suited to the fabric (see Laundry) using a warm water temperature setting.
3. If stain is not fresh, sponge with a diluted solution of white vinegar and water, then launder.

Rust

Washable *(Try one of the recommended products first)*

1. Apply lemon juice to the stain, but do not let it dry.
2. Rinse with warm water and launder.
3. Do not iron a garment before rinsing out the rust stain remover.

Recommended Products

Barkeepers Friend Cleanser & Polish (SerVaas Laboratories, Inc.)—powder for use on ceramic tile or porcelain.

Pumie Scouring Stick (United States Pumice Company)—stick of pumice for use on ceramic tile and porcelain.

RoVer Rust Remover (Hach Chemical Company)—to be added to wash water for laundering fabrics.

Putnam's Color Remover (Putnam Color and Dye Corporation)—to be added to wash water for laundering fabrics.

Whink Rust Stain Remover (Whink Products Co.)—liquid in squeeze bottle; for use on colorfast clothing and carpeting, sinks, and toilets.

Nonwashable

Recommended Product

Whink Rust Stain Remover (Whink Products Co.)—liquid in squeeze bottle; for use on colorfast clothing and carpeting.

Scorch

Washable

1. For slight scorches, launder as usual with chlorine bleach added to the washwater for fabrics that may be bleached.
2. On more severe scorches, dampen a cloth with 3% hydrogen peroxide, place it over the stain, and place a dry cloth over the dampened one.

3. Press with an iron that is as hot as is safe for the fabric.
4. Rinse with clear water.
5. Launder. If scorch is severe and persists after these steps, nothing can be done.

Nonwashable

1. Follow steps 2–4 for washable fabrics.
2. If stain persists, try rubbing it gently with an emery board or fine sandpaper.

Urine

Washable *(Try one of the recommended products first)*

Delicate Fabrics. 1. Sponge (see Stain Removing Techniques) with club soda, then soak stained area for 30 minutes in a solution of 1 quart warm water, ½ teaspoon liquid dishwashing detergent (see Recommended Basic Products), and 1 tablespoon ammonia.
2. Rinse with water.
3. Soak in a solution of 1 quart warm water and 1 tablespoon white vinegar for 1 hour.
4. Rinse with water and dry.
5. If traces of the stain remain, test for colorfastness.
6. If color doesn't change, apply denatured or rubbing alcohol and cover with an absorbent pad dampened with alcohol.
7. Let stand as long as the stain is being removed, changing the pad as it picks up stain.
8. Keep both the stain and pad moist with alcohol.
9. Rinse with water.

Sturdy Fabrics. 1. Sponge (see Stain Removing Techniques) with club soda, then soak stained area in a solution of 1 quart warm water, ½ teaspoon liquid dishwashing detergent (see Recommended Basic Products), and 1 tablespoon ammonia.
2. Rinse with water.
3. Soak in a solution of 1 quart warm water and 1 tablespoon white vinegar for 1 hour.
4. Rinse with water and dry.
5. If traces of the stain remain, test for colorfastness.
6. If color doesn't change, apply denatured or rubbing alcohol and tamp or scrape (see Stain Removing Techniques), keeping the stain moist with alcohol and blotting occasionally with clean, absorbent material.
7. Continue applying alcohol and tamping or scraping as long as any stain is being removed.
8. Rinse with water.
9. If stain persists, bleach with a solution of 1 teaspoon chlorine bleach to 1 tablespoon water, applying the solution to the stain with a medicine dropper.
10. Allow the solution to remain on the stain for no more than 2 minutes, then flush (see Stain Removing Techniques) with water onto clean, absorbent material.
11. Apply 1 teaspoon white vinegar and flush again with water.
12. Make sure all bleach is removed.

Recommended Products

Stain-X Carpet Stain Remover (Positive Products Laboratories, Inc.)—squeeze bottle with squirt-spout; for use on all colorfast fabrics, carpets, leather and vinyl, or upholstery.

Read manufacturer's cautions and warnings before using any product.

Spots and Stains

Spot Shot (Sifers Chemicals, Inc.)—aerosol liquid; designed to remove greasy, nongreasy, and combination stains from carpets.

Nonwashable *(Try recommended product first)*

Delicate Fabrics. 1. Sponge (see Stain Removing Techniques) with water.
2. Apply Wet Spotter and a few drops of ammonia.
3. Let stand as long as stain is being removed, pressing the stain every 5 minutes with clean, absorbent material.
4. Keep the stained area moist with Wet Spotter and ammonia.
5. Flush (see Stain Removing Techniques) with water.
6. Apply Wet Spotter and a few drops of white vinegar.
7. Let stand as long as stain is being removed, pressing the stain every 5 minutes with clean, absorbent material.
8. Keep the stained area moist with Wet Spotter and vinegar.
9. Flush with water.
10. If traces of the stain remain, test for colorfastness.
11. If color doesn't change, apply rubbing or denatured alcohol to the stain and cover with an absorbent pad that has been dampened with alcohol.
12. Let it stand as long as stain is being removed, pressing hard on the pad occasionally.
13. Replace the pad as it picks up stain, keeping the pad and stained area moist with alcohol.
14. Flush with water.

Sturdy Fabrics. 1. Follow steps 1–13 for delicate fabrics.
2. If the stain persists, bleach with a solution of 1 teaspoon chlorine bleach to 1 tablespoon water, applying the solution to the stain with a medicine dropper.
3. Allow the solution to remain on the stain for no more than 2 minutes, then flush (see Stain Removing Techniques) with water onto clean, absorbent material.
4. Apply 1 teaspoon white vinegar and flush again with water.
5. Make sure all bleach is removed.

For Carpets

1. Blot up excess before the spot dries to help prevent yellowing from the acid content.
2. Sponge (see Stain Removing Techniques) with cold water.
3. Apply a solution of 1 tablespoon ammonia in 1 cup water with a sponge.
4. Make a dry suds solution of 1 teaspoon liquid dishwashing detergent (see Recommended Basic Products) in 1 cup water that has been beaten with an eggbeater to make a high volume of suds.
5. Apply only the foam with a sponge, wetting as little as possible.
6. Remove the foam with a solution of equal parts white vinegar and water.
7. Sprinkle dry borax on the spot and let dry.
8. Brush or vacuum to remove the dried borax.

Recommended Product

Stain-X Carpet Stain Remover (Positive Products Laboratories, Inc.)—squeeze bottle with squirt-spout; for use on all colorfast fabrics, carpets, leather and vinyl, or upholstery.

Vomit

Washable *(Try recommended product after step 1)*

Delicate Fabrics. 1. Remove the solids.
2. Soak stained area for 15 minutes in a solution of 1 quart warm water, ½ teaspoon liquid dishwashing detergent (see Recommended Basic Products), and 1 tablespoon ammonia.
3. Blot occasionally with an absorbent pad, continuing as long as stain is being removed.
4. Soak article again in the solution for 15 minutes.
5. Rinse thoroughly with water to remove all ammonia.
6. Soak in a solution of 1 quart warm water and 1 tablespoon enzyme presoak (see Laundry) for 30 minutes.
7. Launder.
8. If stain persists after washing, soak in the warm water/presoak solution for another 30 minutes and relaunder.

Sturdy Fabrics. 1. Remove the solids.
2. Soak stain for 15 minutes in a solution of 1 quart warm water, ½ teaspoon liquid dishwashing detergent (see Recommended Basic Products), and 1 tablespoon ammonia.
3. Tamp or scrape (see Stain Removing Techniques).
4. Blot occasionally with an absorbent pad.
5. Follow steps 4–8 for delicate fabrics.

Recommended Product

Stain-X Carpet Stain Remover (Positive Products Laboratories, Inc.)—squeeze bottle with squirt-spout; for use on all colorfast fabrics, carpets, leather and vinyl, or upholstery.

Nonwashable *(Try recommended product after step 1)*

Delicate Fabrics. 1. Remove the solids.
2. Sponge (see Stain Removing Techniques) with water.
3. Apply Wet Spotter and a few drops of ammonia.
4. Cover with an absorbent pad dampened with Wet Spotter and let stand as long as stain is being removed.
5. Keep the stained area moist with Wet Spotter and ammonia and blot occasionally with absorbent material.
6. Flush (see Stain Removing Techniques) with water to remove all ammonia.
7. Moisten the stain with a solution of ½ teaspoon enzyme presoak (see Laundry) and ½ cup warm water.
8. Cover with a clean pad moistened with presoak solution and squeezed nearly dry.
9. Let stand for 30 minutes, adding more warm presoak solution as needed to keep stain warm and moist, but avoid letting the wet area spread.
10. Flush with water.
11. If stain persists, repeat the entire procedure.

Sturdy Fabrics. 1. Remove the solids.
2. Sponge (see Stain Removing Techniques) with water.
3. Apply Wet Spotter and a few drops of ammonia.
4. Tamp or scrape (see Stain Removing Techniques).
5. Follow steps 5–11 for delicate fabrics.

Read manufacturer's cautions and warnings before using any product.

Spots and Stains

For Carpets

1. Immediately remove solids and blot up moisture.
2. Spray shaving foam on the spot.
3. Let the foam penetrate for 5 minutes, then sponge the foam away.
4. Apply a small amount of plain club soda to the stain and allow it to fizz on the stain before wiping it up.
5. Sponge (see Stain Removing Techniques) with clean water.

Recommended Product

Stain-X Carpet Stain Remover (Positive Products Laboratories, Inc.)—squeeze bottle with squirt-spout; for use on all colorfast fabrics, carpets, leather and vinyl, or upholstery.

Directory of Manufacturers

Absorene Manufacturing Co., Inc.
1609 N. 14th St.
St. Louis, MO 63106
314/231-6355

Afta Solvents Corporation
Express Drive North
Brentwood, NY 11717
516/234-0300

Airwick Industries, Inc.
Consumer Products Division
380 North St.
Teterboro, NJ 07608
201/933-8200

Alberto-Culver Company
2525 Armitage Ave.
Melrose Park, IL 60160
312/681-5200

American Cyanamid Company
Consumer Products Div.
859 Berdan
Wayne, NJ 07470
201/831-2000

American Sponge & Chamois Company, Inc.
Sales Coordinator
47-00 34th Street
Long Island City, NY 11101
212/361-9190

Amway Corp.
7575 E. Fulton Rd.
Ada, MI 49355
616/676-6000

Armor All Products
P.O. Box 19039
Irvine, CA 92713
714/549-2200

Armour-Dial Inc.
Consumer Services Dept.
Greyhound Tower
Phoenix, AZ 85077
602/248-5557

Atlas Textiles Division of the Ohio Wiping Cloth Mfg. Co.
1719 East 39th Street
Cleveland, OH 44114
216/361-2100

Barton Chemical Corp.
5331 W. 66th St.
Chicago, IL 60638
312/767-4140

The George Basch Co.
P.O. Box 188
Freeport, NY 11520
516/378-8100

Beecham Products Division of Beecham Inc.
Church Hill Rd.
P.O. Box 1467
Pittsburgh, PA 15230
412/928-1000

Benson Optical Company
Vice-President, Region I Manager
6600 France Avenue South
Minneapolis, MN 55435
612/925-3233

Bissell Inc.
P.O. Box 1888
Grand Rapids, MI 49501
616/453-4451

Boyle-Midway Inc.
685 3rd Ave.
New York, NY 10017
212/YU6-1000

Brondow Incorporated
550 Mamaroneck Ave.
Harrison, NY 10528
914/698-6544

Brushtech, Inc.
P.O. Box 1194
Plattsburgh, NY 12901
518/563-8420

The Butcher Polish Co.
120 Bartlett St.
Marlborough, MA 01752
617/481-5700

Canden Company
P.O. Box 161721
Sacramento, CA 95816
916/392-9712

Carbona Products Company
330 Calyer
New York, NY 11107
212/383-5599

Carpet Magic, A Division of Hartz Mountain
700 S. 4th St.
Harrison, NJ 07029
201/481-4800

Church & Dwight Co., Inc.
Two Pennsylvania Plaza
New York, NY 10001
201/885-1220

Classic Chemical
1305 E. Ave. H
Grand Prairie, TX 75050
214/647-2990

The Clorox Company
P.O. Box 24305
Oakland, CA 94623
415/271-7283

Directory of Manufacturers

Colgate-Palmolive Company
300 Park Ave.
New York, NY 10022
212/PL1–1200

Cromwell Products, Inc.
P.O. Box 368
180 Post Road East
Westport, CT 06881
203/226–4745

Discwasher, Inc.
Consumer Information
  Department
1407 N. Providence Rd.
Columbia, MO 65201
314/449–0941

The Dow Chemical Co.
Midland, MI 48640
517/636-1000

The Drackett Company
Sub. of Bristol Meyers Co.
5020 Spring Grove Ave.
Cincinnati, OH 45232
513/632–1500

**E. I. Du Pont De Nemours &
  Co., Inc.**
F & F Department
B-4233
Wilmington, DE 19898
302/774–8136

**Ecological & Specialty
  Products, Inc.**
P.O. Box 451
River Street Station
Paterson, NJ 07524
201/278–4935

Economics Laboratory, Inc.
Four Corporate Park Dr.
White Plains, NY 10604
914/694–8626

Empire Brushes, Inc.
P.O. Box 1606
Greenville, NC 27834
919/758–4111

Empire Scientific Corp.
Distributor for C. E. Watts
1055 Stewart Ave.
Garden City, NY 11530
516/222–1400

Empire White Products Co.
45 Hermon St.
Newark, NJ 07105
201/344–5307

Enterprise Paint Co.
1191 S. Wheeling Rd.
Wheeling, IL 60090
312/541–9000

**Faultless Starch/Bon Ami
  Company**
1025 W. 8th St.
Kansas City, MO 64101
816/842–1230

**Fiberglass Cleaning
  Products, Inc.**
1085 N. Main St., Suite W
Orange, CA 92640
714/771–0532

Fiebing Chemical Company
516 S. Second
P.O. Box 041204
Milwaukee, WI 53204
414/271–5011

**Flambeau Products
  Corporation**
Housewares Department
801 Lynn Avenue
Baraboo, WI 53913
608/356–5551

Formby's Inc.
10136 Mills
P.O. Box 788
Olive Branch, MS 38654
601/895–5594

The R. T. French Co.
One Mustard St.
Rochester, NY 14609
716/482–8000

A. J. Funk & Co.
1471 Timber Dr.
Elgin, IL 60120
312/741–6760

**Garry Laboratories Inc.,
  Division of Northeast
  Chemical Co.**
260 Creekside Dr.
Amherst, NY 14150
716/691–8822

Glenwood Laboratories Inc.
83 N. Summit St.
Tenafly, NJ 07670
201/569–0050

Golden Star Polish Mfg. Co.
400 E. 10th Ave.
N. Kansas City, MO 64116
816/842–0233

Gold Seal Co.
210 N. 4th
Bismarck, ND 58501
701/223–4800

**Gorham Division of Textron
  Inc.**
333 Adelaide Ave.
Providence, RI 02907
401/785–9800

Guardsman Chemicals, Inc.
Consumer Products Division
3503 Lousma Drive
Grand Rapids, MI 49508
616/247–7651

Hach Chemical Company
P.O. Box 389
Loveland, CO 80537
800/525–5940

**W. J. Hagerty & Sons, Ltd.,
  Inc.**
P.O. Box 1496
3801 W. Linden
South Bend, IN 46624

**The Herbert Stanley
  Company**
8140 N. Ridgeway Ave.
Skokie, IL 60076
312/675–4575

Hollywood Shoe Polish, Inc.
7 E. 43rd St.
New York, NY 10017
212/490–3163

Horian Engineering, Inc.
600 Lake Emma Road
Lake Mary, FL 32746
305/323–2400

International Silver Company
550 Research Parkway
Meriden, CT 06450
203/634–2000

Interstate Oil Co., Inc.
87 Shawnee Ave.
Kansas City, KS 66119
913/371–3470

Jelmar Co.
666 N. Lake Shore Dr.
Chicago, IL 60611
312/565–1150

S. C. Johnson & Son, Inc.
Consumer Services
  Department
1525 Howe
Racine, WI 53403
414/554–2000

Kimberly-Clark Corporation
North Lake Street
Neenah, WI 54956
414/721–2000

The Kirby Company
Division of Scott & Fetzer Co.
1920 West 114th Street
Cleveland, OH 44102
216/228–2400

The Kiwi Polish Company Pty. Ltd.
Route 662
Douglassville, PA 19518
215/385-3041

K mart Corporation
Customer Relations Department
3100 Big Beaver Road
Troy, MI 48084
313/643-1000

Knomark Inc.
132-20 Merrick Blvd.
Jamaica, NY 11434
212/276-3400

Lehn & Fink Products Division of Sterling Drug Inc.
225 Summit Ave.
Montvale, NJ 07645
201/391-8500

Lever Brothers Company
390 Park Ave.
New York, NY 10022
212/668-6000

Lewal Industries, Inc.
65 Plain Ave.
New Rochelle, NY 10801
914/235-1203

Lewis Research Labs. Co. Inc.
One Blue Hill Plaza
Pearl River, NY 10965
914/735-2400

Lundmark Wax Company
3509 S. Maplewood Ave.
Chicago, IL 60632
312/847-3774

Magic American Chemical Corp.
23700 Mercantile
Cleveland, OH 44122
216/464-2353

Martens Mfg., Inc., A Div. of Foley Mfg. Co.
3300 N.E. Fifth St.
Minneapolis, MN 55418
612/789-8831

Meeco Mfg. Inc.
1137 S.W. Hanford
Seattle, WA 98134
206/624-2266

Miles Laboratories, Inc.
7123 W. 65th St.
Chicago, IL 60638
312/458-6100

Missouri Hickory Corp.
410 N. Michigan Ave.
Chicago, IL 60611
312/943-3793

Multi-Care Corporation
P.O. Box 87
Scarsdale, NY 10583
914/725-2096

Nankee Aluminum Paint Co.
Engineer Lane
Farmingdale, NY 11735
212/886-5858

Noxell Corporation
P.O. Box 1799
Baltimore, MD 21203
301/628-7300

Oakite Products, Inc.
c/o Rasco Incorporated
P.O. Box 193
Lakeville, CT 06039
203/435-2565

Oil-Dri Corp. of America
520 N. Michigan Avenue
Chicago, IL 60611
312/321-1515

C. W. Parker Company
1415 Second Ave.
Des Moines, IA 50314
515/243-6610

Pickwick Int'l.
7500 Excelsior Blvd.
St. Louis Park, MN 55426
612/932-7412

Positive Products Laboratories, Inc.
28-11 Astoria Blvd.
Long Island City, NY 11102
212/721-5881

Premier Dye & Polish Co., Inc.
25 Bridgewater St.
Brooklyn, NY 11222
212/388-9474

J. L. Prescott Co.
Passaic, NJ 07055
201/777-4200

Procter & Gamble
P.O. Box 599
Cincinnati, OH 45201
800/543-0485

Purex Corporation
P.O. Box 6200
24600 S. Main St.
Carson, CA 90749
213/518-2350

Putnam Color and Dye Corporation
P.O. Box 1267
Galesburg, IL 61401
800/332-8183 (Ill. residents)
800/447-8192 (other states)

Quickie Manufacturing Corp.
2605 River Road
Cinnaminson, NJ 08077
609/829-7900

Radiator Specialty Company
P.O. Box 34689
Charlotte, NC 28234
704/377-6555

Redken Laboratories, Inc.
Consumer Relations Department
Canoga Park, CA 91303
213/992-3037 (collect for Calif. residents)
800/423-5369 (other states)

Revere Copper & Brass, Incorporated
P.O. Box 250
Clinton, IL 61727
217/935-3111

John Ritzenthaler Co.
40 Portland Road
West Conshohocken, PA 19428
215/825-9321

I. Rokeach & Sons, Inc.
560 Sylvan Ave.
Englewood Cliffs, NJ 07632
201/568-7550

Rubbermaid Incorporated
Consumer Services Department
1147 Akron Road
Wooster, OH 44691
216/264-6464

David Rubin
42 Somerset Street
Springfield, MA 01108
413/733-2401

Rug Doctor, Inc.
2788 N. Larkin Ave.
Fresno, CA 93727
209/291-5511

The Savogran Co.
259 Lenox St.
Norwood, MA 02062
617/762-5400

Scott Paper Company
Consumer Information Center
Scott Plaza I
Philadelphia, PA 19113
215/521-5000

Directory of Manufacturers

Scott's Liquid Gold-Inc.
4880 Havanna St.
Denver, CO 80239
303/373–4860

SerVaas Laboratories, Inc.
P.O. Box 7008
Indianapolis, IN 46207
317/634–1100

Sifers Chemicals, Inc.
P.O. Box 8316
Shawnee Mission, KS 66208
913/648–6644

Sponge, Inc.
1294 West 70th Street
Cleveland, OH 44102
216/961–6161

A. E. Staley Mfg. Co.
Consumer Products Group
2222 Kensington Ct.
Oak Brook, IL 60521
312/986–1150

Stanley Home Products, Inc.
333 Western Ave.
Westfield, MA 01085
413/562–3631

Star Brite Inc.
P.O. Box 300
Coral Gables, FL 33134
305/858–3636

Sterling Products
15922 Strathern St.
Van Nuys, CA 91406
213/785–4918

STP Corp.
1400 W. Commercial Blvd.
Ft. Lauderdale, FL 33310
305/771–1010

Suburbanite Industries
P.O. Box 3235
Saxonville, MA 01701
617/877–6500

Sunbeam Appliance Service Co.
5300 W. Roosevelt Rd.
Chicago, IL 60650
312/854–3500

Texize Chemicals Company
P.O. Box 368
Greenville, SC 29602
803/963–4261

3M
3M Center
St. Paul, MN 55101
612/733–1110

Trager Mfg. Co., Inc.
1200 Wheeler Ave.
Scranton, PA 18510
717/346–7531

Trewax Company
11558 South St.
Suite 41
Cerritos, CA 90701
213/860–0197

Turtle Wax, Inc.
5655 W. 73rd St.
Chicago, IL 60638
312/284–8300

Union Carbide Corp.
270 Park Ave.
New York, NY 10017
212/551–2345

United Gilsonite Laboratories
Box 70
Scranton, PA 18501
717/344–1202

United States Borax & Chemical Corporation
3075 Wilshire Blvd.
Los Angeles, CA 90010
213/381–5311

United States Pumice Company
2890 Empire Avenue
Burbank, CA 91504
213/843–8553

Vigilant Products Co., Inc.
27 Main St.
Ogdensburg, NJ 07439
201/827–3333

Vistron/Pro Brush
221 Pine St.
Florence, MA 01060
413/584–1780

Westley Industries, Inc.
5300 Harvard Ave.
Cleveland, OH 44105
216/641–5490

Whink Products Co.
1901 15th Avenue
Eldora, IA 50627
712/858–3456

White Laboratories
3768 Silver Star Road
P.O. Box 15335
Orlando, FL 32858
305/293–0606

Wilbert Products Co., Inc.
805 E. 139th St.
Bronx, NY 10454
212/292–8200

Woodhill Permatex
18731 Cranwood Parkway
Cleveland, OH 44128
216/475–3600

J. A. Wright & Co.
60 Dunbar St.
Keene, NH 03431
603/352–2625

Index

A

Abrasives, 243
Absorbent powders, 243
Absorbing technique for stains, 246
Absorene, 11, 51, 75, 89, 155
Acetate, 143, 234
Acetone, 212
Acoustical tile ceilings, 11–12
Acrylic
  awnings, 186
  countertops, 12
  cultured marble made from, 14
  fabric, 143–44
  furniture, 72–73
  paintings, 80
  sweaters, 158–59
Action Neatsfoot Oil Compound, 71, 209
Afta
  Carpet Stain Remover, 245, 254
  Cleaning Fluid, 245, 251, 252, 254, 255, 259, 260, 264, 269
  Silver Dip, 181
  Tile Cleaner, 14, 50, 94, 98
Ajax Cleanser, 49, 92, 189
Ajax Dishwashing Liquid, 159, 226
Alcohol
  denatured, 212
  isopropyl, 166, 214
  rubbing, 54, 84, 161
Alcoholic beverage stains, 247
All-purpose cleaners, 225–26
All-purpose laundry detergents, 232–33
All Temperature Cheer, 232
All Temperature Punch, 233
All-weather coats, 152–54
Aluminum, 169–70
  cookware, 101–3, 169–70
  outdoor furniture, 191–93
Amino Pon Concentrate Shampoo, 168
Ammonia, 13, 25, 48, 92, 97, 98, 112, 123, 127, 159, 161, 163, 227, 232, 243
  clear, 13, 19, 24, 26, 28, 29, 30, 33, 40, 44, 50, 51, 55, 93, 94, 162, 227
  sudsy, 162, 165, 166, 227
Amway
  Buff Up, 54, 57, 73, 86
  Metal Cleaner, 22
  Multi-Purpose L.O.C. Cleaner (High Suds), 187, 225
  Multi-Purpose L.O.C. Cleaner (Regular), 196, 225
  Remove Fabric Spot Cleaner, 153, 245, 249, 259, 262
  Rug & Upholstery Shampoo, 68
  Zoom Spray Cleaner Concentrate, 16, 21, 95, 98, 192, 194, 225
Amyl acetate, 243
Andirons, brass, 22–23, 170
Angora sweaters, 158–59
Arm & Hammer
  Baking Soda, 14, 94
  Laundry Detergent, 60, 65, 87, 232
  Oven Cleaner, 128
  Washing Soda, 188, 231
Armor All Cleaner, 200, 203, 206
Armor All Protectant, 202
Artgum eraser, 52, 88, 154, 157, 209
Artists' brushes, 212
Art objects. See Objets d'art.
Ashes
  in fireplace, 17, 18, 20
  gold cleaned by cigarette, 165
  in self-cleaning ovens, 126–27
Asphalt tile floors, 23–25
Automatic clothes dryers, 118–19
Automatic clothes washers, 236–37
Automatic dishwashers, 116–17
Automobiles, 197–207
  bumper guards on, 202
  bumpers on, 200
  carpeting in, 197–98
  chrome on, 198–99
  cloth upholstery in, 203
  fenders on, 200
  floor mats in, 197, 199–200, 202
  hubcaps on, 200, 202–3
  paint finish on, 200–202
  side moldings on, 202
  taillights on, 206–7
  tires on, 202–3
  vinyl tops on, 205–6
  white sidewall tires on, 202–3
  windows on, 206–7
  windshields on, 206–7
  wood-grain trim on, 207
Automotive grease and oil stains, 260
Awnings, 186–87
Axion, 230

B

Baby formula stains, 230
Baby shampoo, 167–68
Bac-Tex Bacteriostatic Rug Shampoo Concentrate, 68, 198
Baking soda, 13, 14, 15, 17, 21, 48, 50, 51, 81, 92, 93, 94, 95, 97, 98, 101, 102, 103, 104, 106, 107, 108, 112, 114, 115, 117, 118, 119, 120, 121, 124, 125, 129, 130, 131, 132, 134, 136, 137, 138, 139, 148, 161, 164, 165, 166, 169, 170, 173, 176, 180, 181, 182, 184, 191, 192, 193, 198, 200, 211, 227, 245
Bamboo furniture, 74
Barbecue grills, 187–88
Bar-B-Q and Oven Grill Brush, 218
Bar Keepers Friend Cleanser & Polish, 92, 105, 171, 175, 178, 185, 195, 244, 270
Bar soaps for laundry, 233
Bathroom fixtures, 95–96
Bathroom Scrubber, 221
Bathtubs, 91–92
Beacon Floor Wax, 25, 27, 29, 34, 35, 37, 39, 41, 43, 45
Bedding, 58–66
  bedspreads, 58
  blankets, 59–60
  box springs, 62–63
  comforters, 60–62
  mattresses, 62–63
  pillows, 63–65
  quilts, 60–62
  sleeping bags, 65–66
Bed linens, polyester, 146
Bedspreads, 58
Befresh, 100
Big Wally, 89, 98, 196, 203, 226
Bissell
  Foam Rug Cleaner with Resoil-Fighter Additive, 68
  One Step Wood Floor Care, 32, 47
  Upholstery Shampoo for Home & Auto, 63, 71, 203
  Wall to Wall Rug Shampoo, 67
Biz, 149, 230
Black Wonder Dusting Cloth, 219
Blankets
  electric, 59
  modacrylic in, 145

Index

wool in, 59
Bleach, 234
  chlorine, 16, 49, 50, 86, 99,
    107, 114, 116, 140, 141,
    144, 145, 146, 148, 194,
    234, 243
  oxygen-type, 141, 144, 147,
    230, 234, 243
  sodium perborate, 147, 243
  3% hydrogen peroxide acting
    as, 91, 141, 234, 243
Blenders, electric, 131–32
Blinds, 85–86
Blood stains, 230, 248
Blouses, hand washing, 238
Boiled linseed oil, 19, 53, 56, 72,
    115, 215
Bold 3, 59, 61, 62, 149, 232
Bon Ami Cleaning Powder, 92,
    102, 108, 109, 170, 183, 193
Bon Ami Deluxe Polishing
    Cleanser, 14, 15, 91, 94, 108,
    116, 126, 134, 183, 184
Bone
  art objects, 77
  hairbrushes and combs, 161
Books, 208–9
  mildew stains on, 267
Boots, 153–54, 156
Borax powder, 91, 148
Bounce, 235
Bounty Towels, 221
Box springs, 62–63
Bras, hand washing, 238
Brass, 170–71
  andirons and fire tools, 22–23,
    170
Brasso, 105, 109, 171, 175, 179,
    183
Breath O' Pine Multi-Purpose
    Cleaner, 92, 191, 226
Brick, 189
  floors, 25–27
  patio floors, 189
  walls, 49, 189
Brillo Steel Wool Soap Pads, 20,
    102, 103, 109, 183, 192, 202,
    216, 222
Brite For No-wax Floors, 43
Brocade, acetate in, 143
Broilers, 137
Brooms, 217
Bruce
  Acrylic, 32, 47
  Clean & Wax, 32, 47
  Deep Cleaner, 32, 46
  One Step, 31, 45
Brushes, 217–18
Bumpers, automobile, 200, 202
Butcher's Bowling Alley Paste
    Wax, 27, 32, 34, 37, 39, 43,
    47, 74
Butcher's Fireplace & Stove
    Glass Cleaner, 19
Butter stains, 248–49

C

Cabbage leaves for polishing
    pewter, 179
Cabinet Magic, 53, 54, 56, 57
Calgonite Automatic
    Dishwashing Detergent, 110,
    112

Calgon Water Softener, 149, 231
Cameo Aluminum and Stainless
    Steel Cleaner, 102, 108, 170,
    174, 182, 192
Cameo Copper Cleaner, 105,
    171, 175
Candlesticks, 77, 80–81
Candle wax stains, 249
Cane furniture, 74
Can openers, electric, 133
Cans, garbage, 190–91
Canvas awnings, 186
Carbona
  Cold Water Wash, 159, 233
  1 Hour Rug Cleaner, 67
  Spot Remover with Applicator
    Top, 245, 249, 250, 251,
    255, 256, 258, 259, 260,
    261, 265, 268
  Spray Foam Rug Shampoo, 68
Carpet Magic "Steam" Cleaning
    Cleaner, 68
Carpet Magic "Steam" Machine, 67
Carpets, 66–68, 145
  alcoholic beverage stains on,
    247
  in automobiles, 197–98
  urine stains on, 272
  vomit stains on, 274
Carpet sweepers, 218
Cars. See Automobiles.
Carvings
  bone, 77
  jade, 78–79
Cascade Automatic Dishwashing
    Detergent, 110, 113
Cashmere sweaters, 158–59
Cast iron
  cookware, 103–4
  fireplace tools, 20
Catsup stains, 249–51
Ceilings, 11–12
Ceiling tile, 12
Cellulose sponges, 223
Ceramic. See also Ceramic tile.
  cooktops, 126
  cookware, 106–7
  hot tray surfaces, 136–37
Ceramic tile
  countertops, 13–14, 93–94
  glazed floors, 27–28
  unglazed floors, 28–30
  walls, 49–50
Chamois, 218, 219
Chamois gloves, 150
Chassis, automobile, 200
Chenille robes, 229
Chewing gum spots, 251–52
Chimneys, 17–18
China
  dinnerware, 109–10
  toilet bowls made of vitreous,
    99–100
Chlorine bleach, 16, 49, 50, 86,
    99, 107, 114, 116, 140, 141,
    144, 145, 146, 194, 234
Chocolate stains, 230, 252–53
Chrome, automobile, 198–99
Chromium, 173–74. See also
    Chrome, automobile.
Citrus fruits to clean garbage
    disposers, 136
Classic
  Car Wax, 201

Finish Restorer, 207
  Whitewall Tire Cleaner, 200
Clay cookware, 103–4
Cleaner, all-purpose, 225–26
Clean-Sweep Record Purifier, 215
Cleaners, window, 224
Clear ammonia, 13, 19, 24, 26,
    28, 29, 30, 33, 40, 44, 50, 51,
    55, 93, 94, 162, 227
Cling Free, 235
Cling Free Fabric Softener
    Sheets, 235
Clorox Bleach, 14, 94, 149, 234,
    244
Clorox 2 All Fabric Bleach, 234,
    244
Cloth. See also Fabric.
  awnings made from, 186, 187
  rainwear made from, 152–53
  upholstery in automobiles, 203
Clothes dryers, 118–19
Clotheslines, 239
Clothespins, 239
Clothes washers, 118–19
Cloths, 218–19
Club soda, 245
Coats, 150–52
  all-weather, 152–54
Coconut oil, 244
Coffee
  for cleaning black suede shoes,
    157
  stains from, 253–54
Coffeemakers, 107, 132–33
Cold Power XE, 232
Cold water laundry detergent,
    232–33
Colorfastness test
  for bedspreads, 58
  before bleaching, 234, 242
  for carpets and rugs, 66
  for down-filled comforters and
    quilts, 60
  for draperies, 87
  for dyed silk, 141
  for quilts/comforters of
    undetermined fiber, 61
  for shoe uppers, 154
  for window shades, 88
Combination stains, 242
Combs, hair, 161
Comet Cleanser, 20, 92, 117
Comforters
  cotton-filled, 61–62
  down-filled, 60–61
  polyester fiber-filled, 61–62
  silk-covered, 60, 61
  synthetic-filled, 61–62
  velvet-covered, 60, 61
  wool-covered down, 60
  wool-filled, 61–62
Compactors, trash, 129–30
Complete All Purpose Polishing
    Cleaner, 22, 90
Concentrated All Detergent, 233
Concrete floors, 30
Conditioners, water, 230–31
Cooking oil, 170, 259
Cooktops
  ceramic-glass, 126
  electric, 126, 128–29
  gas, 126, 128–29
Cookware
  aluminum, 101–3

cast iron, 103
ceramic glass, 106–7
clay, 103–4
copper, 104–5
enamelware, 106
glass, 106–7
nonstick-coated, 107–8
stainless steel, 108–9
Copper, 174–75
cookware, 104–5
mixed with gold for jewelry, 176
and tin to form bronze alloy, 172
water pipes, 174
Copper Glo, 105, 109, 171, 174, 175, 183
Corduroy, cotton. See Cotton.
Cork tile floors, 31–32
Cornmeal, 66, 78, 88, 243
Cornstarch, 52, 154, 200, 243
Cotton, 140, 236
cleaning cloths, 218, 219
curtains, 86–87
flame retardant, 140
lampshades, 74–75
shoes, 154–55
sweaters, 158–59
sweat socks as cleaning mitts, 220
Countertop Magic, 16, 95
Countertops, 12–14, 93–95
acrylic, 12
ceramic tile, 13–14, 93–94
cultured marble, 14–15, 94
marble, 14
plastic laminate, 15–16, 94–95
wood, 16–17
zinc, 184–85
Cosmetics stains, 263–65
Crayon marks, 243, 254–55
Cream of tartar, 91, 102
Creosote, 17, 20
Crepe
acetate in, 143
wool in, 142
Crystal Drano Drain Opener, 211
Cultured marble
countertops, 14–15, 93–94
shower stalls, 97–98
Cultured pearls, 163
Curtains, 86–87
Cutlery, 78, 111
Cut oats, 78

D

Dash, 233
Dawn, 226
Dazzle, 226
Decorator tile walls, 50
Degreaser, 110, 123
Delete Polishing Cleanser, 126
Denim. See Cotton.
Deodorant stains, 255
Dermassage Dishwashing Liquid, 159, 226
Detergents, 231–33
all-purpose laundry, 232–33
light duty laundry, 233
liquid dishwashing, 226
Diaper pails, 148, 149, 230
Diapers, 148–49, 231, 235
Dinnerware, 109–10
Dip-It Coffee Pot Destainer, 110, 133

Discwasher Record Cleaning System, 215
Dishes, 109–10
Dishpans, 219
Dishwasher All, 110, 113
Dishwashers, automatic, 116–17
Dishwashing detergents, liquid, 226
Disposers, garbage, 135–36
Dobie Cleaning Pad, 222
Doors, storm, 169–70
Double knits, acetate in, 143
Dove Dishwashing Liquid, 159, 226
Dow Disinfectant Bathroom Cleaner, 14, 15, 50, 92, 94, 98
Down and feather filling
in comforters and quilts, 60–61
in cushions, 69
drying articles made with, 239
in outerwear, 150–51
in pillows, 63–65
in sleeping bags, 65–66
Downy Fabric Softener, 235
Dow Oven Cleaner, 128
Drain Power, 210
Drains, 210–11
fixtures for, 95–96
plastic or rubber boards for, 113–14
Dresses, hand washing, 238
Dry cleaning solvents, 244
Drip coffeemakers, 132–33
Dry detergent method
cloth automotive upholstery cleaned with, 203
fabric upholstery on furniture cleaned with, 70
lampshades cleaned with, 75
mattresses or box springs cleaned with, 63
vinyl wall coverings cleaned with, 52
window shades cleaned with, 89
Dryers, clothes, 118–19
Dry sinks, zinc, 184–85
Dry spotter, 244
Du Pont
Car Wash Concentrate, 201
Rain Dance Car Wax, 201
Rally Cream Wax, 201
Duriklens Plastic Lens Cleaner, 160
Duro Aluminum Jelly, 103, 170, 193
Duro Naval Jelly, 216
Dust Bug, The, 214
Dust jackets for books, 208
Dustmops, 219
Dustpans, 219
Dynamo, 233

E

Easy-Off Oven Cleaner, 127, 137
Easy-Off Window Cleaner, 55, 174
Easy-On Speed Starch, 140
Egg stains, 256–58
Electrasol, 110, 113
Electric can openers, 133

Electric irons, 134–35
Electric stovetops, 126
Empire Dust-R-Magic Brush, 217
Empire Handled Hand & Nail Brush, 217
Enamel
cookware, 106
waffle iron surfaces, 139
Endust, 69, 82, 85
Enzyme presoaks, 58, 140, 146, 151, 154, 230
Epic Brush & Roller Cleaner, 213
Era, 232
Esquire Boot Polish, 156
Esquire Spray Shine, 156
Eyeglasses, 160–61

F

Fab All Temperature Laundry Detergent, 232
Fabric, 231
dinginess, 240
flowers, 77–78
furniture upholstery, 70–71
gloves, 150
grayness, 240
harshness, 241
rainwear, 152–53
shoes, 154–55
softeners, 235
Fake furs, modacrylic in, 145
Fans, rangehood, 122–23
Fantastik Multi-Surface Spray Cleaner, 21, 65–66, 86, 89, 98, 117, 119, 120, 122, 123, 125, 129, 130, 154, 192, 194, 203, 225
Faucets, bathroom, 95–96
Faultless Hot-iron Cleaner, 134
Favor, 73
Fels-Naptha Heavy Duty Laundry Bar Soap, 83, 186, 233
Felt, wool in, 142
Fenders, automobile, 200
Fiberglass
automobile surfaces, 200
bathtubs, 91–92
curtains, 86–87, 144
draperies, 144
fabric, 144, 239
lampshades, 74–75
shower stalls, 97–98
Fiber scouring pads, 221–22
Fiebing's Saddle Soap, 71, 156
Filters
microwave oven, 121–22
rangehood, 122–23
vacuum cleaner, 223
Final Touch Concentrated Fabric Softener, 235
Finish, 110, 113
FINIS High Gloss Furniture Polish, 53, 56, 72
Fireboxes, 17, 18–19
Fireplaces, 17–23
ashes in, 17
brass tools for, 22–23
cast iron tools for, 20
chimneys, 17
creosote in, 17
fireboxes in, 17
fire screens for, 19

Index

flues in, 17
glass enclosures for, 19–20
grates in, 20
hearths on, 17, 20–22
lintels in, 18
mantels on, 20–22
Fire screens, 19
"500"-XL Windshield Washer
Anti-Freeze & Solvent, 207
Flagstone floors, 32–34
Flambeau Nylon Pan Scraper,
222
Flatware, 111
Fleece robes, modacrylic in, 145
Floor mats for automobiles, 197,
199–200, 202
Floor polishers, 219
Floors, 23–47
asphalt tile, 34–36
brick, 36–38, 189
buffable waxes and polishes
for, 27, 30, 32, 34, 37, 39,
43, 47
ceramic tile, glazed, 27–29
ceramic tile, unglazed, 28–30
cleaner/polishes, 24, 41, 45
cleaners for, 30, 34, 46–47
concrete, 30
cork tile, 31–32
flagstone, 32–34
linoleum, 34–36
marble, 36–37
no-wax vinyl, 43
polishes—self-polishing for,
25, 26–27, 29, 32, 33–34,
35, 37, 39, 41, 43, 45, 47
quarry tile, 38–39
removing heelmarks from, 23,
31, 34, 40, 44, 46, 221
rubber tile, 39–41
slate, 32–34
terrazzo, 42–43
vinyl, 43–45
wax strippers and cleaners for,
25, 27, 29–30, 34, 35–36,
37, 39, 41, 43, 45
wood, 45–47
Floor scrubbers, 219
Flour, 88, 105, 137, 139, 164,
171, 172, 173, 175, 177, 179,
180, 227
Flowers, fabric, 77–78
Flues, 17, 18
Flushing technique for stains, 246
Foam filling, 63–65, 239
Food processors, 131–32
Food scrapers, 113–14
Formby's Furniture Cleaner, 22,
53, 56, 74, 90
Formby's Lemon Oil Furniture
Treatment, 22, 53, 56, 74, 90
Formica plastic laminate
countertops, 15, 94
Formula 409 All Purpose Cleaner,
16, 20, 21–22, 65, 86, 89, 92,
95, 117, 119, 120, 122, 123,
125, 129, 130, 153, 188, 192,
193, 194, 202, 216, 225
Formula stains, baby, 230
Foundation garments, spandex
in, 147
Free 'n Soft, 235
Freezers, 119–21, 124–25
Freezing technique for stains, 246

French chalk, 243
Fruit stains, 230
Fuller's earth, 243
Furniture, 69–74. See also
Outdoor furniture.
antique, 73
bamboo, 74
cane, 74
fabric upholstery on, 70–71
leather upholstery on, 71
metal, 69
oiled wood, 72
painted wood, 73
plastic, 70
polished wood, 73–74
rattan, 74
rush, 74
specialty wood, 74
vinyl upholstery on, 72
wicker, 74
wood television cabinets, 84
Furniture cream, 72, 82
Fur rugs, 66
Future Acrylic Floor Finish, 25,
26, 27, 29, 34, 35, 37, 39, 41,
43, 45

G

Gain, 233
Galoshes, 153–54
Garbage cans, 190–91
Garbage disposers, 135–36
Garden furniture. See Outdoor
furniture.
Garden tools, 169–70, 215–16
Garry's
Black Knight Tar and Bug
Remover, 201
Foaming Glass Cleaner, 207
Knight's Armor Chrome
Cleaner & Polish, 198
Prince Regent Concentrated
Car Wash, 201
Really White Whitewall Speed
Kleener, 202
Royal Satin, 201
VLP Vinyl-Leather-Plastic
Cleaner and Conditioner,
204, 205–6
Gas stovetops, 126
Gentle Fels, 159, 226
Glamorene Spray 'N Vac, 68
Glamorene Upholstery Shampoo,
63, 71, 203
Glass
cookware, 106–7
covering paintings, 80
crystal, 112
dinnerware, 109–10
fireplace enclosures, 19–20
microwave oven trays, 121–22
milk, 112
shower stalls, 97–98
windows on automobiles,
206–7
windshields on automobiles,
206–7
Glass Plus, 16, 20, 55, 95, 103,
109, 170, 174, 183
Glassware, 112–13. See also
Glass.
Glass Wax, 55, 117, 120, 181

Glory Professional Strength Rug
Cleaner, 68, 197, 247
Gloves, 150, 220
Glycerin, 54, 155, 158, 244, 245
Goddard's
Cabinet Makers Polish With
Lemon Beeswax, 73
Cabinet Makers Wax, 73
Dry Clean Spot Remover, 244,
248–49, 253, 265
Long Shine Brass & Copper
Polish, 105, 171, 175
Long Term Silver Polish, 165,
181
Goddards Marble Polish, 80
Gold, 176–77
book edges, 208
cutlery, 111
dinnerware, 109–10
flatware, 111
jewelry, 164–65
Gorham Silver Polish, 109, 179,
181, 182
Grabber, The, 223
Granular detergents, 232–33
Grass stains, 154–55, 230, 258–
59
Grates, fireplace, 20
Gravy stains, 230
Grease
in drains, 210, 211
on filters in microwave ovens,
121–22
on filters in rangehoods, 122–
23
on glass fireplace enclosures,
20
on hubcaps, 202
on metal utensils, 113
on nonwashable shoes, 154
on plastic laminate
countertops, 16
on redwood garden furniture,
194
on sleeping bags, 66
spots from, 240, 242, 259–60
Grease Relief, 16, 20, 66, 123,
188, 190
Grills, barbecue, 187–88
Grout, 13–14, 27–30, 32–34, 49–
50, 93–94, 97–98
Gr-reat 'n Easy, 91, 97, 98
Guardsman Furniture Polish, 74
Gum spots, chewing, 251–52
Gunk Garage Floor, Bar-B-Q and
Mower Cleaner, 188

H

Hagerty
Heavy-Duty Copper Brass &
Metal Polish, 105, 109,
171, 174, 175, 183
Jewel Clean, 164, 166
Silver Foam, 177, 181
Hairbrushes, 161
Hair combs, 161
Hairpieces. See Wigs.
Hair spray stains, 260–61
Handi Wipes, 219
Handle Scrub Brush w/Scraper,
218
Handle With Care, 159, 233

Hard Gloss Glo-Coat, 25, 26, 29, 33, 35, 37, 39 41, 43, 45
Hardware, bathroom, 95–96
Hearths, 17, 20–22
Heat returns, 47–48
Heat stains, 101, 108
Heat vents, 47–48
Heavy Duty Mister Plumber Drain Opener, 211
Heel marks, 23, 31, 34, 40, 44, 46, 221
Hollywood Sani-White, 157
Hosiery, nylon, 145
Hot trays, 136–37
Household products, common, 227
Hubcaps, 200, 202–3
Human hair wigs, 167–68
Hydrogen peroxide, 91, 141, 234

I

Ice cream stains, 261–62
Ink stains, ballpoint, 263
Instant-Dip Silver Cleaner, 181
Instant Fels Dishwashing Soap, 159, 226
International Silver Polish, 165, 181
Iron Klean, 135
Irons, electric, 134–35
Irons, waffle, 139
Isopropyl alcohol, 166, 214
Ivory
  cutlery handles made from, 78
  in ornamental objects, 78
  piano keys made from, 78, 81–82
Ivory Liquid, 159, 226
Ivory Snow, 71, 149, 150, 163, 204, 233

J

Jackets, 150–52
Jade, 78–79, 165–66
Janitor In A Drum, 226
Jersey
  triacetate in, 147
  wool in, 142
Jewelry, 162–66
  cameo, 166
  ceramic glazes on, 162
  clasps for, 162–66
  copper in, 164
  coral, 165–66
  costume, 162–63
  cultured pearl, 163
  diamond, 165–66
  emerald, 165–66
  foil-back, 166
  glass, 162–63
  gold, 164–65
  guard chains for, 162
  ivory, 166
  jade, 78–79, 165–66
  metal, base, 162
  metal, precious, 164–65
  mirror-back, 166
  mother-of-pearl, 163
  opal, 162, 165–66
  pearl, 162, 163

plastic, 162–63
platinum, 164–65, 179–80
prongs for, 162–66
ruby, 165–66
silver, 164–65
simulated pearl, 162–63
stone, precious, 162, 165–66
turquoise, 162, 165–66
wooden, 162
Johnson Paste Wax, 26, 32, 34, 37, 39, 43, 47
Joy, 159, 226
Jubilee Kitchen Wax, 16, 116, 118, 120, 122, 125, 128, 130
J/Wax
  Car-Plate, 201
  Chrome Cleaner-Polish, 199
  Kit, 201
  Sprint No-Buff Car Wax, 201
  Vinyl Top & Interior Cleaner, 198, 205, 206

K

Kapok filling in pillows, 63–65
Kerosene, 177, 192, 196, 216
Keyboards, piano, 81–82
Kirby Vacuum Cleaner with a Rug Renovator, 68
Kirkman Borax Soap, 233
Kitchen magic, 117, 119, 120, 122, 125, 129, 130
Kiwi
  Liquid Wax, 157
  Patent and Vinyl, 156
  Saddle Soap, 157
  Scuff Magic, 157
  Shoe White, 156
  Sneaker Shampoo, 155
  Spray Shine, 157
Klean 'n Shine, 73, 86, 119, 120, 122, 125, 129, 130, 174, 180
Klear Floor Finish, 24, 26, 29, 33, 34, 39, 40, 41, 43, 44, 45
Kleen Guard Furniture Polish with Lemon Oil, 72, 73, 82
K mart Rug Shampoo, 67
K2r Spot-lifter, 153, 244, 249, 250, 251, 259, 264, 265, 268
Kwikeeze Water Rinsing Brush Cleaner, 213

L

Lacquer, 212–13
  on brass, 170–71
  on bronze, 172
  on copper, 104, 174
  on piano cases, 81–82
  on simulated pearls, 162
  thinner for, 212–13
  on unpainted aluminum garden furniture, 192
Laminate, plastic. See Plastic laminate.
Lamp bases
  alabaster, 76
  jade, 78–79
  porcelain, 80–81
Lampshades, 74–75
Latex-based paint, 212–13
  stains from, 268–69

Laundry, 228–41
  all-purpose detergents for, 232–33
  automatic washers used for, 236–37
  chlorine bleach for, 234
  detergents for, 231–33
  fabric softeners for, 235
  hand washing, 238
  hydrogen peroxide used as bleach for, 234
  light duty detergents for, 233
  light duty soaps for, 233
  line drying, 239
  machine drying, 239
  oxygen bleach for, 234
  preparing, 229–30
  presoaks for, 230
  prewash spot and stain removers for, 229–30
  problems with, 240–41
  products to use for, 230–35
  sorting, 228–29
  water conditioners for, 230–31
  water temperatures for, 236–37
  wringer washers used for, 237–38
Laundry products, 230–35
  chlorine bleaches as, 234
  detergents as, 232–33
  fabric softeners as, 235
  hydrogen peroxide as, 234
  light duty soaps as, 233
  oxygen bleaches as, 234
  water conditioners as, 230–31
Leather
  book covers, 208–9
  furniture upholstery, 71
  gloves, 150
  shoes, 154, 155–57
  upholstery in automobiles, 204–5
Leather Works, The, 71, 157, 204, 206, 209
Lemon, 16, 78, 112, 114, 171, 175
Lemon Behold Furniture Polish, 16, 22, 57, 86, 90
Lemon juice, 91, 102, 227, 245
Lemon Pledge, 22, 57, 90
Lestoil Deodorizing Rug Shampoo, 68
Lestoil Heavy Duty Cleaner, 117, 119, 120, 123, 125, 129, 130, 190, 225
Light duty laundry detergent, 233
Like Magic All Purpose Cleaner, 12, 75, 84, 86, 225
Lime A-Way, 98, 101
Linen, 141, 236
  cleaning cloths, 218, 219
  dish towels, 219
  lampshades, 74–75
  shoes, 154
Lingerie, 145, 238
Linoleum floors, 34–36
Linseed oil, boiled, 17, 53, 56, 72, 115, 215
Lipstick stains, 263–64
Liquid bleach. See Chlorine bleach.
Liquid detergents for laundry, 232–33
Liquid dishwashing detergents, 226

Index

Liquid Drano Drain Opener, 211
Liquid-plumr Drain Opener, 211
Liquid Woolite, 159, 233
Lubricating oil, 215
  stains, 260
Lundmark High Power Wax
  Remover, 25, 27, 30, 34, 36,
  37, 39, 41, 43, 45
Lundmark's Acrylic Floor Wax,
  25, 27, 29, 34, 35, 37, 39, 41,
  43, 45
Lux Dishwashing Liquid, 52, 63,
  65, 70, 75, 87, 89, 186, 203,
  226
Lysol
  Basin/Tub/Tile Cleaner, 13,
    15, 50, 92, 93, 94, 98
  Deodorizing Cleaner II, 92,
    100, 187, 190, 225
  Disinfectant Spray, 96, 194
  Liquid Disinfectant Toilet Bowl
    Cleaner, 99

M

Machine cycles in automatic
  clothes washers, 237
Machine Wash Woolite, 59, 61,
  62, 159, 233
Magic
  Handycan, 216
  Plastic Window Cleaner, 84
  Pre-Wash, 83, 230
Makeup stains, 264–65
Mantels, 20–22
Manual Parastat Model MKIIA, 215
Marble
  countertops, 14
  floors, 36–37
  objets d'art, 79–80
Marble, cultured. See Cultured
  marble.
Marble Magic, 80
Margarine stains, 248–49
Mar-Glo Marble Polish, 79
Martens Wood Preservative, 17,
  115
Masonry tile, 20–21
Mattresses, 62–63
  mildew stains on, 267
Meat juice stains, 265–66
Medium-bristled brushes, 217–18
Metal
  awnings, 186
  blinds for windows, 85–86
  clothes washer and dryer parts,
    188–19
  furniture, 69
  garbage cans, 190–91
  hairbrushes and combs, 161
  jewelry, 162, 164–65
  pails, 221
  tile walls, 50
  utensils, 113
  waffle iron surfaces, 139
Mex Multi-Purpose Cleaner, 25,
  27, 29, 30, 34, 35, 37, 39, 41,
  43, 45, 48, 49, 123, 188, 189,
  225
Mica-Lustre, 16, 84, 95
Microwave ovens, 121–22
Mildew stains, 244, 266–67
  on awnings, 187

on books, 267
on ceramic tile and grout, 13
on mattresses, 267
on rainwear, 152
on shower curtains, 96
on shower stalls, 97, 98
on vinyl and plastic garden
  furniture, 193, 194
Milk stains, 230
Mineral deposits, 101, 107, 116,
  134. See also Waterspots.
Miracle White Laundry Soil &
  Stain Remover, 230
Mirrors, 76
Mirror tile walls, 51
Mr. Clean All-Purpose Cleaner,
  123, 188, 194, 196, 213, 225
Mr. Muscle Overnight Oven
  Cleaner, 20, 128
Mr. Rust, 216, 244
Mitts, 220
Mohair, 142
Mold on clay cookware, 103–4
Mop & Glow, 24, 35, 40, 44
Mops, 220–21
Mother of pearl, 163
Mothproofing
  piano felts and hammers, 81
  sweaters, 158
Motor oil, 215
Mustard stains, 267–68

N

Natural sponges, 223
Needles, phonograph, 214
Nevr-Dull Magic Wadding Polish,
  102, 108, 164, 169, 171, 172,
  174, 176, 178, 181, 183, 185,
  193
Nickel, 176
Nongreasy stains, 242
Nonprecipitating water
  conditioners, 231
Non-Slip Liquid Floor Wax, 27,
  30, 34, 37, 39, 43
Nonstick coating
  on barbecue grills, 187
  on cookware, 107–8
Norsan Blue Automatic Toilet
  Bowl Cleaner, 100
No-wax vinyl floors, 43
Noxon Liquid 7 Metal Polish, 103,
  105, 109, 170, 171, 172, 175,
  179, 183, 193
Nylon, 145
  carpets, 145
  hairbrushes and combs, 161
  hosiery, 145
  lampshades, 74–75
  lingerie, 145
  rainwear, 145
  shoes, 154–55
  sweaters, 158–59
  tents, 145
  windbreakers, 152–53
Nylon Clean 'n Sweet, 222
Nylonge Super Surface Sponge, 223

O

Oakite All Purpose Cleaner, 24,
  30, 35–36, 37, 39, 41, 45, 51,

85, 96, 117, 119, 120, 125,
  129, 130, 226
Oats, cut, 78
Objets d'art, 76–81
  alabaster, 76
  bone, 77
  candlesticks, 77
  carvings, 77
  fabric flowers, 77–78
  ivory, 78
  jade, 78–79
  knife handles, 77
  marble, 79–80
  paintings, 80
  porcelain, 80–81
  statues, 76
  sword handles, 77
  vases, 76, 78–79, 80–81
O-CEDAR Angler Broom, 217
O-CEDAR Every-Which-Way,
  219
Octagon, 233
Odorless Paint Thinner, 213
Oil-based paint, 212–13
Oil-Dri, 30
Old English Lemon Creme
  Furniture Polish, 22, 73
Old English Furniture Polish
  Lemon Oil, 74, 90
Olive oil, 166, 215, 216
One-Wipe Dust Cloth, 219
Outdoor furniture, 191–95
  aluminum, painted, 191–92
  aluminum, unpainted, 192–93
  plastic, 193–94
  redwood, 194
  vinyl, 193–94
  wood, 194
  wrought iron, 195
Outerwear, 150–52
Oven Cleaner, 127
Ovens, 126–28
  continuous-cleaning, 126–27
  microwave, 121–22
  self-cleaning, 126–27
  toaster, 137
Oxco Perc Brush, 218
Oxco Tile & Grout Brush, 218
Oxydol, 233
Oxygen-type bleach, 141, 144,
  147, 230, 234

P

Pads, scouring. See Scouring
  pads.
Pails
  aluminum, 169–70
  diaper, 148, 149, 230
  metal, 221
  plastic, 221
Paint
  on automobiles, 200–202
  on ceilings, 12
  rollers for, 212–13
  stains from, 268–69
  thinner for, 212
Paintbrushes, 212–13
Painted furniture, aluminum,
  191–92
Painted walls, 51
Painted wood
  furniture, 73

outdoor furniture, 194
shutters, 90
woodwork, 55–56
Paintings, 80–81
Palmolive Dishwashing Liquid,
187, 226
Paneling, wood, 52–54
oil finish on, 53
polishes for oil finish, 53
wax finish on, 53–54
wood cleaners for, 53, 54
Panel Magic, 53, 54, 56, 57
Panties, hand washing, 238
Paper
ceilings covered with, 12
towels, 221
walls covered with, 51–52
Parker's Perfect Polish, 53, 72
Parsons'
Clear Detergent Ammonia, 16,
95, 243
Sudsy Detergent Ammonia,
165, 177
Wax & Acrylic Remover, 25, 26,
29, 33, 35, 37, 38, 39, 41,
42, 43, 45
Patio floors, brick, 189
Pearls, 162, 163
Percale. See Cotton.
Percolators, 132–33
Perfume stains, 269
Perspiration stains, 270
Petroleum jelly, 208, 209
Pewter, 178–79
cutlery, 111
flatware, 111, 178
Phonograph needles, 214
Phonograph records, 214–15
Pianos, 81–82. See also Ivory.
Pickwick Pro Care Deluxe Record
Maintenance System, 215
Pickwick Record Cleaning Cloth,
214
Picture frames, 80
Pillows, 63–65
Pine Forest Ajax All Purpose
Cleaner, 190, 226
Pine Sol, 92
Plaster ceilings, 12
Plastic
blinds for windows, 85–86
clothes washer and dryer parts,
118–19
dinnerware, 109–10
furniture, 70
garbage cans, 190–91
gloves, 220
lampshades, 74–75
lining in automatic
dishwashers, 116–17
outdoor furniture, 193–94
pails, 221
piano keys, 81–82
rainwear, 152, 153–54
shoes, 154–55
utensils, 113–14
windows and windshields on
automobiles, 206–7
wood-grain trim on
automobiles, 207
Plastic & Leather Cleaner, 71,
157, 204, 206, 209
Plastic laminate
countertops, 15–16, 93–95

facing on automatic
dishwashers, 117
furniture veneers, 72–73
shower stalls, 97–98
Platinum, 164–65, 179–80
Playtex Handsaver Gloves, 220
Pledge, 74
Plush, 68
Polyester. See also Polyester
fiber-filling.
blends for bed linens, 146
blends for towels, 146
clothing, 146
epoxy finish on piano cases,
81–82
Polyester fiber-filling
in comforters and quilts, 61–62
in outerwear, 150, 151
in pillows, 63–65
in sleeping bags, 65–66
in vests, 150
Porcelain, 80–81
cast iron coated with, 92–93
steel coated with, 92–93
Porcelain enamel
on clothes washers and dryers,
118
drain cleaner damage to, 210
on liners of continuous-
cleaning ovens, 127
Polishers, floor, 219
Potatoes, raw, 183
Potato mashers, 113
Precipitating water conditioners,
231
Premier Sneaker Cleaner, 155
Presoak products, enzyme, 230
Prewash spot and stain
removers, 229–30
Pumice, 221
Pumie Scouring Stick, 221, 270
Purex Liquid Bleach, 234
Purex Toss 'n Soft, 149, 235
Putnam's Color Remover, 244,
270

Q

Quarry tile floors, 38–39
Quickie Automatic Wet Mop, 221
Quilts
cotton-filled, 61–62
down-filled, 60–61
patchwork, 60, 61
polyester fiber-filled, 61–62
silk-covered, 60, 61
synthetic-filled, 61–62
velvet-covered, 60, 61
wool-covered down, 60
wool-filled, 61–62

R

Radiators, 47–48
Rain Barrel Fabric Softener, 60,
149, 235
Rainbow Sundry Products Rotten
Stone, 179
Raincoats, 150–51, 152–54
Rainwear, 152–54
nylon, 145
Rangehoods, 122–23
Ranges. See Stoves.

Rattan furniture, 74
Rayon, 146–47
clothing, 146–47
drapery, 146–47
lampshades, 74–75
upholstery, 146–47
Records, 214–15
Red Devil Fireplace Cleaner, 21
Redwood garden furniture, 194
Refrigerators, 124–25
Returns, heat, 47–48
Reusable Sponge Towel, 222
Revere Ware Instant Copper
Cleaner, 105, 109, 171, 173
Revere Ware Stainless Steel
Cleaner, 182–83
Rings, 176, 177, 179–80
Rinso, 232
Robes, chenille, 229
Rokeach Silver Polish, 181
Rollers, paint, 212–13
RoVer Rust Remover, 244, 270
Rubber
bumpers and bumper guards
for automobiles, 202
floor mats for automobiles, 197,
202
gloves, 220
hairbrushes and combs, 161
rainwear, 153–54
side moldings for automobiles,
202
tile floors, 39–41
utensils, 113–14
Rubbermaid Toilet Bowl Brush
Set, 218
Rubbers, 153–54
Rubbing alcohol, 54, 84, 161, 166
Rubin-Brite Metal Polish, 102,
109, 170, 171, 173, 175, 177,
181, 182
Rug-cleaning appliances, 67, 68,
219
Rug Doctor Steam Detergent, 68
Rugs, 66–68
Rug shampooers, 219
Rush furniture, 74
Rust stains, 244, 270–71
on automobile chrome, 198,
199
on barbecue grills, 187
around bathtub drains, 92
on cast iron, 103–4, 177–78
on tin, 183
on tools, 215–16
on window screens, 196
on wrought iron, 177–78, 195
Rye bread, 52

S

Sable brushes, 212
Saddle soap, 156
Salad oil, 17, 187
Salt, 78, 105, 171, 172, 175, 211,
243
residues on automobile
carpets, 197
residues on automobile
chrome, 198
residues on automobile
exteriors, 200
stains on leather, 155

Salt, flour, and vinegar paste, 171, 172, 175
Sani-Flush, 100
Satin
acetate in, 143
shoes made from, 154–55
Scarves, hand washing, 238
Scotch-Brite
Cookware Scrub 'N Sponge, 221
Household Scrub 'N Sponge, 15, 94
Scouring Pad, 222
Scotchgard, 152
Scorch marks, 270
Scouring pads
fiber, 221–22
steel, 223
synthetic, 222
Scrapers, 222
Scraping technique for stains, 246
Screens
fire, 19
window, 195–96
Scrubbers, floor, 219
Sea Mist All-Purpose Pine Oil Cleaner, 226
Shades
lamp, 74–75
window, 88–91
Shampoo
baby, 167–68
hair, 141, 167
Shampooers, rug, 219
Shaving cream, 245
Shellac
brushes used to apply, 212–13
on specialty wood furniture, 74
Shoes, 154–57
canvas, 154–55
cleaners/conditioners for, 156–57
cotton, 154–55
duck, 154–55
fabric, 154–55
leather, 155–57
linen, 154–55
nylon, 154–55
patent leather, 155–57
plastic, 154
polishes for, 157
rope-trimmed, 154
satin, 154–55
silk, 154–55
sneakers, 154–55
straw, 154
suede, 157
vinyl, 155–57
wood on, 154
Shout Laundry Soil & Stain Remover, 65, 83, 230
Shower, 97–98
curtains, 96–97
heads, 95–96
rods, 95–96
stalls, 97–98
Shutters, window, 90
Siding, aluminum, 169–70
Silk, 141
flowers made of, 77–78
hydrogen peroxide used to bleach, 234
lampshades made of, 74–75

shoes made of, 154–55
sweaters made of, 158–59
undyed, 230
Silver
candlesticks, 77
cutlery, 111
dinnerware, 109–10
flatware, 111
jewelry, 164–65
SilverStone cookware, 107
Simoniz
Chrome Cleaner, 199
No Buff Car Wax, 201
Shines Like the Sun, 202
Sink pads, 113–14
Sinks. See Washbasins.
Slate floors, 32–34
Sleeping bags, 65–66
Slipcovers, 83
Smoke stains
on automobile window interiors, 206
on barbecue grills, 188
on brick above barbecue grills, 189
on brick walls, 49
on glass fireplace enclosures, 19–20
on wooden mantels, 21
Sneakers, 154–55. See also Tennis shoes.
to fluff down-filled articles in clothes dryer, 60, 239
Sno Bol Toilet Bowl Cleaner, 99
Snowy Bleach, 234
Soap, 233
Soap film
on ceramic tile, 49, 50
on cultured marble, 14
on shower curtains, 96
on shower stalls, 97–98
Sodium carbonate, 140
Sodium perborate bleach, 147. See also Bleach.
Soft-bristled brushes, 217–18
Soft Scrub Cleanser, 15, 16, 21, 22, 92, 94, 95, 102, 105, 106, 109, 113, 117, 119, 120, 122, 125, 129, 130, 136, 170, 182, 184, 185, 191
Soilax, 86, 89, 226
Soleplates, electric iron, 134
Solvents, dry cleaning, 244
Soot
on awnings, 186
in fireplaces, 17, 18, 19, 20
on redwood garden furniture, 194
Sorting technique, laundry, 228–29, 238
S.O.S. Steel Wool Soap Pads, 183
Spandex, 147, 234
Sparkle Glass Cleaner, 55, 109, 117, 119, 121, 125, 129, 130, 132, 160, 174, 183, 206
Sparklens Lens Cleaner, 160
Spic and Span, 24, 26, 28, 29, 30, 33, 40, 44, 86, 89, 117, 119, 120, 123, 125, 129, 130, 190, 226
Sponge mops, 220–21
Sponges, 223
Sponging technique for stains, 246

Spots and stains, 242–78. See also Stains.
agents for removing, 243–45
equipment for removing, 245
procedures for removing, 247–78
products used before washing to remove, 229–30
techniques for removing, 245–46
Spot Shot, 245, 254, 272
Spotter
dry, 244
wet, 245
Spray 'n Wash, 230
Spray-on acoustical finish ceilings, 12
Squeegee, 224
Squeez-a-Matic Sponge Mop, 221
Stained wood
mantels, 22
shutters, 90
Stainless steel, 182–83
cookware, 108–9
cutlery, 111
flatware, 111
lining in copper cookware, 104
Stainless Steel Magic, 137, 138, 139, 174, 182
Stains, 247–78. See also Spots and stains.
alcoholic beverage, 247
baby formula, 230
blood, 230, 248
butter, 248–49
candle wax, 249
catsup, 249–51
chewing gum, 251–52
chocolate, 230, 252–53
coffee, 253–54
crayon, 254–55
deodorant, 255
egg white, 256–57
egg yolk, 257–58
fruit, 230
grass, 154–55, 230, 258–59
gravy, 230
hair spray, 260–61
ice cream, 261–62
ink, ballpoint, 263
lipstick, 263–64
makeup, 264–65
meat juice, 265–66
mildew, 266–67
milk, 230
mustard, 267–68
oil, cooking, 259
oil, lubricating and automotive, 260
paint, latex, 268
perfume, 269
perspiration, 270
rust, 270–71
scorch, 270–71
tea, 253–54
urine, 273–74
vegetable, 230
vomit, 275–76
Stain-X Carpet Stain Remover, 245, 248, 255, 257, 259, 262, 266, 271, 272, 273, 274
Stanhome
Cleaning Mitt, 220

Foam Upholstery Cleaner, 71
Panel & Cabinet Cleaner, 53,
  54, 56, 57
Super Floor Finish, 25, 27, 29,
  33, 35, 37, 39, 41, 43, 45
Upholstery and Rug Shampoo,
  63, 71
Upholstery Brush, 218
Stanley Foam Rug Shampoo, 68
Stanley Jewelry Cleaner, 165,
  166, 177
Sta-Puf Fabric Softener, 235
Star Brite Car Polish, 201
Statues
  alabaster, 76
  marble, 79–80
  porcelain, 80–81
Steam carpet cleaning machines,
  67, 68
Steam irons. See Electric irons.
Steel scouring pads, 222
Steel, stainless. See Stainless
  steel.
Stepladders, 223
Step Saver, 24, 41, 45
Step stools, 223
Stiff-bristled brushes, 217–18
Stockings, hand washing, 238
Storm doors, 169–70
Stoves
  ceramic cooktops on, 126
  gas rangetops on, 126, 128–29
  electric rangetops on, 126,
    128–29
  ovens in, 126–28
  plastic knobs on, 128–29
STP Son of a Gun, 205
String mops, 220–21
Stuffed toys, modacrylic in, 145
Stylus, phonograph, 214
Sudsy ammonia, 162, 165, 166,
  227
Suede
  garments, 157, 221
  shoes, 157, 221
Suede Stone, 157, 221, 243, 255
Sunlight damage
  on acetate, 143
  on automobile finishes, 200
  on book covers, 208
  on pianos, 81
  on rubber tile floors, 39
  on rubber utensils, 113
  on silk, 141
  on sweaters, 158
Super Bravo Floor Finish, 25, 27,
  29, 34, 35, 37, 39, 41, 43, 45
Superwasher, 224
Supreme Steel Wool Balls, 222
Sweaters, 158–59, 238
Sweat socks as mitts, 220
Sweepers, carpet, 218
Swimwear, spandex in, 147
Synthetic fiber wigs, 167, 168
Synthetic scouring pads, 222

T

Tabletops, zinc, 184–85
Taffeta
  acetate in, 143
  triacetate in, 147
Taillights, automobile, 206–7

Talcum powder, 243
Tamping, 246
Tannery, The, 71, 156, 204, 205,
  209
Taps, bathroom, 95–96
Tar deposits, 20, 200
Tarnish
  on brass, 170–71
  on bronze, 172–73
  on copper, 104, 105, 174–75
  on flatware and cutlery, 111
  on pewter, 179
  on silver, 180–81
Tarni-Shield Copper & Brass
  Cleaner, 23, 171, 175
Tarni-Shield Silver Cleaner, 165,
  181
Tarn-X, 23, 105, 165, 175, 181
Teakettles, 101, 107
Tea stains, 253–54
Television sets, 84
Tennis shoes, 64, 65, 154–55.
  See also Sneakers.
Teri Towels, 221
Terrazzo floors, 42–43
Thinsulate fiber filling, 151
Tide, 187, 233
Tile
  acoustical, 11–12
  asphalt, 23–25
  ceiling, 12
  ceramic, 13–14, 27–30, 49–50,
    93–94
  cork, 31–32
  decorator, 50
  masonry, 20–21
  metal, 50
  mirror, 51
  quarry, 38–39
  rubber, 39–41
  in showers, 97–98
Tile 'n Grout Magic, 13, 49, 93, 98
Tin, 104, 183–84
  cookware, 183–84
Tires, 202–3
Toaster ovens, 137
Toasters, 138
Toilets, 99–100
Tools, 215–16
  brass or brass-plated fireplace,
    22
  cast iron fireplace, 20
  garden, 169–70, 215–16
Toothbrush holders, 95–96
Top Job, 89, 226
Toupees. See Wigs.
Towels, 231, 235
  bath, 229
  cotton, 140
  paper, 221
  polyester blends in, 146
  racks for, 95–96
Trash cans, 190–91
Trash compactors, 129–30
Trend Heavy Duty Laundry
  Detergent, 233
Trewax
  Beauty Sealer, 26, 29, 30, 33,
    37, 39, 43
  Clear, 27, 32, 33, 37, 39, 43, 47
  Instant Wax Stripper & Floor
    Cleaner, 25, 27, 29, 34, 36,
    37, 39, 41, 43, 45
  Terrazzo and Slate Sealer/

Finish, 29, 33, 38, 42
  Up & Out, 245, 263, 264
  Wood Cleaner, 32, 47
Triacetate, 147
Trim, wood-grain, 207
Tuff Stuff Foam Cleaner, 193,
  196, 205, 206
Tuffy Cleaning Pad, 222
Turpentine, 53, 56, 72, 177, 212
Turtle Wax
  Auto & Van Carpet Cleaner,
    198
  Instant Saddle Soap, 71, 157
  Turtle Extra, 201
  Whitewall Tire & Mat Cleaner,
    199
  Zip Wax Car Wash, 201
20 Mule Power Industrial Strength
  Bathroom Cleaner, 13, 50,
  92, 93, 97, 98
20 Mule Team Borax, 79, 106,
  149, 190, 231
Twinkle Copper Cleaner Kit, 105,
  171, 175
Twinkle Silver Polish Kit, 181
Ty-D-Bol, 100

U

Umbrellas
  on garden furniture, 193
  rain, 152–54
Unspot Spot Remover, 244
Upholstery
  automobile cloth, 203
  fabric, 70–71
  leather, 204–5
  vinyl, 72, 204–5
Urine stains, 271–72
Utensils, 113–15
  metal, 112
  plastic, 113–14
  rubber, 113–14
  wooden, 114–15

V

Vacuum cleaners, 223
Vanish Automatic Toilet Bowl
  Cleaner, 100
Vanish Bowl Freshener, 100
Varnish, 212–13
  on wooden furniture, 73–74
  on wooden garden furniture,
    194
  on wooden mantels, 22
  on wooden salad bowls, 114–
    15
  on wooden window shutters, 90
  on woodwork, 55–57
Vases
  alabaster, 76
  crystal, 112
  jade, 78–79
Vegetable oil. See Salad oil.
Venetian blinds, 85–86
Vents, heat, 47–48
Vibra Vac, 68
Vigilant's Copper and Brass
  Polishing Cloth, 105, 171,
  175
Vinegar, 13, 24, 48, 50, 51, 52, 55,
  92, 93, 94, 97, 98, 101, 112,

Index

116, 132, 155, 171, 172, 175, 197, 207, 211, 227
cider, 107, 227
white (or clear), 19, 55, 97, 105, 135, 148, 227, 231, 245
Vinegar, ammonia, and baking soda solution, 13, 14, 48, 50, 51, 92, 93, 94, 97, 98
Vinyl
awnings, 186
book coverings, 208–9
floors, 43–45
furniture upholstery, 72
gloves, 150
outdoor furniture, 193–94
rainwear, 152, 153–54
tops on automobiles, 205–6
upholstery in automobiles, 204–5
wall coverings, 52
Vinyl Magic, 72, 194, 204, 205
Viva paper towels, 221
Vomit stains, 273–74

W

Waffle irons, 139
Wallpaper, 51–52. See also Walls.
removing marks from, 52, 221, 243, 255
Walls, 48–54
brick, 49
ceramic tile, 49–50
decorator tile, 50
metal tile, 50
mirror tile, 51
painted, 51
paper coverings for, 51–52
removing marks from, 52, 221
vinyl coverings for, 52
wood paneling on, 52–54
Washbasins, 91–92
zinc, 184–85
Washcloths, 140
Washers, clothes
automatic, 236–37
wringer, 237–38
Washing film, 231. See also Soap film.
Washing agents, 245. See also Laundry.
Washing problems, causing, 240–41
brown stains, 240
dingy fabric, 240
excessive wear, 240
gray fabric, 240
harsh-feeling fabric, 241
linting, 241
scorching, 241
static electricity, 241
yellowing, 241

Washing soda, 210
Watch cases, platinum, 179
Watch fobs, platinum, 179
Water conditioners, 230–31
Water levels in automatic clothes washers, 237
Waterproofing, 152, 235
Waterspots
on ceramic tile, 13, 93
on cultured marble, 94
on fabric, 242
on flatware, 111
on shower curtains, 96–97
on shower stalls, 97–98
on sink and tub hardware, 95–96
on stainless steel cookware, 108
Water temperatures in automatic washers, 236–37
Wax
build-up on polished wood furniture, 73
drips, 77
Weiman Panel Bright, 53
Weiman Wood Furniture Soap, 53, 54, 56, 57
Westley's Automotive Rug & Carpet Cleaner, 198
Westley's Hi-Lustre Car Wash, 201
West Pine Cleaner Deodorizer, 191, 192, 194, 196, 226
Wet spotter, 245
Whink Rust Stain Remover, 244, 270
White shoe polish
stains, 272
on venetian blind tapes, 85
White sidewall tires, 202–3
Wicker furniture, 74
Wigs, 167–68
human hair, 167–68
modacrylic in, 145
synthetic fiber, 167, 168
Wilbert Dri-Finish Lemon Oil, 72
Windex Glass Cleaner, 23, 55, 117, 121, 122, 123, 161, 174, 207
Window, 54–55. See also Automobiles, windows on.
blinds, 85–86
coverings, 85–90
curtains, 86–87
draperies, 87–88
frames, 169–70
screens, 169, 195–96
shades, 88–89
shutters, 90
Window Spray Cleaner, 55, 109, 174, 182
Windshields, automobile, 206–7
Wipe-R Clean, 207
Wisk Laundry Detergent, 233

Wood. See also Woodwork.
blinds, 85–86
bowls, 114–15
counters, 16–17
cutting boards, 114–15
floors, 45–47
furniture, 72–74
outdoor furniture, 194
paneling, 52–54
rolling pins, 114–15
salad utensils, 114–15
sealant, polyurethane, 45
shutters, 90
spoons, 114–15
television cabinets, 84
trays, 114–15
utensils, 114–15
Wood Crafter Lemon Furniture Polish, 74
Woodwork, 55–57
natural, 55–57
oiled finish, 55–56
painted, 55–56
polishes for oil finish, 56
polishes for waxed finish, 57
stained, 55–57
varnished finish, 55–57
waxed finish, 55–57
wood cleaners for, 56, 57
Wood Preen, 31, 46, 56, 57
Wool, 142, 236, 237
cleaning cloths, 218
outerwear, 151–52
rugs, 66–68
sweaters, 158–59
Woolite Self Cleaning Rug Cleaner, 68, 197
Woolite Upholstery Cleaner, 63, 70
Wright's Brass Cleaner & Polish, 105, 171, 173, 174, 175, 179
Wright's Silver Cleaner & Polish, 181
Wringer clothes washers, 237–38
Wrought iron, 177–78
outdoor furniture, 195

X

X-14 Instant Mildew Stain Remover, 13, 50, 94, 98, 244, 267

Y

Yes, 59, 61, 62, 149, 232

Z

Zinc, 184–85
Zud, 109, 171, 173, 175, 178, 179, 183, 195, 216